Practical Android Projects

Lucas Jordan
Pieter Greyling

Apress®

Practical Android Projects

Copyright © 2011 by Lucas Jordan and Pieter Greyling

All rights reserved. No part of this work may be reproduced or transmitted in any form or by any means, electronic or mechanical, including photocopying, recording, or by any information storage or retrieval system, without the prior written permission of the copyright owner and the publisher.

ISBN-13 (pbk): 978-1-4302-3243-8

ISBN-13 (electronic): 978-1-4302-3244-5

Printed and bound in the United States of America 9 8 7 6 5 4 3 2 1

Trademarked names, logos, and images may appear in this book. Rather than use a trademark symbol with every occurrence of a trademarked name, logo, or image we use the names, logos, and images only in an editorial fashion and to the benefit of the trademark owner, with no intention of infringement of the trademark.

The use in this publication of trade names, trademarks, service marks, and similar terms, even if they are not identified as such, is not to be taken as an expression of opinion as to whether or not they are subject to proprietary rights.

President and Publisher: Paul Manning
Lead Editor: Frank Pohlmann
Developmental Editor: Douglas Pundick
Technical Reviewer: Tony Hillerson
Editorial Board: Steve Anglin, Mark Beckner, Ewan Buckingham, Gary Cornell, Jonathan Gennick, Jonathan Hassell, Michelle Lowman, Matthew Moodie, Jeff Olson, Jeffrey Pepper, Frank Pohlmann, Douglas Pundick, Ben Renow-Clarke, Dominic Shakeshaft, Matt Wade, Tom Welsh
Coordinating Editor: Corbin Collins
Copy Editors: Nancy Sixsmith, Sharon Terdeman, Tracy Brown
Compositor: MacPS, LLC
Indexer: BIM Indexing & Proofreading Services
Artist: April Milne
Cover Designer: Anna Ishchenko

Distributed to the book trade worldwide by Springer Science+Business Media, LLC., 233 Spring Street, 6th Floor, New York, NY 10013. Phone 1-800-SPRINGER, fax (201) 348-4505, e-mail orders-ny@springer-sbm.com, or visit www.springeronline.com.

For information on translations, please e-mail rights@apress.com, or visit www.apress.com.

Apress and friends of ED books may be purchased in bulk for academic, corporate, or promotional use. eBook versions and licenses are also available for most titles. For more information, reference our Special Bulk Sales–eBook Licensing web page at www.apress.com/info/bulksales.

The information in this book is distributed on an "as is" basis, without warranty. Although every precaution has been taken in the preparation of this work, neither the author(s) nor Apress shall have any liability to any person or entity with respect to any loss or damage caused or alleged to be caused directly or indirectly by the information contained in this work.

The source code for this book is available to readers at www.apress.com. You will need to answer questions pertaining to this book in order to successfully download the code.

To Sandy Pond.

—Lucas Jordan

To Paula and Guilhem for their love during the good times and the bad times. To precious Caitlin and Aaron, who are my guiding stars. To my relentlessly supportive and loyal mother Christina, my brother Cornelius, and my sister Hester. I could not have done this without all of you. Thank you.

—Pieter Greyling

Contents at a Glance

- Contents v
- About the Authors x
- About the Technical Reviewer xi
- Acknowledgments xii
- Preface xiii
- Chapter 1: Android Fundamentals 1
- Chapter 2: Development Tools in Practice 49
- Chapter 3: Roll Your Own Android Scripting Environment 105
- Chapter 4: Embedding Lua in Android Applications 155
- Chapter 5: Introducing SL4A: The Scripting Layer for Android 193
- Chapter 6: Creating a GUI with HTML/JavaScript and AIR 221
- Chapter 7: Using REST with Facebook and Twitter 251
- Chapter 8: Using the Google App Engine with Android 275
- Chapter 9: Game Development: Graphics 311
- Chapter 10: Game Development: Animation 341
- Chapter 11: App Inventor 361
- Index 387

Contents

- **Contents at a Glance** iv
- **About the Authors** x
- **About the Technical Reviewer** xi
- **Acknowledgments** xii
- **Preface** xiii

- **Chapter 1: Android Fundamentals** 1
  - What Is Android? 2
  - Installing the Android SDK 2
    - Java Development Kit (JDK) 3
    - Android SDK and Target Platforms 3
  - Android SDK Test Drive 9
  - Android Architecture and Background 20
    - The Android Platform Stack 21
    - Android Component Architecture 23
    - The Android Runtime: Dalvik Virtual Machine (DVM) 23
  - Using an Integrated Development Environment (IDE) 27
  - Working with Eclipse 28
    - On the Web: Eclipse for Android Development 28
    - Quickstart: The Eclipse Android Development Tools (ADT) Plugin 29
  - Working with NetBeans 33
    - On the Web: NetBeans for Android Development 33
    - Quickstart: The NetBeans Android (NBAndroid) Plugin 34
  - Working with IntelliJ IDEA Community Edition 42
    - On the Web: JetBrains IntelliJ IDEA for Android Development 42
    - Quickstart: The IntelliJ IDEA Android Plugin 43
  - Summary 47

Chapter 2: Development Tools in Practice 49

Coding with the SDK and a Programmer's Editor 50
Development Environment Dependencies 50
    Ensure that Development Kit Locations Are on the Path 50
    Preparing an Android Virtual Device (AVD) 51
Frequently Used Android Development Kit Tools 52
Working with the Android Tools and a Code Editor 53
    Selecting a Code Editor 53
    Configuring the Editor for Android Work 56
The Example Application Project 58
Generating the Foundation Android Project 59
    The Android Project Directory Structure 60
Preparing to Run the Example Application 61
    Starting a Debugging Session 61
    Replacing the Default Generated Code 63
    Building and Installing the Project Example Code 64
    Creating a Log Filter for the Application in the DDMS 64
Running the Example Application 66
    What Does the Demo Application Do? 67
    A Walk through the Core Application Files 74
Android Coding How to 81
    Using the Android Log API 81
    Centralizing Application GUI Initialization Code 85
    Exiting an Application Activity 86
    Enabling and Disabling Buttons (and other Views) 87
    Creating Controls Dynamically (at Runtime in Code) 88
    Making an Android Toast 90
    Showing an Android Alert Dialog 90
    Creating and Showing an Android System Notification 91
    Using a Private Application File 92
    Making Menus 95
Migrating the Example Application to Eclipse/ADT 97
    Make a Copy of the Project 97
    Open Eclipse with the ADT Plugin Installed 97
    Create a New Android Project from the Copy of the Project 97
    Create and Test a New Run Configuration for the Project 98
    Deploying to a Real Device 99
    Creating a Signed APK Package of the Example Application 101
Summary 104

Chapter 3: Roll Your Own Android Scripting Environment 105

Designing a Scripting Environment 106
    The Components of a Scripting System 106
    The Component Roles in a Scripting System 107
    Designing for Resource-Constrained Systems 109
    Multi-Threading for Background Code 110
Programming with BASIC 110
    A BASIC Backgrounder 111

Cocoa—A BASIC Interpreter for Java 111
Outlining the Code Projects for This Chapter 112
The Cocoa-BASIC AWT Project 112
    Understanding the Cocoa-BASIC AWT Application Design 112
    Running the Cocoa-BASIC AWT Desktop Application 114
    Reviewing the Cocoa-BASIC AWT Source Code 118
The CocoaDroid Project 120
    A Preflight Checklist 120
    Understanding the CocoaDroid Application Design 121
    Running the CocoaDroid Android Application 122
Summary 153

Chapter 4: Embedding Lua in Android Applications 155

Introducing Lua and Kahlua2 156
    Lua Resources 156
    Kahlua2 Resources 157
Using Kahlua2 in Your Android Java Applications 157
    Development Environment Configuration 158
The Kahlua2 Project 158
    Setting up the Kahlua2 Runtime Files Project 159
    Building from the Console 160
    Building from an IDE 160
    The Kahlua2 Runtime Libraries 161
The Kahlua2 Android Interpreter Project 162
    Setting up the Project 162
    Building from the Console 163
    Building from an IDE 163
    Running the Kahlua2 Android Interpreter 164
    Understanding the Basics of Embedding Kahlua2 165
The KahluaDroid Project 168
    Running the KahluaDroid Application 169
    Running Lua Code On or Off the Main GUI Thread 176
    Exposing Android Application Methods to Kahlua2 180
    Calling Application Methods as Lua Functions 183
    Implementing an Application Startup Script 185
Summary 192

Chapter 5: Introducing SL4A: The Scripting Layer for Android 193

What Is Scripting Layer for Android? 194
    About SL4A 194
    The SL4A License 194
    Using SL4A 194
    SL4A Resources 195
    The SL4A Code Repository 195
Running SL4A in the Android Emulator 196
    Development Environment Configuration 196
    Downloading the SL4A APKs 197
    Installing the SL4A APK on the Android Emulator 197
    Running SL4A on the Android Emulator 198

Installing SL4A Interpreters	202
Understanding Scripting Layer for Android	209
Communicating Using JavaScript Object Notation (JSON)	209
Summarizing the SL4A Architecture	210
Reviewing Local Proxy Implementations	211
Getting the SL4A Source Code	215
Cloning the SL4A Source Code	216
SL4A Hello World Examples	219
Summary	220

Chapter 6: Creating a GUI with HTML/JavaScript and AIR — 221

Setting Up an Android Project to Display a Web Application	222
The Android Project	223
Calling Android Methods from JavaScript	225
JavaScript Application	226
Graphics and Animation	231
User Interaction	235
JavaScript Summary	238
Using Flash and Flex Apps on Android with AIR	238
Writing a Flex Application for Android	239
Building and Deploying	240
Creating the Flex UI with MXML	244
Writing ActionScript	246
Summary	250

Chapter 7: Using REST with Facebook and Twitter — 251

Understanding REST	252
REST and JSON	253
REST from an Android Application	255
Asynchronous Tasks	258
Twitter	259
Examples in Code	261
Tweeting on Behalf of the User	265
Confirming the User Wants to Tweet	266
Understanding the Facebook API	268
Facebook and Authentication	268
Facebook's Social Graph API	272
Summary	274

Chapter 8: Using the Google App Engine with Android — 275

Introducing Google App Engine	276
Getting Started with GAE	276
Using Eclipse with GAE	278
GAE Project Structure	280
Charges for the Google App Engine Service	283
Google App Engine Services	284
Examining a Sample GAE Application	287
Adding the HighScore Service	290
Querying the HighScore Service	293
Consuming GAE Services with Android	297

Exploring the Top Ten Activity 300
　　　Viewing the Users of a Game 303
　　　Viewing a User's Location (MapView) 305
　Summary 310

Chapter 9: Game Development: Graphics 311
　Introducing the Android View Package 312
　　　Understanding XML Layout 312
　　　Layout in Code 317
　　　Custom Component 320
　Understanding the Drawable Class 328
　　　Drawable Class 328
　　　Drawable Subclasses 330
　　　NinePatchDrawable 334
　Direct Rendering 336
　Summary 340

Chapter 10: Game Development: Animation 341
　Android Animations 341
　　　Creating Views and Animations 343
　Frame By Frame Animations 353
　　　Mixing Views and SurfaceViews 359
　Summary 360

Chapter 11: App Inventor 361
　Setting Up App Inventor 361
　Working with Blocks 365
　　　Understanding the Types of Blocks 367
　　　Creating Application Logic with the Block Editor 376
　Limitations of App Inventor 383
　　　Limited Set of Components 384
　　　Limitations in Block Editor 385
　Summary 386

Index 387

About the Authors

 **Lucas Jordan** (www.lucasjordan.com) is a lifelong computer enthusiast and has worked for more than 13 years as a Java developer. He worked at the Children's Hospital Boston for a multidisciplinary applied research and education program called CHIP. After leaving Boston, Lucas settled in Rochester, New York and now works for EffectiveUI as a lead developer. He has contributed to his local Java User's Group (RJUG.org), presenting on JavaFX and GWT. In his free time, Lucas is starting a company called ClayWare Games, LLC with his wife Debra Lewis. ClayWare Games, LLC makes accessories and apps for mobile touch devices.

 **Pieter Greyling** (www.pietergreyling.com) is an information technology expert and software architect with two and half decades of software development experience. He has worked on distributed software engineering projects with teams on several continents for many years. Pieter enjoys software programming and sees smartphone mobile technology as a wonderful way to add an extra element of fun into computing. In his copious free time, he likes to play console video games with his family and take a far too occasional bicycle ride.

About the Technical Reviewer

**Tony Hillerson** is a software architect for EffectiveUI. He graduated from Ambassador University with a BA in MIS. On any given day, Tony might be working with Android, Rails, Objective-C, Java, Flex, or shell scripts. He has been interested in developing for Android since early betas. Tony has created Android screencasts, tech reviewed Android books, and spoken on Android at conferences. He also sometimes gets to write some Android code.

Tony is interested in all levels of usability and experience design, from the database to the server to the glass.

In his free time, Tony enjoys playing the bass, playing *World of Warcraft*, and making electronic music. Tony lives outside Denver, Colorado with his wife and two sons.

Acknowledgments

We would like to acknowledge the excellent staff at Apress who managed to get this book completed on time after numerous delays. Good job, everyone!

A very special thank you goes to our coordinating editor, Corbin Collins, and Douglas Pundick, our developmental editor.

We also thank Frank Pohlmann, the lead editor, and Assistant Editorial Director Steve Anglin.

Thank you to our technical reviewer, Tony Hillerson, for giving us really valuable input and feedback.

Preface

Android is a well-thought-out platform for developing mobile applications. Google has done a wonderful job of providing third-party developers with a world-class development environment. The ease of development combined with the enormous user base makes Android a very compelling platform for developers.

What this Book Is

When you're building an Android application, many things are straightforward; however, there are facets to the Android platform for which the voice of experience is an invaluable guide. Each chapter in this book explores one of these facets and aims to guide the reader to a better understanding of the topic. By presenting a concrete example project and the steps required to make it work, the reader will gain insight into Android and avoid some pitfalls along the way.

In addition, we have tried to show alternative ways to develop with the Android SDK Tools and IDEs. There are projects here that not only cover programming Android applications with Java but also get you started working with other languages such as JavaScript and Lua.

What You Will Need

Chapters 1 and 2 cover the groundwork of the Android development environment in detail. These chapters provide full instructions for creating and working with the Android SDK Tools and other development software such as IDEs and plugins.

In summary, to work with the projects in this book you will need the following:

- **A desktop computer running Windows, Linux, or Mac OS X**
  The book projects were developed using a mix of Windows XP, Ubuntu Linux, and Mac OS X. All the projects were tested for compatibility on these platforms.

- **Java SDK**
  The book uses the Java JDK 1.6.0_18 and later.

- **Apache Ant**
  We have found a stand-alone installation of Apache Ant to be very convenient and useful when working with the Android SDK terminal command-line tools. Full coverage of this aspect is given in the first two chapters of the book.

- **Google Android SDK**
  All the projects in this book were developed and built using the Android 2.3 "Gingerbread" SDK.

- **Integrated development environment (IDE)**
  We have used the following IDEs for the projects in the book: Eclipse, NetBeans, and IntelliJ IDEA Community Edition. All the IDE projects have been tested for compatibility, so you are free to choose your own IDE. In fact, we provide enough coverage using only the Android terminal command-line tools and Apache Ant for you to choose to forego an IDE altogether.

As we mentioned, Chapters 1 and 2 cover working with the core Android SDK and the installation and configuration of an Android development environment suited to your tastes.

All other chapters describe the setup and installation of any extra tools and software dependencies required for the content of that particular chapter.

What You Need to Know

We expect you to be proficient in the Java programming language and perhaps JavaScript, plus another scripting language such as Python, Lua, Ruby, or Perl.

Chapter 1

Android Fundamentals

The Android platform is a very exciting yet relatively new player in today's mobile device market. Beyond rating very highly in the number of cool features per device, Android-enabled smartphones are currently enjoying the highest percentage sales growth rate in the mobile industry.

According to Gartner Research,[1] worldwide sales of Android-based smartphones to end users have jumped from the number 6 spot in 2009 to number 4 by the end of the first quarter of 2010. This level of growth is expected to continue. In fact, Gartner has predicted that Android will become the number 2 worldwide mobile operating system in 2010 and will challenge Symbian for the number 1 position by 2014.[2]

We want to share with you some of the enthusiasm we have for this truly remarkable development platform. Throughout the course of this book, we will attempt to do this by showing the wide range of opportunities available at your fingertips when you choose to develop Android applications.

Perhaps you are reading this book in order to gain more background understanding of the Android platform. Perhaps you plan to roll up your sleeves and join us in running and playing with the projects in the emulator or your own device. We want to get you up and running quickly and provide you with sufficient understanding of the Android platform and Android Development Kit (ADK) development environment to have success with your goals.

With those goals in mind, this chapter aims to be as practical an introduction to Android development as possible. It also strives to cover a broad spectrum of required conceptual and theoretical background material in a concise and to-the-point manner.

We will start with a short description of the Android platform and then jump straight into coverage of the installation of the Android SDK and supporting development tools. To fully round out our SDK setup study, we embark on a step-by-step test drive that

---

[1] From Gartner press release: http://www.gartner.com/it/page.jsp?id=1372013

[2] From the Gartner press release: http://www.gartner.com/it/page.jsp?id=1434613

involves generating a bare-bones Android project and getting the resulting skeleton Android application up and running in the Android emulator.

The next order of business will be a tour of the Android platform architecture. Here we will describe the Android platform stack; Android component architecture; and Dalvik, the Android runtime. With this knowledge in hand, we then cover working with the Java IDEs Eclipse, NetBeans, and IntelliJ IDEA Community Edition; plus spend some time learning how to equip them with Android programming capabilities via plugins.

This means we have a lot of ground to cover, so let's get started.

What Is Android?

In a nutshell, Android is an operating system targeted at mobile hardware such as phones and other constrained computing devices such as netbooks and tablet computers.

The concept and platform was the brainchild of Android Inc., a small startup company from Palo Alto, California, that was acquired by Google in 2005. Its stated goal was to create a small, stable, flexible, and easily upgraded operating system for handsets that would be highly attractive for device manufacturers and telephony carriers.

Android platform releases 1.x through 2.x are aimed primarily at smartphone devices, whereas it is reported that Android release 3.x will be the first operating platform specifically designed with high-end support for tablet computers.

The Android platform was originally unveiled in November 2007. The unveiling coincided with the announcement of the formation of the Open Handset Alliance, a group of companies that share the goal of promoting open standards for mobile device platforms such as Android.

In October 2008, Android was released under the Apache 2.0 open-source license.[3] This and the flexible component-based design of the platform present innovative and cost-effective opportunities for manufacturers and software developers alike. We aim to showcase some of these distinguishing platform capabilities during the course of this book.

Installing the Android SDK

We will start by installing the core Android SDK and tools. Our aim is to get the Android emulator with our own simple application up and running on an Android Virtual Device (AVD) as soon as possible. The experience gained will then serve as a basis for further discussion.

---

[3] http://source.android.com/source/licenses.html

The examples and commands you will be shown were run on a mixture of Ubuntu GNU/Linux, Microsoft Windows, and Apple Mac OS X systems. All the tools, including the JDK and the Android SDK toolset, behave in a similar, if not identical, manner across the major supported computing platforms.

Java Development Kit (JDK)

To begin with, you should have a recent version of the Java SDK (JDK) installed on your particular system. It can be obtained either from your operating system distribution package install manager application or directly downloaded from the Internet.[4] We assume that we do not need to go into the details for doing this. Suffice it to say that JDK5 or upward should be fine. This writing is based on JDK6.

> **CHECKING THE JDK VERSION:** To confirm that a compatible version of the JDK is installed and available to the environment, we usually do a quick check on the command line or console terminal, as follows:
>
> ```
> $ java -version
> java version "1.6.0_18"
> OpenJDK Runtime Environment (IcedTea6 1.8.1) (6b18-1.8.1-0ubuntu1)
> OpenJDK Server VM (build 16.0-b13, mixed mode)
> $ javac -version
> javac 1.6.0_18
> ```
>
> If something goes wrong, you should consult the JDK configuration documentation for your particular platform. We will not cover debugging Java installations here.

Android SDK and Target Platforms

Assuming that our Java platform is ready, we now need to download the Android SDK starter package and use it to install our target Android platforms.

The Android SDK starter package can be downloaded from the official Google Android SDK download site.[5] Select the download appropriate for your development platform. The supported platforms currently include Windows, Mac OS X (Intel), and Linux (i386).

In the case of having downloaded an SDK starter package archive for Linux or Mac OS X, unpack the downloaded archive into a directory of your choice.

---

[4] https://jdk6.dev.java.net/

[5] http://developer.android.com/sdk/

In the case of having downloaded the Windows installer (.exe file), run the installer and install into a directory of your choice.

You could call this directory anything you like, but we recommend something similar to the following:

Linux or Mac OS X system: `~/android-sdk-linux_x86`

Windows system: `C:\android-sdk-windows`

Make a note of this directory path name for later use.

Within the root of the unpacked directory structure there should be a text file with a name like `SDK Readme.txt`. This has specific instructions for each platform. What is important to note here is that the downloaded archive does not include the complete SDK. The following note contains an extract from the readme shipped with the latest Android SDK as of this writing.[6]

> **READ THE SDK README!** The Android SDK archive only contains the tools. It no longer comes populated with a specific Android platform or Google add-on. Instead, you use the SDK Manager to install or update SDK components such as platforms, tools, add-ons, and documentation. In order to start developing applications, you must install at least one version of the Android platform using the SDK Manager. This requires an Internet connection, so if you plan to use the SDK offline, please make sure to download the necessary components while online.

At this point, it is recommended to add the Android SDK tools directory to the development environment system `PATH` variable. The tools directory can be found under the preceding unpacked root directory: `<sdk>/tools/`.

Having the binaries and tools on the path will make it a lot more convenient to issue Android SDK commands from anywhere on the terminal console of your development system.

As an example, after adding the appropriate entries to the shell user login script for my GNU/Linux development system, we receive the following output from listing it with the Linux cat command:

```
$ cat ~/.bashrc
.....
#-- google android dev tools --
export PATH="$PATH: ~/android-sdk-linux_86/tools"
export PATH="$PATH: ~/android-sdk-linux_86/platform-tools"
.....
```

---

[6] Android SDK release 8, Android 2.3 platform

> **SETTING THE PATH ON WINDOWS:** From the desktop, right-click My Computer and click Properties. Alternatively, from Control Panel, double-click System. Both options open the System Properties dialog box. Now click the Advanced tab. In the Advanced section, click the Environment Variables button. In the Environment Variables window, select the PATH variable in the User- or System Variable section, depending on whether you want the setting applied for all users or just yourself. Click the Edit button. Add or modify the path. Directories are separated by a semicolon. Click OK when done.

For confirmation, issuing the following command on your development system will print the current value of the system PATH variable to the terminal console window.

Linux and Mac OS X:

echo $PATH

Windows:

echo %PATH%

Android Platform API Levels

The API level targeted by your application is very important for reasons of device compatibility and the software development- and maintenance lifetime of your codebase. If it is not managed properly, the maintenance of your application could potentially become a nightmare, especially if it is deployed to multiple Android devices and operating platforms.

It is also a good idea to become familiar with the folder structures of the Android SDK once it is installed. Again, this is especially valid if your applications will be built for multiple Android hardware targets.

For a better understanding of the subject of API levels, it is well worth the effort of reviewing the documentation found on the official developer's web site for Android API levels.[7] The tie-in between API level numbers and their corresponding platforms are clarified in Table 1–1, which was current at the time of writing.

---

[7] http://developer.android.com/guide/appendix/api-levels.html

Table 1-1. *Android Platform Versions and API Levels*

Platform Version	API Level
Android 2.3	9
Android 2.2	8
Android 2.1	7
Android 2.0.1	6
Android 2.0	5
Android 1.6	4
Android 1.5	3
Android 1.1	2
Android 1.0	1

Android Platform Setup

Here is a short list of dependencies for proceeding with the setup of SDK platforms:

- Android SDK starter package downloaded and unpacked.
- The JDK, ADK, and Ant tools are accessible on the environment path.
- We have a basic understanding of Android platform versions and API levels.
- Last but not least, we should be connected to the Internet.

We can now install the SDK platform components using the Android SDK and AVD Manager programs.

To start the SDK Manager on Linux or Mac OS X, execute the following command:

`$ android`

To start the SDK Manager on Windows, run the following program:

`SDK Manager.exe`

The main user interface of the Android SDK Manager on Linux should appear as in Figure 1-1.

CHAPTER 1: Android Fundamentals

Figure 1–1. *The Android SDK and AVD Manager during initial SDK setup on Linux*

> **WINDOWS USB DRIVER FOR ANDROID DEVICES:** It is worth showing the equivalent Android SDK and AVD Manager for the Windows platform (see Figure 1–2). It contains an important addition, the Windows USB Driver package for Android devices. This will become necessary when you develop, debug, and deploy directly in conjunction with a physical Android phone or other Android hardware device attached via USB cable to a Windows computer.

Figure 1-2. *The Android SDK and AVD Manager during initial SDK setup on Windows*

Note that in both cases we have selected the Android 2.3 platform, API level 9, plus the relevant additions such as documentation and SDK samples. Now click Install Selected. The appropriate SDK resource bundles will now be downloaded and installed into the SDK directory structure where we unpacked the SDK starter archive.

In order to maintain and update your SDK over time, an update session can be directly initiated from the command line by executing the following commands:

- In a terminal session on Linux/Mac OS X:

```
$ android update sdk
```

- Besides the option of simply running SDK Manager.exe again, the same can be achieved from the Windows command prompt with the following:

```
C:\> android.bat update sdk
```

Again, we assume that the Android tools can be found on the system path. Further information about managing your Android SDK installation can be found on the Android Developers "Adding SDK Components" page.[8]

Extra Tools: Apache Ant

There are some development tools that no Java developer should do without. One such an indispensable utility is Apache Ant, which is a build tool that is Java's rough equivalent to make. make is traditionally used in C/C++ development environments. Ant also differs from make in that it uses XML to specify build steps and actions.

The Android SDK extensively uses Ant for its compilation, build, and deployment infrastructure. We will use it to test drive our core tools in the next section. So if it is not already installed on your system, we recommend you grab a copy and install it. If necessary, you can find installation instructions and more information about Ant on the official Ant web site.[9]

> **SOME IDES ALREADY CONTAIN ANT:** If you will be using an IDE exclusively, installing a stand-alone instance of Apache Ant might not be necessary. IDEs such as Eclipse and NetBeans come packaged with an Ant distribution that they invoke behind the scenes during the build process.

If you are planning to work through the examples that follow, ensure that Ant is on the system environment path once it is installed.

Android SDK Test Drive

We will now take our SDK and platform installation for a comprehensive test drive to complete the installation of runtime components and to confirm that everything was set up correctly. We will also get to know the environment better. This is a central part of this chapter and will form the basis of further subjects covered.

Initially, we will do the work from the terminal console, command line, or command prompt, whichever terminology is appropriate for your system or personal preference.

1. Create an application project directory to work in and call it HelloAndroidSdk. From within a parent- or home directory of your choice somewhere on your system, issue the following commands:

    On Linux or Mac OS X:

```
$ mkdir HelloAndroidSdk
$ cd HelloAndroidSdk
```

---

[8] http://developer.android.com/sdk/adding-components.html

[9] http://ant.apache.org/

On Windows:

```
C:\> md HelloAndroidSdk
C:\> cd HelloAndroidSdk
```

2. Next we will create a bare-bones Android application using the SDK tools, but before we do that, let's check the available platform targets. From now on, we will only show the GNU/Linux bash shell version of the command because the equivalents for the other platforms are identical in syntax. Issue the following command:

```
$ android list targets
```

Based on the SDK selections installed earlier, the output should be similar to this listing:

```
Available Android targets:
id: 1 or "android-9"
    Name: Android 2.3
    Type: Platform
    API level: 9
    Revision: 2
    Skins: HVGA (default), QVGA, WQVGA400, WQVGA432, WVGA800, WVGA854
```

3. Now we will use the SDK tools to create a skeleton Android application targeting the previous platform within this folder. Enter the following command code as a single command line on the console:

```
$ android create project --target "android-9" --name MyAndroidSdkApp
--path ./MyAndroidSdkAppProject --activity MyAndroidSdkAppActivity
--package com.example.myandroid
```

NOTE: The `--target "android-9"` argument could also have read as follows: `--target 1`.

The successful completion of the command should result in output similar to this:

```
Created project directory: ./MyAndroidSdkAppProject
Created directory ./MyAndroidSdkAppProject/src/com/example/myandroid
Added file ./MyAndroidSdkAppProject/src/com/example/myandroid/↵
MyAndroidSdkAppActivity.java
Created directory ./MyAndroidSdkAppProject/res
Created directory ./MyAndroidSdkAppProject/bin
Created directory ./MyAndroidSdkAppProject/libs
Created directory ./MyAndroidSdkAppProject/res/values
Added file ./MyAndroidSdkAppProject/res/values/strings.xml
Created directory ./MyAndroidSdkAppProject/res/layout
Added file ./MyAndroidSdkAppProject/res/layout/main.xml
Added file ./MyAndroidSdkAppProject/AndroidManifest.xml
Added file ./MyAndroidSdkAppProject/build.xml
```

The Android SDK has now generated the full source code and resource files to build a complete and functional Android application.

A listing is shown in Figure 1–3 of the Java source code of one of the files, MyAndroidSdkAppActivity.java, that was generated. This is the application's main entry point, a class that extends the Activity class.

> **ABOUT THE CODE:** We will not go into the detailed coding aspects of Android programming in this chapter. This chapter serves as the diving board used by the rest of the book to dive into the details of coding Android applications.

4. Next, we want to build the generated source code into an executable application. To do this, first enter the following into the new application directory:

```
$ cd MyAndroidSdkAppProject
```

Now issue the following command to instruct ant to build a debugging release of the application project:

```
$ ant debug
```

This should result in ample output similar to the following:

```
Buildfile: /HelloAndroidSdk/MyAndroidSdkAppProject/build.xml
    [setup] Android SDK Tools Revision 8
    [setup] Project Target: Android 2.3
    [setup] API level: 9 [setup] ...
BUILD SUCCESSFUL
Total time: 5 seconds
```

Assuming a successful build (as indicated by the message at the end of the listing) the /MyAndroidSdkAppProject/bin directory should now be populated with executable binaries. It should also contain debug versions of the application in the form of Dalvik Virtual Machine (DVM)–compatible classes (classes.dex) and Android application packages (MyAndroidSdkApp-debug.apk). We will cover them in more detail later on in the chapter.

The project directory should look similar to Figure 1–3. Feel free to investigate the project folder structures and the files that were created.

THE MANIFEST FILE: ANDROIDMANIFEST.XML: Another of the files that were generated in the root of the project is called the AndroidManifest.xml file. This is a very special file in that it defines and binds the application together. It is used by the Android SDK to declare essential information about the application for the benefit of the Android runtime system. Among other items, it identifies the application's Java package that serves as its unique name to the system, required permissions, components consumed and implemented, libraries to link against, and so on. Also see the Android Developers site for the Manifest File.[10]

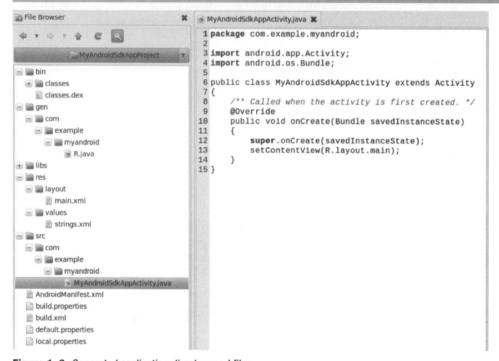

Figure 1–3. *Generated application directory and files*

5. Of course, we are eager to launch our new application, but first we need a device for it to run on. Because we will generally not use a physical device for ongoing development, we require a virtual machine on which to run an emulation of the Android runtime platform. The Android SDK takes care of both requirements.

---

[10] http://developer.android.com/guide/topics/manifest/manifest-intro.html

- An Android virtual machine is called an *Android Virtual Device (AVD)*, and multiple AVDs can be configured using the AVD Manager to model your test- and production target device configurations. Reference material can be found on the Android Virtual Devices web site.[11]
- The Android runtime platform emulation is provided in the Android SDK and is simply called the *Android emulator*. The emulator is the platform that will run our application. Complete information is available Android emulator web site.[12]

6. To create an AVD, we will start the AVD Manager on the terminal command line by issuing the following command:

```
$ android
```

This will launch the familiar Android SDK and AVD Manager (see Figure 1-4).

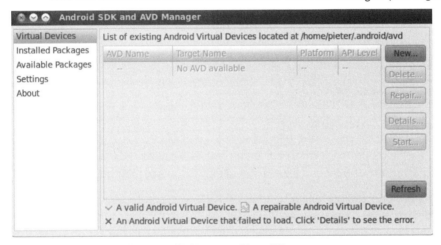

Figure 1-4. *The Android SDK and AVD Manager with no AVDs*

7. Our next task is to create an AVD. Clicking the New button opens the Create new Android Virtual Device (AVD) form (see Figure 1-5).

---

[11] http://developer.android.com/guide/developing/tools/avd.html

[12] http://developer.android.com/guide/developing/tools/emulator.html

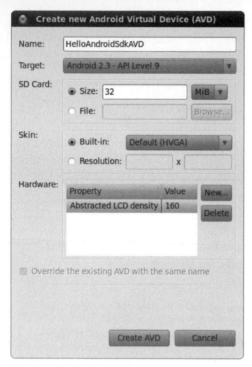

Figure 1–5. *Creating a new AVD with the AVD Manager*

Fill out the text fields on the form to create a new AVD called `HelloAndroidSdkAVD` with a virtual SD card of 32MB in size. Then click the `Create AVD` button.

8. After an informational dialog telling us that the AVD was created successfully, we should be taken back to the main `Android SDK and AVD Manager` form (see Figure 1–6). Here we should now see our new `HelloAndroidSdkAVD` in the list of AVDs available to this instance of the Android SDK.

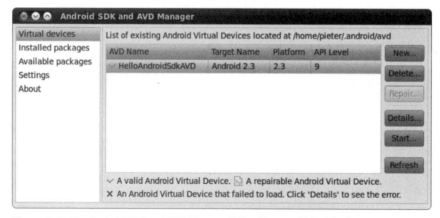

Figure 1–6. *The Android SDK and AVD Manager listing the new Virtual Device*

9. Now that we have created our AVD, we can launch the emulator from the terminal and instruct it to run on top of our `HelloAndroidSdkAVD` virtual AVD. Issue this command on the console:

```
$ emulator -avd HelloAndroidSdkAVD
```

Because this is the first time we launch the emulator with our brand-new AVD, it can take a little while for the startup to complete.

ANOTHER WAY TO LAUNCH THE EMULATOR/AVD COMBINATION: Launching the emulator with our AVD can also be achieved directly from the AVD Manager graphical user interface (GUI) application by selecting the AVD in the `Virtual Devices` list and clicking the `Start` button.

Once the emulator is up and running, we should see the Android platform startup screen (see Figure 1-7). We now have a device to run our test application on. This device is essentially a full implementation of the Android platform stack including the DVM that, along with the AVD, provides us with a complete virtual mobile device. Leave the emulator running or restart it for the next section.

Figure 1-7. *The Android emulator running the new AVD*

If you have not used an Android device before, now might be a good time to play with the emulator to get comfortable with the user interface. Table 1–2 presents a short list of handy emulator keys and the corresponding keyboard keys that will be useful during development. See the Android Developers emulator site for a full list.[13]

Table 1-2. *Convenient Android Emulator Keyboard Keys*

Device Key	Keyboard Key
Home	HOME
Menu	F2 or PAGE UP
Back	ESC
Search	F5
Power	F7
Orientation (portrait, landscape)	KEYPAD_9, CTRL+F12
Full-screen emulator (on/off)	ALT-ENTER
Trackball (on/off)	F6
DPad left/up/right/down	KEYPAD_4/8/6/2
DPad center	KEYPAD_5

10. Our next step is to deploy the application package onto the emulator. With the emulator running on the desktop, enter the following command on the console terminal from within the `MyAndroidSdkAppProject` folder:

```
/MyAndroidSdkAppProject$ ant install
```

---

[13] http://developer.android.com/guide/developing/tools/emulator.html

> **RUN THE EMULATOR IN A SEPARATE PROCESS:** To run the emulator and still have access to issue commands on the same terminal, use the following:
>
> Linux/Mac OS X: `emulator -avd HelloAndroidSdkAVD &`
>
> On Windows: `start emulator -avd HelloAndroidSdkAVD`
>
> The emulator is then launched in a separate operating system process, thus allowing us to continue entering commands, such as the install instruction, on the original console.

Ant will attempt to update and rebuild your application if necessary and then run the `ant install` step to deploy the package to the device.

The `ant install` process should connect with the deployment daemon and copy the application package onto the emulator. The output should be something like the following:

```
install:
     [echo] Installing
     [exec]    pkg: /data/local/tmp/MyAndroi
     [exec] Success
     [exec] 828 KB/s (0 bytes in 13263.000s)
BUILD SUCCESSFUL
Total time: 9 seconds
```

> **IN CASE OF BUILD FAILED:** The build and install might fail with the following output:
>
> ```
> install:
>      [echo] Installing
>      [exec] error: device offline
>      [exec] * daemon not running. starting
>      [exec] * daemon started successfully *
> BUILD FAILED
> ```
>
> Make sure that you have only one instance of the emulator running, verify that it has completely finished starting up and then run `ant install` again. The daemon should be properly started up the next time round.

The daemon referred to is the `Android Debug Bridge` (simply called `adb`) and it performs the actual installation initiated by the `ant install` build step. Issuing the following adb command will list the devices currently running:

```
adb devices
List of devices attached
emulator-5554   device
```

The Android Debug Bridge is a core Android development tool that is worth spending time learning about; you will certainly encounter it again in this book. More information is available on the official Android Developers adb site.[14]

> **LEAVE THE EMULATOR RUNNING:** It is often a good idea to just leave the emulator running in its own session while you are developing. The process is identical to keeping a real phone switched on during the whole time you might need it. This habit also pays when using an IDE such as NetBeans or Eclipse.

11. With the emulator up and running, and the application now installed, we should get the initial Android screen. Drag open the small lock on the left of the initial Android platform startup screen (as seen in Figure 1–7); the Android Home screen appears (see Figure 1–8).

Figure 1–8. *The Android emulator open on the Home activity*

12. Click the Launcher icon for the Application Launcher Activity (see Figure 1–9).

---

[14] http://developer.android.com/guide/developing/tools/adb.html

Figure 1-9. *The Android Emulator open on the Launcher activity*

13. Now click the icon for launching our installed test application (see Figure 1-10).

Figure 1-10. *The Android emulator in the MyAndroidSdkAppActivity Activity*

And there we have it! The `MyAndroidSdkAppActivity` application was run successfully displaying a friendly hello message. That concludes our comprehensive test drive.

Test Drive Summary

It is important to recap our goals with the test drive section because they remain relevant throughout the book:

- A primary goal was introducing the Android SDK core development tools and environment. As with any development platform, having an understanding and feeling comfortable with the core tool culture is very valuable. This will enable the developer to drop down into these tools for problem resolution and to build custom scripting or automation tasks using these command-line tools that can significantly boost productivity.

- We also wanted to see something running as quickly as possible. The intent was to build confidence and a good foundational springboard. Of course, it is also a lot more interesting and a lot more fun to take a practical approach when learning something new.

- Another goal was to demonstrate that it is entirely possible to develop for the Android platform without using a dedicated and monolithic IDE. IDEs, though very useful as productivity- and source code project management tools, can often obscure important details and limit an understanding of core aspects of a platform. Obviously, we would still need other tools such as a good programmer's text editor to code with. The Android SDK complements your personal development tools of choice with a full suite of build, deployment, and debugging utilities.

More information about building Android applications with the out-of-the-box SDK command-line tools is available on the official Android Developers "Developing In Other IDEs" web site.[15]

Android Architecture and Background

This is not intended to be an in-depth coverage of the Android platform architecture. We will try to provide a basic understanding of key Android platform concepts that will serve as background and context for our practical projects. The official Android Developers web site[16] is a good reference for further study.

The Android architecture stack, at its highest level, is broadly made up of three layers:

- Exceptionally rich end-user functionality delivered via a core set of state-of-the-art applications that are pluggable by design.

- Middleware services forming a loosely coupled, reusable, fully open, and extensible component framework with supporting runtime libraries.

- An open-source, highly stable, trusted, and high-performance operating system that forms the foundation of the Android platform.

---

[15] http://developer.android.com/guide/developing/other-ide.html

[16] http://developer.android.com/guide/basics/what-is-android.html

The Android Platform Stack

A breakdown of the layers and components that comprise the system architecture of the Android platform is graphically depicted in Figure 1–11. We will briefly describe them here.

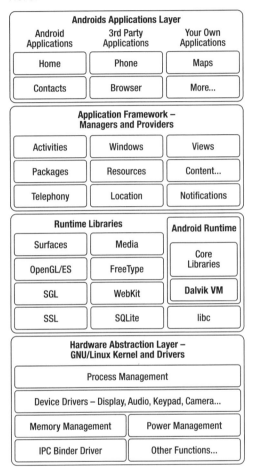

Figure 1–11. *The Android platform system architecture*

The Hardware Abstraction Layer (HAL)

Hardware abstraction layers (HALs) are designed to protect operating platform engineers and applications developers from the idiosyncrasies of a multitude of hardware platforms delivered to the device market by almost equally numerous vendors.

The open-source Linux kernel and appropriate device drivers form the HAL for the Android operating platform. It takes care of core system operations such as hardware driver control, process management, networking, and power- and memory management.

The C/C++ Runtime Libraries

The native C/C++ libraries run directly on the HAL kernel and provide core services to applications and the Android runtime.

These services include graphics support (2D, 3D, SGL, OpenGL), display management, video and audio media playback, structured data storage (SQLite), libc, built-in web browser support via WebKit, and SSL for secure networking.

The Android Runtime

The DVM is the star of the Android applications runtime. Each DVM instance is hosted in its own Linux kernel system process and takes advantage of system-level threading and memory management. Its performance and memory characteristics are such that Android can afford to allocate an instance of the DVM to each running application.

The DVM is supported by a core set of (Java) libraries and APIs that are fully documented, open, and available to software developers. Even though Java code is written to target Dalvik using these libraries, this does not make the DVM a true Java Virtual Machine (JVM). It merely supports a large part of standard Java augmented by libraries and APIs that are Android-specific.

Due to its unique and encompassing role in Android applications development, we will investigate Dalvik in more detail in an upcoming section of this chapter.

The Application Framework

The Android Application Framework directly supports the development of applications. It is the broad set of Java namespaces and classes with which we create our applications.

This framework encompasses a wide range of Android Managers and Providers that abstract the supporting hardware and device resources and services. These include everything from the user interface, to location awareness, acceleration detection, camera, telephony, system notifications etc.

The Applications Layer

Android systems are generally delivered with a highly functional set of core applications that provide the device user with an innovative set of tools. These tools allow the device owner to both leverage and take advantage of the impressive capabilities of the Android hardware platform and to mix and match applications to their taste and special requirements.

The Android SDK supports developing against this high level of flexibility with the same comprehensive set of APIs used by the platform developers themselves. In addition, the open design of the platform allows developers to apply the SDK to reuse, extend, or completely replace the provided core applications with their own creations.

All Android applications are treated equally by the system. Standard Android applications are generally written in Java, and native code libraries can be loaded and called via Java Native Interface (JNI) if needed.

Android Component Architecture

Android is a component-based platform. Applications are built up from loosely coupled, reusable, extendable, and replaceable components that fall within well-defined roles. We will briefly list the types of components here. The "Android Fundamentals" web site[17] provides a deeper treatment of the subject:

- **Activities** (Views). This is the application's primary user interface component. Every individual screen of an Android application is derived from the `Activity` Java class (`android.app.Activity`[18]). They are containers for Views (`android.view.View`[19]).

- **Services** (Controllers). These are background components that behave like UNIX daemons and Windows services. They run invisibly and perform ongoing unattended processing.

- **Content Providers** (Models). Data Managers that are the recommended form of inter-application data sharing.

- **Intents**. Inter-application messaging that can target a specific Service or Activity. It can also be broadcast system-wide to advertise an intended action or request an action to be performed.

- **Broadcast Receivers**. Listeners and consumers for Intents.

- **Notifications**. Visual or aural mechanisms for end-user notification.

- **Widgets**. Special visual components that extend the Home screen.

The Android Runtime: Dalvik Virtual Machine (DVM)

At the heart of the Android Java runtime platform sits the *Dalvik Virtual Machine (DVM)*. We have mentioned some aspects of the DVM previously. The central and unique role that the DVM plays in the Android system justifies looking at it in a little more depth. Furthermore, the positioning and peculiarities of the DVM in the world of JVMs also bear closer scrutiny.

The DVM is Google's fully open-source implementation of the Java SE (JSE) VM. The DVM was optimized by design for attaining the maximum possible performance for a

---

[17] http://developer.android.com/guide/topics/fundamentals.html

[18] http://developer.android.com/reference/android/app/Activity.html

[19] http://developer.android.com/reference/android/view/View.html

Java VM hosted on resource-restricted devices such as mobile phones. It strives to maximize the well-known gains associated with programming in Java while minimizing the penalties of operating a virtual machine in a constricted environment.

The following points regarding Android Java development and the DVM runtime bytecode support are fundamental for Android software developers:

- **Android is not JSE:** The Android API maximizes overlap with the JSE, but there are differences. A notable example is in the GUI department. Android implements its own graphical user interface API and does not support JSE AWT and Swing at all.

- **Android uses Standard Java** Android supports development with the full Java programming language. Even though some packages and APIs of the JSE are not supported, use of the Java language is generally unrestricted. For this reason, your Android Java code is compiled with a standard, vanilla Java compiler, not a Google-specific one.

- **Dalvik runs (.dex) Dalvik Executables:** Your Android code will be compiled by the mainstream Java compiler you have come to love. The resulting bytecode will also be the same familiar format. However, perhaps surprisingly, the DVM does not run this bytecode. It does not execute the standard .class and .jar files you might be used to. Instead, the DVM runs its own form of bytecode compiled as .dex files that are commonly packaged into .apk Android Package files. The Android SDK includes a tool called "dx" that transforms standard compiled class files into .dex files. Figure 1–12 has a graphical representation of this process followed by an overview.

- **Every application has its DVM:** The DVM is, by design, highly optimized in terms of performance and size. This allows (also by design) each Android application to be hosted in its own instance of the DVM. At the cost of a marginal amount of extra system resources, this runtime architecture promotes higher application availability and better security. For example, applications do not share memory and are thus protected from the potential misbehavior and runtime failure of other applications.

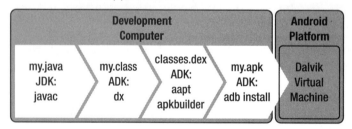

Figure 1–12. *The path from a Java source file to a DVM executable package*

The Path to DEX (and APK)

An overview of the steps required for creating a runnable Android package, as depicted in Figure 1–12, is as follows:

- Life for an Android Java application starts with a programming text editor and stock-standard Java source code that imports Android APIs from the namespaces and libraries provided with the Android SDK.

- This code is compiled with a standard Java compiler (javac) from the standard JDK. The result is a standard set of bytecode class files as one would expect from a normal Java application.

- These class files are consumed by the Android SDK dx program that converts and binds the set of class files into a DVM-compatible classes.dex file. This binary consists of special bytecode meant to run on the DVM. It does not run on the reference JVM.

- All class-, dex and resource files are then prepared, signed, and zipped together as an Android application package (.apk) archive by the aapt and apkbuilder utility programs.

- The .apk application package is then ready for deployment and execution on an Android device. Packages can be installed either via the ant install build step or using the adb install command.[20]

AN ANDROID BUILD FROM JAVA TO DEX TO APK

Tracing through the following build listing extract taken from our earlier "Android SDK Test Drive" section should serve to complement the previous overview. Important names are in bold font, and some sections have been condensed for brevity. It might be useful to refer to this listing later when we have covered more ground and some concepts start to come together.

```
\MyAndroidSdkAppProject> ant debug
Buildfile: \MyAndroidSdkAppProject\build.xml
      [setup] Android SDK Tools Revision 8
   [setup] Project Target: Android 2.3
   [setup] API level: 9
   [setup]
   [setup] ----------------
   [setup] Resolving library dependencies:
   [setup] No library dependencies.
   [setup]
   [setup] ----------------
   [setup]
   [setup] WARNING: No minSdkVersion value set. Application will install on all⤶
 Android versions.
   [setup]
```

---

[20] http://developer.android.com/guide/developing/tools/adb.html#move

```
    [setup] Importing rules file: tools\ant\main_rules.xml

-debug-obfuscation-check:
-set-debug-mode:
 -compile-tested-if-test:
-dirs:
    [echo] Creating output directories if needed...
    [mkdir] Created dir: \MyAndroidSdkAppProject\gen
    [mkdir] Created dir: \MyAndroidSdkAppProject\bin\classes
-pre-build:
-resource-src:
    [echo] Generating R.java / Manifest.java from the resources...
-aidl:
    [echo] Compiling aidl files into Java classes...
-pre-compile:
compile:
    [javac] \android-sdk-windows\tools\ant\ant_rules_r3.xml:336: warning:↵
 'includeantruntime' was not set, defaulting to build.sysclasspath=last; ↵
set to false for repeatable builds
    [javac] Compiling 2 source files to \MyAndroidSdkAppProject\bin\classes
-post-compile:
 -obfuscate:
-dex:
    [echo] Converting compiled files and external libraries into↵
 \MyAndroidSdkAppProject\bin\classes.dex...
-package-resources:
    [echo] Packaging resources
    [aapt] Creating full resource package...
-package-debug-sign:
[apkbuilder] Creating MyAndroidSdkApp-debug-unaligned.apk and signing it with a debug↵
 key...
debug:
    [echo] Running zip align on final apk...
    [echo] Debug Package: \MyAndroidSdkAppProject\bin\MyAndroidSdkApp-debug.apk
BUILD SUCCESSFUL
```

Dalvik and the Apache Harmony JVM

A significant part of the DVM was built with code from the Apache Harmony Java class library. Apache Harmony is a full stack, open-source Java SE implementation that can be used as an alternative JRE.

To quote from the Apache Harmony web site, the project has as its primary goal the implementation of a complete Java SE, including virtual machine, class library areas, and all related and common tooling.

The fact that Harmony is a full stack reimplementation of Java SE also has implications for Android. Both platforms essentially attempted to create full and free JSE implementations that are not bound to licensing anomalies that had historically plagued Java. Harmony and the lion's share of the Android code fall under Apache License Version 2.0. The notable exceptions in the case of Android are the Linux kernel patches that are released under the GPLv2 license. However, the stated preferred license for new Android derived code is Apache 2.0.

The relationship between Android Dalvik and Harmony might at some point in the future lead to a reconciliation phase where compatible code contributions are merged from the Android codebase back into Harmony. Regardless, this does highlight the often subtle but powerful possibilities that the effective use of the open-source model creates for those willing to embrace it.

One important aspect to remember is that although Apache Harmony aims to be a full JSE implementation, as mentioned earlier, the Android implementation is not.

> **DALVIK COMES FROM DALVÍK:** For the curious (and we're sure many of you are), the name "Dalvik" apparently stems from the name of the fishing village, Dalvík, in the north of Iceland. This is believed to have been the home of some ancestors of the DVM creator, Dan Bornstein.

Dalvik JVM Performance

With the Android 2.2 "Froyo" release and onward, the DVM includes a just-in-time compiler. This is especially important for the future of the Android platform because performance and perceived performance are of the utmost relevance for end-user applications running on resource-restricted devices such as mobile phones.

The DVM architecture is register-machine–based as opposed to stack-machine–based. Stack-machines are commonly used for virtual machines in general and for most JVMs in particular. We will try to avoid the debate about virtual stack versus virtual register VM performance. Suffice it to say that, theoretically, even though register-machine based implementations tend to result in larger machine code; they also tend to execute faster than stack machines after being loaded into memory. This is partly due to fewer resulting VM instructions that need to be executed by the real machine to fetch and perform the actual computation work, despite the larger overall code size.

Again, this has direct relevance for the execution profile of applications and services on restricted devices. There are always trade-offs, especially when betting on factors such as improved memory resource availability at relatively lower expense than processor cost.

Using an Integrated Development Environment (IDE)

This section presents an overview of applying the Eclipse and NetBeans IDEs to your Android development tasks. It gives resource references, shows how to install the relevant supported plugins that will convert these Java IDEs into full-blown Android development tools, and provides quickstart information on creating an Android project in the respective IDE.

Working with Eclipse

From the moment the Android SDK was released, Eclipse has been the de facto standard IDE for Android development and remains so to this day.

From our perspective, these are the main reasons for this:

- With the release of the Android SDK, Google immediately made available the extensive Android Development Tools (ADT) plugin for Eclipse. It has a clear head start.
- ADT is used and maintained by the Google Android platform developers themselves.
- Eclipse enjoys huge Java development market penetration. This applies to both open-source environments that build on Eclipse RCP and commercial development suites from big vendors.
- Eclipse/ADT, like the Android SDK itself, is open source and available free of charge.

These motivators combine to make choosing Eclipse for Android development a no-brainer for most developers and organizations. Clearly, one (beneficial) side effect of this situation is that there is a huge amount of official (and less than official) information available for using Eclipse/ADT. It has also been covered almost by default in many books and tutorial publications.

We are trying to present a comprehensive introduction to Android development in only one chapter of this book. Considering this and the vast amount of Eclipse/ADT information available, we will strive only to deliver an Eclipse/ADT quickstart plus convenient references to additional information. We assume that the reader has, at the very least, sufficient experience to know what `Eclipse Update Sites` are and how to manage them in the IDE.

On the Web: Eclipse for Android Development

Official information and references for Eclipse and the Google ADT plugin for Eclipse can be found at the following online locations:

Eclipse Home and Download Area

- http://www.eclipse.org
- http://www.eclipse.org/downloads/

Android Development Tools Plugin for Eclipse ADT

- http://developer.android.com/sdk/eclipse-adt.html
- http://developer.android.com/sdk/eclipse-adt.html#installing

Android Development in Eclipse with ADT

- `http://developer.android.com/guide/developing/eclipse-adt.html`

Official Google ADT Eclipse Update Site

- `https://dl-ssl.google.com/android/eclipse/`
- `http://dl-ssl.google.com/android/eclipse/`

If you do not have Eclipse on your system, go ahead with downloading and installing it. The Eclipse version that the author uses (Eclipse 3.6.x Helios JEE) is displayed (using the Help ➤ About Eclipse menus) in Figure 1–13.

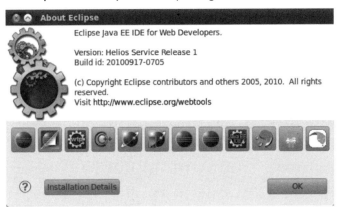

Figure 1–13. *Eclipse version*

Quickstart: The Eclipse Android Development Tools (ADT) Plugin

We will now cover the setup procedure for the Eclipse/ADT plugin.

Installing ADT

1. To install the Eclipse ADT plugin, go to the Eclipse **Help ➤ Install New Software** menu and click the Add (a New Software Site) button. This should display the dialog shown in Figure 1–14.

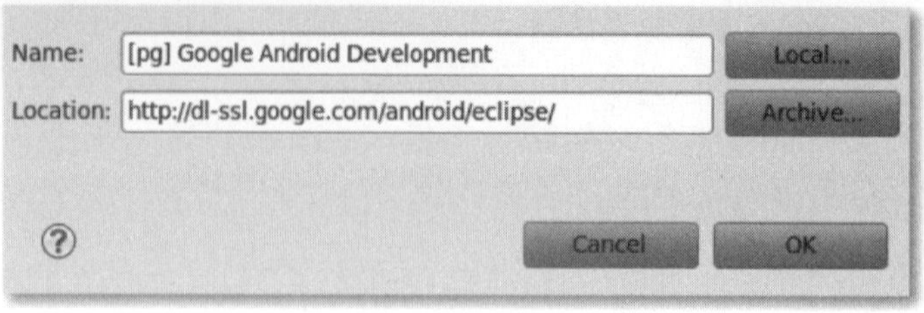

Figure 1-14. *Add the ADT Eclipse software site.*

2. Enter your own preferred Name and in the Location use either of the following resource locators:

    https://dl-ssl.google.com/android/eclipse/

    http://dl-ssl.google.com/android/eclipse/

    Try the second URL if the former fails to connect. Click the OK button.

3. The Eclipse Available Software dialog shown in Figure 1–15 displays with the ADT listed. Select all the tools and click Next or Finish. Continue with the setup workflow until the installation is complete.

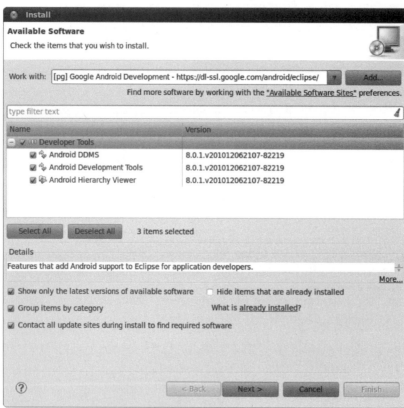

Figure 1-15. *Eclipse Add ADT Available Software*

4. Now follow the **Window ➤ Preferences** menus and select the `Android` entry in the tree view on the left. The `Android Preferences` editor should now be visible, as in Figure 1–16.

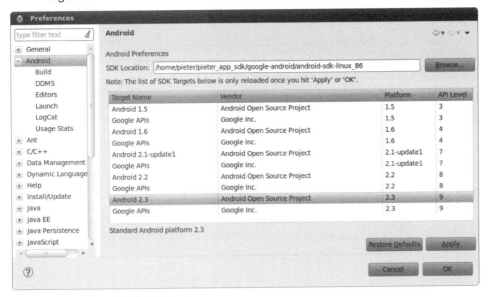

Figure 1–16. *Eclipse ADT Android preferences*

5. Use the `Browse` button to find the root directory of the location where the Android SDK is installed on your system. Click the `Apply` button.

6. If the updated list of installed SDK Targets appears, the Eclipse ADT plugin is now installed correctly. Click `OK` to dismiss the dialog.

It might be a good idea to restart Eclipse and double-check the `Android Preferences` setting again. If this procedure did not work, please follow up with the Eclipse/ADT online references given earlier.

> **THE ANDROID SDK AND AVD MANAGER IN ECLIPSE:** After successful ADT installation, the `Android SDK and AVD Manager` can be launched from the Eclipse menu system. Follow **Window ➤ Android SDK and AVD Manager**.

Android Projects in Eclipse

Create new Android projects by clicking **File ➤ New ➤ Project** and selecting `Android Project` from the `Android` node. See Figure 1–17.

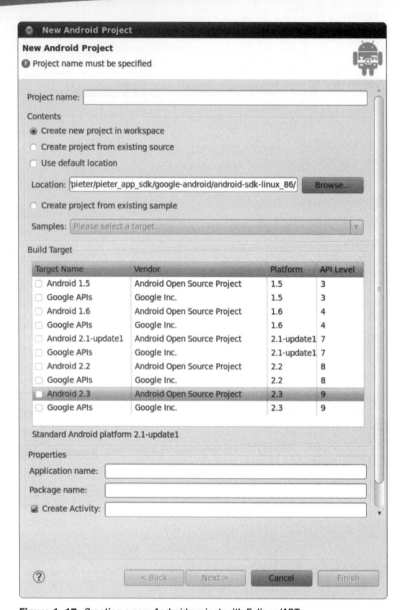

Figure 1-17. *Creating a new Android project with Eclipse/ADT*

From the same dialog (refer to Figure 1-17), new Android projects can also be created from the existing source by enabling the `Create project from existing source` radio button and then following the selection workflow.

Another option, which is handy when getting to know the Android SDK, is to select `Create project from existing sample`. This then populates the `Samples` drop-down with a list of Android SDK sample projects retrieved from the contents of your SDK installation. Here you will be able to select a sample as the basis for your new project.

Working with NetBeans

No, Eclipse is no longer the only free Android development IDE game in town. Over the last years, the NetBeans[21] IDE has become a fully viable alternative to Eclipse in the IDE arena. Not only that, but the NetBeans platform[22] is also making a serious challenge to Eclipse RCP for a stake in the rich client platform development space. The NetBeans platform has been used as the development foundation of choice for many high-profile products in the defense, geospatial, network management, retail, bio-informatics, and myriad other commercial and open-source domains.[23]

As mentioned before, we are presenting a wide introduction to Android development in only one chapter of this book. Yet we still feel that it is a good idea to cover Android development with NetBeans. NetBeans has many easy-to-use qualities that make it a great choice for both teaching and getting started with Java development in general and Android development in particular. Furthermore, we would like to contribute to the growing body of documentation that supports Android development with NetBeans. Experience has shown that having a choice of high-quality development tools available is always a good thing.

On the Web: NetBeans for Android Development

Official information and references for NetBeans and the NBAndroid plugin for NetBeans can be found at the following online locations.

NetBeans Home and Download Area

- http://netbeans.org/
- http://netbeans.org/downloads/

Android Plugin for NetBeans: NBAndroid

- http://kenai.com/projects/nbandroid/
- http://kenai.com/projects/nbandroid/pages/Install

Android Development In NetBeans, with NBAndroid

- http://wiki.netbeans.org/IntroAndroidDevNetBeans

---

[21] http://netbeans.org/downloads

[22] http://netbeans.org/features/platform

[23] http://netbeans.org/features/platform/showcase.html

Official NBAndroid NetBeans Update Site

- http://kenai.com/downloads/nbandroid/updates.xml

If you do not have NetBeans on your system, download and install it. The NetBeans version that the author currently uses (NetBeans 6.9.1) is displayed (using the **Help ➤ About** menus) in Figure 1–18.

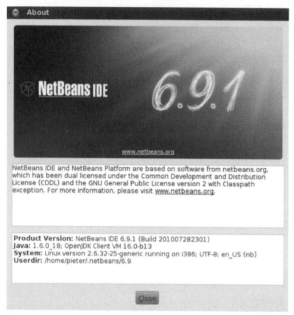

Figure 1–18. *NetBeans version*

Quickstart: The NetBeans Android (NBAndroid) Plugin

We will now cover the setup procedure for the NetBeans/NBAndroid plugin. To install NBAndroid, follow these steps:

1. To install the NetBeans NBAndroid plugin, go to the NetBeans **Tools ➤ Plugins** menu and click the Settings tab.

2. Click the Add button to show the Update Center Customizer, as shown in Figure 1–19.

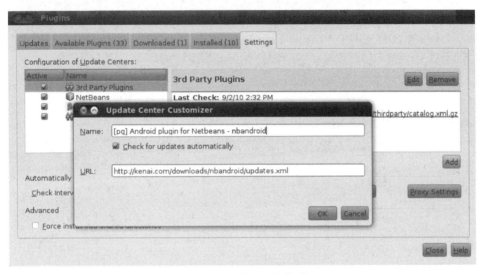

Figure 1–19. *Adding the NBAndroid plugin Update Center in NetBeans*

3. Enter your own preferred Name for the Update Center and in the URL text box enter the following:

   http://kenai.com/downloads/nbandroid/updates.xml

4. Click the OK button.

   You should now be able to see the NBAndroid plugin Update Center visible in the list on the Settings tab (see Figure 1–20).

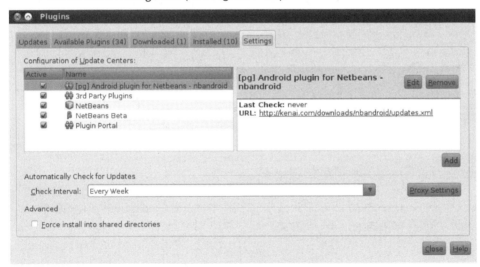

Figure 1–20. *The NBAndroid plugin Update Center added to NetBeans*

5. Click the Available Plugins tab. Find and select Android. The description should appear on the right side (see Figure 1–21).

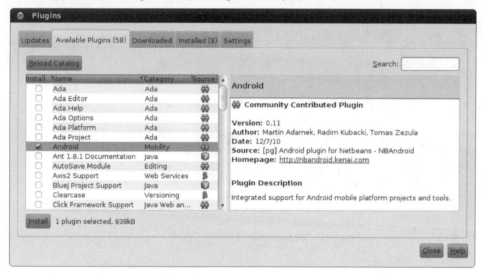

Figure 1-21. *The NBAndroid plugin listed in NetBeans*

6. Now click the Install button on the bottom left of the dialog.

7. Click Next (see Figure 1-22), accept the license agreement, and let the installation continue until it is complete.

Figure 1-22. *Installing the NBAndroid plugin in NetBeans*

8. Click the Installed tab. Check Show Details. Sort the Name column. The Android plugin should be Active (see Figure 1-23). Click Close.

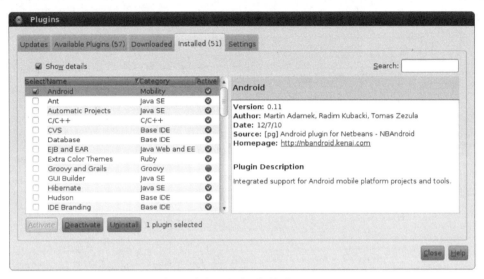

Figure 1–23. *Completed NBAndroid plugin installation in NetBeans*

9. Click the left Navigator Services tab. The Android Devices node should now be visible in the tree of services (see Figure 1–24).

Figure 1–24. *The Android Devices node in NetBeans Services*

10. Now go to menu **Tools ➤ Java Platforms**.
11. Click Add Platform (see Figure 1–25).

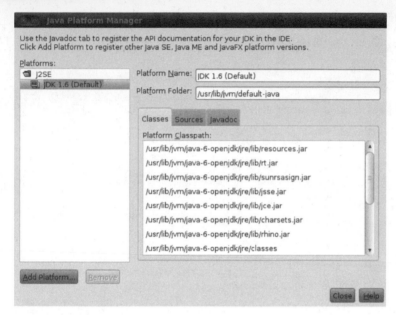

Figure 1–25. *Managing Java platforms in NetBeans*

12. Select the Google Android Platform. Click Next (see Figure 1–26).

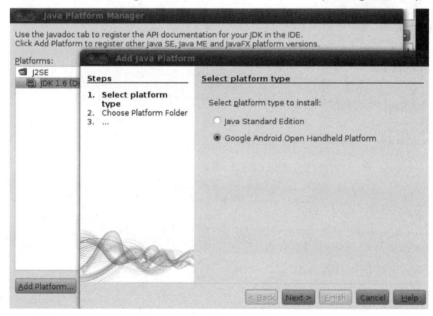

Figure 1–26. *Adding the Android Java platform to NetBeans*

13. Browse to the Android SDK root folder. Click Next (see Figure 1–27).

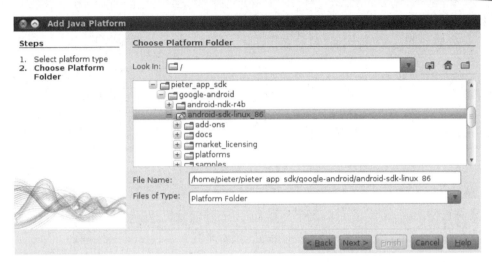

Figure 1–27. *Setting the Android SDK folder*

14. Select a target and give it a name. Click `Finish` (see Figure 1–28).

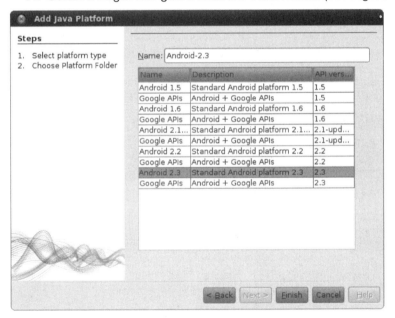

Figure 1–28. *Setting the Android SDK target*

15. The Android platform target is now registered with NetBeans and ready for use. Click the `Close` button (see Figure 1–29).

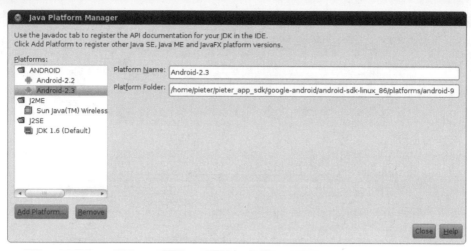

Figure 1-29. *The Android Java platform target is now registered with NetBeans.*

Android Projects in NetBeans

Here we present a tutorial on how to create a new Android project using NetBeans and NBAndroid:

1. Create new Android projects in NetBeans by going to the main menu and clicking File ➤ New Project. Select Android from the Categories list. Click Next (see Figure 1-30).

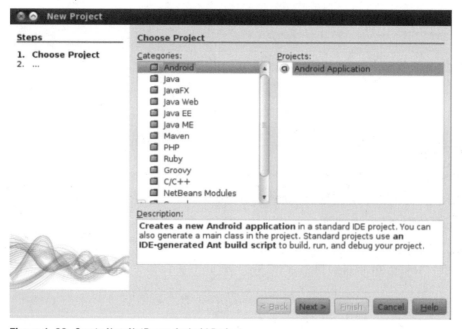

Figure 1-30. *Create New NetBeans Android Project*

The New Android Application screen opens (see Figure 1–31).

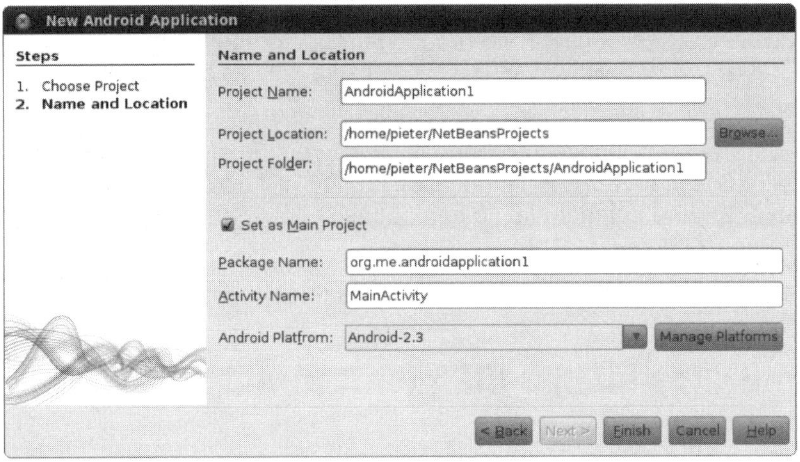

Figure 1–31. *Create New NetBeans Android project name and location*

2. Fill in your Project Name, Location, Folder, Package Name, and Activity Name. Pick an Android platform from the drop-down.

3. Click Finish.

The main NetBeans development environment and code editor opens in the new project (see Figure 1–32).

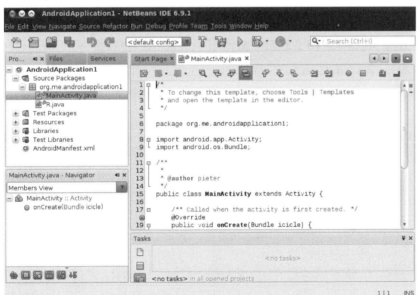

Figure 1–32. *Create New NetBeans Android application*

Your NetBeans IDE is ready to be used for coding Android projects.

Working with IntelliJ IDEA Community Edition

IntelliJ IDEA[24] from JetBrains[25] has long had a reputation for being one the most outstanding Java IDEs ever created. However, it was available only as a commercial closed-source product.

Just over a year ago, JetBrains announced an open source[26] version of IntelliJ IDEA called the Community Edition.[27] A year later, it released its official Android plugin, previously only available with the commercial edition of the IDE, as part of the free Community Edition starting with version 10.[28]

This gives Android Java developers a very serious and attractive no-cost IDE alternative.

On the Web: JetBrains IntelliJ IDEA for Android Development

Official information and references for JetBrains IntelliJ IDEA Community Edition and using it for Android development can be found at the following online locations:

IntelliJ IDEA Community Edition Home and Download Areas

- http://www.jetbrains.org
- http://www.jetbrains.org/display/IJOS/Download
- http://www.jetbrains.com/idea/download/

IntelliJ IDEA Early Access Program and Download Areas

- http://www.jetbrains.com/idea/nextversion/
- http://confluence.jetbrains.net/display/IDEADEV/IDEA+X+EAP

Android Development with IntelliJ IDEA

- http://www.jetbrains.com/idea/features/google_android.html

---

[24] http://www.jetbrains.com/idea/

[25] http://www.jetbrains.com/

[26] http://www.jetbrains.org

[27] http://blogs.jetbrains.com/idea/2009/10/intellij-idea-open-sourced/

[28] http://blogs.jetbrains.com/idea/2010/10/intellij-idea-10-free-ide-for-android-development/

Official IntelliJ IDEA Documentation and Blog Site

- http://www.jetbrains.com/idea/documentation
- http://blogs.jetbrains.com/idea/

IntelliJ IDEA Community Edition Project and Code Repository

- http://git.jetbrains.org/
- http://git.jetbrains.org/?p=idea/community.git;a=summary

If you do not have IntelliJ IDEA Community Edition on your system, now is a good time to download and install it. The IntelliJ IDEA version that the author currently uses (IntelliJ IDEA 10 Preview) is displayed (using the Help ➤ About menus) in Figure 1–33.

Figure 1–33. *IntelliJ IDEA Community Edition version*

Quickstart: The IntelliJ IDEA Android Plugin

The IDEA Android plugin comes bundled with the IDE installation so there is nothing extra to set up for Android development as far as the IDE itself is concerned. The only other task to perform is identifying the location of your Android SDK and platform target for your project. We will demonstrate how to do this shortly.

Android Projects in IntelliJ IDEA Community Edition

Here we will present a short tutorial on how to create a new Android project using the IntelliJ IDEA Community Edition:

1. Create new Android projects in IntelliJ IDEA by going to the main menu and clicking File ➤ New Project. The first New Project wizard screen opens (see Figure 1–34).

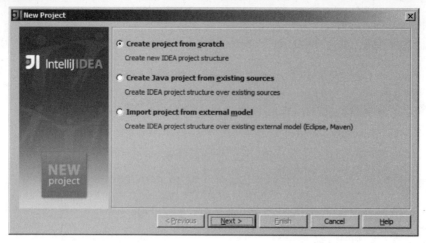

Figure 1-34. *Creating a new IntelliJ IDEA Community Edition project*

2. Select Create project from scratch and click Next. The next New Project wizard screen should appear (see Figure 1–35).

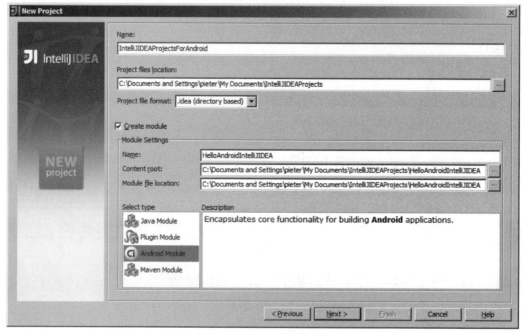

Figure 1-35. *Creating a new IntelliJ IDEA Community Edition Android project*

3. Select a project type of Android Module, fill out the Name and Location directories entry fields with appropriate values, and click Next. The following New Project wizard screen for the source directory configuration should appear (see Figure 1–36).

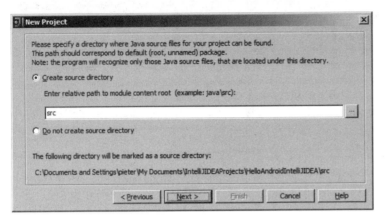

Figure 1–36. *Configuring the New Project source directory*

4. Decide whether and where to configure the source directory and click Next. The following New Project wizard screen for the Android SDK and platform target configuration should appear (see Figure 1–37).

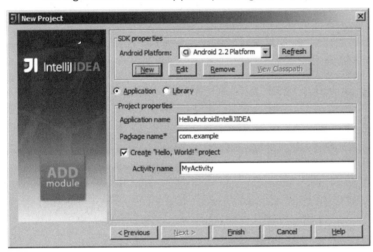

Figure 1–37. *Configuring the Android platform for a project*

5. Optionally select an Android Platform from the list and click Next, or click New to configure a new platform. The following Select Path dialog form should appear (see Figure 1–38) if you perform the latter.

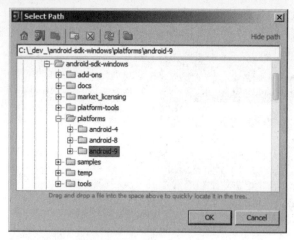

Figure 1-38. *Adding a New Android platform target to an IntelliJ IDEA Community Edition project*

6. Browse to the required `Android Platform` directory on your development system and click `OK`. The previous dialog form should now appear with the new platform in the list (see Figure 1-39). Select the platform and fill out the remaining fields with your settings. Click `Finish`.

Figure 1-39. *Selecting an Android SDK platform target for an IntelliJ IDEA Community Edition project*

7. The `New Project` wizard is now complete, and the main IntelliJ IDEA development environment and code editor opens in the new project (see Figure 1-40).

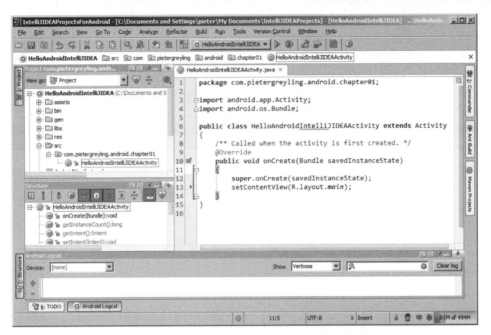

Figure 1-40. *Creating a new IntelliJ IDEA Android application and IDE code editor*

Your IntelliJ IDEA Community Edition IDE is now ready for use in programming Android projects.

Summary

In this chapter, we have used a fairly broad brush to give you a good introductory background and knowledge of the Android development platform. Without getting distracted with too much detail, we have covered multiple aspects from theory to tools. We have also complemented this material with references to the official online Android developer resources and encouraged their habitual use.

In addition, we provided quickstart recipe guides for beginning with Android programming using the most popular Java developer IDEs. These tools are purpose-built and maintained to complement and leverage the core Android SDK tools. They should serve to streamline and accelerate your development work while not distracting from the use of the SDK programs and utilities directly when needs dictate.

The knowledge and understanding you gained should equip you with a good foundation for starting your practical journey into programming software using the Android SDK and your own tools of choice. This springboard will allow you to dive into deeper waters in any specific Android technology direction you wish to pursue.

Chapter 2

Development Tools in Practice

In the first chapter of the book we presented a broad coverage of the Android platform from both a theoretical and practical viewpoint. You had the opportunity to learn about the overall architecture and components of the platform. You also had the chance to test drive the tools that ship with the Android software development kit (SDK) by creating a skeleton Android project from the command line and stepping through the development lifecycle all the way to installation of the application on the Android emulator.

We also included an introduction to the three major noncommercial Java integrated development environments (IDEs), Eclipse, NetBeans, and Intellij IDEA Community Edition, showed you how to equip them with Android development capabilities via freely available plugins.

This chapter has a dual goal: first, it aims to leave you with a firm grasp of how to use the Android SDK development tools for real Android development projects. Second, and no less important, it will provide an introduction to the structure and components of Android projects and the Android application programming interface (API).

We will cover the creation of a capable Android development environment with nothing but the Android SDK command line and graphical user interface (GUI) tools plus a stock programmer's text editor. As part of this discussion, we will present a project containing reusable code sections and techniques that also give us the chance to demonstrate specific SDK tools and Android API features.

Finally, we will import the example project into the Eclipse integrated development environment (IDE) in order to demonstrate how to take advantage of some of the Android productivity features of Eclipse with the Android Development Tools (ADT) plugin.

Coding with the SDK and a Programmer's Editor

It is entirely feasible to do serious Android development using the Android SDK in combination with a programmer's editor. This approach requires minimal setup overhead and is worth becoming familiar with for the sole reason of enriching your understanding of core Android development. This will help you to understand what your IDE of choice is doing behind the scenes and empower you to dig right in to debugging tasks without an IDE.

As an example, we have often saved time by diving straight to the root cause of an Android application crash during debugging simply by issuing the following Android Debug Bridge command in a terminal window:

```
adb logcat
```

Thereafter repeating the same steps that caused the runtime failure in the application and watching the logging output as it is streamed to the logcat terminal often makes the real problem (such as a missing permission in the application manifest file) clearly evident.

For further information on the adb tool, and as a general approach to learning the core ADK utilities and programs, we suggest running the adb `help` command. Reviewing the official Android developer site for, in this case, the Android Debug Bridge is also recommended.[1]

> **NOTE ON DEVELOPMENT OPERATING SYSTEMS:** We use a mixture of Ubuntu GNU/Linux, Apple Mac OS X, and Microsoft Windows development systems. The code listings, screen captures and commands we demonstrate generally apply to all platforms. We will draw attention to any notable exceptions.

Development Environment Dependencies

Before we proceed, we need to review some dependencies and ensure that we can run the necessary Android SDK utilities and commands on our development system.

Ensure that Development Kit Locations Are on the Path

For doing serious work with the Android SDK, always ensure that the appropriate binaries and tools (<Java JDK/bin>, <Android SDK/tools>, <Android SDK/platform-tools>, and <Ant/bin>) are on the system path. We covered the subject of path setup and issues in some depth in the first chapter of this book. Please refer to that chapter for more information if necessary.

---

[1] http://developer.android.com/guide/developing/tools/adb.html

Preparing an Android Virtual Device (AVD)

To be able to run our test project for this chapter we will need an Android Virtual Device. It is probably ideal that this AVD is not cluttered with previous debugging applications and leftover user data.

We can either reuse the `HelloAndroidSdkAVD` we created in the first chapter or create a new one. The AVD should be configured with at least Android 2.3 (API Level 9) compatibility like the one depicted in Figure 2–1. I chose to create a fresh AVD and give it the more meaningful name of `android23api9_hvga_32mb` for easier reference.

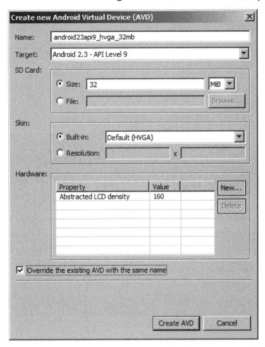

Figure 2–1. *Preparing a new Android Virtual Device (AVD)*

Creating (and Deleting) an AVD from the Command Line

The Android SDK also supports the creation of AVDs from the command line.[2] So we could also have made our new AVD using the following terminal command:

`android create avd -n android23api9_hvga_32mb -t android-9 -s HVGA -c 32M`

If you want to get rid of the AVD for some reason, simply use the following command:

`android delete avd -n android23api9_hvga_32mb`

---

[2] http://developer.android.com/guide/developing/tools/avd.html#options

> **BE CAREFUL!** The android delete terminal command does not ask for confirmation of the requested operation. So this makes it really easy to accidentally purge an AVD you might still need. Make sure to keep backups of development AVDs that contain useful test data.

AVD File and Image Locations

AVD configuration and image files are created on your development computer under the .android directory in your home folder. Depending on your system, the default locations are as shown in Table 2–1.

These locations can be overridden by using the –p switch on the android create avd command as in the next example command on Linux / Mac OS X:

`android create avd -n avd23api9 -t android-9 -c 32M -p mydroiddev/avds/avd23api9`

Or on Windows:

`android create avd -n avd23api9 -t android-9 -c 32M -p C:\mydroiddev\avds\avd23api9`

Table 2–1. *Default AVD Locations by Operating System Platform*

Platform	Default Android Virtual Device Location
Linux and Mac OS X	~/.android/avd/
Windows XP	C:\Documents and Settings\<user>\.android\avd\
Windows Vista	C:\Users\<user>\.android\avd\

As always, more information is available on the Android Developers web site.[3]

Frequently Used Android Development Kit Tools

Becoming comfortable with using the Android SDK tools from the terminal command line will add a lot of value to your Android development efforts. The various IDEs and their Android plugins come packed with a lot of functionality. These features are often standard out-of-the-box Android SDK tools in a repackaged or embedded form. Familiarity with the core tools will enrich your understanding of your IDE of choice as well as allow you to drop down to these tools when the IDE implementation falls short.

There are a handful of tools that will prove themselves useful on a daily basis. Launching some tools brings up GUIs from which other core functionality can be reached conveniently via menus. Table 2–2 provides a list of commands that will allow a

---

[3] http://developer.android.com/guide/developing/tools/avd.html#location

developer to perform the majority of Android development tasks in combination with a code editor.

Table 2-2. *Indispensable Android SDK Development Tool Commands*

Android SDK Development Tool	Linux/Mac OS X	Windows
Android SDK and AVD Manager	android	android.bat
Dalvik Debug Monitor	ddms	ddms.bat
Ant Compile	ant compile	ant.bat compile
Ant Clean	ant clean	ant.bat clean
Ant Build Debug	ant debug	ant.bat debug
Ant Build Install	ant install	ant.bat install
Ant Build Uninstall	ant uninstall	ant.bat uninstall

> **NOTE:** All ant commands must be run in your Android application project root directory where the ant build.xml file should reside. The `android create project` command generates a build.xml file containing the relevant ant build actions and targets.

Working with the Android Tools and a Code Editor

The purpose of this section is to give you an idea of what is possible using the frequently used Android tools from the previous section, plus a code editor that is configured to invoke these tools directly from its own user interface.

Selecting a Code Editor

For our demonstration, we have decided to use the Geany[4] programmer's editor. It was selected because it suited our intentions in this instance particularly well, not because we are suggesting that it should become your editor of choice. The main aspects that made it applicable for demonstrating the goals of this section are as follows:

- It is a GUI that can easily and clearly be presented in a book.
- It is freely and easily obtainable for many operating systems for readers who want to try the examples.

---

[4] http://www.geany.org/

- It supports the grouping of files into projects with user customizable build commands.

References for Editor Alternatives

Before we go on, we thought it would be appropriate to list some references for other editor environments that some readers will certainly know and might even be using as their preferred choice. We fully understand that the subject of the programmer's code editor can spark very animated discussions and should be treated with sensitivity.

So here is a short and by no means definitive list of editors and editing environments that can be well suited to Android development:

- **Emacs and Android-Mode:** The GNU Emacs manual describes it as "the extensible, customizable, self-documenting, real-time display editor." Emacs is open source and runs on almost all known platforms.
    - Emacs home: http://www.gnu.org/software/emacs/
    - Java-Mode: http://sourceforge.net/projects/jdee/
    - Android-Mode: https://github.com/remvee/android-mode
    - Using Emacs for Android Development: http://blog.fmaj7.me/?p=18
- **Eclim, Vim with Eclipse:** Vim is a highly configurable text editor built to enable efficient text editing. It is an improved version of the vi editor distributed with most UNIX systems. Vim is open source and runs on almost all known platforms.
    - Vim home: http://www.vim.org/
    - Eclim Eclipse for Vim: http://eclim.org/index.html
    - Using Vim + Eclim for Android Development: http://jyro.blogspot.com/2009/05/android-development-with-vim-eclim.html
- **jEdit:** jEdit is a mature programmer's text editor with hundreds (counting the time developing plugins) of person-years of development behind it. It is open source and written in Java, so it runs on Mac OS X, OS/2, UNIX, VMS, and Windows.
    - jEdit home: http://www.jedit.org/
- **TextMate:** TextMate is a powerful, general-purpose GUI text editor for Mac OS X that is very popular with programmers and technology professionals. It is highly configurable and focuses on productive automation. It is currently only available for Mac OS X and is a proprietary, commercial product.
    - TextMate home: http://www.macromates.com/

- **Bluefish:** Bluefish is a powerful editor targeted toward programmers and web designers, with many options to write web sites, scripts, and programming code. It is released under the GNU GPL license and runs on most operating systems including Linux, FreeBSD, Mac OS X, OpenBSD, Solaris, and Windows.
  - Bluefish home: http://bluefish.openoffice.nl/

Working with Geany

Releases of Geany are either available from your system package distribution site or can be downloaded as source code,[5] installers, or third-party packages.[6] It is also available in a portable[7] format that can be installed on a USB stick.

Geany has the following important characteristics that we list here because we believe they apply as practical considerations to whichever editor or editors you decide to use instead:

- Cross-platform (Linux, Windows, Mac OS X, *BSD, Solaris, and so on)
- Open source and easily built from source code
- Small and fast, allowing rapid use also on constrained systems
- Good documentation set
- Active project with frequent releases and a supportive community
- Code syntax coloring, completion, and symbol navigation tree
- Organization of code folders into projects with build commands
- Configurable menu tools based on external commands
- Extensible architecture and a stable set of core plugins

> **AN IMPORTANT NOTE ON CODE EDITORS:** You are clearly free to use any programming editor of your choice. Indeed, many good development text editors available in the open-source and commercial markets have the characteristics and features we have outlined.

---

[5] http://www.geany.org/Download/Releases

[6] http://www.geany.org/Download/ThirdPartyPackages

[7] http://www.geanyportable.org/

Configuring the Editor for Android Work

Ideally, we want to be able to conveniently invoke the Android SDK tool commands listed in Table 2–2 from the user interface of our editor. Geany supports this customization through a concept called `Build Commands` that results in new application menu entries. Indeed, this is one of the characteristics we listed previously and one of the reasons why we chose it for this section.

Most good open-source and commercial code editors support this feature in some fashion and to some extent. Our goal is to simply introduce this concept of external tool commands as an alternative to a full-blown IDE, not to focus too much on the specific editor at hand.

Whether you decide to use Geany or another equivalent editor, we recommend researching the relevant documentation. Geany's manual is also posted on the official web site.[8]

The ability to customize the Geany build commands is available from the `Set Build Commands` menu item on the `Build` menu. This opens the `Project Properties` dialog on the `Build` tab, as shown in Figure 2–2.

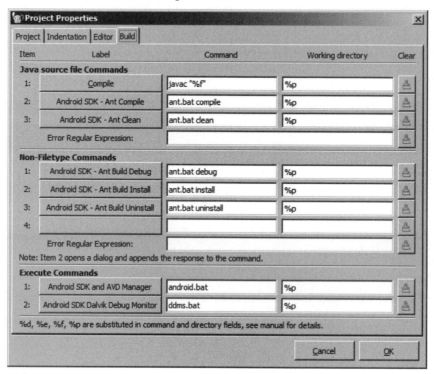

Figure 2–2. *Android SDK Build commands for Geany code editor on Windows*

---

[8] http://www.geany.org/Documentation/Manual

The Project Properties dialog Build tab depicted in Figure 2–2 is for Geany on a Windows development system.

Incidentally, the %p substitution symbol is Geany-specific and is substituted at invocation time with the current project directory as a working directory for the command. More information on substitutions is available in the user manual.[9]

The equivalent configuration and Android SDK tool commands for a Linux development system are shown in Figure 2–3.

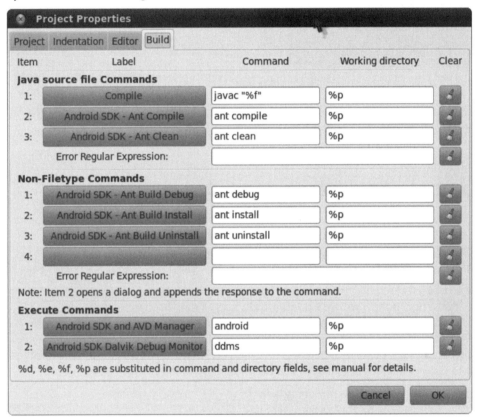

Figure 2–3. *Android SDK Build commands for Geany code editor on Linux*

Configuring Geany in this fashion results in a Geany Build Menu similar to that shown in Figure 2–4.

---

[9] http://www.geany.org/manual/current/#substitutions-in-commands-and-working-directories

Figure 2-4. *Android SDK commands on Geany code editor Build menu*

We now have the Android SDK development tools conveniently at hand directly in the user interface of the tool. This essentially converts our code editor into a very lean but functional mini–Android development IDE.

The Example Application Project

The example project we present in this section is not meant to be a useful application in itself. It has a dual purpose: to serve as a container for reusable bits of code and as a vehicle for demonstrating the use of several development tools that ship with the Android SDK.

We will first present the full source code of relevant sections of the project and then take a step-by-step approach to work through a grab bag of small reusable code chunks. These code pieces cover the kinds of things we generally want to know how to do as soon as possible when learning a new development platform. Quickly composing such code snippets allows us to rapidly create small, quick-and-dirty, but functional prototype applications. The project code will cover areas such as the following.

- Fixed text labels that communicate instructions, application help, or other usage information to the user
- Editable text fields that gather user input, data modifications, and deletions for application processing
- Conditionally active or inactive buttons that trigger code actions and afford the user the opportunity to control application functionality
- Mouse and Keyboard Event listeners on buttons and text fields that trap user input actions and alter application state accordingly
- Extracting Views and String values from application layout files and string tables at runtime

- Storing and loading basic application data to and from simple, "flat" text files
- Flexible runtime logging that traces application behavior for debugging, production problem resolution, accountability, security and other purposes
- Notifications and alarms that keep the user and the system up to date with application state and functioning or elicit user decision-making actions
- Creation and layout of user interface controls using static XML files during application build
- Programmatic, or dynamic, creation and layout of user interface controls at runtime in code
- Creation and interaction with application menus

Generating the Foundation Android Project

The first step to developing a new Android application with the core tools is to generate the base project folder structure and files. This was covered in the first chapter of this book, but we will provide the required knowledge for this section here.

Since we called our project MyAndroidSdkAppProject in the first chapter, and we are dealing with an assortment of generic Android SDK features, we will simply call the project for this section MyAndroidSdkAppProject2.

Open your terminal (command-line console) in a parent folder of your choice and then issue the following command on your platform shell (cmd.exe, bash, etc):

```
android create project
--target "android-9"
--name MyAndroidSdkApp2
--path ./MyAndroidSdkAppProject2
--activity MyAndroidSdkAppActivity2
--package com.example.myandroid
```

Note that we have added line breaks to the command for convenient reading. Please refer to the first chapter for more information on the android create project command. The official documentation is available on the Android developer web site.[10] For more background information, also try issuing the following command:

```
android -h create
```

This will list some useful help and usage information to the terminal console window.

---

[10] http://developer.android.com/guide/developing/other-ide.html

The Android Project Directory Structure

The android create project command generates a project directory structure and files that can immediately be compiled with Ant from the project root directory using the ant compile command. A debugging release of the application can also be directly built using ant debug.

If you have decided to use the Geany editor according to our earlier discussion, you can create a Geany project using the MyAndroidSdkAppProject2 directory as the base directory for the project. Having done this, you can then configure the project build commands according to our previous instructions. It will then be possible to invoke the Ant Build Debug command from the Build menu. We will cover this in further detail.

Should you prefer not to use the editor for this section, you can also just run the build from a terminal session on the command line instead.

After a successful debug build, the directory structure and content of the project folder should appear similar to that listed in Listing 2–1. This is the standard layout of an Android SDK Ant-based project so it is prudent to become familiar with it. We will not delve into detailed discussion of each element here. The relevant information is conveniently accessible from the official Android Developers web page.[11]

We will be covering appropriate segments of an Android project directory as we work through the code projects in this chapter and the rest of the book.

Listing 2–1. *Basic Android Create Project Directory Structure*

```
\MyAndroidSdkAppProject2
|    AndroidManifest.xml
|    build.properties
|    build.xml
|    default.properties
|    local.properties
|    proguard.cfg
+---bin
|    |    classes.dex
|    |    MyAndroidSdkApp2-debug-unaligned.apk
|    |    MyAndroidSdkApp2-debug.apk
|    |    MyAndroidSdkApp2.ap_
|    \---classes\com\example\myandroid
|                MyAndroidSdkAppActivity2.class
|                     R$attr.class
|                     R$drawable.class
|                     R$layout.class
|                     R$string.class
|                     R.class
+---gen\com\example\myandroid
|                R.java
+---libs
+---res
|    +---drawable-hdpi
```

---

[11] http://developer.android.com/guide/developing/other-ide.html#CreatingAProject

```
|   |           icon.png
|   +---drawable-ldpi
|   |           icon.png
|   +---drawable-mdpi
|   |           icon.png
|   +---layout
|   |           main.xml
|   \---values
|               strings.xml
\---src\com\example\myandroid
                MyAndroidSdkAppActivity2.java
```

You have already seen the application that was generated for us in action. If you refer to the "Android SDK Test Drive" sections of Chapter 1, you will find an image of it running in the Android emulator (refer to Figure 1-10). The only difference should be that it now says MyAndroidSdkAppProject2 instead of MyAndroidSdkAppProject.

Preparing to Run the Example Application

In the following sections, we will be covering the source code for the example application while running through the application workflow in the Android emulator. This will help you understand what the code does in practice.

Starting a Debugging Session

To begin the debugging session we need to launch both the Dalvik Debug Monitor (DDMS) and the Android emulator with our AVD. We can do this from the terminal command line with the following commands.

On Linux/Mac OS X:

```
emulator -avd android23api9_hvga_32mb &
ddms &
```

On Windows:

```
start emulator -avd android23api9_hvga_32mb
start ddms
```

Clearly, we also can use the convenient shortcuts we set up on the Geany editor menu as depicted in Figure 2–5.

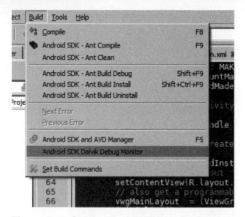

Figure 2–5. *Starting the DDMS from the Geany customized Build menu*

To launch the emulator with our AVD, we first start the Android SDK and AVD Manager. When the Manager application user interface is open, select android23api9_hvga_32mb from the AVD Name list and then click the Start button. The DDMS application can be launched directly from the menu entry.

During the loading of the Android emulator, the DDMS should appear as in Figure 2–6. The emulator instance is selected, and DVM events are listed on the Log tab.

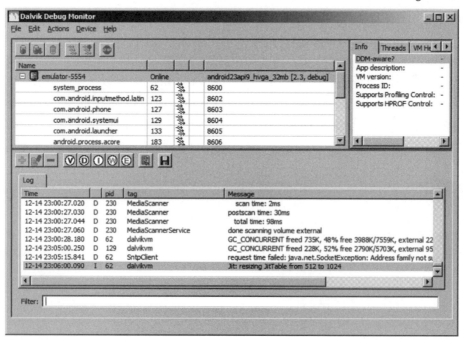

Figure 2–6. *Android DDMS with loading emulator instance selected*

The emulator should now be visible as in Figure 2–7. Note that for convenience we have switched the orientation to Landscape using the CTRL+F12 keyboard sequence.

Figure 2–7. *Android emulator instance in Landscape view mode*

> **NOTE:** We will leave the emulator and the Android Debug Bridge (ADB) running in the background while doing development using the same AVD. Unless we need to switch AVDs, there should generally be no need to restart these tools for each recompilation, rebuild, or reinstall of the application debug package (MyAndroidSdkApp2-debug.apk).

Replacing the Default Generated Code

We need to replace the code for the following three files in the project folder, /MyAndroidSdkAppProject2, with our own[12] versions:

- The application main layout file: We will be adding new GUI controls

    /res/layout/**main.xml**

---

[12] The book example source code and listings are available as download archives from the Apress web site.

- The default strings table file: To show how to read string resources

    /res/values/**strings.xml**

- The main activity class code file: New Java demonstration code

    /src/com/example/myandroid/**MyAndroidSdkAppActivity2.java**

You are free to edit the existing generated files or simply overwrite them with the files from the code listings of this book. We will discuss the files in detail later on.

Building and Installing the Project Example Code

We now want to build and deploy the new code to the AVD in one step (Figure 2–8).

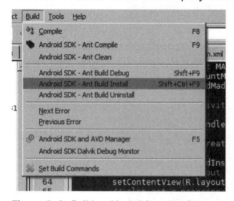

Figure 2–8. *Build and install from the Geany customized Build menu*

We can either do this from the Geany custom menu as before or execute the command directly from the terminal in the root project directory as follows. This command should work from Linux, Mac OS X, and Windows:

ant install

If you click the Application Launcher icon of the emulator, you should now see MyAndroidSdkAppActivity2 among the application icons.

Creating a Log Filter for the Application in the DDMS

To make things easier during debugging, the Dalvik Debug Monitor (DDMS) application offers the ability to create application filters based on custom criteria. We can create a new log filter by clicking the button with the large green cross (marked in Figure 2–9). One of the criteria is called the Log Tag. Fill in the Filter Name and Log Tag text fields with MyAndroidSdkAppActivity2.

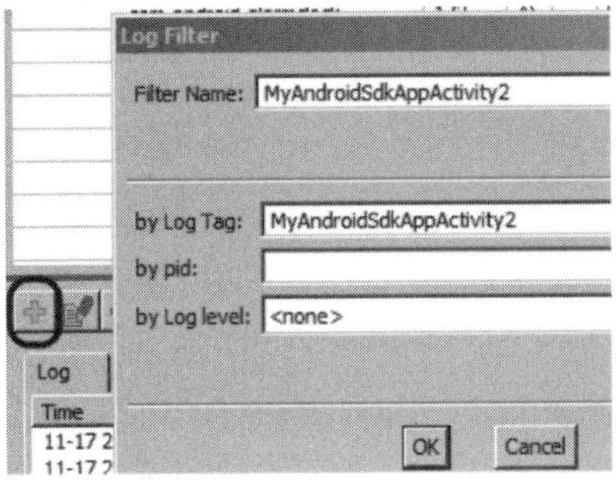

Figure 2-9. *Creating a new log filter based on the application Log Tag*

The following segment of code is an extract from Listing 2-8:

```
public class MyAndroidSdkAppActivity2 extends Activity
{
    /** TAG for debug logging purposes - used as a filter in DDMS */
    private static final String TAG = "MyAndroidSdkAppActivity2";
```

[--code omitted--]

It shows the main entry point for the main application class that inherits the Android Activity class. All Android applications that interact with the end user have to extend this class. The central role of the Activity class is well explained on the Android Developers web site.[13]

For the moment, we are mainly interested in the Log Tag. In this code segment, we have declared the code necessary to implement and later use an application Log Tag. More information on the Log[14] class and debugging tasks[15] are available on the official Developers site.

You will soon see how to use this tag in your code.

> **NOTE:** It is highly recommended to always implement and use the Android Log API during development and debugging of your own code.

As shown in Figure 2–10, you should now be able to see a new tab for the application log filter in the DDMS user interface.

---

[13] http://developer.android.com/reference/android/app/Activity.html

[14] http://developer.android.com/reference/android/util/Log.html

[15] http://developer.android.com/guide/developing/debug-tasks.html

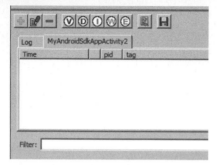

Figure 2–10. *A new log filter in DDMS based on the application Log Tag*

Running the Example Application

Now that we have built and deployed our code, and we have a convenient log filter in place, we can proceed to launch the application in the emulator. Be sure to keep the DDMS open on your desktop with the `MyAndroidSdkAppActivity2` log filter tab active.

Figure 2–11 depicts the initial screen of the application after startup. Note that for convenience we have again switched the orientation to Landscape using the `CTRL+F12` keyboard sequence. Once we start testing the application, it will make more sense to switch back to Portrait orientation.

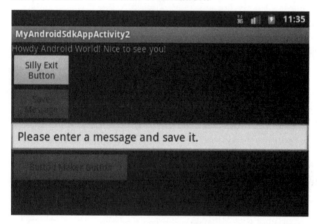

Figure 2–11. *The MyAndroidSdkAppActivity2 Application in the emulator*

The logging activity of the first time launch of the application code is visible in Figure 2–12. For interest, our application code looks for a private file on startup. If it does not find it, it logs the exception and proceeds. These exception log entries are visible in Figure 2–12.

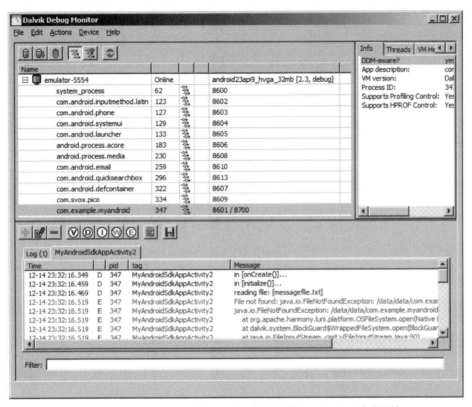

Figure 2-12. *The MyAndroidSdkAppActivity2 application log filter and output in DDMS*

What Does the Demo Application Do?

As shown in Figure 2–11, the initial screen of the application after startup is fairly simple on the surface. It presents five basic visible GUI controls:

- A fixed text view that acts as a label with a hello message. We will not spend time on this control since it is very straightforward.

- An enabled button with the text "Silly Exit Button". When clicked, this button will cause the application to seemingly close. We will discuss this in more detail in a coming section. Suffice it to say that we called it "Silly" since Android applications, or activities, do not normally need specific exit support. The platform already has facilities for this.

- An initially disabled button called "Save Message", which allows the user to save any text entered into the editable text field below. This text will appear the next time the application is launched. It also pops up an Android toast message when pressed.

- An editable text field initially filled with the text "Please enter a message and save it." When edited with contents, it will trigger code that will enable the previously disabled Save and Maker buttons. If the text message is left blank the buttons will be disabled.

- An initially disabled button called "Button Maker Button". When this button is enabled as described previously, it will dynamically create another button below it each time it is pressed. This code will be used to demonstrate the creation of GUI controls at runtime. The created buttons will also have data tags and event handlers attached to them at creation time. These will invoke routines that implement a mix of Android notification mechanisms (toasts, alerts, and system notifications).

We suggest you play around with the application to get a feel for it before diving into the code discussions below.

Here follows a sequence of screen captures and comments of the application demonstration features in action.

Figure 2–13 shows the application after opening for the first time. Note that some of the buttons are not enabled.

Figure 2–13. *The MyAndroidSdkAppActivity2 Application after first-time launch*

Figure 2–14 shows the application after entering a text message. The previously disabled buttons have now been activated.

Figure 2–14. *The MyAndroidSdkAppActivity2 Application after entering a new text message*

Figure 2–15 depicts the application after clicking on Save Message. If the application is closed and reopened, this text message will be reloaded from a private application file.

Figure 2–15. *The MyAndroidSdkAppActivity2 Application shows a toast after saving the new text message*

Figure 2–16 shows the application after clicking the Button Maker Button three times.

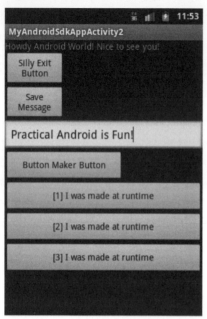

Figure 2–16. *The Application with new buttons after pressing the Button Maker Button three times*

Figure 2–17 shows that clicking the first created button raises an OK alert dialog.

Figure 2–17. *MyAndroidSdkAppActivity2 Dynamic Button 1 shows an alert*

Figure 2–18 shows that clicking the second created button raises an Android toast. Note that the label text for each dynamic button is also changed as it is pressed.

Figure 2–18. *MyAndroidSdkAppActivity2 Dynamic Button 2 shows a toast*

Figure 2–19 shows that clicking the third button creates an Android system notification. System Notifications are normally reserved for Android services or other background applications, but here we have decided to demonstrate how to create one in an interactive manner.

Figure 2–19. *MyAndroidSdkAppActivity2 Dynamic Button 3 creates a notification*

Figure 2–20 shows the opened notification in Landscape orientation. Clicking Clear should dismiss it.

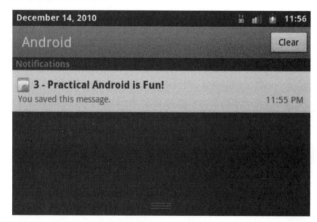

Figure 2–20. *MyAndroidSdkAppActivity2 Dynamic Button 3 system notification*

Note that the demonstration application consistently carries the custom text message through to all the user notification types.

If we close and reopen the application (see Figure 2–21), the user interface is now aware that a message was previously persisted, and all buttons are consequently also available for use.

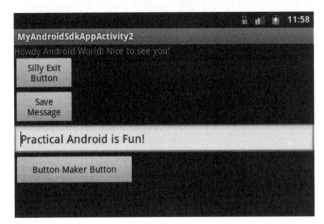

Figure 2-21. *Application after reopening and automatic reloading of persisted text message*

Figure 2-22 shows the demonstration menu group with a menu item highlighted.

Figure 2-22. *Application demonstrating menu groups after pressing the F2 MENU key*

Figure 2-23 shows a toast based on the menu item that was selected.

Figure 2-23. *Application showing a toast after selecting a menu item*

That concludes our tour of the example application. You should now have a good enough understanding of the interactions of the application to dive into the project files and source code.

A Walk through the Core Application Files

As mentioned earlier, we have replaced the following first three files of the generated application with our own. We will discuss each of these files in overview.

- Application main layout: `/res/layout/main.xml`
- Default strings table: `/res/values/strings.xml`
- Activity: `src/com/example/myandroid/MyAndroidSdkAppActivity2.java`

Even though we have not altered it, we will also discuss the Application Manifest file.

- Android Manifest file: `/AndroidManifest.xml`

The Application Manifest File

We will start with the Android Manifest file. One basic aspect that is vital to understand when developing Android software is the process by which the Android runtime finds the startup class in an Android application package.

The keys to this process lie within the application manifest. If we review Listing 2–2, we can follow the process described as follows based on the contents of our example manifest file.

Listing 2–2. *The Generated Application Manifest File: AndroidManifest.xml*

```xml
<?xml version="1.0" encoding="utf-8"?>
<manifest xmlns:android="http://schemas.android.com/apk/res/android"
      package="com.example.myandroid"
      android:versionCode="1"
      android:versionName="1.0">
    <application android:label="@string/app_name" android:icon="@drawable/icon">
        <activity android:name="MyAndroidSdkAppActivity2"
                  android:label="@string/app_name">
            <intent-filter>
                <action android:name="android.intent.action.MAIN" />
                <category android:name="android.intent.category.LAUNCHER" />
            </intent-filter>
        </activity>
    </application>
</manifest>
```

From the manifest the Android runtime will look up the name within the activity tag that wraps a MAIN action and a category of LAUNCHER. It then takes this name and appends it to the package tag value specified in the manifest tag. The full name of the startup class in this case will then be com.example.myandroid.MyAndroidSdkAppActivity2.

The Application Main Layout File

As mentioned elsewhere, the original layout file that was generated by the android create project command is presented in Listing 2–3 for reference only. We replaced it with the one in Listing 2–4.

Listing 2–3. *The Original Generated Application Layout File: main.xml*

```xml
<?xml version="1.0" encoding="utf-8"?>
<LinearLayout xmlns:android="http://schemas.android.com/apk/res/android"
    android:orientation="vertical"
    android:layout_width="fill_parent"
    android:layout_height="fill_parent"
    >
<TextView
    android:layout_width="fill_parent"
    android:layout_height="wrap_content"
    android:text="Hello World, MyAndroidSdkAppActivity2"
    />
</LinearLayout>
```

Android GUIs and the Role of the View Class

Before we go any farther, it is worth covering some background surrounding activities, layouts, views, and how Android GUIs are built up. There are some core Android GUI concepts, their relationships, and their roles that will underpin all our GUI work as Android developers. The essence of these concepts can be summarized as follows:

- **Activities:** All Android application screens or forms are instances of the Activity class or descendants thereof. Activities are the foundation of Android applications with a user interface. In contrast, background or long-running applications like services are not derived from the Activity class, but rather from the invisible Android Service class. An activity normally takes on a visible appearance by being assigned a specific Layout class instance.

- **Layouts:** The Layout class forms the unseen container for all visible controls in an activity screen or form. Layouts are built on the ViewGroup class and can be specified declaratively in an XML layout file or created programmatically in the runtime code of the application.

- **View Groups:** The ViewGroup class is a container class and a direct subclass of the View class. It also serves as the base class for all Layout classes including LinearLayout, RelativeLayout, AbsoluteLayout, FrameLayout, and other composites.

- **Views:** The View class is the base class for the ViewGroup class and the root for all user interface components, controls, or widgets in the Android GUI world. The View class handles all on-screen drawing and event processing. This class is the root GUI class and is second to only one other class in the inheritance hierarchy, java.lang.Object. In order to create your own, highly specialized and distinguishing user interfaces, you will generally implement your own direct View descendant classes and base your interfaces on them.

The previous background should now serve as a basis for understanding the user interface aspects of our example application better.

The Layout for the Example Code

The layout file for the example application (see Listing 2–4) declares the five View controls initially visible in the application's activity.

Listing 2–4. *The Project Example Application Layout File: main.xml*

```xml
<?xml version="1.0" encoding="utf-8"?>
<LinearLayout xmlns:android="http://schemas.android.com/apk/res/android"
    android:id="@+id/layout_main"
    android:orientation="vertical"
    android:layout_width="fill_parent"
    android:layout_height="fill_parent">
    <TextView
```

```
            android:layout_width="fill_parent"
            android:layout_height="wrap_content"
            android:text="Howdy Android World! Nice to see you!"
        />
        <Button
            android:id="@+id/cmd_silly_exit_button"
            android:layout_width="96px"
            android:layout_height="wrap_content"
            android:text="Silly Exit Button"
        />
        <Button
            android:id="@+id/cmd_save_message"
            android:layout_width="96px"
            android:layout_height="wrap_content"
            android:text="Save Message"
        />
        <EditText
            android:id="@+id/txt_toast"
            android:layout_width="fill_parent"
            android:layout_height="wrap_content" >
        </EditText>
        <Button
            android:id="@+id/cmd_make_button"
            android:layout_width="192px"
            android:layout_height="wrap_content"
            android:text="Button Maker Button"
        />
</LinearLayout>
```

A subtle but important addition to the layout file is the bold line of XML code:

`android:id="@+id/layout_main"`

The original layout did not contain this line. We added it for the purpose of demonstrating how to get access to the id of the root `LinearLayout ViewGroup` instance. If we browse forward to Listing 2–8, our replacement `MyAndroidSdkAppActivity2.java` source file, we can find the following code:

```
private ViewGroup vwgMainLayout = null;
[--code omitted--]
vwgMainLayout  = (ViewGroup)findViewById(R.id.layout_main);
```

These code segments demonstrate how to get a reference to the main activity layout. This is then used later to add controls dynamically to the `ViewGroup` layout instead of declaring them in the XML layout file before build time. See Listing 2–11 for more on this.

The `findViewById(int id)` method is the standard Android API for retrieving a handle to a `View` instance that was created by the Android platform from declarations in a `Layout` file. We will see it in almost all Android application code. It takes as an argument the id of the View that was declared in an XML layout file.

These ids are generated by the Android SDK from the application's resource XML files during build time. The `R.java` Java class source code file is generated (in the gen directory) based on the XML resource files declared in the project structure. Here follows an extract from the `R.java` file with the relevant `R.id.layout_main` id highlighted in bold:

```
[--code omitted--]
public static final class id {
    public static final int cmd_make_button=0x7f050004;
    public static final int cmd_save_message=0x7f050002;
    public static final int cmd_silly_exit_button=0x7f050001;
    public static final int layout_main=0x7f050000;
    public static final int txt_message=0x7f050003;
}
public static final class layout {
    public static final int main=0x7f030000;

[--code omitted--]
```

> **DO NOT EDIT R.JAVA:** The `R.java` class file serves as a list (index) of all application resources identified by a unique build time–generated reference. It should never be edited by hand.

The Default String Table File

The String table is a container for string resources, which are generic software development artifacts used to minimize the impact of changes in the international aspects of applications, among others. In general, these aspects do not directly affect the logic of the compiled application, and the latter should ideally not be affected when the former needs to vary.

For example, when an application user interface needs to support a new natural language B, as well as an existing language A, string resources can be the answer for retrieval of the correct language values based on locale. Embedding (or "hard-coding") both sets of values in the application code is not a sustainable alternative. This becomes especially relevant when a potential support requirement for a third language C might be just around the corner.

The example application demonstrates how to extract values from the String table, `strings.xml` (see Listing 2–6), using the Android API `getString()` method call as in the following code extract from Listing 2–9:

```
    public void initialize()
    {

[--code omitted--]

        /** get string values from the default string table */
        message_def  = getString(R.string.default_message);
        label_toasts = getString(R.string.label_toasts);
        label_alerts = getString(R.string.label_alerts);
        label_notify = getString(R.string.label_notify);


[--code omitted--]
```

More information on Android string resources can be found online at the Android Developers web site.[16]

Listing 2–5 presents the original String table.

Listing 2–5. *The Original Generated Application String Table File: strings.xml*

```xml
<?xml version="1.0" encoding="utf-8"?>
<resources>
    <string name="app_name">MyAndroidSdkAppActivity2</string>
</resources>
```

Listing 2–6 shows the replacement String table.

Listing 2–6. *The Project Example Application Replacement String Table File: strings.xml*

```xml
<?xml version="1.0" encoding="utf-8"?>
<resources>
    <string name="app_name">MyAndroidSdkAppActivity2</string>
    <string name="default_message">Please enter a message and save it.</string>
    <string name="label_toasts">I make Toasts!</string>
    <string name="label_alerts">I make Alerts!</string>
    <string name="label_notify">I just Notify!</string>
</resources>
```

The Main Activity Java Source File

As earlier, we will first present the generated Android Activity class source file shown in Listing 2–7 and then provide the full code listing of our chapter project replacement example in segments from Listing 2–8 onward.

Listing 2–7. *The Original Generated Application Main Activity Java File: MyAndroidSdkAppActivity2.java*

```java
package com.example.myandroid;

import android.app.Activity;
import android.os.Bundle;

public class MyAndroidSdkAppActivity2 extends Activity
{
    /** Called when the activity is first created. */
    @Override
    public void onCreate(Bundle savedInstanceState)
    {
        super.onCreate(savedInstanceState);
        setContentView(R.layout.main);
    }
}
```

Our replacement MyAndroidSdkAppActivity2.java source file (see Listing 2–8) is fairly long and extensive. It also covers several distinct technical areas of Android programming. We will systematically work through code segments from the full source code file as extracts in the chapter "How to" sections that follow. We strongly suggest

---

[16] http://developer.android.com/guide/topics/resources/string-resource.html

that you build and work through the code project with us to get the best from the discussion.

Listing 2-8. *The Application Main Activity Java Source File: MyAndroidSdkAppActivity2.java (Partial)*

```java
package com.example.myandroid;

import android.app.Activity;
import android.app.AlertDialog;
import android.app.Notification;
import android.app.NotificationManager;
import android.content.Intent;
import android.app.PendingIntent;
import android.os.Bundle;
import android.util.Log;
import android.content.Context;
import android.view.View;
import android.view.ViewGroup;
import android.view.ViewGroup.LayoutParams;
import android.view.KeyEvent;
import android.view.Menu;
import android.view.MenuItem;
import android.widget.LinearLayout;
import android.widget.Button;
import android.widget.EditText;
import android.widget.Toast;
import java.lang.Runtime;
import java.lang.CharSequence;
import java.lang.Integer;
import java.lang.Object;
import java.io.BufferedReader;
import java.io.File;
import java.io.InputStream;
import java.io.InputStreamReader;
import java.io.OutputStream;
import java.io.OutputStreamWriter;

public class MyAndroidSdkAppActivity2 extends Activity
{
    /** TAG for debug logging purposes - used as a filter in DDMS */
    private static final String TAG = "MyAndroidSdkAppActivity2";

    /** our message text file - used to store arbitrary bits of text */
    private static final String MESSAGEFILE = "messagefile.txt";

    /** handles to our static controls in the XML layout */
    private Button          cmdSilly      = null;
    private Button          cmdMaker      = null;
    private Button          cmdSave       = null;
    private EditText        txtMessage    = null;
    private CharSequence    message_def   = null;
    private CharSequence    message       = null;
    private String          label_toasts  = null;
    private String          label_alerts  = null;
    private String          label_notify  = null;

    /** handles to our dynamic controls created programmatically */
    private ViewGroup       vwgMainLayout = null;
```

```
    private static final int MAKE_MAX   = 3;
    private int              countMade  = 0;
    private Button           cmdMade    = null;

    /** Called when the activity is first created. */
    @Override
    public void onCreate(Bundle savedInstanceState)
    {
        Log.d(TAG, "in [onCreate()]...");

        super.onCreate(savedInstanceState);
        // set the main layout
        setContentView(R.layout.main);
        // also get a programmable handle to the main layout
        vwgMainLayout   = (ViewGroup)findViewById(R.id.layout_main);
        initialize(); // our init method
    }
[--code omitted--]
```

Android Coding How to

In this section we will break down the example application source code into segments that demonstrate distinct coding techniques. We will be doing this in a "how-to" format.

The goal is to clarify the overall code structure and to create a small reference of reusable code snippets for common Android programming tasks.

Using the Android Log API

Since application logging is something that applies to all code, the first aspect we want to cover in this how-to section is about using the built-in Android Log API.

We want to remind you that reference reading on the Log API is available on the official Android Developers site.[17] There is also good coverage of Android debugging techniques on the site.[18]

Log API Methods and Styles

The Android API includes a standard logging class simply called Log, which supports several static methods that allow the programmer to implement logging facilities in a program at several levels. The most commonly used of these levels and methods are listed in Table 2–3. You will see some of these levels and methods used throughout the demonstration project source code.

---

[17] http://developer.android.com/reference/android/util/Log.html

[18] http://developer.android.com/guide/developing/debug-tasks.html

Table 2-3. *Android Log API Levels and Methods*

Logging Level	Log API Static Method	Overloaded Method with Exception Argument
Verbose	Log.v(String tag, String msg)	Log.v(String tag, String msg, Throwable tr)
Debug	Log.d(String tag, String msg)	Log.d(String tag, String msg, Throwable tr)
Information	Log.i(String tag, String msg)	Log.i(String tag, String msg, Throwable tr)
Warning	Log.w(String tag, String msg)	Log.w(String tag, String msg, Throwable tr)
Error	Log.e(String tag, String msg)	Log.e(String tag, String msg, Throwable tr)

Some aspects of logging in Android code were covered during an earlier section that showed how to create log filters in the DDMS. We also presented a snippet of code there which is worth reviewing again. It shows the declaration for the Log Tag:

```
public class MyAndroidSdkAppActivity2 extends Activity
{
    /** TAG for debug logging purposes - used as a filter in DDMS */
    private static final String TAG = "MyAndroidSdkAppActivity2";
```

In general, we use a logging call style similar to the following snippet for standard debug tracing:

```
public void onCreate(Bundle savedInstanceState)
{
    Log.d(TAG, "in [onCreate()]...");
```

For logging exceptions we use the following type of call:

```
catch (Throwable t) {
    Log.e(TAG, "File write failed: " + t.toString(), t);
    throw t; /** other unexpected exception - rethrow it */
}
```

As we will show next, the effects of such logging calls can be graphically viewed using the ample logging tools provided by the Android SDK.

Android SDK Log Viewers

Besides log filters, the DDMS menu system (see Figure 2–24) shows another way to view the Android log. Select **Device ➤ Run logcat** to do this.

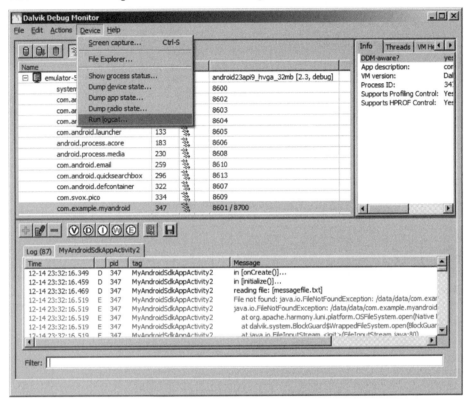

Figure 2–24. *Starting logcat from the DDMS menus*

Figure 2–25 shows the resulting logcat remote window after opening it from the DDMS menu system.

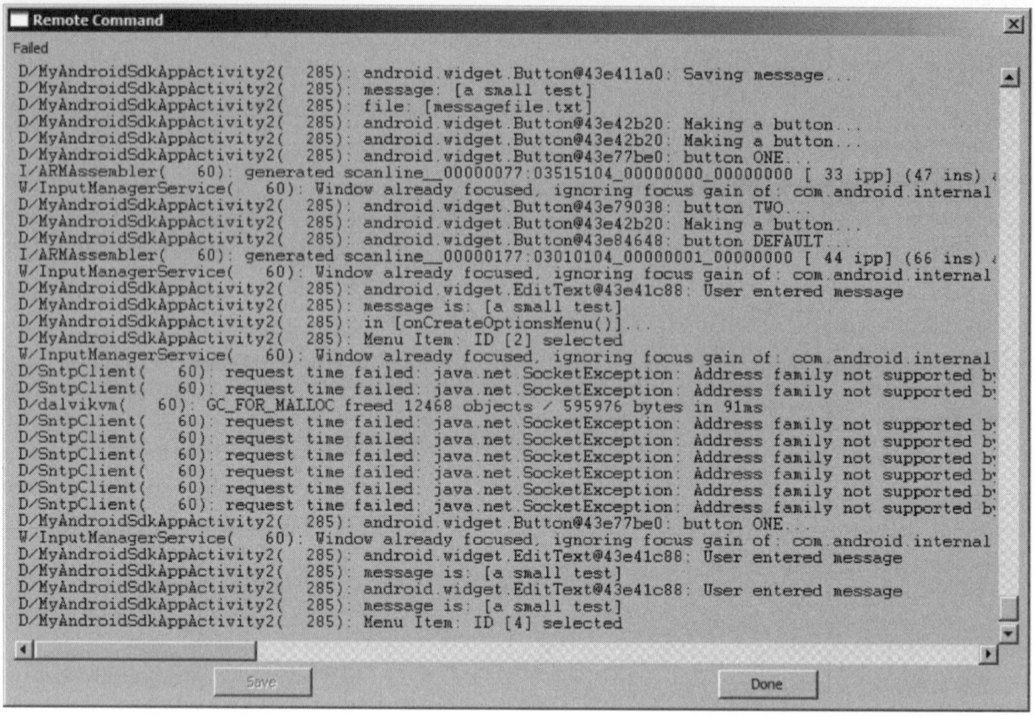

Figure 2-25. *Running logcat from the DDMS menus*

We can also issue `adb logcat` from a separate terminal window to track log entries as they are written. Figure 2-26 depicts `logcat` open on a Windows development computer.

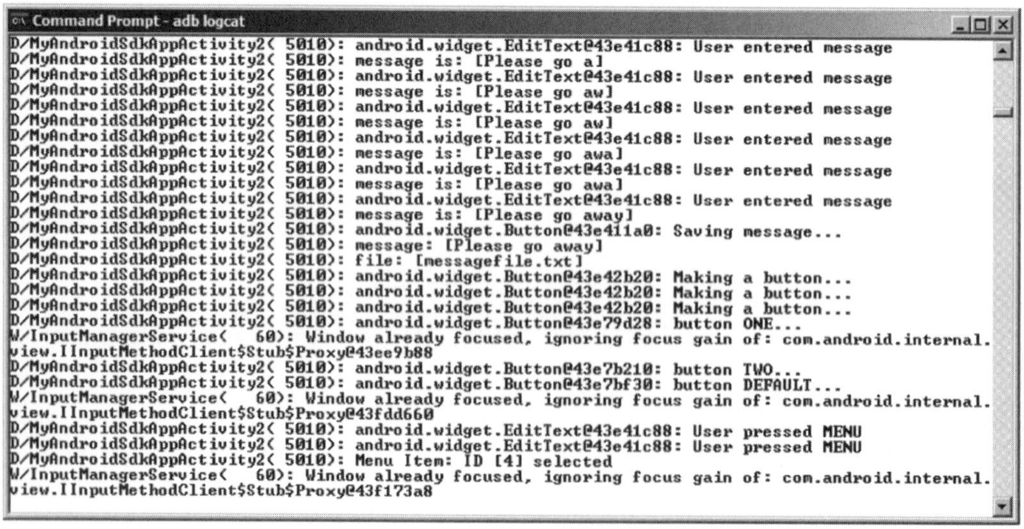

Figure 2-26. *Running adb logcat on the Windows command line*

Centralizing Application GUI Initialization Code

Listing 2–9 presents a centralized method in which all GUI control and supporting element setup for the application is performed. This is not so much a specific technique as it is a good programming practice. It has the advantage that it reduces noise and clutter in the onCreate() method.

The method, initialize(), is invoked at the end of the Activity onCreate() method. It is responsible for delegating to the set of how-to methods you will see later. These methods implement the lower level Android API functionality that the example project attempts to demonstrate.

Listing 2–9. *MyAndroidSdkAppActivity2.java : GUI Setup Grouped Within an Initialize() Method*

```java
public void initialize()
{
    Log.d(TAG, "in [initialize()]...");

    /** get string values from the default string table */
    message_def  = getString(R.string.default_message);
    label_toasts = getString(R.string.label_toasts);
    label_alerts = getString(R.string.label_alerts);
    label_notify = getString(R.string.label_notify);

    cmdSilly = (Button)findViewById(R.id.cmd_silly_exit_button);
    cmdSilly.setOnClickListener(
        new Button.OnClickListener() {
            public void onClick (View v){
                Log.d(TAG, v.toString() + ": Leaving activity...");
                Runtime.getRuntime().exit(0);
            }
        }
    );

    cmdSave = (Button)findViewById(R.id.cmd_save_message);
    cmdSave.setOnClickListener(
        new Button.OnClickListener() {
            public void onClick (View v) {
                Log.d(TAG, v.toString() + ": Saving message...");
                message = txtMessage.getText();
                Log.d(TAG, "message: [" + message + "]");
                Log.d(TAG, "file: [" + MESSAGEFILE + "]");
                writeMessageFile(message);
                makeToast("[" + message + "] is now saved");
            }
        }
    );

    txtMessage = (EditText)findViewById(R.id.txt_message);
    txtMessage.setOnKeyListener(new View.OnKeyListener() {
        public boolean onKey(View v, int keyCode, KeyEvent event) {
            final int action = event.getAction();
            boolean ret = false; // we are not consuming the event by default
            if (keyCode == KeyEvent.KEYCODE_MENU) { // ignore menu key
                Log.d(TAG, v.toString() + ": User pressed the MENU key");
            }
```

```
            else {
                Log.d(TAG, v.toString() + ": User worked in the message");
                message = txtMessage.getText();
                setButtonsEnabled();
            }
            return ret;
        }
    });

    cmdMaker = (Button)findViewById(R.id.cmd_make_button);
    cmdMaker.setOnClickListener(
        new Button.OnClickListener() {
            public void onClick (View v) {
                Log.d(TAG, v.toString() + ": Making a button...");
                makeWideButton( "I was made at runtime");
            }
        }
    );

    Log.d(TAG, "reading file: [" + MESSAGEFILE + "]");
    message = readMessageFile();
    txtMessage.setText(message);
    Log.d(TAG, "retrieved: [" + message + "]");
    setButtonsEnabled();
    if (0 == message.length()) { // only show default message if empty
        txtMessage.setText(message_def);
    }
}
```

Exiting an Application Activity

The top button you see when you open the application is a button called "Silly Exit Button". The reason for this name stems from the fact that, by design, Android applications should not, in theory and in practice, need "Exit" buttons or any other such mechanisms. Normally a device user will simply abandon the current application and directly go off to another application as needed. The Android platform already supports mechanisms for doing this such as Back, Home, and so on.

Be that as it may, it is interesting to note how such functionality can be achieved. It might also be useful in certain circumstances where there is a need to achieve the same result programmatically without user initiation.

The following segment of code is extracted from Listing 2–9 and shows the implementation of this button:

```
    cmdSilly = (Button)findViewById(R.id.cmd_silly_exit_button);
    cmdSilly.setOnClickListener(
        new Button.OnClickListener() {
            public void onClick (View v){
                Log.d(TAG, v.toString() + ": Leaving activity...");
                Runtime.getRuntime().exit(0);
            }
        }
    );
```

As highlighted by the code in bold, the effect of an Exit is achieved by asking the JVM runtime implementation, in this case the DVM, to shut itself down.

Enabling and Disabling Buttons (and other Views)

Until the user has actually entered a text message or activated the text area to accept the default message already there, some of the buttons on the activity will remain inactive (or disabled).

The method shown in Listing 2–10, setButtonsEnabled(), is responsible for centrally checking the state of the text message and enabling or disabling the relevant buttons accordingly. It uses the setEnabled() method of the subject View instances. In this case, these subjects are Button instances. The Android Button class is descended from the View class and thus supports the setEnabled() method. We pass the boolean false or true depending on whether to disable or enable the target control instance respectively.

Listing 2–10. *MyAndroidSdkAppActivity2.java: Button Availability State Control Is Centralized*

```
public void setButtonsEnabled()
{
    if (0 == message.length()) {
        Log.d(TAG, "message is EMPTY");
        cmdMaker.setEnabled(false);
        cmdSave.setEnabled(false);
    }
    else {
        Log.d(TAG, "message is: [" + message + "]");
        cmdMaker.setEnabled(true);
        cmdSave.setEnabled(true);
    }
}
```

When studying this method it is worth also reviewing and keeping in mind the following snippet from the initialize() method in Listing 2–9:

```
txtMessage = (EditText)findViewById(R.id.txt_message);
txtMessage.setOnKeyListener(new View.OnKeyListener() {
    public boolean onKey(View v, int keyCode, KeyEvent event) {
        final int action = event.getAction();
        boolean ret = false; // we are not consuming the event by default
        if (keyCode == KeyEvent.KEYCODE_MENU) { // ignore menu key
            Log.d(TAG, v.toString() + ": User pressed the MENU key");
        }
        else {
            Log.d(TAG, v.toString() + ": User worked in the message");
            message = txtMessage.getText();
            setButtonsEnabled();
        }
        return ret;
    }
});
```

The preceding code implements a View OnKeyListener for the message text field. As the user interacts with the message EditText field using the keyboard, it delegates control to the `setButtonsEnabled()` method. This ensures that the state of availability of the buttons is constantly kept synchronized with whether the user has actually entered or accepted any text in the message field.

Creating Controls Dynamically (at Runtime in Code)

One of the techniques we wanted to demonstrate in the example code was how to create a GUI control programmatically. In Listing 2–11, we present this by implementing a helper method `makeWideButton()` that creates instances of the `Button` class in the particular sense.

These techniques can also be used in the general sense for other GUI controls since Buttons are descended from the `View` class, and all other Android GUI artifacts have the `View` class as their root. The method on the layout container class (`ViewGroup`) that adds the subject GUI control (`View`) to itself is predictably called `addView()` and takes a View instance as its primary argument.

Listing 2–11. *MyAndroidSdkAppActivity2.java:- Dynamic View (Button) Control Creation*

```
/**
 * class to demonstrate tagging an Android View instance with user data
 * */
public class MyButtonTagData {
    public Integer myUserId = 0;
    public CharSequence myUserData = "--empty--";
    public MyButtonTagData(Integer id, CharSequence data) {
        this.myUserId   = id;
        this.myUserData = data;
    }
}

public void makeWideButton(CharSequence label)
{
    countMade++;
    if (MAKE_MAX >= countMade) {
        cmdMade = new Button(this);
        cmdMade.setText("[" + countMade + "] " + label);
        cmdMade.setTag( /** attach our structure instance to the control */
            new MyButtonTagData(new Integer(countMade), label_notify)
        );
        cmdMade.setOnClickListener(
            new Button.OnClickListener() {
                public void onClick (View v) {
                    MyButtonTagData tagdata = (MyButtonTagData)v.getTag();
                    Integer tag = tagdata.myUserId;
                    switch (tag.intValue()) {
                        case 1:
                            ((Button)v).setText(label_alerts);
                            Log.d(TAG, v.toString() + ": button ONE...");
                            showOkAlertDialog(tag + " - " + message);
                            break;
                        case 2:
                            ((Button)v).setText(label_toasts);
                            Log.d(TAG, v.toString() + ": button TWO...");
```

```
                            makeToast(tag + " - " + message);
                            break;
                        default:
                            ((Button)v).setText(tagdata.myUserData);
                            Log.d(TAG, v.toString() + ": button DEFAULT...");
                            showNotification(tag + " - " + message);
                            break;
                    }
                }
            }
        );
        LayoutParams parms = new LayoutParams(
            LayoutParams.MATCH_PARENT, LayoutParams.WRAP_CONTENT);
        vwgMainLayout.addView(cmdMade, parms);
    }
}
```

If we review Listing 2–8, our replacement MyAndroidSdkAppActivity2.java source file, we can find the following code:

```
private ViewGroup vwgMainLayout = null;
[--code omitted--]
vwgMainLayout  = (ViewGroup)findViewById(R.id.layout_main);
```

This shows us retrieving a reference to the main activity layout. This is required to serve as the target upon which to call the addView() method as per the implementation of makeWideButton() in Listing 2–11.

It is also worth noting the LayoutParams class instance (parms), which we create to set some attributes for the dynamically created Button View instance(cmdMade). The method addView() will use this parms instance as its second argument upon adding the button to the main layout instance (vwgMainLayout). These attributes are normally declaratively controlled from an XML layout file but we wanted to demonstrate how to do this with Java code.

Another detail worth drawing attention to is the setTag() method call. The signatures for this method are as follows:

- void   setTag(int key, Object tag): Sets a tag associated with the current view instance and a key.
- void   setTag(Object tag): Sets the tag associated with the current view instance.

We use the first form to attach a reference to an arbitrary class called MyButtonTagData for demonstration purposes and then retrieve it later using the getTag() method. In this fashion, tags can be used to store data that is associated with a view without having to create separate data structures.

Making an Android Toast

Listing 2–12 presents the code we use in the example application to raise all the Android toast notifications. We want to point you to the official online documentation for the Toast class[19] and the tutorial on creating Android toasts.[20] The code for our bare-bones toast requirement is quite straightforward and intuitive.

Listing 2–12. *MyAndroidSdkAppActivity2.java: Making a Toast*

```
public void makeToast(CharSequence message)
{
    Toast.makeText(
        this,
        message,
        Toast.LENGTH_SHORT).show();
}
```

NOTE: Having forgotten to call the `show()` method when making toasts have often caught us by surprise. This appears to be a common mistake, so be on the lookout for it when your toasts won't show.

Showing an Android Alert Dialog

Listing 2–13 presents the code we use in the example application to create and show the Android OK alert dialogs. The alert dialog builder is a powerful mechanism with a lot of flexibility. We recommend that you have a look at the Android Developers site reference for the `AlertDialog.Builder` class[21] and the tutorial on creating dialogs.[22] Again, the code is straightforward and self-explanatory.

Listing 2–13. *MyAndroidSdkAppActivity2.java: Showing a Basic Alert Dialog*

```
public void showOkAlertDialog(CharSequence message)
{
    new AlertDialog.Builder(this)
      .setMessage(message)
      .setPositiveButton("OK", null)
      .show();
}
```

---

[19] http://developer.android.com/reference/android/widget/Toast.html

[20] http://developer.android.com/guide/topics/ui/notifiers/toasts.html

[21] http://developer.android.com/reference/android/app/AlertDialog.Builder.html

[22] http://developer.android.com/guide/topics/ui/dialogs.html

Creating and Showing an Android System Notification

Android system notifications are normally used by background applications without a user interface, Android services in particular. We will not cover Android services here but wanted to demonstrate how notifications work (see Listing 2–14).

Listing 2–14. *MyAndroidSdkAppActivity2.java: Creating and Showing a System Notification*

```java
public void showNotification(CharSequence message)
{
    final int notifyRef = 1;
    final int notifyIcon = R.drawable.icon;
    final long notifyWhen = System.currentTimeMillis();
    final String notifyService = Context.NOTIFICATION_SERVICE;

    NotificationManager notifyManager = (NotificationManager)
        getSystemService(notifyService);

    Notification notification = new Notification(
        notifyIcon, message, notifyWhen);

    Context context = getApplicationContext();
    CharSequence notifyTitle = message;
    CharSequence notifyText = "You saved this message.";

    Intent notifyIntent = new Intent(
        this, MyAndroidSdkAppActivity2.class);
    PendingIntent contentIntent = PendingIntent.getActivity(
        this, 0, notifyIntent, 0);
    notification.setLatestEventInfo(
        context, notifyTitle, notifyText, contentIntent);

    notifyManager.notify(notifyRef, notification);
}
```

A key step in creating system notifications is getting a handle on the Android notification service. This handle is an instance of the `NotificationManager` class and is the engine behind the creation and triggering of notifications.

The notification is then instantiated from the `Notification` class and populated with an icon integer handle, our message character buffer, and a timestamp in milliseconds for the notification.

We then fill out the notification with the current application Context, a custom title and text, and an Intent instance to launch when we click the notification in expanded form. Of course, we could have added the title and text as arguments to our method signature, but we will only use it in one call in our example code and it is a simple matter to make it more generic. The focus is on demonstrating the concepts involved.

Using a Private Application File

The two wrapper methods shown in Listing 2–15 take care of storing and retrieving the custom string message we entered. They do this by calling our Android private application file helper methods presented in Listing 2–16. Note that here we catch and handle any exceptions that were bubbled up by our general file helper methods in a manner visible to the user (with a toast).

Listing 2–15. *MyAndroidSdkAppActivity2.java: Loading and Storing a Demonstration Text Message in a File*

```
    /**
     * application specific wrapper to read a message that might be in a file
     * */
    public String readMessageFile()
    {
        String ret_str = "";
        try {
            ret_str = stringFromPrivateApplicationFile(MESSAGEFILE);
        }
        catch (Throwable t) {
            makeToast("Message read failed: " + t.toString());
        }
        return ret_str;
    }

    /**
     * application specific wrapper to write a message to a file
     * */
    public void writeMessageFile(CharSequence message)
    {
        try {
            stringToPrivateApplicationFile(MESSAGEFILE, message.toString());
        }
        catch (Throwable t) {
            makeToast("Message write failed: " + t.toString());
        }
    }
```

The two methods in Listing 2–16 encapsulate the generic functionality of storing and loading string data to and from what are known as private application files.

Listing 2–16. *MyAndroidSdkAppActivity2.java: Reading from and Writing to a Private Android Application File*

```
    /**
     * general method to read a string from a private application file
     * */
    public String stringFromPrivateApplicationFile(String name)
        throws java.lang.Throwable
    {
        String ret_str = "";
        try {
            InputStream is = openFileInput(name);
            if (null != is) {
                InputStreamReader    tmp_isr = new InputStreamReader(is);
                BufferedReader       tmp_rdr = new BufferedReader(tmp_isr);
                String               tmp_str = "";
```

```
            StringBuilder        tmp_buf = new StringBuilder();
            while ( (tmp_str = tmp_rdr.readLine()) != null) {
                tmp_buf.append(tmp_str);
            }
            is.close();
            ret_str = tmp_buf.toString();
        }
    }
    catch (java.io.FileNotFoundException e) {
        /** file has not been created - log this */
        Log.e(TAG, "File not found: " + e.toString(), e);
    }
    catch (Throwable t) {
        Log.e(TAG, "File read failed: " + t.toString(), t);
        throw t; /** other unexpected exception - rethrow it */
    }
    return ret_str;
}

/**
 * general method to write a string to a private application file
 */
public void stringToPrivateApplicationFile(String name, String data)
    throws java.lang.Throwable
{
    try {
        OutputStreamWriter tmp_osw = new OutputStreamWriter(
                openFileOutput(name, Context.MODE_PRIVATE));
        tmp_osw.write(data);
        tmp_osw.close();
    }
    catch (Throwable t) {
        Log.e(TAG, "File write failed: " + t.toString(), t);
        throw t; /** other unexpected exception - rethrow it */
    }
}
```

NOTE: These helper methods, in the spirit of being generic and reusable, do not make exceptions visible to the end user. This would limit the scope of their applicability. Instead, exceptions are logged and propagated to calling client code for handling.

Browsing the Device File System with the DDMS File Explorer

The Android SDK tools enable us to browse the file system of the Android device or emulator that we are using for development. Figure 2–27 shows a way to access this functionality graphically from the DDMS. Open **Device ➤ File Explorer** from the DDMS menu system.

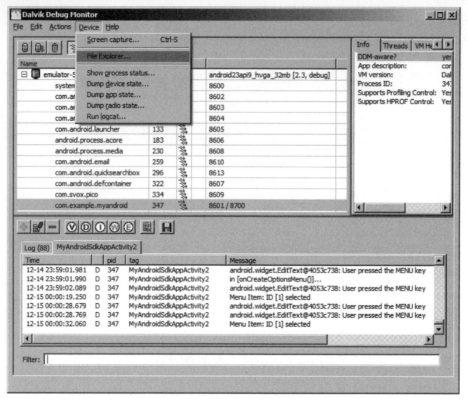

Figure 2–27. *Opening the File Explorer from the DDMS menu system*

Figure 2–28 shows the File Explorer browsing the data subdirectories for the example application. You can clearly see the demonstration message file.

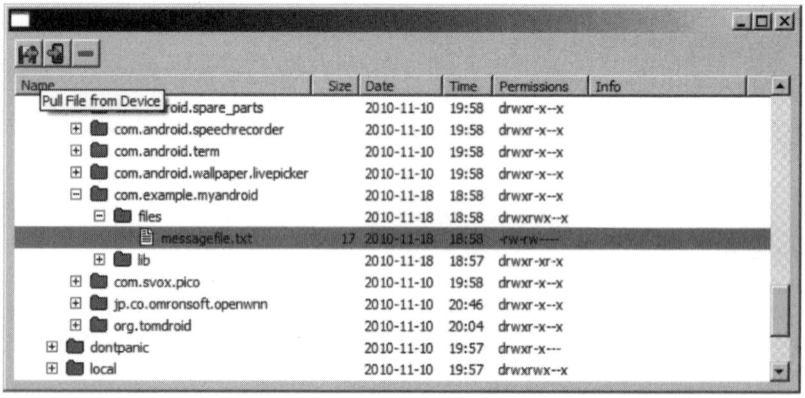

Figure 2–28. *The File Explorer window with a view on the file system and the example message file*

The File Explorer also allows us to push and pull files to and from the device or emulator.

Navigating the Device File System with the ADB Shell

In addition to graphically navigating the device file system, the Android SDK tools also allow us to run a remote shell on an attached device, whether the device is an AVD emulated instance or an actual physical device.

The SDK utility that supports this functionality is the ADB. To see how this works, issue the following commands in a terminal command-line window:

```
adb -e shell
# cd /data/data/com.example.myandroid/files/
# ls
# cat messagefile.txt
```

The output of running this session on Windows can be seen in Figure 2–29. The preceding commands are compatible with Linux, Mac OS X, and Windows systems. In fact, it might be worth a mention that the # (hash) prompt belongs to the remote Linux shell on the device, not the local host system.

Figure 2–29. *Navigating the file system and the ADB shell*

For clarity, a transcript of this session for Windows follows here:

```
C:\>adb -e shell
# cd /data/data/com.example.myandroid/files/
cd /data/data/com.example.myandroid/files/
# ls
messagefile.txt
# cat messagefile.txt
Practical Android is Fun!
#
```

Making Menus

Per Listing 2–17, Android activity menus are mainly created by overriding two methods on the Activity class: onCreateOptionsMenu() and onOptionsItemSelected().

The onCreateOptionsMenu() method is invoked with the activity's default root menu item as an argument. This can then be used to add additional menu groups and menu items. We should always return true from this method if the menu structure is to be visible, or else return false.

The onOptionsItemSelected() method takes care of menu actions that are triggered by events as the user selects menu items. When we handle a known application menu item in our menu event code, we should always return true from this method. For all other (perhaps unknown) menu items, we should delegate the return processing to the base class' implementation of this method.

Listing 2–17. *MyAndroidSdkAppActivity2.java: Creating Menus and Responding to Menu Selection Events*

```java
/**
 * how to make a menu - implement onCreateOptionsMenu()
 * */
@Override
public boolean onCreateOptionsMenu(Menu menu)
{
    // always first delegate to the base class in case of system menus
    super.onCreateOptionsMenu(menu);

    /** our 1st demo menu grouping - menu sub-item titles should be
     * read from the strings table rather than embedded in app code */
    final int mnu_grp1 = 1;
    menu.add(mnu_grp1, 1, 1, "My Menu Item 1-1");
    menu.add(mnu_grp1, 2, 2, "My Menu Item 1-2");

    // our 2nd demo menu grouping
    final int mnu_grp2 = 2;
    menu.add(mnu_grp2, 3, 3,"My Menu Item 2-1");
    menu.add(mnu_grp2, 4, 4,"My Menu Item 2-2");

    return true; // true for a visible menu, false for an invisible one
}

/**
 * how to respond to a menu - implement onOptionsItemSelected()
 * */
@Override
public boolean onOptionsItemSelected(MenuItem item)
{
    final int mnu_id = item.getItemId();
    Log.d(TAG, "Menu Item: ID [" + mnu_id + "] selected");
    switch(mnu_id) {
        case 1: // our own items
        case 2:
        case 3:
        case 4:
            makeToast("Menu [" + mnu_id + "] " + message);
            return true; // true when we have handled al our own items
        default: // not our items
            Log.d(TAG, "Menu Item: UNKNOWN ID selected");
            return super.onOptionsItemSelected(item); // pass item id up
    }
}
```

Migrating the Example Application to Eclipse/ADT

Now that you are comfortable with the Android SDK tools and the inner workings of our example project, we will complete the chapter by stepping through a migration of the project to an Eclipse/ADT (Android Development Tools) environment.

Make a Copy of the Project

To keep things simple, we will make a copy of the project folder, /MyAndroidSdkAppProject2, and its contents to a new directory called /MyAndroidSdkAppProject2_Eclipse without altering anything. You are free to do this in any way you wish.

> **NOTE:** The project files for the book examples are available for download from the Apress book web site.

Open Eclipse with the ADT Plugin Installed

We will need a fully functioning Eclipse installation with the ADT plugin correctly installed. Setting this up was covered in the first chapter of the book. Please refer to that section of the book if necessary.

Create a New Android Project from the Copy of the Project

Use the Eclipse menu sequence File ➤ New ➤ Android Project. The dialog shown in Figure 2–30 should be visible.

Now ensure that the Create project from existing source radio button is selected and enter the project name as MyAndroidSdkAppProject2_Eclipse.

Use the Browse button to navigate to the location where we made our /MyAndroidSdkAppProject2_Eclipse copy of the project earlier.

Select the Android 2.3 Build Target. If this build target does not appear in the list it means that ADT was not properly set up according to the instructions in the first chapter. Please refer to Chapter 1 for troubleshooting.

Now click the Finish button to import the project into the Eclipse workspace.

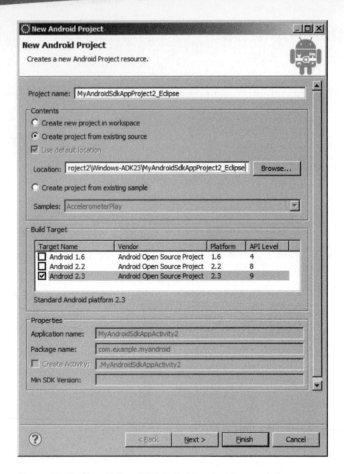

Figure 2–30. *New Eclipse/ADT Android project from existing sources*

Once the project has been imported, perform a `Refresh` and `Build Project` in the IDE.

Create and Test a New Run Configuration for the Project

Use the Eclipse menu sequence **Run ➤ Run Configurations**. The dialog depicted in Figure 2–31 should be now be visible.

Set up the configuration accordingly and name it to your preference. We used the name MyAndroidSdkAppProject2_Eclipse.

Now click the Run button and verify that the application behaves as it is supposed to from previous experience outside Eclipse.

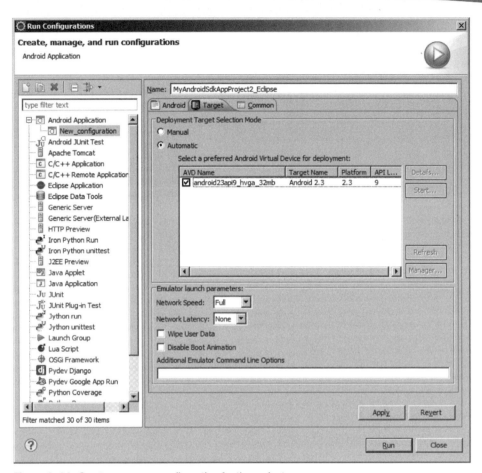

Figure 2-31. *Create a new run configuration for the project*

Deploying to a Real Device

We can test with a real device by attaching it to our development computer via USB. Normally it is as simple as plugging in the device and ensuring that your phone has the USB Debugging setting turned on.

> **NOTE:** If you are developing on Windows, the USB Driver Package for Windows should have been selected and installed as part of the initial Android SDK setup.

Follow the instructions on the "Developing on a Device"[23] page of the Android Developers site for full background and troubleshooting, if necessary, for your platform.

---

[23] http://developer.android.com/guide/developing/device.html

Once the device is connected, switch the Automatic setting on the Target tab of the Run Configuration to Manual, click Apply, and then click Run.

The Eclipse ADT plugin should now present an Android Device Chooser dialog as shown in Figure 2–32 and Figure 2–33.

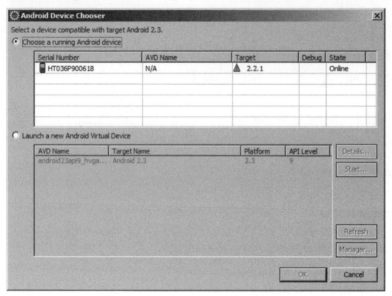

Figure 2–32. *The Eclipse/ADT Android Device Chooser dialog with running device selected*

Your physical device should appear as a valid target along with a list of AVD targets.

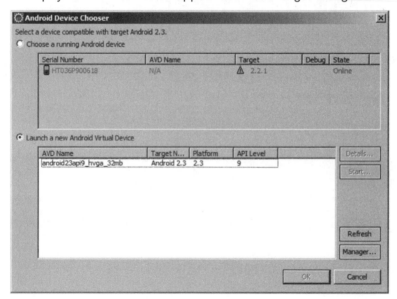

Figure 2–33. *The Eclipse/ADT Android Device Chooser dialog with AVD selected*

If you select the Choose a running Android device option, the example application should be installed and opened on your phone. You can then test the known functionality.

Creating a Signed APK Package of the Example Application

We will now present the steps necessary to export a signed and certificated APK package of an application using Eclipse/ADT. The ADT plugin provides by far the most convenient way for performing this otherwise tedious task:

1. Open the application Android Manifest tab and click the Use the Export Wizard link in the Exporting section. See Figure 2–34.

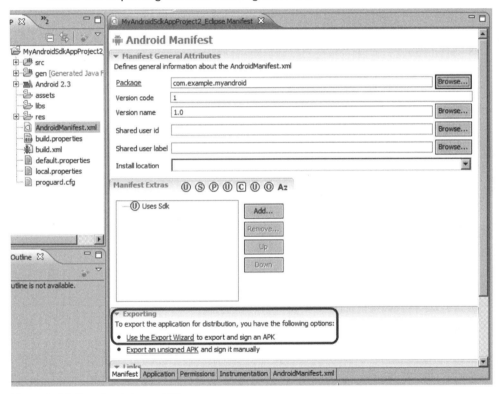

Figure 2–34. *Export and sign an APK*

2. The Project Checks dialog should appear. Click the Next button. See Figure 2–35.

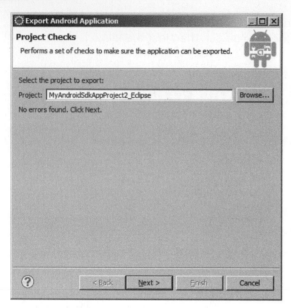

Figure 2–35. Eclipse/ADT Wizard for exporting a signed APK: project verification

3. Now the Keystore selection dialog should appear. Select Create (unless you already have a keystore) and click the Next button when you are done with all the required input fields. Make sure you record the password you selected for the keystore. If this is lost, you will need to create a new keystore from scratch. See Figure 2–36.

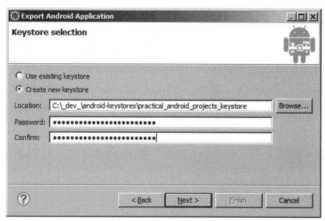

Figure 2–36. Eclipse/ADT Wizard for exporting a signed APK: keystore creation

4. Per Figure 2–37, we should now be prompted for the configuration of a keystore Alias. Follow the same procedure as in the previous step. Take care to select a Validity (duration) period that makes sense. Click the Next button when you are done.

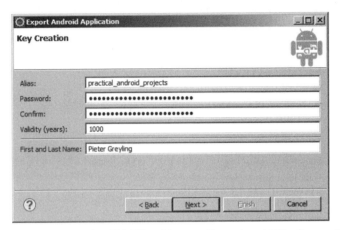

Figure 2–37. *Eclipse/ADT Wizard for exporting a signed APK: alias creation*

5. As depicted in Figure 2–38, we should now be on the last step: Destination and key/certificate checks. This verifies our selections and allows us to pick a destination folder for the final signed APK file. Click the Finish button when done.

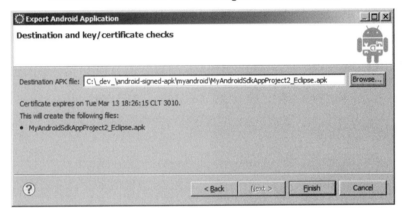

Figure 2–38. *Eclipse/ADT Wizard for exporting a signed APK: checking and saving the APK file*

The certificated APK file can now be deployed to your users.

That completes our migration of the chapter example project to the Eclipse/ADK development environment. You should now be sufficiently comfortable with the spectrum of Android development tools to be able to make full use of an IDE such as Eclipse to boost your productivity significantly.

Summary

In this chapter, you learned how to create and use a fully functional Android development environment using a selection of out-of-the-box Android SDK tools and an open-source programming text editor. In addition, the work was based on a practical demonstration project with several reusable code sections as its subject matter.

This was followed by walking through a migration of the example project to the Eclipse IDE by importing the source code using the Eclipse/ADT plugin wizards. This allowed us to demonstrate taking advantage of some of the Android-specific development features of the Eclipse ADT plugin while building on the understanding of the core toolset covered during the earlier part of the chapter.

Chapter 3

Roll Your Own Android Scripting Environment

A device running Android is by definition a full-blown computing platform.

Considering this, it's not a giant leap of the imagination to wonder about the feasibility of entering programming code directly on the device and having this code execute immediately without any intervening compilation, build, and deployment cycle. In other words, can an Android device work as a handheld, onboard environment for writing and running small scripts and programs?

Perhaps you've found yourself wanting the convenience of tinkering on your phone with a small algorithm or piece of code logic while on the bus, train or plane. Ideally, you'd be able to do this in an iterative manner so that each bit of logic can be run instantly, resulting in immediate feedback.

Maybe you've wished for the ability to customize and configure the behavior of a favorite application by attaching bits of instantly runnable code to well-defined user modifiable points in the software. These sections of code could then be invoked at runtime and, based on the input, would change the way the application performed its tasks.

In these scenarios, our application would effectively become the host for a guest programming-language interpreter. Assuming that the interpreter is component-based, it could, in theory, be plugged into host applications of widely varying design and functional purpose.

In general, such dynamic and interpretive programming activities are known as scripting, and they fall within the realm of scripting languages, interpreters, and domain specific languages (DSLs). The sequence of actions that read the code to be executed and finally end up with a result is also commonly called "evaluation"; hence the frequent existence of methods or functions called "eval" in the implementation code of such environments.

As we've learned so far, the Android OS is by design a flexible, componentized, configurable, and pluggable open source operating platform. Thus, it makes sense to expect we can implement our own scripting environment for our handheld Android device.

In this chapter we will show you how to do just that. We will build our own scripting environment that uses an embedded interpreter to evaluate small scripts and programs written in the BASIC programming language. This interpreter, or engine, was originally written over a decade ago to demonstrate the flexibility and capabilities of Java and the JVM, as well as to show how to implement such a scripting engine using just Java. It is called Cocoa-BASIC and is fully implemented in the Java programming language, making it a good candidate for integration into a standard Android Java-based application.

We assume here that you, as a developer who knows Java, will understand enough of the BASIC language constructs and syntax to follow along. The COCOA programming documentation that we'll refer to also covers the syntax elements and functions supported by the Cocoa-BASIC implementation.

First we'll run through some architectural and design considerations in order to give context and meaning to the practical implementation. We will then demonstrate the BASIC interpreter running in a standard or classic Java AWT (Abstract Window Toolkit) desktop GUI configuration as it was originally conceived. Next we'll cover porting the interpreter to the Android platform where we embed the engine into an Android Activity that acts as the host application for the interpreter. Not only is this application a controller for the interpreter, it also has some basic features that make it a convenient environment for using the interpreter.

This will essentially create a no-frills but complete onboard environment that will enable you to write and run small BASIC scripts and programs directly on your Android device. This implementation will not be an industrial-strength programming tool, but it will certainly provide the foundation and understanding necessary for building one.

Along the way, the project will also allow us to gain further insights into the function and potential of the Android development platform.

Designing a Scripting Environment

Before we dive in, let's have a short planning session and think through the core architectural and design concepts relevant to making our own scripting environment.

The Components of a Scripting System

A scripting system can consist of several components and these can be arranged in a number of configurations.

Seen from a very high level, you'll generally find three components overall, two of which are the main building blocks:

- **The Application:** The logical container and owner of our functionality and features. In summary, the application is what a particular piece of software is all about. It embodies the purpose of the software. No matter how many hidden, self-contained bits and pieces of other software are running behind the scenes, from the user's perspective the application is the sum total of the software.

- **The Interpreter:** The engine that processes the script code and evaluates it to end up with some result.

These two logical components can both be implemented to be run in either of two roles:

- **The Host:** Also known as the controller or the client, this is the part of the application the user will see and interact with. It makes calls or requests to the guest via some form of interface, such as IPC, sockets, files, I/O streams etc. In essence, the host is extended by the guest.

- **The Guest:** Also known as the provider or the server, generally this component will not be seen by the user since it is embedded within the host. It services the host with responses to its requests via an interface such as local or remote method calls, sockets, files, I/O streams, etc.

The third part of the picture is not strictly a design component but rather the unavoidable basis upon which the scripting system functions:

- **The Platform:** The operating system or virtual machine, which can be viewed as one of the building blocks even though it is not strictly a direct structural component of the architecture. Our application code should generally interface only with the operating platform via a well-known and officially published set of platform APIs. In our case, these will be the Android APIs that are published and documented in the Android SDK.

The Component Roles in a Scripting System

As part of the foundation for our interpreter environment design, we will quickly summarize and clarify the possible roles of the guest and host components.

Extending the Application by Embedding the Interpreter

In this scenario, the application performs the role of host for the interpreter. As depicted in Figure 3–1, the interpreter is embedded within the overall application and hidden from the direct view of the end user. The application might present some kind of interface for directing the functioning of the interpreter engine, but always acts as the final controller in this configuration.

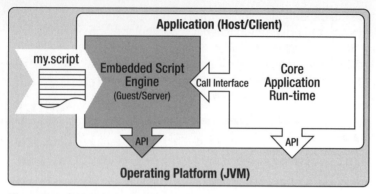

Figure 3-1. *Embedding scripting architecture*

As you will see, we will use this design for our scripting environment implementation.

Extending the Interpreter by Embedding the Application

Even though we will not be using this design approach, we will cover it for the sake of completeness. As shown in Figure 3-2, the roles have now been reversed and the scripting engine itself becomes the primary usage interface for the application. In essence, it becomes the application.

This is a common configuration where the application services an end-user base consisting of skilled or specialist users with technical know-how and advanced requirements.

For instance, the application could be an interactive domain-specific command-line or console terminal shell that allows direct execution of script commands by its users. These script commands then invoke application-specific core functionality from business libraries wrapped as modules embedded within the script environment.

Database engines often ship with such applications that allow the interpretation and execution of backend database administration or data-query commands interactively from a shell.

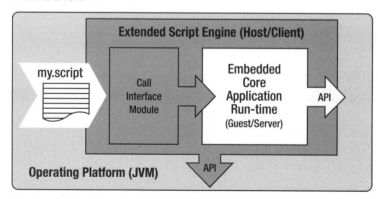

Figure 3-2. *Extending scripting architecture*

It is worth mentioning that it's often useful to apply a cross-over or mix-and-match approach that melds these two design strategies. This can be the case in scenarios where we implement a shell-like scripting interpreter in a graphical toolkit environment. In other words, this can be desirable when the interpreter is lightly wrapped in a thin GUI shell that may be significantly more code-intensive than if the interface were a lean console shell.

Designing for Resource-Constrained Systems

Operating systems such as Android are designed to execute on resource-constrained hardware. As such, these platforms do not take kindly to lax application response times. When these become extreme and regular enough, they certainly affect the perception and popularity of the application with its intended end users.

In fact, the Android system enforces and encourages responsive user interface applications by applying timeouts on long-running application processes, particularly GUI code. The system does this mostly to avoid a state known as ANR, or Application Not Responding, which generally results in the Android system presenting the user with an ANR Dialog as shown in Figure 3–3. This dialog is something we want to avoid as a matter of course when we develop Android applications.

Figure 3–3. *The Android "Application Not Responding" dialog*

What does all of this imply for our onboard interpreter design? It means that our script can't just go off and leave the application's user interface to its own devices. Such behavior will very likely hang of freeze the user interface while it waits for the script interpreter process to rejoin the application.

More information and guidelines on this subject can be found on the Android Developers "Designing for Responsiveness" web site.[1]

Multi-Threading for Background Code

Whenever we predict—or even just have a suspicion, however vague—that our scripting code might at times take a relatively long time to execute, it is always a good idea to consider using asynchronous processing via threads. This is especially appropriate when our script interpreter engine is being hosted in an end-user application with a single-threaded graphical user interface.

GUI frameworks commonly execute on a single main application thread, and it is imperative that this thread is not in any way choked or blocked into unresponsive behavior. When the application defers to performing background work, such as network access or database queries running on the main GUI thread, this can result in a user interface that no longer responds to GUI events for intermittent periods of time—or worse.

The Android operating environment is no exception when it comes to its user interface toolkit threading model. By default, Android applications are run by the system on a single thread called main. This is also known as the UI thread, and it is the thread that is responsible for dealing with the user interface and interacting with the UI components of the Android platform.

You'll find more information regarding threading on the Android Developers Application Fundamentals web page under the "Processes and Threads" heading.[2]

As a final word on threading here, we will mention that in our scripting environment implementation, we will also demonstrate running the interpreter engine on a separate thread using the recommended Android asynchronous processing pattern.

Programming with BASIC

Some readers may wonder about our choice of the BASIC programming language for this chapter. It may come as a surprise to learn that selecting BASIC for the essential "roll your own" aspects of the chapter was, in fact, a no-brainer.

This is due to the history, design, popularity, and, indeed, the very nature of BASIC. It fairly concisely wraps up fundamental and core programming constructs and concepts in a small language that is easy to learn. Most of its relatively few core statements and function names are short and easy to remember. Notably, they are also easy to type on a device with a small keyboard and screen.

---

[1] http://developer.android.com/guide/practices/design/responsiveness.html

[2] http://developer.android.com/guide/topics/fundamentals.html#procthread

These attributes and the language's approachability for a potentially large audience of users make it a very appropriate choice for running on popular and highly mobile small devices.

A BASIC Backgrounder

The BASIC programming language was designed to be easy to teach and easy to learn. Unlike many other languages that were created for the same reason, BASIC can claim a huge number of programmers who were introduced to programming with the language and used it as their first coding environment.

> **WHAT IS BASIC?** BASIC is an acronym that stands for "Beginner's All-purpose Symbolic Instruction Code." It was originally created in 1964 by the computer scientists Kemeny and Kurtz. The main purpose was to teach programming skills to those who weren't scientists or mathematicians, who produced most software applications at the time. There was growing demand for software applications and it was felt that the pool of programming talent could be significantly extended through the introduction of a new generation of high-level programming languages such as BASIC.

BASIC is also unique in that many of its implementations are interpreters. This significantly tightens the feedback loop between the programmer and the development system. Such an iterative programming environment leads to rapid prototyping of systems and a highly accelerated learning pace.

It therefore comes as no surprise that most modern scripting languages follow the same interpretive route and should concede this as one of the main reasons for their rapid growth and adoption by the programming community.

Cocoa—A BASIC Interpreter for Java

For this project, we selected the Cocoa-BASIC interpreter for Java. It was originally created in 1996 by Chuck McManis and featured in a series of articles for JavaWorld[3] entitled "How to build an interpreter in Java."[4] These articles are still available on the JavaWorld web site at the time of this writing and some of the pages are included in the code download archives as part of the documentation.

The source code and documentation for Cocoa BASIC are downloadable and free for learning and noncommercial purposes from the Cocoa home page.[5]

---

[3] http://www.javaworld.com/

[4] http://www.javaworld.com/jw-05-1997/jw-05-indepth.html

[5] http://www.mcmanis.com/chuck/java/cocoa/

> **COCOA-BASIC IS *NOT* OPEN SOURCE:** Please note that Cocoa-BASIC is not published under an open source license. The author has kindly given permission for us to use the Cocoa-BASIC code for the chapter project, and you are free to explore and use it for learning although it remains copyrighted.

More programming documentation for Cocoa-BASIC is available in the code distribution download and on the reference web site.[6]

Outlining the Code Projects for This Chapter

This chapter presents two code projects. Both can be downloaded from the book web site as part of the resources for this chapter:

- **Cocoa-BASIC AWT** (`cocoa-basic-awt`): This is the original Java AWT-based hosting code. It is directly based on the code that can be downloaded from the Cocoa-BASIC home web site. We have collected and organized the code into packages with only the relevant source files and dependencies actually needed by the interpreter and the AWT GUI host application. The project is in the form of an IntelliJ IDEA IDE project but can easily be imported and built in other IDEs.

- **CocoaDroid** (`cocoadroid`): This is the full implementation of our Android-based onboard scripting environment that embeds the BASIC interpreter engine. It is also in the form of an IntelliJ IDEA IDE project.

We will go through the functioning, source code, and relevant resources of these two projects in detail during the remainder of this chapter.

The Cocoa-BASIC AWT Project

Before we dive into the Java AWT desktop GUI version of the scripting environment, let's take a quick look at the overall design paradigm of the application. We will meet these design aspects and component classes again in the Android application implementation, so it's worth covering this material now.

Understanding the Cocoa-BASIC AWT Application Design

Building on our earlier overall logical architecture and design diagrams, we present a similar depiction relevant to the AWT-based Java desktop host application in Figure 3–4.

---

[6] http://www.mcmanis.com/chuck/java/cocoa/basic_doc.html

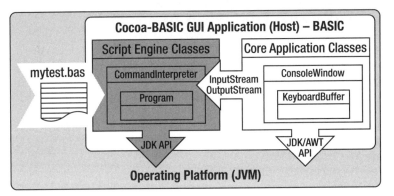

Figure 3-4. *Cocoa-BASIC AWT embedded scripting architecture*

We have added slightly more detail relating to the main classes for the script engine and the core application. As you can see, the key actors in terms of classes are:

- The Application
    - BASIC: The startup application class that contains the Java `main` method. It instantiates the two main classes of the GUI application (`ConsoleWindow`) and the interpreter (`CommandInterpreter`) and hooks up their mechanism of communication: one instance each of `InputStream` and `OutputStream` derived classes, which, in this case, is `DataInputStream` for interpreter input and `PrintStream` for output.
    - `ConsoleWindow`: This class manages the user interface. It is the View of the application. It also embeds an instance of the `KeyboardBuffer` class, which manages the lower-level aspects of the Input- and OutputStream communications with the `CommandInterpreter` class instance.
    - `KeyboardBuffer`: This class manages the interaction between the commands typed via the keyboard and the resulting output received from the interpreter.
- The Interpreter
    - `CommandInterpreter`: The class that encapsulates the script engine. All host application interaction and communication with the script interpreter occurs through this class.
    - `Program`: The backend class that wraps an executable unit of code that can be logically described as a "program."

We will look at the source code for these classes shortly. First let's step through what the application actually does and see what it looks like when it runs.

Running the Cocoa-BASIC AWT Desktop Application

We are not going to go into the details of building and running the application from the IDE. We assume you are proficient enough with Java development tasks to be able to do this on your own.

Assuming we've built the project according to the downloadable book sample code project, the condensed project file directory should be similar to the one in Listing 3–1.

Listing 3–1. *The Cocoa-BASIC AWT Condensed Project Folder*

```
cocoa-basic-awt
+---cocoa
|   +---basic
|   |       BASIC.java
|   |       CommandInterpreter.java
|   |       Program.java
|   |       ...
|   +---dlib
|   |       ConsoleWindow.java
|   |       KeyboardBuffer.java
|   \---util
|   |       ...
+---out
|   +---artifacts
|   |       atest1.bas
|   |       atest2.bas
|   |       cocoa-basic-awt.jar
|   |       ...
\---test-scripts
    |       ...
```

Take note of the location of the `cocoa-basic-awt.jar` file. We will start the application by issuing the following command from the terminal where the `jar` file resides:

```
java -jar cocoa-basic-awt.jar
```

This should start the application with the main window displayed as in Figure 3–5.

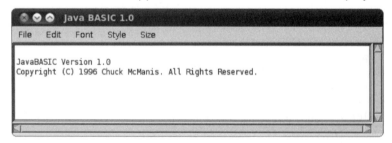

Figure 3–5. *Cocoa-BASIC AWT main window*

This displays a small application banner. To actually run any code, we select **File ➤ New** from the menu as in Figure 3–6.

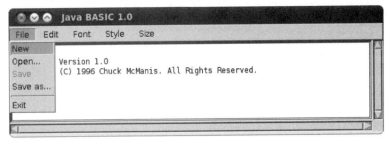

Figure 3–6. *Opening a new Cocoa-BASIC AWT buffer*

This should present the new window buffer in Figure 3–7.

Figure 3–7. *Running code in a new buffer*

Enter some code as per Figure 3–7 and Listing 3–2 into the window text buffer to exercise the interpreter. Don't type the ">>" characters; they are for clarity only. The expected interpreter response is indicated by the absence of these characters.

Listing 3–2. *Simple BASIC Test Code*

```
>> let a$ = "we will make this work on android too…"
>> print a$
we will make this work on android too…
```

Assume that we have, for testing convenience, placed our `cocoa-basic-awt.jar` file and the `atest2.bas` BASIC test code file in certain folders, as follows.

On Linux and Mac OS X:

`/home/<user>/cocoa-basic-awt/`

And on Windows:

`C:\_dev_\cocoa-basic-awt\`

Now we run the application as before and enter the following commands into a new file buffer. The expected interpreter response is also listed in the transcripts.

On Linux and Mac OS X (see Figure 3–8):

```
>> load "/home/<user>/cocoa-basic-awt/atest2.bas"
File loaded.
Ready.
```

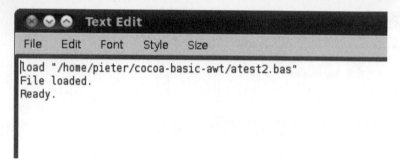

Figure 3-8. *Loading a program's source code file in a new buffer (Linux/Mac OS X)*

And on Windows (see Figure 3-9):

```
C:\_dev_\cocoa-basic-awt\
>> load "C:\_dev_\cocoa-basic-awt\\atest2.bas"
File loaded.
Ready.
```

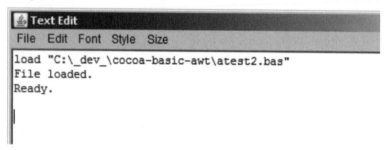

Figure 3-9. *Loading a program's source code file in a new buffer (Windows)*

Now open a new file buffer, type the `list` command and press Enter. The loaded program should be listed in the buffer as in Figure 3-10.

Figure 3–10. *Listing a source code file in a new buffer*

Again, open a new file buffer, type the run command, and press the Enter key. The loaded program should be executed by the BASIC interpreter, producing the output listed in the buffer as shown in Figure 3–11.

Figure 3-11. *Running a loaded program*

This concludes our demonstration of the application.

Reviewing the Cocoa-BASIC AWT Source Code

Now that we understand the flow of the application a little better, let's take a look at some of the source code. Please refer back to the architecture overview diagrams earlier in this chapter for a conceptual refresher if necessary.

Listing 3–3 shows the source code of the main Java startup file for this application, BASIC.java. Code of interest is highlighted in bold.

Listing 3-3. *The Cocoa-BASIC AWT BASIC .java Startup Class*

```
package cocoa.basic;

import java.io.*;
import cocoa.dlib.*;

public class BASIC {
    public static void main(String args[]) {
        char data[] = new char[256];
        ConsoleWindow cw = new ConsoleWindow("Java BASIC 1.0");

        CommandInterpreter ci = new CommandInterpreter(cw.DataInputStream(),
                                                        cw.PrintStream());
        try
        {
            ci.start();
        }
        catch (Exception e)
        {
            System.out.println("Caught an Exception :");
            e.printStackTrace();
            try
            {
```

```
                    System.out.println("Press enter to continue.");
                    int c = System.in.read();
                }
                catch (IOException xx)
                {
                    /* pass */
                }
            }
        }
    }
}
```

As explained earlier, it is important to note that the stream instances, InputStream and OutputStream, of the two classes, `CommandInterpreter` and `ConsoleWindow,` are hooked together upon instantiation via the `CommandInterpreter` class constructor.

```
            ConsoleWindow cw = new ConsoleWindow("Java BASIC 1.0");
            CommandInterpreter ci = new CommandInterpreter(cw.DataInputStream(),
                                                            cw.PrintStream());
```

This causes input into the console window to be streamed into the interpreter, and output from the interpreter to be printed to the console window via the print stream.

Listing 3–4 shows a segment of source code from the `CommandInterpreter` class. Again, code of interest is highlighted in bold. As we can see, the constructor ensures that there are always input and output stream instances available.

Listing 3–4. *I/O Streams and the CommandInterpreter Class (partial)*

```
package cocoa.basic;

import java.io.*;

/**
 * This class is an "interactive" BASIC environment. You can think of it as
 * BASIC debug mode. Using the streams you passed in to create the object, it
 * hosts an interactive session allowing the user to enter BASIC programs, run
 * them, save them, and load them.
 */
public class CommandInterpreter
{
    private DataInputStream inStream;
    private PrintStream outStream;

    final static String commands[] = {
            "new", "run", "list", "cat", "del", "resume",
            "bye", "save", "load", "dump", "cont",
    };

[--code omitted--]
    /**
     * Create a new command interpreter attached to the passed
     * in streams.
     */
    public CommandInterpreter(InputStream in, OutputStream out)
    {
        if (in instanceof DataInputStream)
        {
```

```
            inStream = (DataInputStream) in;
        }
        else
        {
            inStream = new DataInputStream(in);
        }
        if (out instanceof PrintStream)
        {
            outStream = (PrintStream) out;
        }
        else
        {
            outStream = new PrintStream(out);
        }
    }
```

[--code omitted--]

> **NOTE:** We will not be going into the details of the BASIC language interpreter implementation. This is outside the scope of this chapter since this is an Android programming book, not a computer language implementation book. We are focused on the Android platform and the Android programming techniques that make an application such as this possible. As mentioned before, the full source code is available as organized projects for your perusal and study.

Let's move on to the feature project of this chapter, CocoaDroid, our onboard BASIC interpreter and scripting application.

The CocoaDroid Project

To begin the coverage of this project, we present a short table of dependencies (Table 3–1) to serve as a reminder of what to check before running the application in an emulator on our development system. Then, as with the previous project, we take a quick look at the conceptual architecture of the application.

A Preflight Checklist

Table 3–1 lists some configuration items you'll need to take care of in order to test the project. Of course, you are free to set up your configuration to your own liking, but these dependency items should generally be checked in any case.

> **AVD ANDROID PLATFORM LEVEL:** The dependency list in Table 3–1 assumes that the Android platform API Level `android-9` has been installed on your system. This is for Android 2.3, the latest version at the time of this writing. Be sure you know which platform you are creating your AVD for. At the time of this writing, CocoaDroid was built for running on the Android 2.2 (Froyo) and the Android 2.3 (Gingerbread) platforms.

We will not be covering how to run the project on the emulator in any depth here because we assume you've been brought up to speed by reading our first two chapters of this book. Table 3–1 is meant to be simply a convenient reminder.

Table 3–1. *CocoaDroid Project Debugging Dependency Checklist*

Item	Value or Command
PATH	`<Android SDK Directory>/tools`
PATH	`<Android SDK Directory>/platform-tools`
Create an AVD	`android create avd -n android23api9_hvga_32mb -t android-9 -c 32M`
List AVDs	`android list avd`
Delete an AVD	`android delete avd -n android23api9_hvga_32mb`

Understanding the CocoaDroid Application Design

It is a good idea to have a mental map of how our application's main components fit together, so let's take a look at the conceptual architecture diagram in Figure 3–12.

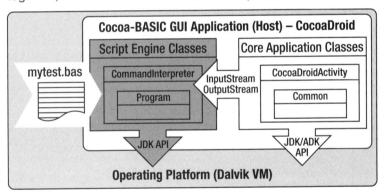

Figure 3–12. *CocoaDroid Embedded Scripting Architecture*

As you can see, the overall logical design of the application remains very similar to that of the earlier Java AWT version.

The main actors in terms of classes are:

- The Application
  - `CocoaDroidActivity`: The main entry point of the application. The Cocoa-BASIC interpreter will be embedded in the `CocoaDroidActivity` Android Activity, which will set up an InputStream and an OutputStream, create an instance of a CommandInterpreter, and pass in references to the two stream instances. These streams will be used to direct communication back and forth between the `CocoaDroidActivity` and the `CommandInterpreter` instances. Note further down that our particular flavor of this class is a subclass called `CocoaDroidCommandInterpreter`. Figure 3-12 still depicts the name of the parent class since logically nothing has really changed in the conceptual design.
  - `CommonAndroidCodeLibrary`: This class services the application with several common operations. They are loosely organized as a set of static methods.
- The Interpreter
  - `CocoaDroidCommandInterpreter`: The class that encapsulates the script engine. All host application interaction and communication with the script interpreter occurs through this class. In the case of the CocoaDroid application, we created a subclass of `CommandInterpreter` called `CocoaDroidCommandInterpreter` that has been altered slightly to fit an Android Activity based environment better.
  - Program: The backend class that wraps an executable unit of code that can be logically described as a "program." It remains exactly as before in the AWT desktop-based project.

We will review some application source code as we go along, but first let's see what the application looks like.

Running the CocoaDroid Android Application

Building and running the application with the IDE and the Android emulator is, once again, assumed to be within the proficiency and skill set of the reader. We will not cover those steps here.

When we've built our application and installed it to an emulator or a physical device, we should see the CocoaDroid application icon on the Application Launcher, as per Figure 3-13.

Figure 3-13. *The CocoaDroid application launcher*

The Elements of the CocoaDroid Main Activity Screen

When we launch the application, we should see the "CocoaDroid – BASIC for Android" startup Activity as shown in Figure 3-14.

Figure 3-14. *The CocoaDroid main Activity screen on startup*

The application prints a startup banner and a ready message. This means that CocoaDroid is now prepared to accept and evaluate strings or listings of commands and statements in the BASIC programming language.

The CocoaDroid application main Activity screen is organized with the following elements:

- **The Input (or Code) Text Field:** An Input entry field for the interpreter and programming language commands. This is an instance of the Android `EditText` View class.

- **The Toolbar:** A tool layout with four buttons. The first button is an instance of the `ImageButton` View class and the others are standard `Button` instances. They are arranged within an embedded `LinearLayout` instance.

  - Run (the black box with the green arrow). This initiates the creation of an interpreter instance and pushes the code in the input text field onto an input stream. This stream feeds into the interpreter `CocoaDroidCommandInterpreter` instance. The interpreter evaluates this code and streams the result back via an output stream from which it is pulled and placed into the output text field.

  - `Load`. This button loads text that was previously saved to two persistent scratch files, one each for input and output, using the `Save` button. The feature allows you to keep a single record of the last input and output session text values.

  - `Save`. This button saves the text currently in the input and output text fields, which can then be reloaded with the `Load` button. It keeps only a single session record at a time, overwriting the previous input and output scratch files with the new values.

  - `Clear`. This button clears the input and output text field values in order to present a clean working area. The output of the last execution run is not lost but pushed onto the top of the history list (described shortly).

- **The Output (or Results) Text Field:** An output field that lists the result of the interpreter evaluation. This is also an instance of the Android `EditText` View class, so its contents can be manipulated.

- **The History List:** A list of previous interpreter output results that scroll downward from the second-most recent to the earliest. Each evaluation result is added to the top of this list when it is replaced by the output of a new interpreter run. This list is an instance of `ListView`.

- **The Main Menu:** CocoaDroid also has an Android application menu that is not immediately visible. It provides the user with a few more features and is portrayed in Figure 3–15.

- Load Samples. The CocoaDroid application package ships with a file containing small snippets of BASIC code that you can copy and paste into the input text filed to use as a basis for your own programs. The file is stored internally as a raw resource file asset. We will cover this in more detail later.

- Load Work. Besides letting you store a copy of an input/output session, CocoaDroid also lets you save a buffer of text we call Work to an application text file. This menu item retrieves the data currently saved and populates the input text field with it when selected.

- Save Work. This menu item saves the current contents of the input text field and writes it to a private application file as described in the Load Work section.

- About CocoaDroid. When this menu item is selected, a short notice banner is printed by the CocoaDroid interpreter to the output results text field. For the sake of demonstration and technical value, we decided to use Cocoa-BASIC code itself to write this message. We will cover this in more detail later.

The Main XML Layout Resource

We have introduced and explained the main user interface controls of the CocoaDroid application. The content of Listing 3–5, the main XML layout resource file, shows the UI Toolkit types and attributes for the user interface.

Listing 3–5. *main.xml*

```xml
<?xml version="1.0" encoding="utf-8"?>
<ScrollView xmlns:android="http://schemas.android.com/apk/res/android"
        android:id="@+id/scroll_view_main"
        android:layout_width="fill_parent"
        android:layout_height="fill_parent"
        android:fillViewport="true"
    >
    <LinearLayout xmlns:android="http://schemas.android.com/apk/res/android"
            android:orientation="vertical"
            android:layout_width="fill_parent"
            android:layout_height="fill_parent"
        >
        <EditText
                android:id="@+id/txt_input"
                android:layout_width="fill_parent"
                android:layout_height="wrap_content"
                android:scrollbars="vertical">
        </EditText>
        <LinearLayout
                android:layout_width="fill_parent"
                android:layout_height="wrap_content"
                android:background="@android:drawable/bottom_bar"
                android:gravity="center_vertical">
```

```xml
        <ImageButton
                android:id="@+id/cmd_enter"
                android:src="@drawable/btn_run"
                android:layout_width="0dip"
                android:layout_weight="2.0"
                android:layout_height="wrap_content"/>
        <Button
                android:id="@+id/cmd_load_scratch"
                android:layout_width="0dip"
                android:layout_weight="1.0"
                android:layout_height="wrap_content"
                android:text="Load"/>
        <Button
                android:id="@+id/cmd_save_scratch"
                android:layout_width="0dip"
                android:layout_weight="1.0"
                android:layout_height="wrap_content"
                android:text="Save"/>
        <Button
                android:id="@+id/cmd_clear"
                android:layout_width="0dip"
                android:layout_weight="1.0"
                android:layout_height="wrap_content"
                android:text="Clear"/>
    </LinearLayout>
    <EditText
            android:id="@+id/txt_output"
            android:layout_width="fill_parent"
            android:layout_height="wrap_content"
            android:scrollbars="vertical">
    </EditText>
    <ListView
            android:id="@+id/lst_output"
            android:layout_width="fill_parent"
            android:layout_height="fill_parent"
            />
   </LinearLayout>
</ScrollView>
```

The Application Activity Class

To get a better idea of the user interface implementation from the Java code perspective, Listing 3–6 shows a partial representation of the application Activity class source file.

Listing 3–6. *CocoaDroidActivity.java (partial)*

```java
public class CocoaDroidActivity extends Activity implements View.OnClickListener
{
    protected static final String TAG = "CocoaDroidActivity";

    protected EditText _txtInput = null;
    protected EditText _txtOutput = null;
    protected ImageButton _cmdEnter = null;
    protected Button _cmdLoadScratch = null;
    protected Button _cmdSaveScratch = null;
```

```java
    protected Button _cmdClear = null;
    protected ListView _outputListView = null;
    OutputStringArrayAdapter _outputArrayAdapter = null;
    ArrayList<String> _outputArrayList = new ArrayList<String>();
    // The input and output streams that form the communications
    // channels with the Cocoa-BASIC interpreter
    protected ByteArrayInputStream _inputStream = null;
    protected ByteArrayOutputStream _outputStream = null;
    // The embedded Cocoa-BASIC interpreter instance reference
    protected CocoaDroidCommandInterpreter _commandInterpreter = null;

    /**
     * Called when the activity is first created.
     */
    @Override
    public void onCreate(Bundle savedInstanceState)
    {
        Log.d(TAG, "onCreate(): ...");
        super.onCreate(savedInstanceState);
        setContentView(R.layout.main);
        initialize();
    }

    /**
     * Sets up Activity user interface controls and resources.
     */
    protected void initialize()
    {
        // set a custom title from the strings table
        setTitle(getString(R.string.app_desc));

        // get a handle on and configure the input and text fields
        _txtInput = (EditText) findViewById(R.id.txt_input);
        _txtInput.setTextSize(TextSize.NORMAL);
        _txtInput.setTypeface(Typeface.MONOSPACE);
        _txtOutput = (EditText) findViewById(R.id.txt_output);
        _txtOutput.setTextSize(TextSize.NORMAL);
        _txtOutput.setTypeface(Typeface.MONOSPACE);
        _txtOutput.setTextColor(Color.GREEN);
        _txtOutput.setBackgroundColor(Color.DKGRAY);

        // get a handle on the enter command button and its event handler
        _cmdEnter = (ImageButton) findViewById(R.id.cmd_enter);
        _cmdEnter.setOnClickListener(this);

        // get a handle on the scratchpad buttons and event handling
        _cmdLoadScratch = (Button) findViewById(R.id.cmd_load_scratch);
        _cmdLoadScratch.setOnClickListener(this);
        _cmdSaveScratch = (Button) findViewById(R.id.cmd_save_scratch);
        _cmdSaveScratch.setOnClickListener(this);

        // button for clearing buffers
        _cmdClear = (Button) findViewById(R.id.cmd_clear);
        _cmdClear.setOnClickListener(this);

        // set up and get a handle on the output list view using an array adapter
        _outputListView = (ListView) findViewById(R.id.lst_output);
```

```
            _outputArrayAdapter = new OutputStringArrayAdapter(this, _outputArrayList);
            _outputListView.setAdapter(_outputArrayAdapter);

            // show the startup about banner
            showAbout();

            // and let the interpreter show a little sample
            String print_hello = "print \">> ready...\"";
            evalCodeStringSync(print_hello);
            _txtInput.setText("");
    }
[--code omitted--]
```

As highlighted in bold, to keep the onCreate method cleaner we have split most of the initialization code into a separate initialize method.

The snippet of code below, extracted from Listing 3–6, shows the input and output stream references we discussed earlier. They are the variables we will use to feed code to the interpreter and to receive results back. The code also shows the reference, CocoaDroidCommandInterpreter, to the CocoaBASIC interpreter engine itself. We will discuss this later when we look at the methods that use it.

```
    // The input and output streams that form the communications
    // channels with the Cocoa-BASIC interpreter
    protected ByteArrayInputStream _inputStream = null;
    protected ByteArrayOutputStream _outputStream = null;
    // The embedded Cocoa-BASIC interpreter instance reference
    protected CocoaDroidCommandInterpreter _commandInterpreter = null;
```

Implementing a Custom ArrayAdapter

From Listing 3–6, we also draw attention to this piece of code:

```
    // set up and get a handle on the output list view using an array adapter
    _outputListView = (ListView) findViewById(R.id.lst_output);
    _outputArrayAdapter = new OutputStringArrayAdapter(this, _outputArrayList);
    _outputListView.setAdapter(_outputArrayAdapter);
```

You might be wondering about the OutputStringArrayAdapter class we refer to in the snippet above. When we build up our ListView, we use a custom ArrayAdapter class, OutputStringArrayAdapter, instead of the standard Android one. Its implementation is shown in Listing 3–7.

Listing 3–7. *OutputStringArrayAdapter — CocoaDroidActivity.java (partial)*

```
/**
 * Custom String ArrayAdapter class that allows us to manipulate the row colors etc.
 */
protected class OutputStringArrayAdapter extends ArrayAdapter<String>
{
    OutputStringArrayAdapter(Context context, ArrayList<String> stringArrayList)
    {
        super(context, android.R.layout.simple_list_item_1, stringArrayList);
    }

    public View getView(int position, View convertView, ViewGroup parent)
```

```
        {
            TextView txt = new TextView(this.getContext());
            txt.setTextColor(Color.GREEN);
            txt.setTextSize(TextSize.SMALL);
            txt.setText(this.getItem(position));
            return txt;
        }
    }
}
```

The purpose of this class is essentially cosmetic—it serves mainly to override the getView method in order to apply a different look to the command history list child rows, and it changes the text font size and text color to fit in with the rest of the Activity. We want the history text entries slightly smaller and in green on a black background.

The Application XML Strings Table

The application code extensively (but not exclusively) uses strings stored in an XML strings table (strings.xml). We show the contents of the strings table in Listing 3-8. These values are retrieved throughout the application source code using the API getString method.

Listing 3-8. *strings.xml*

```xml
<?xml version="1.0" encoding="utf-8"?>
<resources>
    <string name="app_name">CocoaDroid</string>
    <string name="app_desc">CocoaDroid - BASIC for Android</string>
    <string name="app_copy_cocoabasic">CocoaBASIC Version 1.0 Copyright (C) 1996
Chuck McManis. All Rights Reserved.</string>
    <string name="app_copy_cocoadroid">CocoaDroid Android Port Copyright (C) 2010
Pieter Greyling. All Rights Reserved.</string>
    <string name="app_usage_01">Type in BASIC commands, scripts or programs and
press Enter...</string>
    <string name="app_usage_02">Save and reload your session with Save and
Load.</string>
    <string name="app_usage_03">Clear the buffers with Clear.</string>
    <string name="file_name_scratch_input">cocoadroid_scratch_input.txt"</string>
    <string name="file_name_scratch_output">"cocoadroid_scratch_output.txt"</string>
    <string name="file_name_work">"cocoadroid_work.txt"</string>
    <string name="file_name_samples">"program_templates/cocoadroid_basic_templates
.bas"</string>
    <string name="menu_work_load">Load Work</string>
    <string name="menu_work_save">Save Work</string>
    <string name="menu_samples_load">Load Samples</string>
    <string name="menu_app_about">About CocoaDroid</string>
    <string name="title_samples_file_load">Samples File Load</string>
    <string name="title_scratch_files_load">Scratch Files Load</string>
    <string name="title_scratch_files_save">Scratch Files Save</string>
    <string name="title_work_file_load">Work File Load</string>
    <string name="title_work_file_save">Work File Save</string>
    <string name="exception_on_samples_file_load">The Samples File could not be
loaded! Please check your CocoaDroid installation.</string>
    <string name="exception_on_scratch_files_load">The Scratch Files could not be
loaded! Save first.</string>
    <string name="exception_on_scratch_files_save">The Scratch Files could not be
```

```
saved!</string>
    <string name="exception_on_work_file_load">The Work File could not be loaded! Save
Work first.</string>
    <string name="exception_on_work_file_save">The Work File could not be
saved!</string>
</resources>
```

Using XML Menu Layout Resources

We spoke earlier of the application menu. Figure 3–15 depicts its appearance.

Figure 3–15. *CocoaDroid main menu*

Instead of using pure Java code, our application menu is defined in the XML layout resource shown in Listing 3–9.

Listing 3–9. *cocoadroid_main_menu.xml*

```
<?xml version="1.0" encoding="utf-8"?>
<menu xmlns:android="http://schemas.android.com/apk/res/android">
    <item
            android:id="@+id/menu_itm_work_load"
            android:icon="@drawable/mnu_load_work"
            android:title="@string/menu_work_load">
    </item>
    <item
            android:id="@+id/menu_itm_work_save"
            android:icon="@drawable/mnu_save_work"
            android:title="@string/menu_work_save">
    </item>
    <item
            android:id="@+id/menu_itm_samples_load"
```

```
                android:icon="@drawable/mnu_load_samples"
                android:title="@string/menu_samples_load">
        </item>
        <item
                android:id="@+id/menu_itm_app_about"
                android:icon="@drawable/mnu_about"
                android:title="@string/menu_app_about">
        </item>
</menu>
```

Declaring Android UI layouts[7] in XML resources like this provides more flexibility to support multiple physical screen configurations dynamically. Moreover, it supports changes to the user interface without recompilation of the code. This technique also follows the generally recommended principle of separating the presentation layout (UI) from the application logic (code).

Using an Android Menu Inflater

The menu[8] is created using an Android `MenuInflater`[9] inside the overridden method of the `CocoaDroidActivity` class (see Listing 3–10). This loads our `cocoadroid_main_menu.xml` resource file and inflates the menu at runtime.

Listing 3–10. *onCreateOptionsMenu — CocoaDroidActivity.java*

```
/**
 * Implement our app menu using an XML menu layout and the ADK MenuInflater.
 */
@Override
public boolean onCreateOptionsMenu(Menu menu)
{
    // always first delegate to the base class in case of system menus
    super.onCreateOptionsMenu(menu);
    MenuInflater inflater = getMenuInflater();
    inflater.inflate(R.menu.cocoadroid_main_menu, menu);
    // true for a visible menu, false for an invisible one
    return true;
}
```

Our First Script, Hello Android BASIC!

We now understand some of the basic operations and the core ideas behind CocoaDroid. Let's finally try to run some code with it!

Type this code into the input field and press the Run button with the green arrow.

```
let hi$ = "Hello Android"
print hi$, "Practical Book!"
```

---

[7] http://developer.android.com/guide/topics/ui/declaring-layout.html

[8] http://developer.android.com/guide/topics/ui/menus.html

[9] http://developer.android.com/reference/android/view/MenuInflater.html

CocoaDroid should respond by printing the following to the evaluation output text field.

`Hello Android Practical Book!`

The output should look something like what's shown in Figure 3–16.

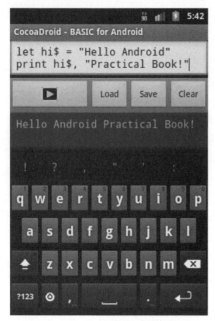

Figure 3–16. *Hello Android in BASIC*

Recall from the earlier partial Listing 3–6 of `CocoaDroidActivity.java` that this class handles clicks on UI Views centrally by implementing `OnClickListener`[10] as follows:

`public class `**`CocoaDroidActivity`**` extends Activity `**`implements View.OnClickListener`**

Thus, when we click on the Run button, the `onClick` method in Listing 3–11 is invoked.

Listing 3–11. *onClick — CocoaDroidActivity.java*

```
/**
 * Centralized onClick listener for all views, particularly buttons.
 *
 * @param v
 */
public void onClick(View v)
{
    Log.d(TAG, "onClick(): ".concat(v.toString()));
    String codeString = _txtInput.getText().toString();
    switch (v.getId()) {
        case R.id.cmd_enter:
            new EvalCodeStringAsyncTask().execute(codeString);
            break;
```

---

[10] http://developer.android.com/guide/topics/ui/ui-events.html

```
                case R.id.cmd_load_scratch:
                    loadScratchFiles();
                    break;
                case R.id.cmd_save_scratch:
                    saveScratchFiles();
                    break;
                case R.id.cmd_clear:
                    clearBuffers();
                    break;
                default:
                    // do nothing
                    break;
            }
        }
```

The method extracts the textual code from the interpreter input field and then drops into the case statement condition for the run button based on the id of the View that was clicked (in this case the run `Button cmd_enter`). It then creates a new instance of the `EvalCodeStringAsyncTask` class, passing in the code that needs to be interpreted. This class takes care of running our code interpreter on a separate thread that doesn't block the user interface main thread while the interpreter is evaluating the code.

Running BASIC Code Asynchronously Using an Android AsyncTask

To run our code safely on a separate thread, we will create our own subclass of the Android AsyncTask[11] class. The Android Developers web site has a good introduction on the subject of writing threading code in Activities called "Painless Threading."[12]

Our threaded class is called `EvalCodeStringAsyncTask` and its implementation is shown in Listing 3–12.

Listing 3–12. *EvalCodeStringAsyncTask — CocoaDroidActivity.java*

```
    /**
     * Handle program code interpretation as asynchronous operations.
     * android.os.AsyncTask<Params, Progress, Result>
     */
    protected class EvalCodeStringAsyncTask extends AsyncTask<String, Integer, String>
    {
        protected String doInBackground(String... codeString)
        {
            String result = "";
            Log.d(TAG, "doInBackground() [code]: \n" + codeString[0]);
            result = evalCodeString(codeString[0]);
            Log.d(TAG, "doInBackground() [eval]: \n" + result);
            publishProgress((int) (100)); // just to demonstrate how
            return result;
        }
```

---

[11] http://developer.android.com/reference/android/os/AsyncTask.html

[12] http://developer.android.com/resources/articles/painless-threading.html

```java
        /**
         * We leave this here for the sake of completeness.
         * Progress update is not implemented.
         *
         * @param progress
         */
        @Override
        protected void onProgressUpdate(Integer... progress)
        {
            setProgressPercent(progress[0]);
        }

        /**
         * Update the GUI output work result edit field.
         *
         * @param result
         */
        @Override
        protected void onPostExecute(String result)
        {
            writeOutput(result);
        }
    }
```

The AsyncTask generic class takes the following arguments when declared:

`android.os.AsyncTask<Params, Progress, Result>`

- Params indicates the types that our implementation of the subclass's overridden execute method will take. This is the same as for the doInBackground method.

- Progress is the type for the overridden onProgressUpdate method.

- Result declares the type for the overridden method onPostExecute that executes when the work is done and is the return value of the doInBackground method.

As per Listing 3–12, our implementation looks like this:

`EvalCodeStringAsyncTask <String, Integer, String>`

When our task is fired, it runs the doInBackground method, which in turn calls the evalCodeString method. This method is shown in Listing 3–13.

Listing 3–13. *evalCodeString — CocoaDroidActivity.java*

```java
    /**
     * Interpret and execute (evaluate) the given code fragment.
     * It is invoked by the EvalCodeStringAsyncTask.
     *
     * @param codeString
     * @return The result of the evaluation drawn off the interpreter output stream.
     */
    protected String evalCodeString(String codeString)
    {
        Log.d(TAG, "evalCodeString(): " + codeString);
```

```
        String result = null;

        // set up and direct the input and output streams
        try {
            _inputStream = inputStreamFromString(codeString);
            _outputStream = new ByteArrayOutputStream();

            // fire up the command interpreter to evaluate the source code buffer
            _commandInterpreter =
                    new CocoaDroidCommandInterpreter(_inputStream, _outputStream);
            try {
                _commandInterpreter.eval();
                // extract the resulting text output from the stream
                result = stringFromOutputStream(_outputStream);
            }
            catch (Throwable t) {
                result = ("UNSUPPORTED OPERATION!\n[\n" +
                        codeString + "\n]\n" + t.toString());
            }
        }
        catch (Throwable t) {
            result = ("UNSUPPORTED OPERATION!\n[\n" +
                    codeString + "\n]\n" + t.toString());
        }

        return result;
    }
```

First, the method creates an instance of a `ByteArrayInputStream` from the code string and an instance of `ByteArrayOutputStream` to act as OutputStream for the interpreter results. The code string is converted to a stream using a utility helper method, `stringFromInputStream`, which essentially does the following:

```
return (new ByteArrayInputStream(codeString.getBytes(_encoding)));
```

The `evalCodeString` method next instantiates a new instance of the CocoaBASIC interpreter class, `CocoaDroidCommandInterpreter`, and passes in the references to the two stream instances. It then calls the eval method on the interpreter instance. The eval method is the entry point into the CocoaBASIC engine black box, which works with what is on the input stream and pipes the result back out via the output stream. This is then passed into another stream utility method, `stringFromInputStream`, which reads the bytes from the input stream and puts this buffer into a string as follows:

```
// extract the resulting text output from the stream
result = stringFromOutputStream(_outputStream);
```

This result is returned from the `evalCodeString` method and finally passed into a call on the `onPostExecute` method by the `AsyncTask` implementation. Our override of `onPostExecute` calls `writeOutput`, which is shown in Listing 3–14. This writes the previous result to the history list and the new result to the output text field where it appears to the user.

Listing 3-14. *writeOutput — CocoaDroidActivity.java*

```
/**
 * Write code evaluation output to the result text view and roll the array list
 * with the stack of previous output results.
 */
protected void writeOutput(String result)
{
    if (0 == result.length() || "".equals(result.trim())) {
        result = "-- null or empty result --";
    }
    Log.d(TAG, "writeOutput(): " + result);
    // always add previous result to index 0; it is the top of the list
    _outputArrayList.add(0, _txtOutput.getText().toString());
    _outputArrayAdapter.notifyDataSetChanged();
    _txtOutput.setText(result); // to the scratch output area
}
```

Now that we've looked in detail at the mechanisms at work when we submit a piece of code, let's move on to some other useful little features of the CocoaDroid application.

Saving Your Latest Session in Scratch Files

As mentioned previously in the section about the elements of the main CocoaDroid Activity screen, the application supports saving the current contents of the input and output text fields into two private application text files we call session "scratch files."

When we first try to use the Load button, the application complains about not finding the scratch files. It presents the alert dialog shown in Figure 3–17. Since it looks for the input scratch file first, that's the one listed in the error alert dialog.

Figure 3-17. *Scratch files not found alert*

> **NOTE:** As a rule, end-user applications should not give away too many details about the implementation of their internals. However, since this is a technical book for learning about implementation details, we decided to show the path and file name in the alert dialog. For a production release of the application, we would replace this alert message with something less revealing but perhaps more useful for an end-user.

The implementation of the method that wraps this functionality is shown in Listing 3–15. It is quite straightforward so we will not explain it further.

Listing 3–15. *loadScratchFiles — CocoaDroidActivity.java*

```java
/**
 * Reads work previously saved to the scratch files.
 * Note that we provide illustrative exception alerts which might or
 * might not be a wise thing for end-user applications in general.
 */
protected void loadScratchFiles()
{
    String scratch_input = "";
    String scratch_output = "";
    try {
        scratch_input = stringFromPrivateApplicationFile(this,
                getString(R.string.file_name_scratch_input));
        scratch_output = stringFromPrivateApplicationFile(this,
                getString(R.string.file_name_scratch_output));
        _txtInput.setText(scratch_input);
        _txtOutput.setText(scratch_output);
    }
    catch (Throwable t) {
        Log.e(TAG, "loadScratchFiles(): LOAD FAILED!", t);
        showOkAlertDialog(this,
                String.format("%s\n%s",
                        getString(R.string.exception_on_scratch_files_load),
                        t.toString()),
                getString(R.string.title_scratch_files_load));
    }
}
```

The stringFromPrivateApplicationFile and showOkAlertDialog methods we use in the listing were described in a previous chapter and can be reviewed from the downloadable book source code.

Clicking the Save button causes the application to save the scratch files and to be able to load them again later, so it should no longer complain about not finding the scratch files. Figure 3–18 shows the toast that is displayed when we do this. We will not list the implementation code for this. It is the inverse of the loading code we've already shown and holds no revelations from an Android programming perspective.

Figure 3–18. *Saving scratch files*

The Clear button shown in Figure 3–19 behaves predictably and simply clears the input and output fields. It does, however, also preserve a record of the contents of the output field by rolling it to the top of the history list.

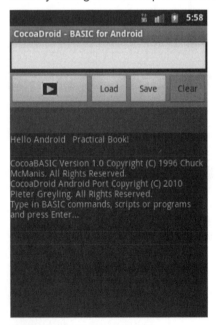

Figure 3–19. *Clearing text fields*

Figure 3–20 shows that when we now click the Load button, our previous session reappears. This works even if we exit the application and it gets unloaded by the Android runtime, even when the device or emulator is restarted. Only by explicitly deinstalling the application or by removing the application data using the system settings application can these files be removed.

Figure 3–20. *Loading the previous session*

Using the Work File

Besides the scratch files, the application also supports saving the current contents of the input text field into another private application text file we call the "Work File." This provides users with the opportunity to keep a separate little work area with snippets of code or a bigger program they are working on that will not be lost when they overwrite the scratch files.

As per Figure 3–21, the Load Work menu item is on the left of the top row of the main, and currently the only, application menu.

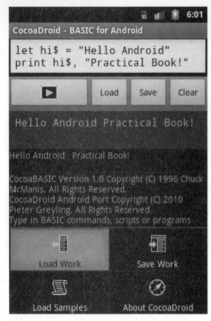

Figure 3–21. *The Load Work menu item*

When we first try to use this menu, the application will, as with the scratch files, complain about not finding the work file. It will present the alert dialog shown in Figure 3–22.

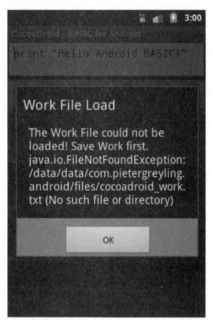

Figure 3–22. *Work File Load alert*

Like the scratch files, we create the work file by saving from the menu, as shown in Figures 3–23 and 3–24.

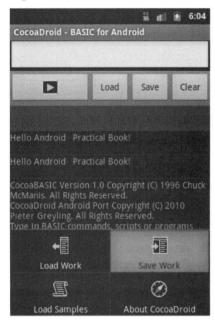

Figure 3–23. *Save Work menu item*

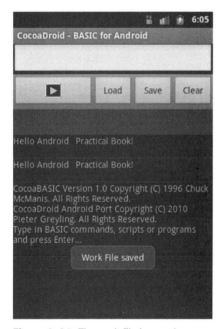

Figure 3–24. *The work file is saved*

We won't spend more time on the work file since its implementation is identical to that of the scratch files.

Viewing the Files in the DDMS File Explorer

We should at this point be able to view the application files with the Dalvik Debug Monitor (DDMS) File Explorer which is part of the Android SDK Tools. Figure 3–25 shows the files in the application package namespace.

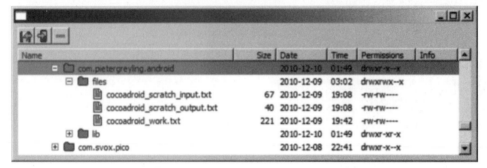

Figure 3–25. *CocoaDroid application scratch and work files viewed with the DDMS File Explorer*

We covered the DDMS and File Explorer tool in an earlier chapter as part of the Android Tools.

> **EMULATOR DATA DIRECTORY:** You can find the application package data location in the /data/data/ directory on the AVD when using the emulator.

Using the CocoaDroid BASIC Samples

Since we are now comfortable with the application menus, go to the Load Samples menu item and select it. You should see the file contents as in Figure 3–26 loaded into the input edit text field.

At the top of the file you should see the SCRIPTS area. These are snippets of code with no line numbers. By scrolling down you'll find the PROGRAMS area. See Figure 3–27. These are more involved code snippets with BASIC line numbers, which allow statements like GOSUB to function.

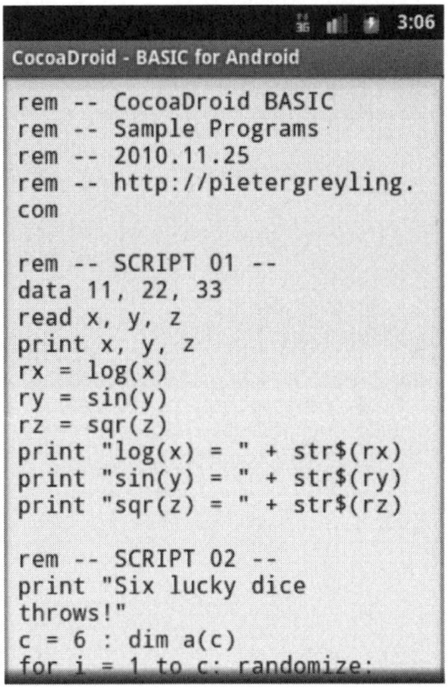

```
CocoaDroid - BASIC for Android

rem -- CocoaDroid BASIC
rem -- Sample Programs
rem -- 2010.11.25
rem -- http://pietergreyling.com

rem -- SCRIPT 01 --
data 11, 22, 33
read x, y, z
print x, y, z
rx = log(x)
ry = sin(y)
rz = sqr(z)
print "log(x) = " + str$(rx)
print "sin(y) = " + str$(ry)
print "sqr(z) = " + str$(rz)

rem -- SCRIPT 02 --
print "Six lucky dice throws!"
c = 6 : dim a(c)
for i = 1 to c: randomize:
```

Figure 3-26. *Loading Samples — Scripts*

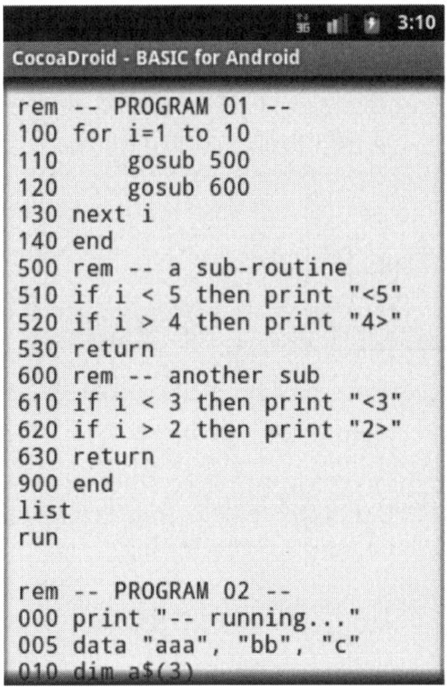

```
CocoaDroid - BASIC for Android

rem -- PROGRAM 01 --
100 for i=1 to 10
110     gosub 500
120     gosub 600
130 next i
140 end
500 rem -- a sub-routine
510 if i < 5 then print "<5"
520 if i > 4 then print "4>"
530 return
600 rem -- another sub
610 if i < 3 then print "<3"
620 if i > 2 then print "2>"
630 return
900 end
list
run

rem -- PROGRAM 02 --
000 print "-- running..."
005 data "aaa", "bb", "c"
010 dim a$(3)
```

Figure 3-27. *Loading Samples — Programs*

Loading an Application Asset Resource

As mentioned before, the file containing the BASIC samples are stored in an application asset file. The data from this file is retrieved by the implementation of the load samples functionality as shown in Listing 3–16.

Listing 3–16. *loadSamplesAssetFile — CommonAndroidCodeLibrary.java*

```java
/**
 * Loads the example snippets from the samples asset file.
 * Note that we provide illustrative exception alerts which might or
 * might not be a wise thing for end-user applications in general.
 */
private void loadSamplesAssetFile()
{
    String buffer = "";
    try {
        buffer = stringFromAssetFile(this,
                getString(R.string.file_name_samples));
        _txtInput.setText(buffer);
    }
    catch (Throwable t) {
        Log.e(TAG, "loadSamplesAssetFile(): LOAD FAILED!", t);
        showOkAlertDialog(this,
                String.format("%s\n%s",
                        getString(R.string.exception_on_samples_file_load),
                        t.toString()),
                getString(R.string.title_samples_file_load));
    }
}
```

If we refer back to the XML strings table section, we can see that the asset file name is declared as follows in `strings.xml`:

```
<string name="file_name_samples">"program_templates/cocoadroid_basic_templates.bas"</string>
```

Our `program_templates` directory lives under the standard application `assets` directory.

The implementation for the utility helper method, `stringFromAssetFile`, is shown in Listing 3–17.

Listing 3–17. *stringFromAssetFile — CommonAndroidCodeLibrary.java*

```java
/**
 * Reads the contents of an Asset File into a String and returns the String.
 */
public static String stringFromAssetFile(Context context, String filename)
    throws   IOException
{
    AssetManager am = context.getAssets();
    InputStream is = am.open(filename);
    String result = stringFromInputStream(is);
    is.close();
    return result;
}
```

And the implementation method, `stringFromInputStream`, is in Listing 3–18.

Listing 3–18. *stringFromInputStream — CommonAndroidCodeLibrary.java*

```java
/**
 * Reads the stream contents of an InputStream into a String and returns the String.
 */
public static String stringFromInputStream(InputStream from)
        throws IOException
{
    return stringFromInputStream(from, 8192);
}

public static String stringFromInputStream(InputStream from, int buffSize)
        throws IOException
{
    ByteArrayOutputStream into = new ByteArrayOutputStream();
    byte[] buf = new byte[buffSize];
    for (int n; 0 < (n = from.read(buf));) {
        into.write(buf, 0, n);
    }
    into.close();
    return (new String(into.toByteArray(), _encoding));
}
```

These methods require knowledge of the data encoding (the variable _encoding) that should be used for the buffer contents. The encoding for the runtime is retrieved by the code in Listing 3–19 in a static block in the class `CommonAndroidCodeLibrary`:

Listing 3–19. *Encoding — CommonAndroidCodeLibrary.java (partial)*

```java
protected static final String _encoding;
protected static final String _newline;
static {
    _encoding = System.getProperty("file.encoding");
    _newline = System.getProperty("line.separator");
}
```

Running the CocoaDroid BASIC Sample Scripts

To run the samples, we will need to copy and paste snippets from the samples file into our input text field. This is a fairly intuitive process but we will present some images in order to give context for the more technical discussion that follows.

Figure 3–28 shows us selecting a section of script code.

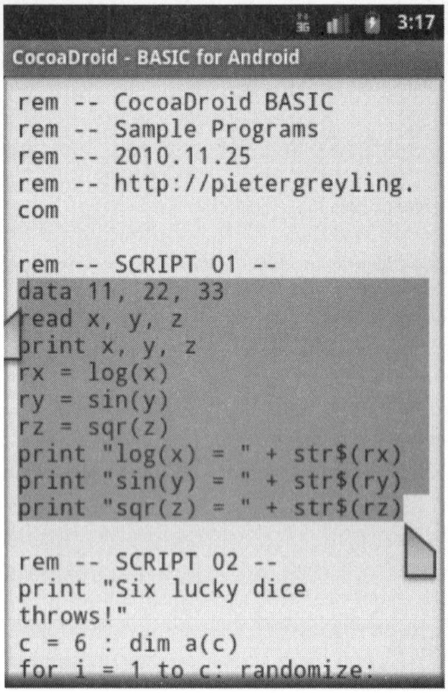

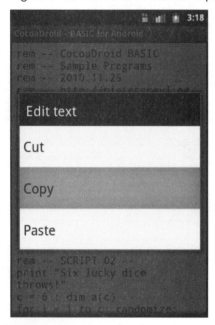

Figure 3–28. *Selecting sample script code*

Figure 3–29 shows the Android clipboard Copy operation.

Figure 3–29. *Copying sample script code*

As in Figure 3–30, we should click `Clear` to cleanse the input edit text field before pasting in the code.

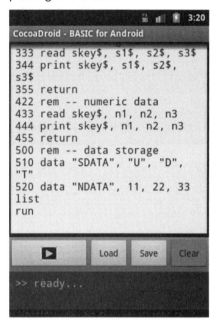

Figure 3–30. *Clearing the buffer for sample code*

Figure 3–31 shows the Android clipboard `Paste` operation.

Figure 3–31. *Pasting sample script code*

And Figure 3-32 shows the BASIC code pasted into the input work area and ready to run.

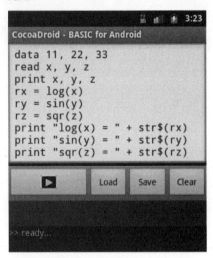

Figure 3-32. *The sample script is ready*

In Figure 3-33 we have run the code and can see the resulting output.

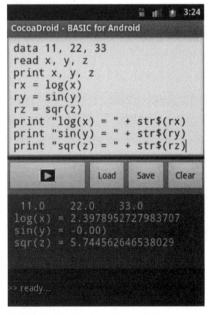

Figure 3-33. *Running the sample script*

Running the CocoaDroid BASIC Sample Programs

Now we will demonstrate following the same procedure with a program. A program is loosely defined as having BASIC line numbers and can thus take advantage of constructs like GOSUB/RETURN, which require a code line address.

We won't go through all the steps in the routine as we did for scripts, but will give you just the required information to get started. We will also draw attention to what is new in working with programs.

Figure 3–34 shows the program we will use for the demonstration. It simulates rolling dice six times.

Figure 3–34. *Selecting the sample program*

Copy and paste this program into the input text field as before. As you can see from Figure 3–35, we have edited the code to roll the dice only twice.

Figure 3-35. *The edited program*

Run this program and you should something similar to Figure 3-36 (We got two sixes!).

Notice the LIST and RUN commands at the end of the source file. And no, like in most dialects of BASIC, the case of commands and statements is not significant. So print is the same as PRINT.

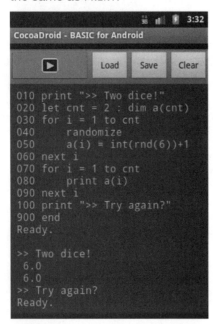

Figure 3-36. *Running the program with LIST*

Try removing the LIST statement and running it again (see Figure 3-37).

Figure 3-37. *Running the program without LIST*

At this point, we believe you now know enough to play around with bits of code and CocoaDroid on your own.

Running BASIC Code Synchronously

Before we finish the chapter, we want to show you the implementation of the CocoaDroid About menu item.

This might seem somewhat roundabout but the reason is that the banner message uses CocoaBASIC to display itself. The way it does this is different from executing other pieces of BASIC in that it does it synchronously. It uses a method called evalCodeStringSync that bypasses the AsyncTask infrastructure and calls the core evalCodeString method directly.

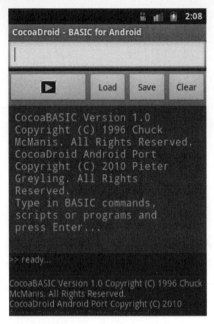

Figure 3–38. *The About menu item*

We provide the implementation for the About banner in Listing 3–20.

Listing 3–20. *showAbout — CocoaDroidActivity.java*

```
/**
 * Start up our script engine with a copyright notice.
 * This also demonstrates the general principle of reusing the BASIC interpreter
 * by passing commands into the input stream and letting it do the work.
 */
protected void showAbout()
{
    // ask the BASIC interpreter to print the startup banner
    String aboutCommand =
            "PRINT \"" + getString(R.string.app_copy_cocoabasic) + "\"\n";
    aboutCommand = aboutCommand +
            "PRINT \"" + getString(R.string.app_copy_cocoadroid) + "\"\n";
    // also ask it to print a little usage message
    aboutCommand = aboutCommand +
            "PRINT \"" + getString(R.string.app_usage_01) + "\"";
    // now submit the work using the synchronous evaluation
    evalCodeStringSync(aboutCommand);
    _txtInput.setText("");
}
```

Listing 3–21 shows the implementation for the evalCodeStringSync method.

Listing 3–21. *evalCodeStringSync — CocoaDroidActivity.java*

```
/**
 * Interpret and execute (evaluate) the given code fragment.
 * This version of evalCodeString is reserved by convention for internally
 * invoking non-user initiated interpreter code evaluation, i.e., from code.
```

```
     * It is not invoked by the EvalCodeStringAsyncTask whereas the companion
     * evalCodeString() method is.
     * @param codeString
     * @return The result of the evaluation drawn off the interpreter output stream.
     */
    protected String evalCodeStringSync(String codeString)
    {
        Log.d(TAG, "evalCodeStringSync(): " + codeString);
        // invoke eval bypassing use of an EvalCodeStringAsyncTask instance
        String result = evalCodeString(codeString);
        if (0 == result.length() || "".equals(result.trim())) {
            result = "-- null or empty result --";
        }
        writeOutput(result);
        // also place on input area since the user might not have entered this
        // the method might have been initiated by code and not by the Enter button
        _txtInput.setText(codeString);
        return result;
    }
```

Recall that we reviewed the core evalCodeString method in Listing 3–13. Feel free to refer back to that section.

In essence the evalCodeStringSync method allows us to issue short-lived pieces of code to the interpreter directly on the main thread of the user interface. Of course, all the usual caveats we discussed earlier then come into play.

Summary

In this chapter we have shown you how to create a no-frills but functionally complete onboard interpreter environment for CocoaBASIC, a dialect of the BASIC programming language.

Besides creating a useful and diverting application, we have also covered a large number of core Android programming techniques, including implementing asynchronous processing, using asset resources, creating custom array adapters, using XML menu resources and menu inflators, and more.

We hope you have fun playing with the CocoaDroid scripting environment!

Chapter 4

Embedding Lua in Android Applications

In this chapter we will show you how to embed the Lua programming language into your Android applications. We will do this using the Kahlua2 implementation of Lua. Kahlua2 is a native port of the Lua programming language to the Java Virtual Machine (JVM). This implementation of Lua is written in the Java programming language and as such makes it very practical for us to host Lua in an Android Java application.

In Chapter 3 of this book, we covered the subject of hosting, or embedding, a programming language interpreter engine as a guest module in an application. There we presented a practical project that embedded the CocoaBASIC language engine into an Android application. This application was designed to run scripts and programs interactively using the BASIC programming language.

You might ask yourself what is different about this chapter. Why are we showing you how to run scripting code from your applications when we have already demonstrated this in a previous chapter? And why have we picked another programming language to do so?

The fundamental difference is that we will now take the integration of the host and guest runtimes to the next step. In this chapter, we will treat the concept of script code calling back into code implemented in our Android application.

Not only will our application implement code to run scripts but it will also implement code to allow those very same scripts to call into methods implemented within our application. Since such methods have access to the Android platform, our scripts can gain equal access to Android functionality as long as we take care to follow the proper protocols.

In addition, this chapter will build on these concepts to show you how easy it is to create a startup script that can configure your own Android applications.

Introducing Lua and Kahlua2

The Lua web site describes Lua as follows:

> "Lua is a powerful, fast, lightweight, embeddable scripting language. Lua combines simple procedural syntax with powerful data description constructs based on associative arrays and extensible semantics. Lua is dynamically typed, runs by interpreting bytecode for a register-based virtual machine, and has automatic memory management with incremental garbage collection, making it ideal for configuration, scripting, and rapid prototyping. Lua is free open-source software, distributed under a very liberal license (the well-known MIT license). It may be used for any purpose, including commercial purposes, at absolutely no cost. Lua is designed, implemented, and maintained by a team at PUC-Rio, the Pontifical Catholic University of Rio de Janeiro in Brazil. "Lua" (pronounced LOO-ah) means "Moon" in Portuguese."

As such, Lua is an excellent choice as an embedded scripting language with which you can allow your users to leverage and extend your applications with custom scripts.

Quoting from the Kahlua[1] site:

> "Kahlua is a Virtual Machine together with a standard library, all implemented in Java. It tries to emulate Lua as much as possible, while still reusing as much as possible from Java."

Kahlua is then an equally good choice for embedding the Lua language into your Java applications.

Lua Resources

For more background on the Lua programming language, you can consult the following online resources:

- The Programming Language Lua:
    - http://www.lua.org/
- Lua Documentation:
    - http://www.lua.org/docs.html

---

[1] http://code.google.com/p/kahlua/

- Lua 5.1 Online Reference Manual:
  - http://www.lua.org/manual/5.1/
- Programming in Lua (first edition):
  - http://www.lua.org/pil/

Kahlua2 Resources

Material about Kahlua and Kahlua2 is available from the following links:

- Kahlua Home:
  - http://code.google.com/p/kahlua/
- Kahlua2 Home:
  - https://github.com/krka/kahlua2
- Kahlua2 Documentation:
  - http://krkadev.blogspot.com/2010/05/getting-started-with-kahlua2.html
- Using the Kahlua2 J2SE runtime platform:
  - http://krkadev.blogspot.com/2010/06/kahlua-j2se-goodies.html
- Kahlua2 on Android:
  - http://krkadev.blogspot.com/2010/06/kahlua-on-android.html
- Differences between Kahlua2 and Lua 5.1:
  - http://krkadev.blogspot.com/2010/06/differences-between-kahlua2-and-lua-51.html

Using Kahlua2 in Your Android Java Applications

This chapter presents the following code projects. They can be downloaded from the book web site as part of the resources for this chapter:

- **Kahlua2** (kahlua2): This is the original Kahlua2 open-source code from Kristofer Karlsson[2] as hosted on the Kahlua2 GitHub site.[3] The project format supports the IntelliJ IDEA integrated development environment (IDE), but can easily be imported and built in other IDEs.

---

[2] http://krkadev.blogspot.com/

[3] https://github.com/krka/kahlua2

- **Kahlua2 Android Interpreter** (`kahlua2interpreter`): This is the code from the Kahlua2 contrib subfolder. We provide it as a separate project that can be built from the command line using Ant as well as using the IntelliJ IDEA IDE. It is a bare-bones Android Lua interpreter application that demonstrates the essentials of hosting the Kahlua2 framework on Android.

- **KahluaDroid** (`kahluadroid`): KahluaDroid is the main project of this chapter. It demonstrates how to embed the Kahlua2 runtime in your own Android applications. This project takes us to the next level by making use of Kahlua2 functionality to allow calling Android application programming interface (API) functions from Lua scripts. It also shows how to implement a simple application startup script infrastructure which supports running Lua code that can configure the Android application when the main Activity is created.

Working through these projects should give you a good understanding of what can be achieved by extending your Android applications with a scripting engine such as Kahlua2.

Development Environment Configuration

As a quick reference, Table 4–1 lists some development environment configuration settings that we find useful for working with the Android software development kit (SDK). It also repeats from previous chapters the command needed to create a compatible Android Virtual Device (AVD) for running the code.

Table 4–1. *Development Environment Configuration Quick Reference*

Item	Value or Command
PATH	`<Android SDK Directory>/tools`
PATH	`<Android SDK Directory>/platform-tools`
PATH	`<Apache Ant Directory>/bin`
Create an AVD	`android create avd -n android23api9_hvga_32mb -t android-9 -c 32M`

The Kahlua2 Project

In order to be able to embed the Kahlua2 Lua runtime into our applications we will need the runtime library files. These dependencies are embedded into our hosting applications as Java archives (`jar` files). We will show you how to build these runtime libraries from the Kahlua2 source code. This will enable us to stay up to date with Kahlua2 changes and help us to understand the process from end-to-end.

Setting up the Kahlua2 Runtime Files Project

To build the Kahlua2 dependency packages, first download the sample project archives from the book web site. Assuming that we have unpacked the chapter sample code, the Kahlua2 project file directory should appear similar to that shown below:

```
+---kahlua2
|   +---.idea
|   |   +---copyright
|   |   \---libraries
|   +---cldc11
|   |   \---src
|   +---contrib
|   |   +---androidinterpreter
|   |   |   +---gen
|   |   |   +---res
|   |   |   |   +---layout
|   |   |   |   \---values
|   |   |   \---src
|   |   |       \---se
|   |   |           \---krka
|   |   |               \---kahlua
|   |   |                   \---android
|   |   +---j2me-lib
|   |   +---midlet
|   |   |   \---src
|   |   +---midlet-interpreter
|   |   |   \---src
|   |   \---midlet-minimal
|   |       \---src
|   +---core
|   |   +---resources
|   |   \---src
|   +---core-dep
|   +---docs
|   +---interpreter
|   |   +---lib
|   |   +---resources
|   |   +---src
|   |   \---test
|   +---j2se
|   |   +---resources
|   |   +---src
|   |   \---test
|   +---javadoc
|   |   \---src
|   +---lib
|   +---testsuite
|   |   +---lua
|   |   +---src
|   |   +---test
|   |   \---util
|   \---webstart
```

Building from the Console

Open a terminal (command-line) window in the kahlua2 directory and issue the following command:

ant package

This should build the project resulting in output similar to the following:

```
kahlua2> ant package
Buildfile: ...\kahlua2\build.xml
[--output omitted--]
setup:
    [mkdir] Created dir: ...\kahlua2\bin\classes\core
    [mkdir] Created dir: ...\kahlua2\bin\classes\j2se
    [mkdir] Created dir: ...\kahlua2\kahlua2\bin\classes\interpreter
    [mkdir] Created dir: ...\kahlua2\bin\classes\cldc11
    [mkdir] Created dir: ...\kahlua2\bin\core-src-replaced
[--output omitted--]
package:
      [jar] Building jar: ...\kahlua2\bin\kahlua-5.1_2.0.0-core.jar
      [jar] Building jar: ...\kahlua2\bin\kahlua-5.1_2.0.0-cldc11.jar
      [jar] Building jar: ...\kahlua2\bin\kahlua-5.1_2.0.0-j2se.jar
      [jar] Building jar: ...\kahlua2\bin\kahlua-5.1_2.0.0-interpreter.jar

BUILD SUCCESSFUL
Total time: 2 seconds
```

Building from an IDE

The Kahlua2 project, as downloaded from its home site, includes support for the IntelliJ IDEA IDE. It can also be imported into other IDEs such as Eclipse. Figure 4–1 shows the Kahlua2 project Ant `build.xml` file and the `package` step in the Ant Build view of this IDE.

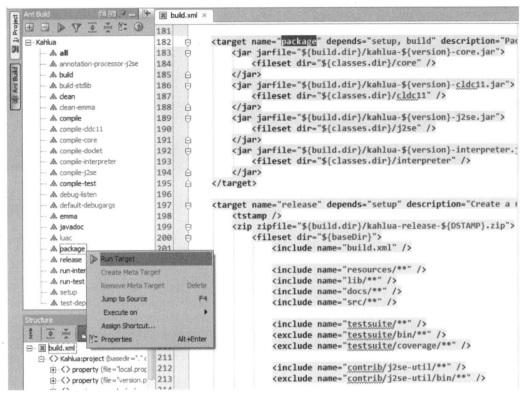

Figure 4–1. Kahlua2 Ant Build and run package target step

This allows us to issue the build step command directly from the IDE instead of running it in a terminal session. The results are identical.

The Kahlua2 Runtime Libraries

You will notice in Listing 4–2 that we highlighted two of the Java archive files in bold:

```
\kahlua2\bin\kahlua-5.1_2.0.0-core.jar
\kahlua2\bin\kahlua-5.1_2.0.0-j2se.jar
```

These library files contain the implementation of the core Kahlua2 language plus a supporting JVM platform, in this case a J2SE-compatible runtime. Kahlua2 also runs on other Java mobile platforms such as CLDC.[4] For more information on Java Micro Edition[5] (J2ME) and CLDC, see the official online documentation.[6]

---

[4] Connected Limited Device Configuration

[5] http://java.sun.com/products/cldc/overview.html

[6] http://java.sun.com/products/cldc/

We will be using the Kahlua2 J2SE platform for our Android work since it is currently the one that is most compatible with the Android platform.

The Kahlua2 Android Interpreter Project

Looking at Listing 4-1, the Kahlua2 project folder, notice that the project includes a subproject under the `contrib` folder called `androidinterpreter`. Here is an extract from the listing:

```
+---kahlua2
|   +---.idea
|   +---cldc11
|   +---contrib
|   |   +---androidinterpreter
```

For convenience, we decided to demonstrate the functionality of this interpreter project in a separately prepared project we called `kahlua2interpreter`. The main reason for this is to add support for building the project using the latest Android SDK Tools as well as allowing us to import it into an IDE without polluting the original code base.

Setting up the Project

In order to demonstrate and understand the interpreter project properly, we will cover the essentials of how we set it up here. The process is common enough when working with Android projects to justify a review.

> **NOTE:** You do not have to perform all these steps. The downloadable project code we provide for the chapter already has everything you need to get it building and running immediately from both the terminal command line and the IDE.

As the first step of setting up the Android interpreter project for this chapter, we used the following Android SDK Tools command to create a baseline Android project directory structure:

```
android create project --target "android-9"
    --name Kahlua2Interpreter
    --path ./kahlua2interpreter
    --activity Kahlua2Interpreter
    --package se.krka.kahlua.android
```

We then copied the Kahlua2 runtime archives we built earlier into the `libs` subdirectory and also copied the main Java source file, renamed from `KahluaInterpreter.java` to `Kahlua2Interpreter.java`, into the `src` folder. The source code references for the `KahluaInterpreter` class were also changed to `Kahlua2Interpreter`.

To preserve credit, and since we are not adding any functionality to the code for this iteration, we made sure to keep the package name, `se.krka.kahlua.android`, the same as that created by the original author[7] of the Kahlua2[8] project.

Building from the Console

As mentioned before, the downloadable project code we provide for the chapter already has everything you need to get it building and running immediately from both the terminal command line and the IDE.

This can be verified by running the following compile command in a terminal window in the `kahlua2interpreter` project root directory:

`ant compile`

This is followed by the following build command:

`ant debug`

In both cases, the result should be a BUILD SUCCESSFUL status and in the case of the latter should end up listing something similar to the following:

```
kahlua2interpreter> ant debug
Buildfile: ...\kahlua2interpreter\build.xml
    [setup] Android SDK Tools Revision 8
    [setup] Project Target: Android 2.3
    [setup] API level: 9
[--output omitted--]
-package-debug-sign:
[apkbuilder] Creating Kahlua2Interpreter-debug-unaligned.apk and signing it with a
 debug key...
debug:
     [echo] Running zip align on final apk...
     [echo] Debug Package: ...\kahlua2interpreter\bin\Kahlua2Interpreter-debug.apk

BUILD SUCCESSFUL
Total time: 4 seconds
```

Building from an IDE

As the final step to confirm that all our changes worked correctly, we imported the project into the Eclipse IDE and set up the Kahlua2 runtime library archives (`kahlua-5.x.x-core/j2se.jar`), as shown in Figure 4–2. You may, of course, choose to import the code into another IDE or environment.

---

[7] http://krkadev.blogspot.com/

[8] https://github.com/krka/kahlua2

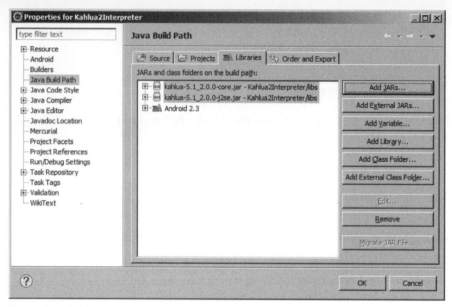

Figure 4–2. *Kahlua2 runtime libraries in the Kahlua2Interpreter Eclipse project*

With this, we can build and debug the project directly from the Eclipse IDE.

Running the Kahlua2 Android Interpreter

Now that we have built the Kahlua2 source distribution, let's run it and enter the following code:

```
from = "Kahlua2!"
print("Hello Android from "..from)
```

Figure 4–3 shows the application after entering the code.

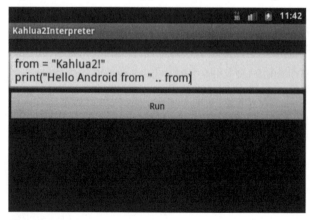

Figure 4–3. *The Kahlua2 Android interpreter—Hello World*

Clicking the Run button should present the image in Figure 4–4. It shows the output from the Lua `print` function.

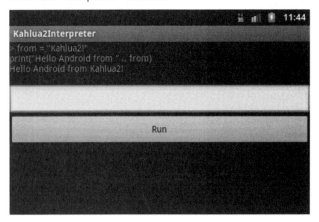

Figure 4–4. *The Kahlua2 Android interpreter*

Understanding the Basics of Embedding Kahlua2

Listing 4–1 shows the implementation for the Kahlua2 Android interpreter constructor. The code is from the main Activity of the application and encapsulates the steps necessary to create an embedded Kahlua2 runtime environment with which to run our Lua scripts.

Listing 4–1. *Kahlua2Interpreter.java (partial)*

```
[--code omitted--]
import se.krka.kahlua.converter.KahluaConverterManager;
import se.krka.kahlua.integration.LuaCaller;
import se.krka.kahlua.integration.LuaReturn;
import se.krka.kahlua.integration.annotations.LuaMethod;
import se.krka.kahlua.integration.expose.LuaJavaClassExposer;
import se.krka.kahlua.j2se.J2SEPlatform;
import se.krka.kahlua.luaj.compiler.LuaCompiler;
import se.krka.kahlua.vm.KahluaTable;
import se.krka.kahlua.vm.KahluaThread;
import se.krka.kahlua.vm.KahluaUtil;
import se.krka.kahlua.vm.LuaClosure;
import se.krka.kahlua.vm.Platform;

[--code omitted--]

private final Platform platform;
private final KahluaTable env;
private final KahluaConverterManager manager;
private final LuaJavaClassExposer exposer;
private final LuaCaller caller;
private final KahluaThread thread;

[--code omitted--]
```

```java
public Kahlua2Interpreter() {
    platform = new J2SEPlatform();
    env = platform.newEnvironment();
    manager = new KahluaConverterManager();
    KahluaTable java = platform.newTable();
    env.rawset("Java", java);
    exposer = new LuaJavaClassExposer(manager, platform, env, java);
    exposer.exposeGlobalFunctions(this);
    caller = new LuaCaller(manager);
    thread = new KahluaThread(new PrintStream(new OutputStream() {
        @Override
        public void write(int i) throws IOException {
            buffer.append(Character.toString((char) i));
        }
    }), platform, env);
}
```

[--code omitted--]

The `KahluaDroid` application project that we will see later also uses this boilerplate code. In order to have a basic understanding of the operations in Listing 4–1, we will go through the essentials of executing Lua code with Kahlua2 here. The Kahlua2 blog web site[9] has good information available, and we encourage you to refer to it.

Kahlua2 requires a platform to run its environment within. The Kahlua2 J2SE platform[10] implementation is currently the most compatible with the Android runtime. A platform instance is created with the `J2SEPlatform` constructor as follows:

```
platform = new J2SEPlatform();
```

Having set up a platform instance, the `platform.newEnvironment` call creates a new environment table filled with runtime library functions using the following snippet of code:

```
env = platform.newEnvironment();
```

This environment is essentially a global namespace in which the Kahlua2 runtime data structures and supporting runtime library code items live. For reference, a source code extract from the implementation of the `J2SEPlatform` `newEnvironment` method can be seen in Listing 4–2.

Listing 4–2. *J2SEPlatform.java (partial)*

[--code omitted--]

```
package se.krka.kahlua.j2se;
```

[--code omitted--]

```java
public class J2SEPlatform implements Platform {
        private static J2SEPlatform INSTANCE = new J2SEPlatform();
```

---

[9] http://krkadev.blogspot.com/2010/05/getting-started-with-kahlua2.html

[10] http://krkadev.blogspot.com/2010/06/kahlua-j2se-goodies.html

```java
        public static J2SEPlatform getInstance() {
                return INSTANCE;
        }
```
[--code omitted--]

```java
    @Override
    public KahluaTable newTable() {
        return new KahluaTableImpl(new ConcurrentHashMap<Object, Object>());
    }

    @Override
    public KahluaTable newEnvironment() {
        KahluaTable env = newTable();

        env.rawset("_G", env);
        env.rawset("_VERSION", Version.VERSION + " (J2SE)");

        MathLib.register(this, env);
        BaseLib.register(env);
        RandomLib.register(this, env);
        UserdataArray.register(this, env);
        StringLib.register(this, env);
        CoroutineLib.register(this, env);
        OsLib.register(this, env);
        TableLib.register(this, env);
        LuaCompiler.register(env);

        KahluaThread workerThread = setupWorkerThread(env);
        KahluaUtil.setupLibrary(env, workerThread, "/stdlib");
```
[--code omitted--]

```java
        return env;
    }
```
[--code omitted--]

As you can see, the following runtime support libraries are registered within this global environment: `MathLib`, `BaseLib`, `RandomLib`, `UserdataArray`, `StringLib`, `CoroutineLib`, `OsLib`, `TableLib`, and `LuaCompiler`. The `J2SEPlatform.java` class can be inspected in more detail as part of the Kahlua2 project source code.

> **NOTE:** The `KahluaDroid` project that we present later is based on the same core code, so it is worth making a mental note of this section in case you need to refer to it. We will not cover these implementation details again under that project.

Let's go back to Listing 4-1 and the following code:

```java
manager = new KahluaConverterManager();
```

The `KahluaConverterManager` supports data type conversion operations. Since Kahlua supports fewer data types (String, Double, Boolean, KahluaTable) than Java, this class does the work of automatic conversion between the two languages.

We also create a new Kahlua2 table instance with the `J2SEPlatform` `newTable` method as follows:

```
KahluaTable java = platform.newTable();
env.rawset("Java", java);
```

This instance will be required to expose our Java class methods to the Kahlua2 runtime as part of the following code:

```
exposer = new LuaJavaClassExposer(manager, platform, env, java);
exposer.exposeGlobalFunctions(this);
```

The `LuaJavaClassExposer` class exposes global methods of the given class referred to with the `exposeGlobalFunctions` call to the Kahlua2 script engine. As you will see in more detail later, with a little extra work this will allow us to call these methods as global Lua functions directly from our Kahlua2 scripts.

Last but not least, our code will need a thread to run on, along with some way of communicating results back to the hosting (or client) environment. This is achieved via the following code:

```
thread = new KahluaThread(new PrintStream(new OutputStream() {
    @Override
    public void write(int i) throws IOException {
        buffer.append(Character.toString((char) i));
    }
}), platform, env);
```

The `KahluaThread` instance is made aware of the runtime platform and the current environment plus has the ability to feed back results via an overridden `write` method on a `PrintStream` instance reference.

The KahluaDroid Project

The main project of this chapter is the KahluaDroid application. This is a Java Android application that embeds the Kahlua2 runtime and also allows Lua scripts executing in that runtime to call back into code in the KahluaDroid application. It builds upon the previous Kahlua Interpreter project and makes use of the tools provided by the Kahlua2 infrastructure in order to provide closer interaction between the worlds of Android and Lua.

> **NOTE:** The KahluaDroid project is compatible with both Eclipse and IntelliJ IDEA Community Edition, so using any or both of these IDEs should work fine. Importing the projects into a NetBeans IDE environment or any other IDE of your choice should also present no problems. We will not cover how to do this here.

Running the KahluaDroid Application

Let us now run KahluaDroid using the emulator with a compatible AVD, as specified before. This will allow us to exercise the behavior of the KahluaDroid application interactively. At the same time, we will also study the elements of the application that implement its behavior and characteristics.

The Application User Interface Controls

When the application has finished loading, it should present us with the Activity depicted in Figure 4–5.

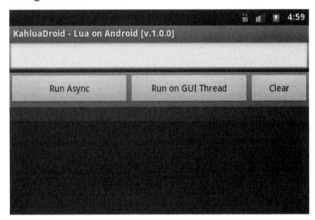

Figure 4–5. *KahluaDroid main activity screen*

The main screen consists of an entry field, followed by three buttons and an output field. Per Listing 4-3, the main application layout resource file, these user interface controls are as follows:

- **Code Input Text Field** (`edittext_input`): Here is where we enter our Lua code.

- **Run Code Asynchronously Button** (`button_run_async`): Clicking this button will run the Lua code on the background using an implementation of the Android AsyncTask class.

- **Run Code Synchronously (on GUI Thread) Button** (`button_run_sync`): Clicking this button will run the Lua code on the main thread, allowing for full interaction with the user interface foreground.

- **Clear Button** (`button_clear`): Causes the contents of the input text field to be deleted.

- **Results Output Field** (`textview_output`): Displays both the input code and the results from code execution.

Listing 4–3, the main application layout resource file, declares the user interface controls that make up the main application interface.

Listing 4–3. *KahluaDroid Main Layout Resource ̄ main.xml*

```xml
<?xml version="1.0" encoding="utf-8"?>
<ScrollView xmlns:android="http://schemas.android.com/apk/res/android"
            android:id="@+id/scrollview_main"
            android:layout_width="fill_parent"
            android:layout_height="fill_parent"
            android:fillViewport="true">
  <LinearLayout android:orientation="vertical"
            android:layout_width="fill_parent"
            android:layout_height="fill_parent"
            android:id="@+id/linearlayout_main">
    <EditText android:layout_height="wrap_content"
            android:layout_width="fill_parent"
            android:id="@+id/edittext_input"></EditText>
    <LinearLayout android:layout_width="fill_parent"
            android:layout_height="wrap_content"
            android:background="@android:drawable/bottom_bar"
            android:gravity="center_vertical">
      <Button android:id="@+id/button_run_async"
            android:layout_width="0dip"
            android:layout_weight="2.0"
            android:layout_height="wrap_content"
            android:text="@string/button_run_async_text_wait"></Button>
      <Button android:id="@+id/button_run_sync"
            android:layout_width="0dip"
            android:layout_weight="2.0"
            android:layout_height="wrap_content"
            android:text="@string/button_run_sync_text_wait"></Button>
      <Button android:id="@+id/button_clear"
            android:layout_width="0dip"
            android:layout_weight="1.0"
            android:layout_height="wrap_content"
            android:text="@string/button_clear_text"></Button>
    </LinearLayout>
    <TextView android:layout_height="wrap_content"
            android:layout_width="fill_parent"
            android:id="@+id/textview_output"></TextView>
  </LinearLayout>
</ScrollView>
```

Entering and Running Lua Code

Since we created KahluaDroid in order to demonstrate how to host Lua code in a standard Java Android application, we will immediately enter and run some code to get a feel for the application.

Enter the following code into the input text field:

```lua
local droidinfo = android_version()
print("This is Android:\n" .. droidinfo)
```

> **THE ANDROID_VERSION FUNCTION:** The android_version function you see in the Lua code is not part of the Kahlua2 runtime. It is actually part of our Android Java code. You will see how we implemented this function later in the chapter.

The application appearance should now be similar to what is shown in Figure 4–6.

Figure 4–6. *Entering Lua Code on the KahluaDroid Main Activity Screen*

Now click the Run Async button.

The expected result should be similar to that portrayed in Figure 4–7.

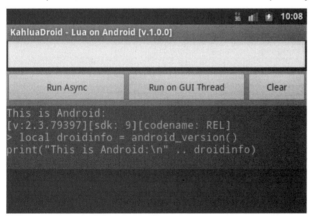

Figure 4–7. *Running Lua code on the KahluaDroid main activity screen*

The application has forwarded the Lua code we entered to the embedded Kahlua2 scripting engine. This ran the code and fed back a printable result stream to the application via the output stream that it uses to communicate computation results to its clients.

Recall that we went into some depth regarding the implementation details of this earlier in the chapter under the "Understanding the Basics of Embedding Kahlua2" section.

The Application Menu

As mentioned earlier, the KahluaDroid application also implements a menu. This menu is portrayed in Figure 4–8.

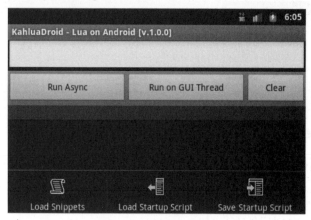

Figure 4–8. *KahluaDroid application menu*

The menu consists of the following menu items:

- **Load Snippets** (menu_itm_snippets_load): This item triggers the loading a small file of Lua code snippets into the input text field. From there, selected sections of these items can be copied and used for getting started with trying the application.

- **Load Startup Script** (menu_itm_startup_script_load): This menu item loads the contents of a user-defined startup file into the input text field. From there, it can be edited and resaved.

- **Save Startup Script** (menu_itm_startup_script_save): This item saves the contents of the input text field as a startup script. This script will be executed the next time the application is launched. To be exact; the next time that the application Activity's onCreate method is invoked.

These items are identified in Listing 4–4, the menu layout resource file.

Listing 4–4. *KahluaDroid Main Menu Resource–kahluadroid_main_menu.xml*

```
<?xml version="1.0" encoding="utf-8"?>
<menu xmlns:android="http://schemas.android.com/apk/res/android">
    <item
            android:id="@+id/menu_itm_snippets_load"
            android:icon="@drawable/mnu_load_snippets"
            android:title="@string/menu_snippets_load">
    </item>
    <item
```

```xml
            android:id="@+id/menu_itm_startup_script_load"
            android:icon="@drawable/mnu_startup_script_load"
            android:title="@string/menu_startup_script_load">
    </item>
    <item
            android:id="@+id/menu_itm_startup_script_save"
            android:icon="@drawable/mnu_startup_script_save"
            android:title="@string/menu_startup_script_save">
    </item>
</menu>
```

By now, the contents of both the menu layout Listing 4–4 and the creation and event handling implementations in Listing 4–5 should be familiar.

Listing 4–5. *Menu Implementation Methods in KahluaDroid.java (partial)*

```
[--code omitted--]

    /**
     * Implement our application menu using an XML menu layout and the ADK MenuInflater.
     */
    @Override
    public boolean onCreateOptionsMenu(Menu menu)
    {
        // always first delegate to the base class in case of system menus
        super.onCreateOptionsMenu(menu);
        MenuInflater inflater = getMenuInflater();
        inflater.inflate(R.menu.kahluadroid_main_menu, menu);
        // true for a visible menu, false for an invisible one
        return true;
    }

    /**
     * Respond to our application menu events.
     */
    @Override
    public boolean onOptionsItemSelected(MenuItem item)
    {
        final int mnu_id = item.getItemId();
        switch (mnu_id) {
            case R.id.menu_itm_snippets_load:
                loadSnippetsAssetFile();
                return true;
            case R.id.menu_itm_startup_script_load:
                loadStartupScript();
                return true;
            case R.id.menu_itm_startup_script_save:
                saveStartupScript();
                return true;
            default: // not our items
                return super.onOptionsItemSelected(item); // pass item id up
        }
    }

[--code omitted--]
```

The Application Strings Table

The KahluaDroid application code uses the strings table resource extensively. It is presented in Listing 4–6 for reference if you are trying to follow all the code using only the text of the book.

Listing 4–6. *KahluaDroid Main String Table Resource–strings.xml*

```xml
<?xml version="1.0" encoding="utf-8"?>
<resources>
    <string name="app_name">KahluaDroid</string>
    <string name="app_version">1.0.0</string>
    <string name="app_desc">KahluaDroid - Lua on Android</string>
    <string name="file_name_snippets">program_templates/lua_snippets.lua</string>
    <string name="file_name_startup_script">kahluadroid_startup.lua</string>
    <string name="button_run_async_text_wait">Run Async</string>
    <string name="button_run_async_text_busy">Running Async...</string>
    <string name="button_run_sync_text_wait">Run on GUI Thread</string>
    <string name="button_run_sync_text_busy">Running Sync...</string>
    <string name="button_clear_text">Clear</string>
    <string name="menu_snippets_load">Load Snippets</string>
    <string name="menu_startup_script_load">Load Startup Script</string>
    <string name="menu_startup_script_save">Save Startup Script</string>
</resources>
```

The Application Initialization Code

Listing 4–7 shows the startup and initialization code for KahluaDroid. This should be self-explanatory based upon what we have covered so far.

Listing 4–7. *KahluaDroid Startup and Initialization Implementation in KahluaDroid.java (partial)*

```java
package com.pietergreyling.android.kahluadroid;

[--code omitted--]

public class KahluaDroid extends Activity
{
    protected static final String           TAG     = "KahluaDroid";
    protected String                        APP_TITLE;
    protected String                        STARTUP_SCRIPT_CODE;

    /**
     * Kahlua reference variables
     */
    protected final Platform                _platform;
    protected final KahluaTable             _env;
    protected final KahluaConverterManager  _manager;
    protected final LuaJavaClassExposer     _exposer;
    protected final LuaCaller               _caller;
    protected final KahluaThread            _thread;

    /**
     * GUI reference variables
     */
    protected EditText                      _txtInput;
```

```java
    protected TextView                      _txtOutput;
    protected Button                        _cmdRunAsync;
    protected Button                        _cmdRunSync;
    protected Button                        _cmdClear;
    protected final StringBuffer            _buffer  = new StringBuffer();

    public KahluaDroid()
    {
        _platform = new J2SEPlatform();
        _env = _platform.newEnvironment();
        _manager = new KahluaConverterManager();
        KahluaTable java = _platform.newTable();
        _env.rawset("Java", java);
        _exposer = new LuaJavaClassExposer(_manager, _platform, _env, java);
        _exposer.exposeGlobalFunctions(this);
        _caller = new LuaCaller(_manager);
        _thread = new KahluaThread(new PrintStream(new OutputStream()
        {
            @Override
            public void write(int i) throws IOException
            {
                _buffer.append(Character.toString((char) i));
            }
        }), _platform, _env);
    }

    @Override
    public void onCreate(Bundle savedInstanceState)
    {
        Log.d(TAG, "onCreate(): ...");
        super.onCreate(savedInstanceState);
        setContentView(R.layout.main);
        initialize();
        runStartupScript();
    }

    /**
     * Sets up Activity user interface controls and resources.
     */
    protected void initialize()
    {
        APP_TITLE = getString(R.string.app_desc) + " [v."
                + getString(R.string.app_version) + "]";
        setTitle(APP_TITLE);
        _txtInput = (EditText) findViewById(R.id.edittext_input);
        _txtInput.setTextSize(TextSize.NORMAL);
        _txtInput.setTypeface(Typeface.MONOSPACE);

        _cmdRunAsync = (Button) findViewById(R.id.button_run_async);
        _cmdRunAsync.setOnClickListener(new View.OnClickListener()
        {
            public void onClick(View view)
            {
                executeAsync();
            }
        });
```

```java
        _cmdRunSync = (Button) findViewById(R.id.button_run_sync);
        _cmdRunSync.setOnClickListener(new View.OnClickListener()
        {
            public void onClick(View view)
            {
                executeSync();
            }
        });

        _cmdClear = (Button) findViewById(R.id.button_clear);
        _cmdClear.setOnClickListener(new View.OnClickListener()
        {
            public void onClick(View view)
            {
                _txtInput.getText().clear();
            }
        });

        _txtOutput = (TextView) findViewById(R.id.textview_output);
        _txtOutput.setTextSize(TextSize.NORMAL);
        _txtOutput.setTypeface(Typeface.MONOSPACE);
        _txtOutput.setTextColor(Color.GREEN);
        _txtOutput.setBackgroundColor(Color.DKGRAY);
    }
```

```
[--code omitted--]
```

Running Lua Code On or Off the Main GUI Thread

On the KahluaDroid main activity screen there is a button named `Run Async` and one next to it called `Run on GUI Thread`. These buttons provide us with the ability to decide whether we want to execute the Lua code on a separate (asynchronous) background thread or on the main thread of the application. All graphical user interface (GUI) interaction is also running on the main thread, so it is important to understand the distinction and possible consequences.

In Chapter 3, where we covered running BASIC scripts with CocoaDroid, we discussed threading in the Android context and the Android `AsyncTask` class infrastructure. If you have not read that chapter, we recommend it as background for this section since the KahluaDroid implementation of threading follows the same principles and practices.

Thus, assuming that you have background knowledge of Android threading concepts we will have a cursory look at the implementation behind the `Run` buttons here and leave you to peruse the code.

> **NOTE:** We will not delve into Android handlers, binding, and thread pools here since our project threading implementations more than suffices for our purposes. One can go far by avoiding multithreading complications using keep-it-simple design disciplines and implementing a subclass of AsyncTask if necessary. It is also worth remembering that while the Android platform supports multithreading, it is by no means a server platform.

Executing Background Code with AsyncTask

When your scripts are designed to stay within the thread space of the Kahlua2 runtime and will not interact with the Android GUI in any way, use the KahluaDroid executeAsync method to push your Lua code. This provides the additional benefit of avoiding potential blocking of the user interface while background work might be taking place on the main application thread. The implementation is shown in Listing 4–8.

Listing 4–8. *Asynchronous Threading Implementation in KahluaDroid.java (partial)*

```
[--code omitted--]

    protected void executeAsync()
    {
        // prepend source to output
        final String source = _txtInput.getText().toString();
        Log.d(TAG, "executeAsync(): " + source);
        String oldoutput = (_txtOutput.getText()).toString();
        String newoutput = ("> " + source + "\n") + oldoutput;
        _txtOutput.setText(newoutput);
        // run the code asynchronously
        KahluaAsyncTask task = new KahluaAsyncTask();
        task.execute(source);
    }

[--code omitted--]
```

Listing 4–9 presents the implementation of the `KahluaAsyncTask` class. This is derived from the Android `AsyncTask` class and provides developers with the recommended approach for running background Android code on a thread separated from the main application GUI thread. As mentioned before, we have covered this to some length in Chapter 3. The Android Developers web site also has good coverage of Android threading[11] and the `AsyncTask` class[12].

Listing 4–9. *KahluaAsyncTask Class Implementation in KahluaDroid.java (partial)*

```
[--code omitted--]

    private class KahluaAsyncTask extends AsyncTask<String, Void, Void>
    {
        @Override
        protected void onPreExecute()
        {
            _cmdRunAsync.setEnabled(false);
            _cmdRunAsync.setText(getString(R.string.button_run_async_text_busy));
            _txtInput.getText().clear();
            flush();
        }

        @Override
        protected Void doInBackground(String... strings)
```

---

[11] http://developer.android.com/resources/articles/painless-threading.html

[12] http://developer.android.com/reference/android/os/AsyncTask.html

```java
                {
                    // flush();
                    String source = strings[0];
                    try
                    {
                        LuaClosure closure = LuaCompiler.loadstring(source, null, _env);
                        LuaReturn result = _caller.protectedCall(_thread, closure);
                        if (result.isSuccess())
                        {
                            for (Object o : result)
                            {
                                _buffer.append(KahluaUtil.tostring(o, _thread) + "\n");
                            }
                        }
                        else
                        {
                            _buffer.append(result.getErrorString() + "\n");
                            _buffer.append(result.getLuaStackTrace() + "\n");
                        }
                    }
                    catch (Exception e)
                    {
                        _buffer.append(e.getMessage() + "\n");
                    }
                    return null;
                }

                @Override
                protected void onPostExecute(Void result)
                {
                    flush();
                    _cmdRunAsync.setText(getString(R.string.button_run_async_text_wait));
                    _cmdRunAsync.setEnabled(true);
                }

                private void flush()
                {
                    // output.append(_buffer.toString());
                    // prepend _buffer to output
                    String oldoutput = (_txtOutput.getText()).toString();
                    String newoutput = _buffer.toString() + oldoutput;
                    _txtOutput.setText(newoutput);
                    _buffer.setLength(0);
                }
            };

[--code omitted--]
```

Executing UI Code on the Main Thread

If your scripts have side effects such as interaction with Android user interface elements, use the KahluaDroid `executeSync` method. This will allow your code to influence the GUI without crashing. The implementation is shown in Listing 4–10.

Listing 4-10. *Synchronous Threading Implementation Methods in KahluaDroid.java (partial)*

```
[--code omitted--]

    protected void executeSync()
    {
        // prepend source to output
        final String source = _txtInput.getText().toString();
        Log.d(TAG, "executeSync(): " + source);
        String oldoutput = (_txtOutput.getText()).toString();
        String newoutput = ("> " + source + "\n") + oldoutput;
        _txtOutput.setText(newoutput);
        _cmdRunSync.setText(getString(R.string.button_run_sync_text_busy));
        executeSync(source);
    }

    protected void executeSync(String source)
    {
        try
        {
            LuaClosure closure = LuaCompiler.loadstring(source, null, _env);
            LuaReturn result = _caller.protectedCall(_thread, closure);
            if (result.isSuccess())
            {
                for (Object o : result)
                {
                    _buffer.append(KahluaUtil.tostring(o, _thread) + "\n");
                }
            }
            else
            {
                _buffer.append(result.getErrorString() + "\n");
                _buffer.append(result.getLuaStackTrace() + "\n");
            }
        }
        catch (Exception e)
        {
            _buffer.append(e.getMessage() + "\n");
        }
        finally {
            flushSync();
            _cmdRunSync.setText(getString(R.string.button_run_sync_text_wait));
        }
    }

    private void flushSync()
    {
        String oldoutput = (_txtOutput.getText()).toString();
        String newoutput = _buffer.toString() + oldoutput;
        _txtOutput.setText(newoutput);
        _buffer.setLength(0);
    }

[--code omitted--]
```

Exposing Android Application Methods to Kahlua2

Kahlua2 enables the implementation of Lua callable global functions by decorating compatible methods within your Java class with the `@LuaMethod` annotation.

We covered the background earlier with our treatment of the `LuaJavaClassExposer` class. To recap, this class exposes global methods of the given class referred to with the `exposeGlobalFunctions` call to the Kahlua2 script engine. This enables the Kahlua2 runtime to call back to methods of the given class.

Scope does not allow for us to review the full details behind this here, but the code is available within the Kahlua2 project of this chapter.

Sharing Data between Java and Lua

Listing 4–11 provides a listing of a method pair we implemented to demonstrate how to set and get variable values in the Lua environment. This effectively allows us to share variable values between the Android Java application and the Lua environment table.

Listing 4–11. *Lua Environment Variable Manipulation Methods in KahluaDroid.java (partial)*

```
[--code omitted--]

    @LuaMethod(global = true)
    public void lua_setvar(CharSequence varname, CharSequence value)
    {
        _env.rawset(varname, value);
    }

    @LuaMethod(global = true)
    public String lua_getvar(CharSequence varname)
    {
        String value = (String)_env.rawget(varname);
        return value;
    }

[--code omitted--]
```

Modifying the Android application GUI from Lua

Listing 4–12 shows a set of methods that manipulate the GUI of our Android application in some way or other. The implementation of an application startup script later in this chapter will use these methods to demonstrate the alteration of visual aspects of an Android application from within Lua script code.

Listing 4–12. *Android GUI Manipulation Methods in KahluaDroid.java (partial)*

```
[--code omitted--]

    @LuaMethod(global = true)
    public void app_settextsize()
    {
        Double size = (Double)_env.rawget("text_size");
        app_settextsize(size);
```

```java
        }

        @LuaMethod(global = true)
        public void app_settextsize(Double size)
        {
            switch (size.intValue()) {
                case 1:
                    _txtInput.setTextSize(TextSize.SMALL);
                    _txtOutput.setTextSize(TextSize.SMALL);
                    break;
                case 2:
                    _txtInput.setTextSize(TextSize.NORMAL);
                    _txtOutput.setTextSize(TextSize.NORMAL);
                    break;
                case 3:
                    _txtInput.setTextSize(TextSize.LARGE);
                    _txtOutput.setTextSize(TextSize.LARGE);
                    break;
                default:
                    _txtInput.setTextSize(TextSize.NORMAL);
                    _txtOutput.setTextSize(TextSize.NORMAL);
            }
        }

        @LuaMethod(global = true)
        public void app_settextcolor()
        {
            Double color = (Double)_env.rawget("text_color");
            app_settextcolor(color);
        }

        @LuaMethod(global = true)
        public void app_settextcolor(Double color)
        {
            switch (color.intValue()) {
                case 1:
                    _txtOutput.setTextColor(Color.BLACK);
                    _txtOutput.setBackgroundColor(Color.WHITE);
                    break;
                case 2:
                    _txtOutput.setTextColor(Color.GREEN);
                    _txtOutput.setBackgroundColor(Color.DKGRAY);
                    break;
                case 3:
                    _txtOutput.setTextColor(Color.LTGRAY);
                    _txtOutput.setBackgroundColor(Color.BLUE);
                    break;
                default:
                    _txtOutput.setTextColor(Color.GREEN);
                    _txtOutput.setBackgroundColor(Color.DKGRAY);
            }
        }

[--code omitted--]
```

Implementing a Small Lua Callable Android Runtime

Listing 4–13 presents the implementation of a small Lua callable Android runtime. This is a loose set of Android-related operations that we are making accessible from Lua scripts. Again, we will show how we call these methods as Lua functions later.

Listing 4–13. *Lua Callable Android Runtime Methods in KahluaDroid.java (partial)*

```
[--code omitted--]
    @LuaMethod(global = true)
    public void android_alert(CharSequence message)
    {
        new AlertDialog.Builder(this)
            .setTitle(getString(R.string.app_name))
            .setMessage(message)
            .setPositiveButton("OK", null).show();
    }

    @LuaMethod(global = true)
    public void android_alert(CharSequence message, CharSequence title)
    {
        new AlertDialog.Builder(this).setTitle(title).setMessage(message)
                .setPositiveButton("OK", null).show();
    }

    @LuaMethod(global = true)
    public void android_toast(CharSequence message)
    {
        Toast.makeText(this, message, Toast.LENGTH_SHORT).show();
    }

    @LuaMethod(global = true)
    public void android_notify(
            CharSequence title,
            CharSequence tickerText,
            CharSequence message)
    {
        showNotification(
                getApplicationContext(),
                KahluaDroid.class,
                tickerText,
                title,
                message,
                R.drawable.icon_practical_andy_blue);
    }

    @LuaMethod(global = true)
    public String android_version()
    {
        String full_version =
            String.format("[v:%s.%s][sdk: %s][codename: %s]",
                    VERSION.RELEASE,
                    VERSION.INCREMENTAL,
                    VERSION.SDK_INT,
                    VERSION.CODENAME);
        return full_version;
    }
```

```
    @LuaMethod(global = true)
    public String android_release()
    {
        String release = String.format("%s", VERSION.RELEASE);
        return release;
    }

    @LuaMethod(global = true)
    public String android_sdk()
    {
        String sdk_level = String.format("%s", VERSION.SDK_INT);
        return sdk_level;
    }
[--code omitted--]
```

Calling Application Methods as Lua Functions

Having seen the implementation of Lua script-callable methods in our main KahluaDroid class, let us have a look at how to use them. We have provided a few small Lua code samples in the form of a Lua snippets file.

The KahluaDroid Lua Snippets

Under the `assets` folder of the application source code, you should find the `program_templates/lua_snippets.lua` code file.

This is the asset file that gets loaded by the `Load Snippets` (Figure 4–9) menu item.

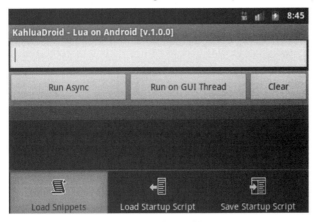

Figure 4–9. *KahluaDroid Load Snippets Menu*

Figure 4–10 depicts the Activity after loading the snippets file into the input text field.

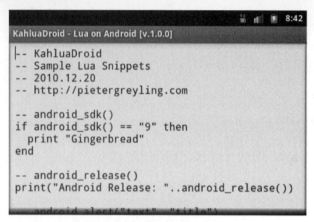

Figure 4-10. *KahluaDroid loaded snippets*

The full content of the snippets file is in Listing 4-14.

Listing 4-14. *KahluaDroid Lua Code Snippets Asset File–lua_snippets.lua*

```lua
-- KahluaDroid
-- Sample Lua Snippets
-- 2010.12.20
-- http://pietergreyling.com

-- android_sdk()
if android_sdk() == "9" then
  print "Gingerbread"
end

-- android_release()
print("Android Release: "..android_release())

-- android_alert("text", "title")
android_alert(
  "Run me on the GUI thread!",
  "Android Alert")

-- android_toast()
android_toast("Run me on the GUI thread!")

-- android_notify(
--    title, tickerText, message)
android_notify(
  "KahluaDroid Notification",
  "KahluaDroid message waiting...",
  "Thanks for reading this message.")

-- app_settextsize() / app_settextcolor()
app_settextsize(1)  -- small
app_settextcolor(3) -- grey on blue
app_settextsize(2)  -- normal
app_settextcolor(2) -- green on dkgrey
app_settextsize(3)  -- large
```

```
    app_settextcolor(1) -- black on white

    -- lua runtime lib: os
    print(os.date())

    -- lua runtime lib: math
    print(math.sin(3))

    -- tables
    a={}; a["num"]=12345; print("n="..a["num"])

    -- functions
    function func(a)
      print("-- func: "..a)
    end
    func ("test argument")

    -- random number generation
    local r = newrandom()
    r:random() -- 0 to 1
    r:random(max) -- 1 to max
    r:random(min, max) -- min to max
    -- seeds with hashcode of object
    r:seed(obj)

    ---[[
    local r = newrandom()
    for i=1,6 do
      print("dice "..i.." rolled "..r:random(6))
    end
    --]]

    -- Sample Startup Script
    msg1 = "Startup script complete.\n"
    msg2 = "KahluaDroid ready..."
    app_settextsize(1)   -- small
    app_settextcolor(3) -- grey on blue
    print(msg1..msg2)
    android_toast(msg1..msg2)
```

Implementing an Application Startup Script

Startup scripts are a common way to configure applications of all types, from personal productivity applications on the desktop to back-end number crunching server applications. Knowing what we have learned so far in this chapter, we can now effectively implement a basic startup script infrastructure for our Android applications.

Saving Lua Code as a Startup Script

To create a small startup script, we will copy some code from the Lua snippets file that we have prepared for this project.

Open the snippets using the `Load Snippets` menu, as addressed earlier. We will pick the following code (see Listing 4–14):

```
-- Sample Startup Script
msg1 = "Startup script complete.\n"
msg2 = "KahluaDroid ready..."
app_settextsize(1)  -- small
app_settextcolor(3) -- grey on blue
print(msg1..msg2)
android_toast(msg1..msg2)
```

Copy the section as shown in Figure 4–11.

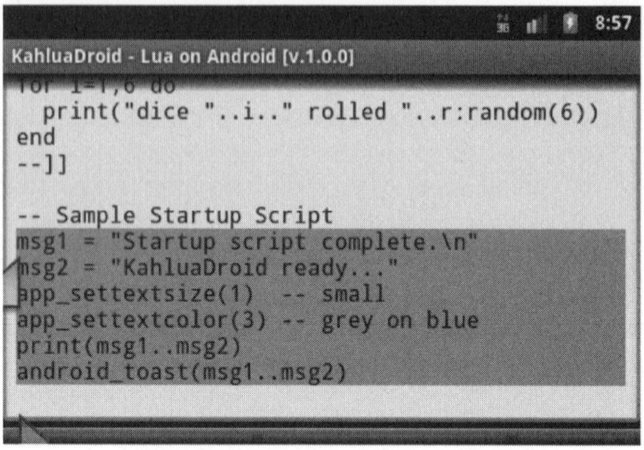

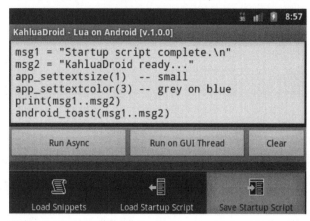

Figure 4–11. *Copying the KahluaDroid startup script from the Lua snippets*

Now paste the selection into the input text field, as shown in Figure 4–12.

Figure 4–12. *Pasting the KahluaDroid startup script code*

Use the `Save Startup Script` menu item to save the code to the startup file. This should result in a toast message similar to that shown in Figure 4–13.

CHAPTER 4: Embedding Lua in Android Applications

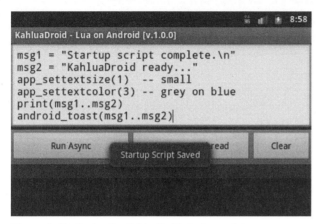

Figure 4-13. *Saving the KahluaDroid startup script*

Running the Application with the Startup Script

When we relaunch the application after saving the startup script, you should see a result similar to that depicted in Figure 4-14. The text size will be smaller, and the output text background will be blue with a gray foreground.

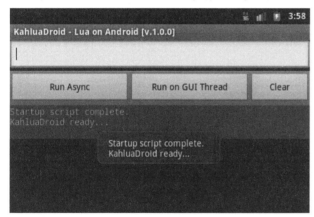

Figure 4-14. *Running the KahluaDroid startup script on application launch*

The startup script load implementation is shown in Listing 4-15.

Listing 4-15. *Startup Script Implementation-KahluaDroid.java (partial)/ CommonAndroidCodeLibrary.java (partial)*

```
[--code omitted--]

    protected void runStartupScript()
    {
      try
      {
        STARTUP_SCRIPT_CODE = readStartupScript();
        Log.d(TAG,
```

```java
                    "runStartupScript(): STARTUP_SCRIPT_CODE:\n" +
                    STARTUP_SCRIPT_CODE);
            executeSync(STARTUP_SCRIPT_CODE);
        }
        catch (Throwable t)
        {
            Log.e(TAG, "runStartupScript(): FAILED!", t);
            STARTUP_SCRIPT_CODE = "";
        }
    }

[--code omitted--]

    protected String readStartupScript()
    {
        String buffer = "";
        try {
            buffer = stringFromPrivateApplicationFile(this,
                    getString(R.string.file_name_startup_script));
            return buffer;
        }
        catch (Throwable t) {
            Log.e(TAG, "readStartupScript(): NO STARTUP SCRIPT!", t);
            //showOkAlertDialog(this, t.toString(), "Read Startup Script");
            return "";
        }
    }

[--code omitted--]

    /**
     * Reads a private application file into a String and returns the String.
     *
     * @param context
     * @param name
     * @return
     * @throws java.lang.Throwable
     */
    public static String stringFromPrivateApplicationFile(Context context, String name)
            throws java.lang.Throwable
    {
        String ret_str = "";
        InputStream is = context.openFileInput(name);
        InputStreamReader tmp_isr = new InputStreamReader(is);
        BufferedReader tmp_rdr = new BufferedReader(tmp_isr);
        String tmp_str = "";
        StringBuilder tmp_buf = new StringBuilder();
        while ((tmp_str = tmp_rdr.readLine()) != null) {
            tmp_buf.append(tmp_str);
            tmp_buf.append(_newline); // readLine drops newlines, put them back
        }
        is.close();
        if(0 < tmp_buf.length()) { // brutally remove the inevitable newline at end
            tmp_buf.setLength(tmp_buf.length() - 1);
        }
        ret_str = tmp_buf.toString();
        return ret_str;
```

```
    }
[--code omitted--]
```

As you will notice, the startup script code is run synchronously on the main application thread using the `executeSync` method since this also allows it to relatively safely cause side-effects that influence the state of the user interface.

Using Lua Comment Blocks in the Startup Script

When working and testing the code in a startup script, it is useful to have a handy way of quickly activating and deactivating blocks of code. A simple technique with which to achieve this is by using the Lua comment block syntax.

In Lua, line comments start with a double hyphen (`--`) at any point in a line and runs until the end of the line:

```
-- This is a Lua line comment and starts with a double-hyphen (--).
-- Such comments only run to the end of the line that they are on.
```

Lua also offers multiline or block comments that start with `--[[` and run until a matching `]]`.

```
--[[ Multi-line strings and comments
    use double square brackets. ]]
```

A common trick, when we want to disable a piece of code, is to write the following:

```
--[[
print("commented")        → nothing (a comment)
--]]
```

Now, if we add a single hyphen to the first line, the code is in again:

```
---[[
print("uncommented")      → uncommented
--]]
```

In the first case, the `--` in the last line is still inside the block comment. In the second case, the `---[[` does not start a block comment, but a line comment instead. This leaves the `print("uncommented")` outside comments and thus active. The last line then forms a separate comment, as it starts with `--`.

This makes it easy to test and save startup script code with KahluaDroid. Simply enclose sections of code in block comments and enable and disable the sections with a single change at the top of the block. This way, you can store pieces of code and not worry about losing any work you might want to retest or apply later.

Figure 4–15 displays a block comment in effect.

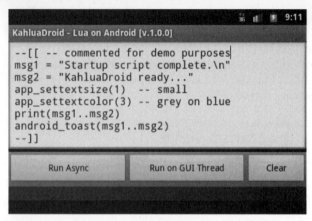

Figure 4–15. *KahluaDroid startup script block commented*

Figure 4–16 displays the same block of code uncommented.

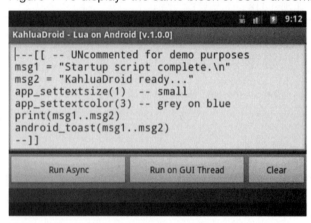

Figure 4–16. *KahluaDroid startup script block uncommented*

Accessing the Startup Script from the DDMS File Explorer

Android application files on the emulator can also be accessed by using the Android SDK Dalvik Debug Monitor (DDMS) File Explorer. Although we demonstrated this in previous chapters, we do so here again (see Figure 4–17).

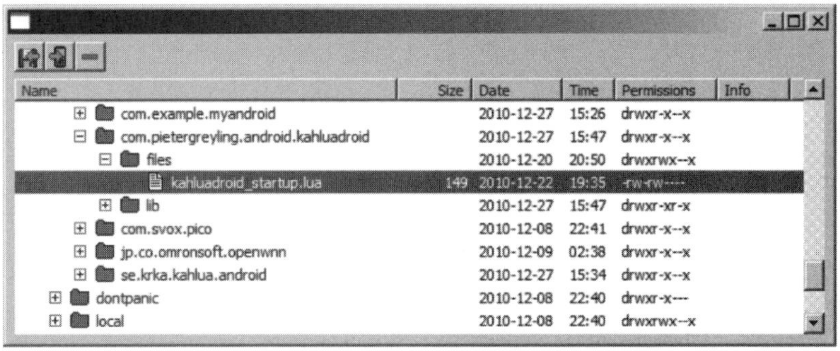

![Figure 4-17 screenshot]

Figure 4–17. *The KahluaDroid Startup Script in the DDMS File Explorer*

Removing a Broken Startup Script

Sometimes we make mistakes in our code. In the case of our startup script, such malfunctioning code might cause moments during which our application cannot launch properly or even refuses to start at all. This can present a "Catch-22" scenario in which we are cannot use the application to fix the problem. Since the application then does not start, or does so in an unpredictable state, we cannot reload the startup script in order to edit the code of the script and fix it.

It might be obvious, but the Android platform comes with functionality to manage applications and clear corresponding application data. This can be accessed from the Settings main menu using the Manage apps menu item. (See Figure 4–18.)

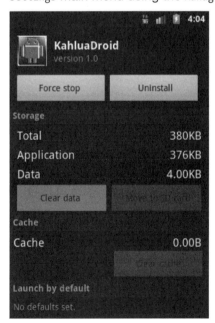

Figure 4–18. *Clearing KahluaDroid application data*

Summary

This chapter showed you the basics of how to use the Lua programming language to extend your own Java-based Android applications.

We chose the Kahlua2 implementation of Lua since it has a native Java code base and was designed to run on mobile devices.

We demonstrated how it is possible to call methods implemented in our Android classes from Lua scripts.

In the next chapter, we will finalize our study of scripting on the Android platform by giving you an introduction to the Scripting Layer for Android (SL4A). SL4A is a platform that enables the running of multiple scripting engines on an Android device.

Our scripting implementations of the last two chapters have run within the processes of our Java Android applications. The design of SL4A currently differs in that scripting engines run in their own Android processes and communicate to an Android RPC server application via a JSON RPC bridge. This Java Android server application then makes Android API calls by proxy on behalf of the scripting engine.

Chapter 5

Introducing SL4A: The Scripting Layer for Android

The main objective of this chapter is to introduce you to the Scripting Layer for Android (SL4A) platform. Our aim is to give you enough basic understanding of how SL4A[1] works and to be able to use it to run your own scripts written in a number of high-level scripting languages.

As you will see, the design of SL4A enables it to support many scripting language interpreters. In order to make practical use of SL4A, you will need to understand at least the rudiments of one high-level scripting language such as Python, Ruby, Perl, Lua, JavaScript, or BeanShell.

For this book, we assume that you have a good level of Java programming language knowledge and this should serve you well if you intend to use a related language such as BeanShell or JavaScript with SL4A.

In this chapter, we will first give you some background about what SL4A is, what it can be used for, where to get it, and where to learn more about it for yourself. We will then show you how to install and run SL4A with small examples. After this, you will get a technical overview of how SL4A works and how its design relates to the scripting architectures we presented in the two previous chapters. To help you on your way to a deeper study of SL4A, we will then show you how to obtain a copy of the complete SL4A source code repository. In conclusion, we will present some equivalent SL4A "Hello World" example code snippets in various scripting languages.

---

[1] From now on, we will use the acronym "SL4A" instead of "Scripting Layer for Android."

What Is Scripting Layer for Android?

In a nutshell, SL4A is an infrastructure for enabling the interoperation of scripting language engines that have been ported to the Android platform with the Android application programming interface (API) via remote procedure calls (RPCs) to a server implemented as a standard Android Java application.

About SL4A

SL4A,[2] originally called Android Scripting Environment (ASE), was brought to us by Damon Kohler[3] and is hosted on Google Code as an open-source project.

From the user perspective, the SL4A Android application lets you edit and run scripts against multiple interactive script interpreters on your Android device. It also supports the ability to install script interpreters into the application directly from the SL4A home site.

In essence, SL4A is more than just a standard end-user Android application; it is also a platform for exposing Android functionality to custom client programs such as scripting engines.

The SL4A License

Like the Android platform, SL4A is open source and is released under the same Apache License Version 2.0,[4] as is most of Android.

Using SL4A

The SL4A system is suited for the following kinds of tasks:

- **RAD programming:** With SL4A it is possible to use a rapid application development (RAD) approach to quickly create a prototype application that allows you to test the feasibility of an idea. Once the practicality of the application is confirmed, you can create a full-blown Android application.

- **Writing test scripts:** Assuming that the supporting Android APIs are exposed to SL4A, it can be used to create test scripts for other functionality.

---

[2] http://code.google.com/p/android-scripting/

[3] http://www.damonkohler.com/search/label/sl4a

[4] http://www.apache.org/licenses/

- **Building utilities:** You can fairly easily and quickly write utility and tool scripts that do small jobs or automate certain aspects of repetitive tasks. These tools probably do not require a complicated user interface; they need just a simple dialog-based user interaction mode.

SL4A Resources

For more background on SL4A, we recommend consulting the following online resources:

- SL4A home:
    - http://code.google.com/p/android-scripting/
- SL4A downloads:
    - http://code.google.com/p/android-scripting/downloads/list
    - http://code.google.com/p/android-scripting/downloads/list?q=label:Featured
- SL4A FAQ:
    - http://code.google.com/p/android-scripting/wiki/FAQ
- SL4A Wiki:
    - http://code.google.com/p/android-scripting/w/list
- SL4A tutorials:
    - http://code.google.com/p/android-scripting/wiki/Tutorials
- SL4A source code:
    - http://code.google.com/p/android-scripting/source/checkout

The SL4A Code Repository

The SL4A project source code is hosted on Google Code in a Mercurial repository.[5]

Mercurial SCM is an open-source, distributed-source, control management tool. Mercurial is designed to be cross-platform and is written in the Python programming language.

---

[5] http://code.google.com/p/android-scripting/source/browse/

Later in the chapter, we will show you how to use the Mercurial client-side tools and integrated development environment (IDE) plugins to bring the SL4A code to your desktop in order to build and run SL4A.

Running SL4A in the Android Emulator

Before we dive into the details of SL4A, we will show you the quickest way to have a look at SL4A in action.

We will download the SL4A Android application package (APK) distribution and install it on a running Android emulator instance. This will allow us to use SL4A to install some scripting engines into the emulator from the SL4A site.

Development Environment Configuration

As a quick reference, Table 5–1 lists some development environment configuration settings and commands that you will find useful for working with the code in this chapter.

Table 5–1. *Development Environment Configuration Quick Reference*

Item	Value or Command
PATH	`<Android SDK Directory>/tools`
PATH	`<Android SDK Directory>/platform-tools`
PATH	`<Apache Ant Directory>/bin`
PATH	`<Mercurial Directory>/`
Create an AVD	`android create avd -n android23api9_hvga_32mb -t android-9 -c 32M`
Start the AVD on Linux / Mac OS X	`emulator -avd android23api9_hvga_32mb &`
Start the AVD on Windows	`start emulator -avd android23api9_hvga_32mb`

Even though the `PATH` entry for the Mercurial executable (hg or hg.exe) is not strictly necessary right now, it will become useful if you decide to get a snapshot of the SL4A code and build it yourself.

Downloading the SL4A APKs

First, we will download the SL4A application archive from the SL4A download site here:

- http://code.google.com/p/android-scripting/downloads/list

Or here:

- http://code.google.com/p/android-scripting/downloads/list?q=label:Featured

Download the latest release of the SL4A APK. At the time of writing, this was the following:

sl4a_r3.apk

Save this to a directory on your file system. We have called ours sl4a-apk.

Also available on the SL4A site were the following scripting engine APKs:

```
beanshell_for_android_r1.apk
jruby_for_android_r1.apk
lua_for_android_r1.apk
perl_for_android_r1.apk
python_for_android_r1.apk
rhino_for_android_r1.apk
```

NOTE: The SL4A APKs are included in the book downloads, so you can get started right away.

Installing the SL4A APK on the Android Emulator

Ensure that you are running the Android emulator using a compatible AVD. For this, follow the instructions in Table 5–1.

Now, in a terminal command-line shell, navigate to the directory where you have saved the downloaded SL4A APK file and enter the following command:

adb install sl4a_r3.apk

This should produce output similar to the following:

```
adb install sl4a_r3.apk
364 KB/s (840827 bytes in 2.250s)
        pkg: /data/local/tmp/sl4a_r3.apk
Success
```

The SL4A launcher icon should now appear on the emulator, as illustrated in Figure 5–1.

Figure 5–1. *SL4A Application Launcher icon*

Running SL4A on the Android Emulator

When we launch the application, you should see the SL4A primary Usage Tracking request, as shown in Figure 5–2.

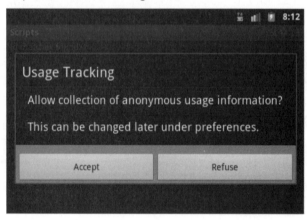

Figure 5–2. *SL4A Usage Tracking*

Simply click one of either the Accept or Refuse buttons. After invoking the SL4A application menu (press the F2 keyboard key while in the emulator), you should now see the image of the main SL4A application Activity screen, as shown in Figure 5–3.

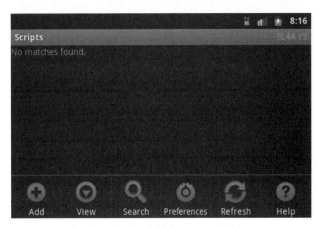

Figure 5–3. *SL4A application initial screen with Menu*

Now select the View menu item and choose the Interpreters entry, as shown in Figure 5–4.

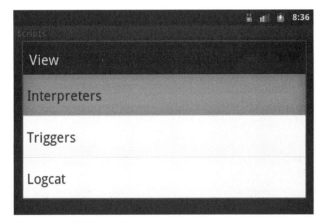

Figure 5–4. *SL4A view interpreters*

As illustrated in Figure 5–5, our SL4A emulator installation is currently equipped only with the Shell interpreter.

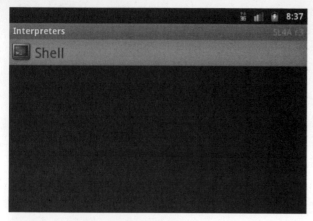

Figure 5–5. *SL4A interpreters: Shell*

If you run the Shell interpreter, you should be presented with Figure 5–6. As you can see, we have entered the following command into the shell:

echo $PATH

We are also about to execute the UNIX top command.

Figure 5–6. *SL4A interpreters: Shell commands*

The result of running the top command is shown in Figure 5–7.

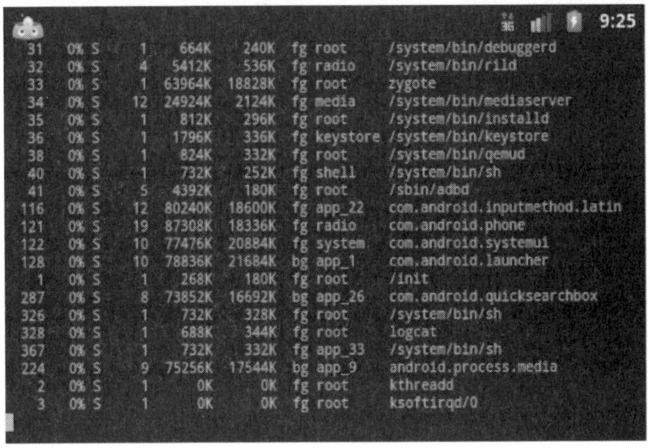

Figure 5-7. *SL4A Interpreters: Shell top*

When you exit the Shell interpreter using the application menu, you are presented with the screen as depicted in Figure 5-8.

Click the Yes button.

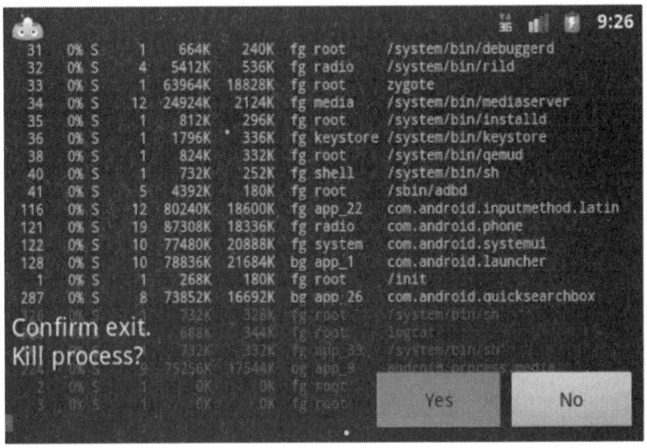

Figure 5-8. *SL4A interpreters: Shell exit*

We are now done with confirming that our SL4A emulator installation is functioning correctly.

Installing SL4A Interpreters

Next we will add some new scripting language interpreters to the SL4A toolbox.

We will first show you how to do so using the SL4A application and then summarize how to install the interpreters from your computer using the downloadable[6] application packages (APKs). This will enable you to install the base interpreter engines slightly faster than doing it from the device using SL4A. It is best thereafter to let the relevant script engine fetch its current and compatible extra ZIP packages under its own control.

Adding Interpreters with SL4A

From within the Interpreters screen, select the Add menu item. After scrolling down to the Python entry in the list, you should see the image depicted in Figure 5–9.

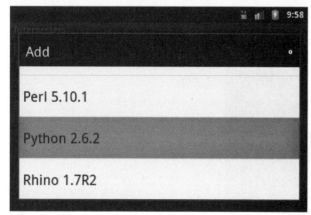

Figure 5–9. *SL4A Add interpreters*

Select the Python entry.

This will start a download of the Python APK from the SL4A site that should show the notification shown in Figure 5–10 when completed.

---

[6] http://code.google.com/p/android-scripting/downloads/list

CHAPTER 5: Introducing SL4A: The Scripting Layer for Android   203

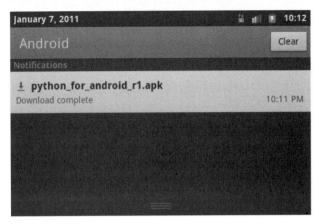

Figure 5–10. *SL4A Add interpreters: Python downloaded*

Clicking the notification entry should display the dialog shown in Figure 5–11.

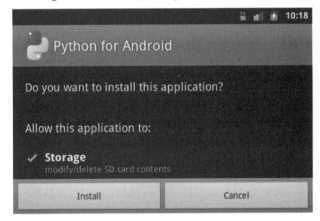

Figure 5–11. *SL4A Add interpreters: Python install*

Now click the `Install` button.

The image shown in Figure 5–12 is what you should see during the download and installation process.

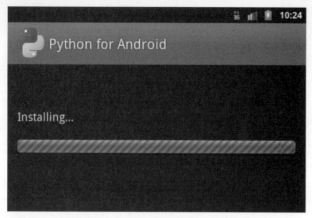

Figure 5–12. *SL4A Add interpreters: Python installing*

Once the installation is complete, you should see something similar to that shown in Figure 5–13.

Figure 5–13. *SL4A Add interpreters: Python installed*

If you now click the Open button, you will be presented with a screen (see Figure 5–14) to initiate the secondary installation sequence. This will download all the supporting archives to the emulator instance.

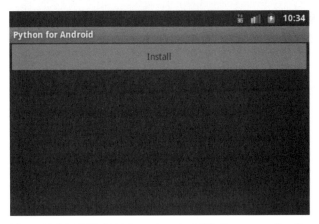

Figure 5–14. *SL4A Add interpreters: Install Python supporting files*

Figure 5–15 depicts the process of downloading the suite of Python interpreter files.

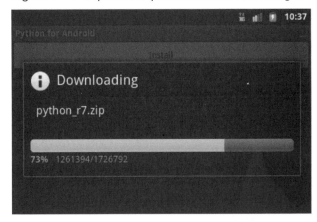

Figure 5–15. *SL4A Add interpreters: Install Python download supporting files*

Once the whole installation download process is complete, you should see the image illustrated in Figure 5–16.

Do not click the Uninstall button.

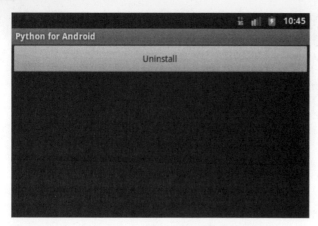

Figure 5-16. *SL4A Add interpreters: Install Python done*

Going back to the SL4A interpreters list, you should now see the Python script language entry, as shown in Figure 5-17.

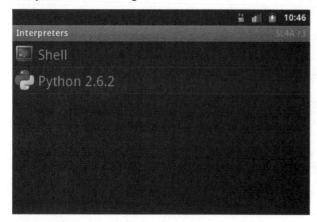

Figure 5-17. *SL4A Add interpreters: Python complete*

This means that you can run Python on Android! The result of clicking the Python interpreter entry is shown in Figure 5-18.

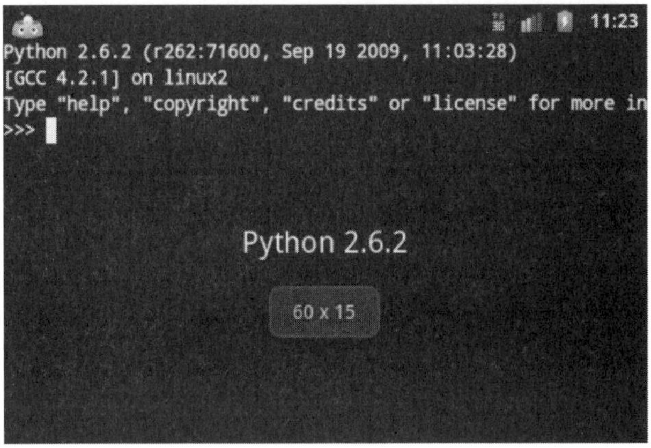

Figure 5-18. *SL4A: Run Python*

Let's enter some code into the interpreter. Try running the following Python statements:

```
import sys
print(sys.platform)
```

The result should be the following:

```
linux2
```

This short session is also shown in Figure 5–19.

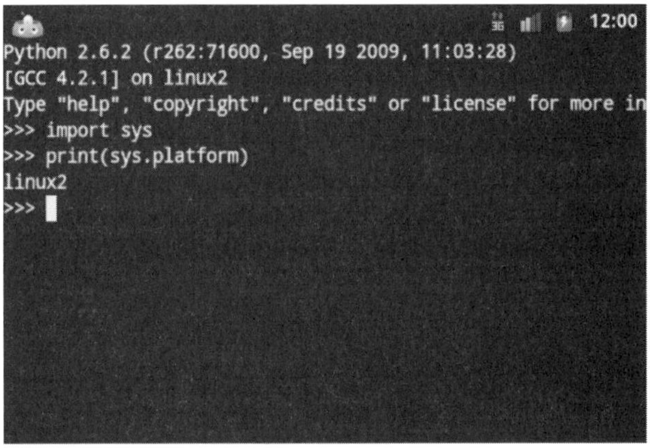

Figure 5-19. *SL4A - Run Python Code*

To demonstrate interaction with the Android API, enter the following code into the interactive interpreter:

```
import android
andy = android.Android()
andy.makeToast('Hello Practical Android Projects!')
```

The result is shown in Figure 5–20.

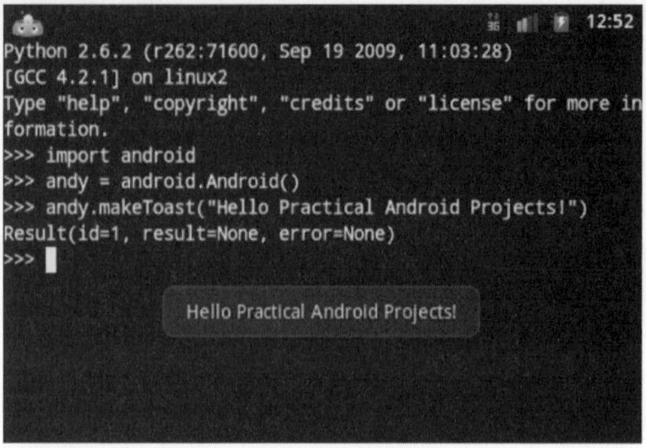

Figure 5–20. *SL4A: Run Python Hello Android*

This concludes our demonstration of how to install SL4A interpreters using SL4A.

> **NOTE:** The SL4A interpreter setup process that we have documented so far will also apply when using a physical device. So when you install SL4A and the supported interpreters on your phone, the same steps will be presented.

Adding Interpreters with Package Archives

As mentioned earlier, it is also possible to install the interpreters from your computer using the downloadable[7] application packages (APKs). This makes script interpreter installation slightly faster than only using the SL4A application as explained before.

Let's assume that you want to install the Perl scripting interpreter in this fashion. In a terminal command-line shell, navigate to the directory where you have saved the downloaded Perl APK file and enter the following command:

```
adb install perl_for_android_r1.apk
```

This should produce output similar to the following:

```
adb install perl_for_android_r1.apk
96 KB/s (33894 bytes in 0.343s)
        pkg: /data/local/tmp/perl_for_android_r1.apk
Success
```

As shown earlier in Figure 5–14 where we installed Python, you can now initiate the secondary installation sequence using the Perl for Android Launcher icon that should now be visible in the emulator or device. This will download all the supporting archives

---

[7] http://code.google.com/p/android-scripting/downloads/list

following on from Figure 5–14 with the same workflow as before. At the very least, it saves having the interpreter package being downloaded.

Understanding Scripting Layer for Android

As mentioned earlier, SL4A enables interoperation between Android agnostic scripting language engines and the Android API. As you will see later, this is not restricted to scripting languages only. Any program that implements a compatible JSON–based RPC[8] interfacing module or set of routines can potentially invoke the SL4A RPC Server.

Communicating Using JavaScript Object Notation (JSON)

Internally, SL4A uses the JavaScript Object Notation (JSON) data format for the interchange of messages and data between the SL4A RPC Server and its clients. This is fundamental to its workings so we will give a quick summary of JSON here.

The acronym JSON was originally specified by Douglas Crockford. The JSON data format is described in RFC 4627.[9]

To quote from the JSON specification:

> "JavaScript Object Notation (JSON) is a lightweight, text-based, language-independent data interchange format. It was derived from the ECMAScript Programming Language Standard. JSON defines a small set of formatting rules for the portable representation of structured data. JSON can represent four primitive types (strings, numbers, booleans, and null) and two structured types (objects and arrays)."

To give you an idea of the data format, the specification also presents an example of a JSON object as follows:

```
{
    "Image": {
        "Width":  800,
        "Height": 600,
        "Title":  "View from 15th Floor",
        "Thumbnail": {
            "Url":    "http://www.example.com/image/481989943",
            "Height": 125,
            "Width":  "100"
        },
        "IDs": [116, 943, 234, 38793]
    }
}
```

---

[8] Remote Procedure Call

[9] http://tools.ietf.org/html/rfc4627

We will not go into more detail about JSON here but instead recommend that you follow up the online resources for more information if you are interested.

Summarizing the SL4A Architecture

SL4A exposes Android API functionality to its clients. It achieves this by implementing a scripting language–compatible module that marshals RPCs and their responses to and from a RPC server implemented as an Android Java application. This enables the RPC server to have direct access to the Android API and it behaves as a remote proxy using a façade that encapsulates and exposes selected Android APIs.

Scripting languages are ported, via cross-compilation or otherwise, to the Android platform in their purest form avoiding any source code changes. This implies that the scripting language has no knowledge of the Android platform at all. It gains access to the Android API using a special module generally implemented in the scripting language itself that accesses the Android API over the remote SL4A RPC server. The current implementation uses the JSON data format for its application layer network messaging package payload content.

The overall design of this infrastructure is illustrated in Figure 5–21.

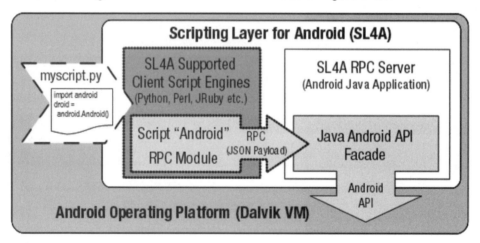

Figure 5–21. *SL4A architecture overview*

To explain things another way, a "generic" script engine, running in a self-contained process, accesses the Android API over bidirectional JSON-RPC via an API façade. The façade is serviced in a separate process, and implemented as a "standard," Java-based, Android server application. The latter has full access to the Android platform API and thus essentially serves as a remote API "proxy" for the scripting engine/interpreter. Each scripting language has a "wrapper" module providing an "Android object" that serves as an in-process, local, API proxy, with the task of packaging RPC calls as scripting methods in the spirit of the particular scripting engine.

To sum this up, an overview of the full-round trip invocation stack looks something like the following:

```
-- Script Interpreter
---- Client/Caller/Consumer Script
------ "Android" Script Object (locally wraps RPC calls) - Local Proxy
-------- Remote Procedure Calls (RPC) - Exchanges contain a JSON payload
------ Android API Java Facade - Remote Proxy
---- API Server/Provider - Android Java application
-- The Android Platform itself
```

> **NOTE:** This decoupled architecture permits any compatible local or remote client to call into SL4A as long as it does so via the JSON RPC call interface.

Reviewing Local Proxy Implementations

We will not go into detailed explanations of the code, but to give you an idea of what is involved, here are some implementations of client RPC proxy wrapper modules.

In Python (see Listing 5–1):

Listing 5–1. *Python Module for Accessing the AndroidProxy (android-scripting/python/ase/android.py)*

```python
# Copyright (C) 2009 Google Inc.
#
# Licensed under the Apache License, Version 2.0 (the "License"); you may not
# use this file except in compliance with the License. You may obtain a copy of
# the License at
#
# http://www.apache.org/licenses/LICENSE-2.0
#
# Unless required by applicable law or agreed to in writing, software
# distributed under the License is distributed on an "AS IS" BASIS, WITHOUT
# WARRANTIES OR CONDITIONS OF ANY KIND, either express or implied. See the
# License for the specific language governing permissions and limitations under
# the License.

__author__ = 'Damon Kohler <damonkohler@gmail.com>'

import collections
import json
import os
import socket
import sys

PORT = os.environ.get('AP_PORT')
HOST = os.environ.get('AP_HOST')
HANDSHAKE = os.environ.get('AP_HANDSHAKE')
Result = collections.namedtuple('Result', 'id,result,error')


class Android(object):

  def __init__(self, addr=None):
```

```python
    if addr is None:
        addr = HOST, PORT
    self.conn = socket.create_connection(addr)
    self.client = self.conn.makefile()
    self.id = 0
    if HANDSHAKE is not None:
        self._authenticate(HANDSHAKE)

def _rpc(self, method, *args):
    data = {'id': self.id,
            'method': method,
            'params': args}
    request = json.dumps(data)
    self.client.write(request+'\n')
    self.client.flush()
    response = self.client.readline()
    self.id += 1
    result = json.loads(response)
    if result['error'] is not None:
        print result['error']
    # namedtuple doesn't work with unicode keys.
    return Result(id=result['id'], result=result['result'],
                  error=result['error'], )

def __getattr__(self, name):
    def rpc_call(*args):
        return self._rpc(name, *args)
    return rpc_call
```

The equivalent functionality is shown in the C programming language (see Listing 5–2) taken from the android-cruft project[10] on Google Code. This project demonstrates how to write C programs that can access the Android API by leveraging SL4A, using the same principles as the earlier Python proxy.

Listing 5–2 presents the C `main` function that is the meat of the code logic. It attempts to invoke the Android API over the SL4A RPC server in order to raise an Android Toast with the message "w00t!" It marshals the message character buffer into a `json_array`, which it then sends over to the SL4A RPC server with a call to the `sl4a_rpc` function.

Listing 5–2. *C Main Module for Accessing SL4A (ndk-to-sl4a.c)*

```c
[--code omitted--]

main(int argc, char **argv) {
  int port = 0;
  if (argc != 2) {
    printf("Usage: %s port\n", argv[0]);
    return 1;
  }
  port = atoi(argv[1]);

  int socket_fd = init_socket("localhost", port);
  if (socket_fd < 0) return 2;
```

---

[10] http://code.google.com/p/android-cruft/wiki/SL4AC

```
    json_t *params = json_array();
    json_array_append(params, json_string("w00t!"));
    sl4a_rpc(socket_fd, "makeToast", params);
}
[--code omitted--]
```

The supporting C functions are shown in Listing 5–3. We will not go into the details, but present the listing here for the sake of completeness.

Listing 5–3. *C Support Functions for Accessing SL4A (ndk-to-sl4a.c)*

```
// Released into the public domain, 15 August 2010
// This program demonstrates how a C application can access some of the Android
// API via the SL4A (Scripting Languages for Android, formerly "ASE", or Android
// Scripting Environment) RPC mechanism.  It works either from a host computer
// or as a native binary compiled with the NDK (rooted phone required, I think)
// SL4A is a neat Android app that provides support for many popular scripting
// languages like Python, Perl, Ruby and TCL.  SL4A exposes a useful subset of
// the Android API in a clever way: by setting up a JSON RPC server.  That way,
// each language only needs to implement a thin RPC client layer to access the
// whole SL4A API.
// The Android NDK is a C compiler only intended for writing optimized
// subroutines of "normal" Android apps written in Java.  So it doesn't come
// with any way to access the Android API.
// This program uses the excellent "Jansson" JSON library to talk to SL4A's
// RPC server, effectively adding native C programs to the list of languages
// supported by SL4A.
// To try it, first install SL4A: http://code.google.com/p/android-scripting/
//
// Start a private server with View->Interpreters->Start Server
//
// Note the port number the server is running on by pulling down the status
// bar and tapping "SL4A service".
// This program works just fine as either a native Android binary or from a
// host machine.
// ------------
// To compile on an ordinary linux machine, first install libjansson.  Then:
// $ gcc -ljansson ndk-to-sl4a.c -o ndk-to-sl4a
// To access SL4A on the phone use "adb forward tcp:XXXXX tcp:XXXXX" to port
// forward the SL4A server port from your host to the phone.  See this
// page for more details:
// http://code.google.com/p/android-scripting/wiki/RemoteControl
// ------------
// To compile using the NDK:
//    1. Make sure you can compile "Hello, world" using the NDK.  See:
//       http://credentiality2.blogspot.com/2010/08/native-android-c-program-
using-ndk.html
//
//    2. If you followed the above instructions, you have a copy of the agcc.pl
//       wrapper that calls the NDK's gcc compiler with the right options for
//       standalone apps.
//
//    3. Unpack a fresh copy of the jansson sources.  Tell configure to build for
//       Android:
//
// $ CC=agcc.pl ./configure --host=arm
// $ make
```

```
//
//    4. Cross your fingers and go!  (I'm quite certain there's a more elegant
//       way to do this)
//
// $ agcc.pl -I/path/to/jansson-1.3/src -o ndk-to-sl4a-arm ndk-to-sl4a.c↵
 /path/to/jansson-1.3/src/*.o
//
//    5. Copy to the phone and run it with the port of the SL4A server!

#include <stdio.h>
#include <jansson.h>
#include <unistd.h>
#include <string.h>

#include <sys/types.h>
#include <sys/socket.h>
#include <netinet/in.h>
#include <netdb.h>

// This mimics SL4A's android.py, constructing a JSON RPC object and
// sending it to the SL4A server.
int sl4a_rpc(int socket_fd, char *method, json_t *params) {
  static int request_id = 0; // monotonically increasing counter

  json_t *root = json_object();

  json_object_set(root, "id", json_integer(request_id));
  request_id++;

  json_object_set(root, "method", json_string(method));

  if (params == NULL) {
    params = json_array();
    json_array_append(params, json_null());
  }

  json_object_set(root, "params", params);

  char *command = json_dumps(root, JSON_PRESERVE_ORDER | JSON_ENSURE_ASCII);
  printf("command string:'%s'\n", command);

  write(socket_fd, command, strlen(command));
  write(socket_fd, "\n", strlen("\n"));

  // At this point we just print the response, but really we should buffer it
  // up into a single string, then pass it to json_loads() for decoding.
  printf("Got back:\n");
  while (1) {
    char c;
    read(socket_fd, &c, 1);
    printf("%c", c);
    if (c == '\n') {
      break;
    }
  }
  fflush(stdout);
  return 0;
```

```
}

// This function is just boilerplate TCP socket setup code
int init_socket(char *hostname, int port) {
  int socket_fd = socket(AF_INET, SOCK_STREAM, 0);
  if (socket_fd == -1) {
    perror("Error creating socket");
    return 0;
  }

  struct hostent *host = gethostbyname(hostname);
  if (host == NULL) {
    perror("No such host");
    return -1;
  }

  struct sockaddr_in socket_address;

  int i;
  for (i=0; i < sizeof(socket_address); i++) {
    ((char *) &socket_address)[i] = 0;
  }

  socket_address.sin_family = AF_INET;

  for (i=0; i < host->h_length; i++) {
    ((char *) &socket_address.sin_addr.s_addr)[i] = ((char *) host->h_addr)[i];
  }

  socket_address.sin_port = htons(port);

  if (connect(socket_fd, (struct sockaddr *) &socket_address, sizeof(socket_address)) ↵
< 0) {
    perror("connect() failed");
    return -1;
  }

  return socket_fd;
}
[--code omitted--]
```

Getting the SL4A Source Code

To quote from the home site of SL4A:

> *"SL4A is designed for developers and is alpha quality software."*

This means that you can expect SL4A to go through relatively frequent changes and releases until it moves out of alpha. For this reason, we will present methods by which you can retrieve the SL4A source code.

Cloning the SL4A Source Code

We will show you several options for getting a local copy of the SL4A source code repository.

Installing Mercurial

We recommend that you install a local copy of Mercurial using the following resources:

- Mercurial source code management home:
    - http://mercurial.selenic.com/
    - http://mercurial.selenic.com/about/
- Mercurial downloads:
    - http://mercurial.selenic.com/downloads/
- Mercurial tools:
    - http://mercurial.selenic.com/wiki/OtherTools

> **NOTE:** The Eclipse IDE plugin for Mercurial that we will present later also includes the option of installing the Mercurial executables and binaries for the Windows platform. We prefer to install Mercurial as a stand-alone application and add it to the system PATH variable.

To verify the Mercurial installation on your development computer, execute the following command from the terminal command line:

```
hg -v
```

This should result in output similar to the following:

```
Mercurial Distributed SCM (version 1.6.2)
Copyright (C) 2005-2010 Matt Mackall <mpm@selenic.com> and others
This is free software; see the source for copying conditions.
[--text omitted--]
use "hg help" for the full list of commands
```

Getting SL4A Using the Mercurial Hg Executable

We assume that you have installed a local copy of Mercurial and that it is on your system PATH variable. Enter into a file system directory of your choice using the terminal command line and execute the following command:

```
hg clone https://android-scripting.googlecode.com/hg/ android-scripting
```

This should result in output somewhat similar to the following:

```
hg clone https://android-scripting.googlecode.com/hg/ android-scripting
requesting all changes
adding changesets
```

```
adding manifests
adding file changes
added 1066 changesets with 34881 changes to 28397 files
updating to branch default
11207 files updated, 0 files merged, 0 files removed, 0 files unresolved
```

Using Mercurial with Eclipse

You can install the Mercurial plugin for Eclipse from the update location below:

- Eclipse Mercurial plugin:
    - `http://javaforge.com/project/HGE`
- Eclipse Mercurial plugin update site:
    - `http://cbes.javaforge.com/update`

Figure 5–22 displays the form required for installing the Eclipse Mercurial plugin.

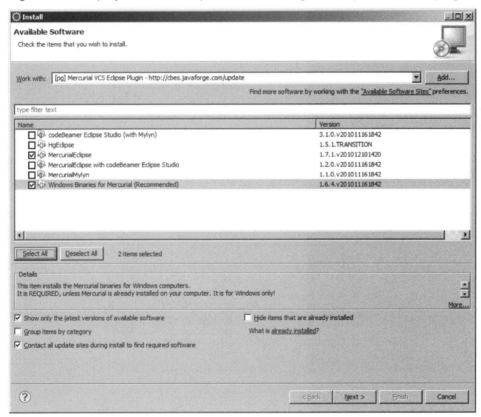

Figure 5–22. *Eclipse Mercurial plugin*

We will not follow the whole sequence here, but Figure 5–23 displays the form required for cloning a Mercurial repository from within Eclipse.

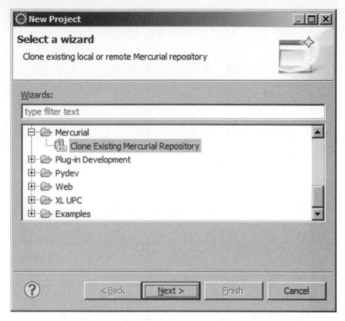

Figure 5-23. *Cloning a Mercurial repository with the Eclipse Mercurial plugin*

Using Mercurial with IntelliJ IDEA

You can install the Mercurial plugin for IntelliJ IDEA from the following location:

- IntelliJ IDEA Mercurial plugin:
    - http://plugins.intellij.net/plugin/?id=3370
    - https://bitbucket.org/willemv/hg4idea

Figure 5-24 displays the form required for using the IntelliJ IDEA Mercurial plugin. This will allow you to clone a Mercurial repository from the IDE.

Figure 5-24. *IntelliJ IDEA Mercurial plugin*

Again, we will not follow the whole sequence here, but Figure 5-25 displays the form required for cloning a Mercurial repository from within IntelliJ IDEA.

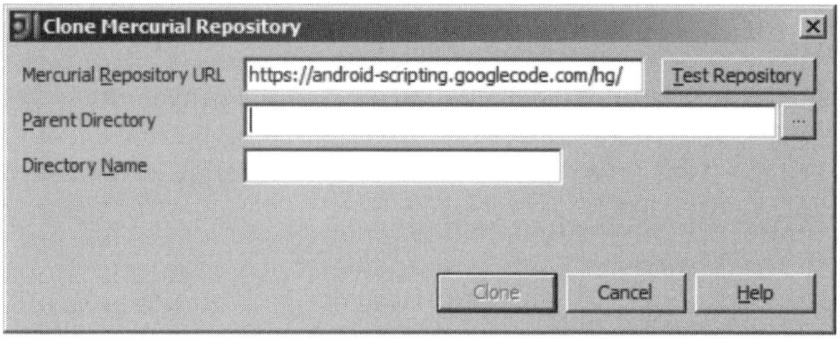

Figure 5–25. *Cloning a Mercurial repository with the IntelliJ IDEA Mercurial plugin*

SL4A Hello World Examples

To get an idea of the spirit of SL4A, here are some basic examples in different scripting languages. Install the interpreters and try them out.

- BeanShell:

```
source("/sdcard/com.googlecode.bshforandroid/extras/bsh/android.bsh");
droid = Android();
droid.call("makeToast", "Hello, Android!");
```

- JavaScript:

```
load("/sdcard/com.googlecode.rhinoforandroid/extras/rhino/android.js");
var droid = new Android();
droid.makeToast("Hello, Android!");
```

- Perl:

```
use Android;
my $a = Android->new();
$a->makeToast("Hello Practical Android Projects!");
```

- Python:

```
import android
andy = android.Android()
andy.makeToast("Hello Practical Android Projects!")
```

- Ruby:

```
droid = Android.new
droid.makeToast "Hello Practical Android Projects!"
```

- TCL:

```
package require android
set android [android new]
$android makeToast "Hello, Android!"
```

We hope that this will encourage you to study SL4A in more depth.

Summary

The main objective of this chapter was to introduce you to the Scripting Layer for Android (SL4A) platform. SL4A is a growing topic and is well worth investigating in depth.

We helped you get a basic understanding of how SL4A works and to be able to use it to run your own scripts on the Android platform.

You now have enough information to clone your own copy of the SL4A source code repository in order to build SL4A yourself.

Chapter 6

Creating a GUI with HTML/JavaScript and AIR

The Android SDK and development environment provide a rich set of tools for developing applications. The biggest drawback to these tools is their lack of cross-platform support. It is true that many of the simpler Java classes provide some level of cross-platform functionality, but when it comes to the UI, it is a different story. It would be a considerable task to write an Android application in a display-agnostic way using the standard Android tool chain. One solution to this cross-platform problem is to write your application in an alternative language and framework that is supported on Android.

At this stage in the game, JavaScript probably provides a developer with the greatest number of supported devices. If you can boil your application down to a web page or two, you have a better chance of getting it working on a larger number of devices. However, JavaScript and HTML bring their own set of cross-platform issues. Consider how much effort web developers must put into cross-browser testing and validation. This same complexity applies to deploying a web-based application on a mobile device, which has its own browser, with its own quirks.

JavaScript and HTML work as a cross-platform solution because browsers must provide a reasonably complete and consistent way of rendering web pages. Similarly, Flash is a good platform for cross-platform application development. Flash applications can also be installed as native applications through Adobe's packaging and deployment tool called AIR. The combination of the large browser penetration of the Flash runtime, along with the potential for more traditional application deployment through AIR, makes the Flash runtime a good choice for cross-platform development. As of Android 2.2, AIR is supported as a first-class citizen.

Developers who consider Flash development an artifact from the 90s are in some ways correct. However, Adobe has done a lot work to bring modern development practices to the Flash runtime. Today, Flash development is done with a set of tools and libraries called Flex. With Flex, you can create modern applications that run on the Flash runtime. Building a UI with Flex is very similar to how Android applications are built, or even

AWT/Swing applications, and should be easy to pick up for any developer who has built a UI with Java.

Though the number of devices that can run Flash is smaller than the number of devices that can render a web page, Flash has at least one advantage: it is written and maintained by a single company. While there are many browsers, written by many different companies, Adobe is the sole author of Flash and this greatly reduces the number of cross-platform surprises, which reduces the overhead for cross-platform development.

Both Flash and JavaScript/HTML have advantages and disadvantages for solving the cross-platform issue. This chapter will explore an application written once in JavaScript/HTML and again in Flex. We will explore what is required to get the applications running on an Android device, and hopefully illuminate each technology enough to help guide a developer looking for a cross-platform solution that includes Android.

We will configure an Android project with the Eclipse plug-in to host our web application as if it was a native app. This will include setting up the basic Android views to view a local web page and describe where the web page should be stored in the project. Once we have the project configured, we will explore the HTML and JavaScript itself, explaining how the application handles user interaction, displaying and animating graphics, and how JavaScript can interact with Java code running on the device.

The second section of this chapter will describe how to set up a Flex/AIR application using Eclipse and the Flash Builder plug-in. Once this project is configured, we will describe how to package it for use with Android and explain how the application works.

Setting Up an Android Project to Display a Web Application

There are two example projects associated with this chapter. We want to look at the one called 06_HtmlOnAndroid first. The basic idea with this application is that it is simply a HTML file bundled in an Android application and is displayed in a `WebView`. In fact, before we look at the Android project at all, look at Figure 6–1, which shows the application in a web browser.

Figure 6–1 shows is a square area in which a number of different circles, or orbs, are drawn. A user can select a pair of orbs to trade places by clicking on them. If orbs of a like type form a complete vertical or horizontal line, they are whisked away and the user's score is incremented. The user's score is presented at the top of the screen along with a high score.

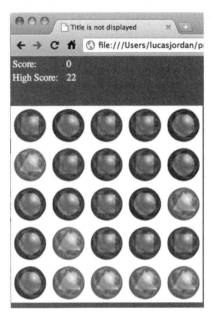

Figure 6-1. *Application running in a web browser*

In this section you will learn how to configure an Android project to display local HTML as if it was a native application. We will also discuss how the HTML and JavaScript works. Lastly, we will cover how to call Java methods from JavaScript.

The Android Project

Android provides a very capable UI component called `WebView` that can be used to display HTML content. The `WebView` class is standard on Android and does not require anything special to use. The entry point in the 06_HtmlOnAndroid project is the class `HtmlOnAndroid` and shows how little code is required to get this type of application set up. Listing 6–1 shows the `onCreate` method of `HtmlOnAndroid`.

Listing 6–1. *HtmlOnAndroid.onCreate()*

```
@Override
public void onCreate(Bundle savedInstanceState) {
        super.onCreate(savedInstanceState);
        webView = new WebView(this);
        webView.getSettings().setJavaScriptEnabled(true);
        webView.loadUrl("file:///android_asset/index.html");
        webView.addJavascriptInterface(new JavaScriptInterface(), "android");
        webView.setScrollBarStyle(WebView.SCROLLBARS_INSIDE_OVERLAY);

        setContentView(webView);
}
```

In Listing 6–1 we see that a new `WebView` is created and set as the `contentView`. This makes the `WebView` the only component visible in the application, allowing us to have a full screen JavaScript/HTML application. After the `WebView` is created, a number of methods are called on the `WebView`. These methods enable functionality that is required by our application.

The call to `webView.getSettings().setJavaScriptEnabled(true)` is critical for our application because it allows the JavaScript to run, which defines the actual game. By default, JavaScript is disabled on new `WebView`s, perhaps for performance or security reasons.

In order to set the web page displayed by the `WebView` a call to `loadUrl` is made. As can be seen in Listing 6–1 we are setting the starting URL to `file:///android_asset/index.html`. The `index.html` file is located in the assets directory of the project. By default, any files stored in the assets directory are available on the device at the path `file:///android_asset/`.

Without modification, an application with a single WebView has a lot of extra stuff on the screen. We want to get rid of as much of this clutter as possible to make room for the application and to make it look more native. See Figure 6–2, which shows the application before and after our cosmetic changes are made.

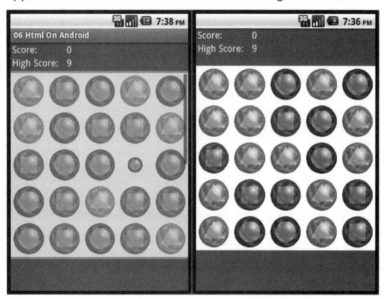

Figure 6–2. *Default Android app vs. cleaned-up app*

You can see on the left that there is a header to the `WebView` and scroll bars on the right. The method call `setScrollBarStyle` is used to remove the default scroll bars of the `WebView`. Since this is a simple, full-screen application, we can remove the scroll bars to increase the viewing area and prevent some user confusion. To further increase the amount of screen area in the `AndroidManifest.xml` file, we set the theme of the application to `@android:style/Theme.NoTitleBar` as can be seen in Listing 6–2.

Listing 6–2. *AndroidManifest.xml*

```xml
<?xml version="1.0" encoding="utf-8"?>
<manifest xmlns:android="http://schemas.android.com/apk/res/android"
      package="org.ljordan.anrdoid.chapter06"
      android:versionCode="1"
      android:versionName="1.0">
    <application android:icon="@drawable/icon" android:label="@string/app_name">
        <activity android:name=".HtmlOnAndroid"
                 android:label="@string/app_name"
                 android:theme="@android:style/Theme.NoTitleBar">
            <intent-filter>
                <action android:name="android.intent.action.MAIN" />
                <category android:name="android.intent.category.LAUNCHER" />
            </intent-filter>
        </activity>
    </application>
    <uses-permission android:name="android.permission.INTERNET" />
        <uses-permission android:name="android.permission.ACCESS_GPS" />
        <uses-permission android:name="android.permission.ACCESS_ASSISTED_GPS" />
        <uses-permission android:name="android.permission.ACCESS_LOCATION" />
        <uses-permission android:name="android.permission.ACCESS_COARSE_LOCATION" />
        <uses-permission android:name="android.permission.ACCESS_FINE_LOCATION" />
</manifest>
```

Listing 6–2 shows the `AndroidManifest.xml` file for this project. Besides setting our theme for the application, we also define the permissions required by this application. It is important to note that the permissions of an application apply to an application that lives in a `WebView` as well. For example, if your application wants to make a call to an external server through JavaScript, you must include the `INTERNET` permission. This is also true for the HTML5 location API, you must set the `ACCESS_GPS` and probably the `ACCESS_FINE_LOCATION` for this feature to work in your web view the way you want.

Calling Android Methods from JavaScript

To make JavaScript applications capable of fully utilizing the host device on which they run, the Android SDK provides a mechanism for JavaScript to make calls into the Android Java environment. This is important, since it frees developers from worrying about whether or not some piece of functionality is available in the `WebView`. In Listing 6–1 the method `addJavascriptInterface` is called on the `WebView` object and a new instance of a class called `JavaScriptInterface` and the String "android" are passed in. This creates a global variable called `android` available to any JavaScript running within this `WebView`. The `android` object is considered to be a `JavaScriptInterface` and JavaScript can call any method defined by that class. The `JavaScriptInterface` class can be named anything, as it is a class defined in this project and can be found in the `HtmlOnAndroid.java` file. Listing 6–3 shows the details.

Listing 6-3. *JavaScriptInterface definition*

```
final class JavaScriptInterface {
    JavaScriptInterface() {
    }

    public int getScreenWidth() {
        return webView.getWidth();
    }

    public int getScreenHeight() {
        // Removing 5 pixels to prevent vertical scrolling.
        return webView.getHeight() - 5;
    }

    public int getHighScore() {
        SharedPreferences preferences = getPreferences(MODE_WORLD_WRITEABLE);
        return preferences.getInt(KEY_HIGH_SCORE, 0);
    }

    public void setHighScore(int value) {
        SharedPreferences preferences = getPreferences(MODE_PRIVATE);
        Editor editor = preferences.edit();
        editor.putInt(KEY_HIGH_SCORE, value);
        editor.commit();
    }

}
```

You can see that the `JavaScriptInterface` class is very simple. It does not even implement an interface. It simply provides a bunch of methods that can be called from JavaScript. The application is going to take advantage of this class by using it to get the size of the `WebView` and to read and write a high score, so it can be saved between sessions. The purpose of this `android` object will become clear in the next section, in which we explore the JavaScript application in detail.

It is important to highlight two issues when exposing an Android object to the JavaScript in a `WebView`. First, a different thread will perform any method call originating in JavaScript than the thread used to created the WebView. The class AsyncTask can be used to help synchronize work between the UI thread and any background thread. The use of the class AsyncTask is covered in Chapter 7. Second, and perhaps more important, these methods are exposed to any JavaScript running within the `WebView`. This may very well include JavaScript from an untrusted site. Take care that the functionally exposed is harmless or that the `WebView` is constrained to only show trusted code. The simplest way to do this is to not link to any external sites or to not include the `INTERNET` permission.

JavaScript Application

Once we have the Android application set up with a `WebView`, we can focus our development attention on creating an application with standard web tools. JavaScript development has come a long way over the years. If you don't have a lot of experience developing JavaScript applications, explore Google's Chrome web browser and the development tools that are included with it. In Chrome, check under the View menu, and you will find a sub-menu called Developer which contains a number of tools. You will find a tree view, showing the DOM of the current page, a list of resources referenced by the page, a JavaScript debugger, and a whole lot more. Figure 6–3 shows an example of these tools.

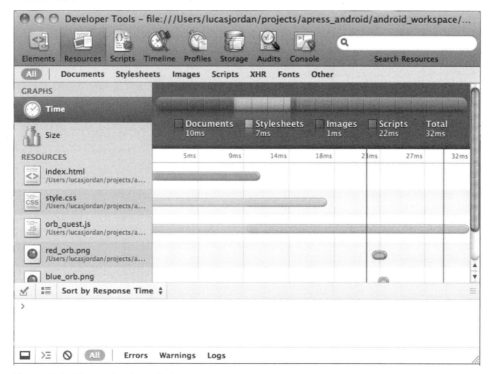

Figure 6–3. *Chrome developer tools*

> **TIP:** Redeploying your JavaScript application onto a mobile device can be a big waste of time during development. Try using a browser like Chrome to develop and debug your web application, then deploy once in a while to your Android device for validation. Download Chrome at www.google.com/chrome.

The starting point for this web application is the file index.html, which is shown in Listing 6–4.

Listing 6–4. *index.html*

```
<!DOCTYPE html>
<html>
<head>

<meta charset="UTF-8">
```

```html
    <title>Title is not displayed</title>

    <link rel="stylesheet" type="text/css" href="style.css" />

    <script type="text/javascript" src="orb_quest.js"></script>

</head>
<body onload="onLoad()" style="background-color: #666666;margin: 0" >
<div>

        <table style="position: absolute;color: #FFFFFF">
          <tr >
            <td><div>Score:</div></td>
            <td><div id="score" style="padding-left: 10px">0</div></td>
          </tr>
          <tr >
            <td><div>High Score:</div></td>
            <td><div id="highScore" style="padding-left: 10px">0</div></td>
          </tr>
        </table>

        <canvas style="position: absolute;" id="canvas" ></canvas>

</div>
</body>
</html>
```

In Listing 6–4 you see the content of the `index.html`. The `index.html` references the style file `style.css` and the script file `orb_quest.js`. In addition to these external files, we have a table for holding the score and high score information, as well as an HTML5 canvas tag. The animation portion of the game is done with a `canvas` element to explore some of the HTML5 features supported by the Android browser. Before we look at the JavaScript code which is the heart of this application, let's consider the CSS file shown in Listing 6–5.

Listing 6–5. *style.css*

```
@CHARSET "UTF-8";

canvas {
        -webkit-tap-highlight-color: rgba(0, 0, 0, 0);
}

body {
        background-color: rgb(128,128,128);
}
```

In Listing 6–5 is a very simple CSS file. In a more complex application, there is no doubt that this file would be much larger, defining many styles used throughout the application. In our case, the only declaration that really matters is the `canvas` element that states that the highlight color should be invisible. More precisely, the color is defined to be black with zero opacity. This is important in our sample application because, by default, images touched in an Android browser become selected and are shown with a blue highlight. For whatever reason a canvas element is treated the same way as an image. Because the user will be tapping this component to play the game, we want to disable this default behavior. Setting the background to gray was done to help the screenshots of this application come though in print.

The body element in the `index.html` file calls the JavaScript function `onLoad` when it is loaded. This function is defined in the JavaScript file `orb_quest.js`. The application logic that drives this game is found in that same JavaScript file. Listing 6–6 shows the `onLoad` function.

Listing 6–6. *orb_quest.js (onLoad Function)*

```
function onLoad(){
        var red_orb = new Image();
        red_orb.src = "images/red_orb.png";
        orb_images.push(red_orb);

        var blue_orb = new Image();
        blue_orb.src = "images/blue_orb.png";
        orb_images.push(blue_orb);

        var green_orb = new Image();
        green_orb.src = "images/green_orb.png";
        orb_images.push(green_orb);

        scoreElement = document.getElementById("score");
        highScoreElement = document.getElementById("highScore");


        highScore = getHighScore();
        highScoreElement.innerHTML = highScore;

        var canvas = document.getElementById("canvas");
        var screenWidth = getScreenWidth();
        var screenHeight = getScreenHeight();

        if (screenWidth < screenHeight){
                canvasSize = screenWidth;
                var top = (screenHeight-canvasSize)/2.0;
                canvas.style.top = top + "px";
        } else {
                canvasSize = screenHeight;
                var left = (screenWidth-canvasSize)/2.0
                canvas.style.left = left + "px";
        }
        canvas.setAttribute("width", canvasSize);
        canvas.setAttribute("height", canvasSize);

        canvas.addEventListener("click", canvasClick, false);

        ctx = canvas.getContext("2d");


        for(var i=0;i<coordCount;i++){
                coord.push(oneFifth*i+oneTenth);
        }
        for (var col=0;col<coordCount;col++){
                for (var row=0;row<coordCount;row++){
                        sprites.push(new Sprite("Orb", randomOrbImage(), coord[col],↵
```

```
            coord[row], oneFifth));
            }
        }

        setInterval("renderScene()", 1000/30);
}
```

The onLoad function in Listing 6–6 handles a number of the things required to get the application up and running. The method defines a number of images, which represent each type of orb, and stores them in the array orb_images. The score, highscore, and canvas elements from the document are identified and stored in global variables, because they will be accessed throughout the life of the application. The canvas element is resized by getting the desired height and width by calling getScreenHeight and getScreenWidth. These methods are shown in Listing 6–7. The last thing that the onLoad function does is register a click listener method on the canvas and add a bunch of starting orbs. Before we move on to some of the details about how this application draws and handles user input, let's look at the getScreenHeight and getScreenWidth functions, because they show how the JavaScript application can communicate with the host Android application.

Listing 6–7. *Functions that call into Android*

```
function getScreenWidth(){
        if (android){
                return android.getScreenWidth();
        } else {
                return 320;
        }
}
function getScreenHeight(){
        if (android){
                return android.getScreenHeight();
        } else {
                return 480;
        }
}
function setHighScore(value){
        if (localStorage && typeof(localStorage) != 'undefined') {
                localStorage.setItem("HighScore", value);
                return value;
        } else {
                if (android){
                        android.setHighScore(value);
                        return value;
                }
        }
        //not actually saved
        return value;
}
function getHighScore(){
        if (localStorage && typeof(localStorage) != 'undefined') {
                var value = localStorage.getItem("HighScore");
                if (value) {
                        return parseInt(value);
                }
                //Maybe it is not set yet.
```

```
                return 0;
        } else {
            if (android){
                    return android.getHighScore();
            }
        }
        //no local storage, not on android... just return zero.
        return 0;
}
```

In Listing 6–7 there are four functions: `getScreenHeight` and `getScreenWidth` are used to set the size of the application, and `getHighScore` and `setHighScore` are used to keep track of any high score that is achieved. The functions that concern themselves with screen size first check to see if the variable named `android` is defined. The variable android is declared in JavaScript, but is only set to a value if this JavaScript is running within the WebView of our application. The variable will be null if the JavaScript is running in any other browser, including a browser on an Android device. If the variable has a value, a call to the corresponding function on the `android` variable is made. Note that the function names are identical to the method names defined in Listing 6–3 for the class `JavaScriptInterface`. Simply put, the function calls made on the JavaScript `android` variable are method calls performed on the `JavaScriptInterface` object created in the `onCreate` method from Listing 6–1.

If the `android` variable is not set, a fallback value is provided. In a more complex application, the values returned could be the size of the browser window, or something else. In our case, we just tell the application to show up in a browser with about the same size at a mobile screen. We would use this fallback pattern if we intended to use this application on a regular web page, beyond our application.

The functions `getHighScore` and `setHighScore` provided a slightly more complex example of mixing browser functionality with Android functionality. Instead of first checking to see if the android variable is set, each function checks to see if a variable `localStorage` is present and defined. The variable `localStorage` is another HTML5 technology used to store user data. The HTML5 local storage API is basically a key value pair. If local storage is not available the application tries to use the `android` variable to store and retrieve data. See Listing 6–3 to see how this is done in Android.

> **TIP:** Learn more than you ever wanted to know about HTML5 at http://dev.w3.org/html5/html-author/.

Graphics and Animation

There are many ways to render content onto a web page: simple HTML, SVG, and now the canvas tag. Although the focus of this book is on Android and not HTML5 or canvas, it is worth exploring the details of how this application works in order to make a valid evaluation of this approach to application development on Android.

The heart of this application is the canvas tag defined in the index.html file. A canvas tag defines a region of the page where graphics will be programmatically drawn. This is different from the HTML DOM or an SVG element, which define a scene graph that can be manipulated with JavaScript. It is true that many visual effects can be achieved with these tools, but not all effects can be efficiently achieved, such as pixel-level drawing. This is where canvas comes in: it allows pixel-level drawing and provides a number of helper functions for things like lines, arcs, paths, text, and images.

To draw on the canvas element, we must get access to a context object for that canvas. In order to get the context, a call to canvas.getContext("2d") is made. By specifying "2d," we get back a context with a number of 2D drawing functions. Those with a Java2D background will find the drawing functions on the canvas context very familiar. There are functions for setting the draw and fill color, functions for drawing lines and arcs to support paths, and functions for setting the rotate, scale, and translate to provide full support for transformations.

In order to achieve an animation instead of just a single static image, we set up a timer to render the scene 30 times a second. This is done by calling setInterval("renderScene()", 1000/30). It is not strictly necessary in our application to draw the scene continuously; we could imagine that we stop rendering while waiting for the user to click the canvas. For simplicity, we render constantly. Each time renderScene is called, we increment a variable called currentTick. The variable currentTick gives us a way to know how many times we have rendered the scene. This is useful when we want to know how far along we are in a particular animation and when we should stop animating.

The basic strategy of this application is to create a list of items drawn on the canvas (Sprites), define a way of expressing their motion, and create a function for drawing them. Let's start with the definitions of the orbs as shown in Listing 6–8.

Listing 6–8. *Sprites*

```
function Sprite(type, img, centerX, centerY, scale) {
        this.type = type;
        this.img = img;
        this.centerX = centerX;
        this.centerY = centerY;
        this.scale = scale;
}
```

In Listing 6–8 we can see a function that creates a Sprite variable. Each Sprite has a type, an image, a location, and a scale. In our case, we are only going to create Sprites with one of the three orb images included with the application. In Listing 6–6, a number of starting orbs are created and placed in the array orb_images. This array is used to store all orbs visible on the screen and generally track game state.

In order to animate the orbs, we create a second type of variables defined by the function Transformation, as seen in Listing 6–9.

Listing 6-9. *Transformation*

```
function Transformation(startTick,endTick,startValue,endValue,field,
tweenFunction,sprite, whenDone) {
        this.startTick = startTick;
        this.endTick = endTick;
        this.startValue = startValue;
        this.endValue = endValue;
        this.field = field;
        this.tweenFunction = tweenFunction;
        this.sprite = sprite;
        this.whenDone = whenDone;
}
```

A `Transformation` describes a change in a `Sprite`'s visual appearance over time. Instead of writing functions that move or scale a sprite as part of a given animation, a `Transformation` provides a simple API for defining these animations. The two values `startTick` and `endTick` define a period of time when this `Transformation` is active. The value `field` describes which value on a `Sprite` this `Transformation` will change. The idea is that during the period between `startTick` and `endTick` this `Transformation` will set a value of a `Sprite` to some value between `startValue` and `endValue`. Let's consider the example `Transformation` shown in Listing 6-10.

Listing 6-10. *Example Transformation*

```
new Transformation(10, 100, .2, .7,"centerX","linear", orb);
```

Listing 6-10 shows a `Transformation` being created that will animate the `centerX` value of an orb from 20 to 70 percent of the way across the canvas. This animation will happen during the period between tick 10 and 100. The `linear` string indicates which `tweenFunction` should be used to describe the motion of the orb. The string `linear` indicates that each passing tick will move the orb the same distance each time. There are two other possible `tweenFunctions` included with this example: `windupovershoot` and `easeboth`. These other functions provide a more pleasant animation than simply linear, and are used to make the scene livelier.

We now have a way of describing the items in the scene and how they move. By creating instances of `Sprite` and `Transformation` and storing them in the arrays `sprites` and `trans`, we can create a scene in a great number of states. These two arrays are used by the function `renderScene` to actually draw the scene onto the `canvas` element, as seen in Listing 6-11.

Listing 6-11. *renderScene*

```
function renderScene(){
        ctx.fillStyle = "rgb(256,256,256)";
        ctx.fillRect(0,0,canvasSize,canvasSize);

        var oldTransIndex = [];

        for (var i=0;i<trans.length;i++){
                var tran = trans[i];
                if (tran.endTick >= currentTick){
                        applyTransformation(tran, currentTick);
                } else {
```

```
                        oldTransIndex.push(i);
                }
        }
        oldTransIndex.reverse();
        for (var i=0;i<oldTransIndex.length;i++){
                trans.splice(oldTransIndex[i], 1);
        }

        for (var i=0;i<sprites.length;i++){
                renderSprite(ctx, sprites[i]);
        }
        currentTick++;
}
```

In Listing 6–11 the first thing done is to set the fill color and then call `fillRect`. These two operations clear the canvas of any visual artifacts from the previous call to `renderScene`, giving us a clean slate on which we can draw. The `renderScene` function then applies each `Transformation` that will change the location or scale values of the `Sprites` they are assigned to. If the range of ticks is less than the value of `currentTick`, the `Transformation` is done and marked for deletion. Then each sprite is rendered to the canvas. Let's consider how `Transformations` are applied and how `Sprites` are rendered in turn. Listing 6–12 shows how `Transformations` update the value of a given `Sprite`.

Listing 6–12. *applyTransformation*

```
function applyTransformation(trans, tick){
        if (tick >= trans.startTick && tick <= trans.endTick){
                if (trans.sprite){
                        var fraction = (tick-trans.startTick)/(trans.endTick -
 trans.startTick);
                        fraction = eval(trans.tweenFunction + "(" + fraction + ")");
                        var value = trans.startValue + (trans.endValue -
 trans.startValue)*fraction;
                        var expression = "trans.sprite." + trans.field + " = " + value;
                        eval(expression);
                }
                if (tick == trans.endTick){
                        if (trans.whenDone){
                                eval(trans.whenDone);
                        }
                }
        }
}
```

In Listing 6–12, after checking that the `tick` value is within range, we calculate what fraction of ticks has passed since `startTick` and the `endTick` of the `Transformation`. The `fraction` value is then passed to the `tweenFunction` that weights the `fraction`. The final value is then calculated based on the modified `fraction` and the defined `startValue` and `endValue`. This final value is then applied to the appropriate field on the `Sprite`. Last, a callback function called `whenDone` is called in case we need to know when this particular `Transformation` is done.

Once each `Sprite` has had chance to be modified by one or more `Transformations`, it is drawn to the canvas. Listing 6–13 shows how this is done.

Listing 6–13. *renderSprite*

```
function renderSprite(ctx, sprite){
        ctx.save();

        var widthInPixels = canvasSize*sprite.scale;
        var scale = widthInPixels/sprite.img.width;
        var centerX = canvasSize*sprite.centerX-(widthInPixels/2.0);
        var centerY = canvasSize*sprite.centerY-(widthInPixels/2.0);

        ctx.translate(centerX, centerY);
        ctx.scale(scale, scale);
        ctx.drawImage(sprite.img, 0, 0);

        ctx.restore();
}
```

In Listing 6–13 we want to translate the drawing location of the `ctx` object in order to draw the `Sprite` at the appropriate place. Since we don't want to keep track of the state of the `ctx` variable, we can use the save and restore functions to modify the state of the `ctx` in any way we want. We know that a call to `restore` will undo all changes. Using the sprites scale and location, we simply call `drawImage` to pass in the image associated with the `Sprite` to draw each `Sprite` on the `canvas`.

User Interaction

We have described how the application is set up and have created a simple but limited API to describe the game scene. The last bit of logic we have to look at is how user interaction affects the game state. User interaction starts with the functions `canvasClick` that is called when a mouse or finger clicks the `canvas` element. Listing 6–14 shows this function in detail.

Listing 6–14. *canvasClick*

```
function canvasClick(e){
        if (trans.length == 0){
                if (selectedOrb){
                        var secondOrb = findOrbForXY(e.layerX, e.layerY);
                        if (secondOrb != selectedOrb){

                                var endOfScale = currentTick + 15
                                trans.push(new Transformation(currentTick, endOfScale,↵
 oneFifth,oneTenth,"scale","windupovershoot",secondOrb));

                                var endOfTranslate = endOfScale + 15;
                                trans.push(new Transformation(endOfScale,↵
 endOfTranslate,secondOrb.centerX,selectedOrb.centerX,"centerX","easeboth",secondOrb,↵
 null));
                                trans.push(new Transformation(endOfScale,↵
 endOfTranslate,secondOrb.centerY,selectedOrb.centerY,"centerY","easeboth",secondOrb,↵
 null));
                                trans.push(new Transformation(endOfScale,↵
 endOfTranslate,selectedOrb.centerX,secondOrb.centerX,"centerX","easeboth",↵
 selectedOrb, null));
```

```
                        trans.push(new Transformation(endOfScale,↵
    endOfTranslate,selectedOrb.centerY,secondOrb.centerY,"centerY","easeboth",↵
    selectedOrb, null));

                        trans.push(new Transformation(endOfTranslate,↵
    endOfTranslate+15,oneTenth,oneFifth,"scale","windupovershoot",secondOrb, null));
                        trans.push(new Transformation(endOfTranslate,↵
    endOfTranslate+15,oneTenth,oneFifth,"scale","windupovershoot",selectedOrb,↵
    "checkForGroups()"));

                    var indexA = sprites.indexOf(secondOrb);
                    var indexB = sprites.indexOf(selectedOrb);

                    sprites[indexB] = secondOrb;
                    sprites[indexA] = selectedOrb;

                    selectedOrb = null;
                }
            } else {
                selectedOrb = findOrbForXY(e.layerX, e.layerY);
                trans.push(new Transformation(currentTick, currentTick +↵
    15,oneFifth,oneTenth,"scale","windupovershoot",selectedOrb, null));
            }
        }
    }
```

In Listing 6–14, we only do anything if the trans array is empty. This means we only care about user input if there are no animations. When a user clicks, we want to know if this is the first or second orb they are clicking. If a click has happened before, the variable selectedOrb will be null; if it is the second time selectedOrb will have a value. We use the function findOrbForXY to figure out where the user clicked and hence, which orb they clicked.

If it was the first orb the user has clicked, we simply record which orb it was in selectedOrb and add a Transformation that scales the selected orb down over the course of 15 ticks (.5 sec). If the user has clicked on a second orb, we want to create a number of Transformations that create the animation of the two orbs changing locations. Last, we swap the locations of the orbs in the array sprites.

We take advantage of the callback function of Transformation to call the function checkForGroups when the last Transformation is done. The checkForGroups function looks for columns and rows that are all of the same type of orb and creates the animations that move the matching orbs off the canvas. Listing 6–15 shows a partial listing of the checkForGroups function.

Listing 6–15. *checkForGroups (partial)*

```
var animatedOrbs = [];

        var endScale = currentTick+15
        var endTrans = endScale+15;
        var matchsFound = 0;

        //check rows
        for (var r=0;r<coordCount;r++){
```

```
                    var allSame = true;
                    var color0 = orbForColRow(0, r).img;
                    for (var c=1;c<coordCount;c++){
                            var colorC = orbForColRow(c, r).img;
                            if (color0 != colorC){
                                    allSame = false;
                                    break;
                            }
                    }
                    if (allSame){
                            matchsFound++;
                            for (var c=0;c<coordCount;c++){
                                    var orb = orbForColRow(c, r);
                                    trans.push(new Transformation(currentTick,↵
 endScale,orb.scale,oneTenth,"scale","windupovershoot",orb));
                                    trans.push(new Transformation(endScale,↵
 endTrans,orb.centerX,orb.centerX+1.0,"centerX","easeboth",orb,↵
 "newOrbAt("+c+","+r+")"));
                            }
                    }
            }
    }
//… ommited column loop
if (matchsFound > 0){
                trans.push(new Transformation(endScale,↵
 endTrans,null,null,null,null,null, "endCheck("+matchsFound+")"));
        }
```

In Listing 6–15 we iterate over each row and column and check to see if all of the orbs are the same type. Listing 6–15 only shows the loop that checks the rows; in the accompanying code you will find the rest of the method that checks the columns. For each row that contains a single type of orb, we create the Transformations that animate each orb off the screen. The Transformation that handles the X (or Y) translation calls the function newOrbAt when it is done; this function simply adds a new orb Sprite to replace the one that is removed. At the end of the checkForMatches function, we check to see if any matches are found. If so, we create one last Transformation whose sole job is to call the function endCheck when all of the Transformations are done animating. Listing 6–16 shows the endCheck function.

Listing 6–16. endCheck

```
function endCheck(numFound){
        score += numFound;
        scoreElement.innerHTML = score;
        checkForGroups();
        if (score > highScore){
                highScore = score;
                highScoreElement.innerHTML = highScore;
                setHighScore(highScore);
        }
}
```

The endCheck function in Listing 6–16 does a little book keeping at the end of our user click event. We update the score by incrementing the variable score and update the display to show this new score. We also call checkForGroups again, in case the orbs generated by the last set of matching rows and columns produce more matches. Last, we update the high score if appropriate by calling `setHighScore`.

JavaScript Summary

The application presented here demonstrates that JavaScript plus HTML5 can be used to create at least a simple game or application. People using web technologies to create applications are probably interested in maximum code reuse, and that is possible. With the new features in HTML5 and the increasing support for these technologies, it is worth exploring this technology fully. In this example we use a `canvas` element to handle a lot of the rendering included in this application. The very simple graphics API creating in this game is just scratching the surface of what is available. Check the numerous and excellent graphics APIs available for rendering to both canvas and SVG. Refer to a library called protovis at `http://vis.stanford.edu/protovis/`. JavaScript is a powerful functional language and can be used to describe not just complex animations but complex applications as well.

Using Flash and Flex Apps on Android with AIR

AIR is an Adobe product that allows Flash applications to be packaged and deployed on many different platforms. The platforms supported are the usual suspects: OS X, Windows, and now Android. Adobe's design philosophy with AIR is that you write an application with their tools and their APIs and they handle the complexity of handling different platforms. This is very similar to the Java philosophy, where the functionality and complexity of the host system is presented with a standard set of APIs. This is great, since we don't have to worry about things like which file system the host application is using. We can simply access the appropriate File API and know that it will work across platforms.

AIR of course does not provided an API for all possible functions of the host device. Like Java, developers find themselves in a tough spot when they are asked to interface with a platform-specific API or hardware component. They may be forced to fall back and make a call to a native library, which by its very nature is not cross-platform and requires special handling code to deal with the case when that native API is absent.

Flex is the tool of choice for creating Flash applications. Flex is a combination of things: it is a set of libraries used by an application to perform basic operations like displaying content or accessing the file system. Flex is also a way of declaratively describing a UI with XML called MXML files. The glue that ties the UI to the libraries is the ActionScript programming language. Finally, the Flex SDK comes with a compiler for turning MXML files and ActionScript files into SWF files. SWF files are analogous to JAR files in Java.

ActionScript is a non-typesafe language that is similar to both JavaScript and Java. ActionScript classes are generally specified in .as files. ActionScript classes are very much like Java classes; they support inheritance and define fields and methods. The non-typesafe nature of ActionScript can be a turn-off to some developers. In practice this makes little difference in day-to-day development, since the Flex compiler is by default configured to generate errors and warnings when code is written in a non-typesafe way. With those protections in place, the majority of ActionScript code is effectively typesafe, and when you need to do something in a non-typesafe way you are free to do so.

In this section you will learn how to set up a Flex project suitable for using with AIR. This project will implement similar functionality as the HTML/JavaScipt version did, so a comparison can be made. We will also look at how an AIR application is packaged for use as an Android application.

Writing a Flex Application for Android

There is a sample project called 06_AirOnAndroid in the accompanying source code. We will be working though the details of this project to give an overview of what is required to write a Flex application with Android in mind.

> **TIP:** The Flex SDK can be downloaded from: www.adobe.com/products/flex/flex_framework/. The Flex SDK includes AIR, which is required to build an Android deployable.

A good way to show that ActionScript is accessible to a Java developer is to look at a simple example class. Listing 6–17 shows the file Orb.as.

Listing 6–17. *Orb.as*

```
package org.orb_quest
{
	import spark.components.Group;
	import spark.primitives.BitmapImage;
	
	public class Orb extends Group
	{
		public var image:BitmapImage;
		
		public function Orb(image:BitmapImage)
		{
			super();
			this.image = image;
			image.smooth = true;
			
			image.x = 512/-2;
			image.y = 512/-2;
			addElement(image);
			
			this.mouseEnabled = false;
			
		}
		public function exampleFunction():String{
			return "example function";
		}
	}
}
```

In Listing 6–17 is the definition of the class Orb. The first difference is the class is contained in a curly bracket block that describes which package this class is in. Besides that cosmetic difference, we see that the definition of the variable image includes the keyword var, and we also notice that the class definition, BitmapImage, comes after the variable name, separated by a colon. I find this variable definition backwards, perhaps from working with Java too much. In any case, after a little time your fingers will retrain themselves. Another difference is the use of the keyword function in both the constructor and the function exampleFunction. This is where a Java developer would expect the return type, which is fact at the end of the definition to the right of the colon. The use of the var and function keywords speaks to the shared history of ActionScript and JavaScript.

Building and Deploying

The example project, 06_AirOnAndroid, is an eclipse project created with the Flash Builder 4 plug-in. Flash Builder 4 is a commercial application and also an eclipse plug-in, and is available for a 30-day trial. While I confess to being a huge fan of open source in its many forms, and would prefer to guide you to an open and free tool, there simply is not one available. The Flex SDK is a free download and can be used without Flash Builder 4, but I find the eclipse integration of Flash Builder 4 critical for my productivity. Besides integrating eclipse with the Flex SDK, it also provides a good editor for MXML and AS files. It also provides code completion, which I can no longer live without.

One catch with Flash Builder 4: if you are running OS X, you must use a build of eclipse that uses the Carbon library. This means the newest version of eclipse you can use is eclipse 3.5 (Galileo).

If you have installed the Flash Builder 4 plug-in and opened the provided sample project, you will notice in the bin-debug directory a number of files. There are two xml files and two swf files. When bundling an application with AIR, you must provided an xml file that describes some properties of the application and an swf file that contains the logic and assets for that application.

As mentioned, there are two xml files and two swf files. This is because there are artifacts generated for a desktop version of the application and a mobile version. If you look in the src directory, you will see the same two XML files, AndroidMain-app.xml and Main-app.xml. The presence of these two files tells Flash Builder 4 to create two sets of applications files. If you want to change a value on one of these xml files, change the one in the src directory, as the one in bin-debug is created as part of the build process.

The reason we need two applications is that, as with the JavaScript version, developing and debugging the application is much easier if you run the application on the desktop. In this case we want to develop and debug the application as an AIR desktop application. In Flex, the root most UI component must be different between desktop applications and Android applications. When we look closer at the actual Flex code, this will become clear.

By default, eclipse automatically builds the project after each file save, so you don't really have to worry about the details of how this gets done. If you are not using Flash Builder 4, at the root of the project directory you will find two hidden files names .actionScriptProperties and .flexProperties. These two files contain all of the information required to build this project with just the Flex SDK.

In the root of the project directory you will also find two scripts, one called `install.sh` and one called `package.sh`. These two files are shown in Listing 6–18 and Listing 6–20.

Listing 6–18. *package.sh*

```bash
#!/bin/bash
cd bin-debug
~/tools/flex/flex_sdk_4.1.0.16076_AIR_2.5/bin/adt -package -target apk-debug↵
 -storetype pkcs12 -storepass password -keystore ../cert.p12 06_AirOnAndroid.apk↵
 AndroidMain-app.xml AndroidMain.swf
```

In Listing 6–18 we see that we use the AIR tool called `adt` to package up the compiled swf with the application description found in the xml file. The `target` command of apk-debug tells AIR to build a deployable suitable for Android. The output of this command is the file `06_AirInAndroid.apk,` which is signed with the `cert.p12` file. Once the signed apk is generated, it is ready to be installed on an Android device or emulator.

One thing you might notice is that there is no AndroidManifest.xml file used in this process. AIR allows us to declare this information with the application xml file. Listing 6–19 shows the Android specific portion of the `AndroidMain-app.xml` file.

Listing 6–19. *AndroidMain-app.xml (partial)*

```xml
<manifestAdditions>

    <!-- Set the manifest properties in AndroidManifest.xml Optional. -->
    <manifest>

    <!-- Set the attributes for manifest. Optional -->
    <!-- <attribute name="android:installLocation" value="auto"/> -->

    <!-- Set the data part for manifest. Optional. -->
    <data>
        <![CDATA[
        <uses-permission android:name="android.permission.INTERNET"/>
        <uses-permission android:name="android.permission.WRITE_EXTERNAL_STORAGE"/>
        <uses-permission android:name="android.permission.ACCESS_FINE_LOCATION"/>
        <uses-configuration android:reqFiveWayNav="true"/>
        <supports-screens android:normalScreens="true"/>
        <uses-feature android:required="true"↵
android:name="android.hardware.touchscreen.multitouch"/>
        ]]>
    </data>
    </manifest>

    <!-- Set the application properties in AndroidManifest.xml Optional. -->
    <!--<application> -->

    <!-- Set the attributes for application. Optional -->
    <!-- <attribute name="android:enabled" value="true"/> -->
```

```
    <!-- Set the data part for application. Optional. -->
    <!-- <data>
        <![CDATA[
          <uses-library android:name="android.view"/>
        ]]>
       </data> -->
<!--</application> -->

<!-- Set the launcherActivity properties in AndroidManifest.xml Optional. -->
<!--<launcherActivity> -->

<!-- Set the attributes for launcherActivity. Optional -->
<!--<attribute name="android:excludeFromRecents" value="false"/> -->

<!--- Set the data part for launcherActivity. Optional. -->
<!-- <data>
       <![CDATA[
          <intent-filter>
          </intent-filter>
       ]]>
       </data> -->
<!-- </launcherActivity> -->

</manifestAdditions>
```

The element manifestAdditions shown in Listing 6–19 contains the information that would normally go in the AndroidManifest.xml file. In our case, the only element that is not commented out is the first data element. It contains the permission XML we would like to include with our application. The rest of the content is commented out, but with the included documentation it is easy to find the right location for anything you might wish to include.

Listing 6–20 shows the Android `adb` tool being used to install the new apk on any running emulator. There is nothing about this command that should be a surprise. We are using the standard method to install an Android application. Listing 6–20 is a script is from my development environment running on OS X. You will need to adjust this script to match your local installation of Android or make your own if you are running Windows.

Listing 6–20. *install.sh*

```
#!/bin/bash
cd bin-debug
~/tools/android/android-sdk-mac_86/tools/adb -e install -r 06_AirOnAndroid.apk
```

Android 2.2 supports AIR applications, but I suspect not all vendors will include AIR on their devices. If an AIR application is installed on a device without the AIR runtime installed, the user will be prompted to install AIR when they first run the application. Figure 6–4 shows the prompt the user will see.

Figure 6–4. *User prompt to install AIR*

This prompt never worked for me. As a result I was forced to find and install the AIR runtime manually on the device before the application would run. Hopefully this is just an issue with the emulator, but it should be noted as a possible hazard of using AIR on Android. Not being able to get the application running seamlessly on a user's device will be a deal breaker for a lot of people. If all goes well, you will see the application running on your device or emulator, it should look like Figure 6–5.

Figure 6–5. *The AIR application running on Android*

In Figure 6–5 we see the application up and running on Android. There is the familiar grid of orbs and the current and high scores. The game is played in exactly the same way: click on two orbs to make them change places. If you create a row or a column of like types, the orbs are cleared and the score is increased. What differs is the implementation.

Creating the Flex UI with MXML

Flex uses the XML markup in the MXML files to describe the component tree of the application. Not every component is necessarily visible at all times. Flex provides special components that can be used to show one set of children or another, like a tabbed view. The basic philosophy of Flex is that you should think of the application, including all possible views, as a single tree of components. The component tree then "binds" to a data model, which dictates which view is visible and what data is displayed. This is similar to the Android philosophy of separating the UI from the application logic. In Android the UI is often defined in XML files that the application instantiates in order to display the UI. Let's consider the entry point for this application, the file AndroidMain.mxml, as shown in Listing 6–21.

Listing 6–21. *AndroidMain.mxml*

```
<?xml version="1.0" encoding="utf-8"?>
<s:Application xmlns:fx="http://ns.adobe.com/mxml/2009"
               xmlns:s="library://ns.adobe.com/flex/spark"
               xmlns:mx="library://ns.adobe.com/flex/mx"
               xmlns:ns="org.orb_quest.*">
    <ns:OrbQuest/>
</s:Application>
```

Listing 6–21 shows that MXML applications are XML files. Like many component-driven UI libraries, the application is composed of a tree of components. In Android the root component is whatever is set using the `setContentView` method of the class `Activity`. In Swing, the root component might be a `JFrame`. In the case of an AIR application running on Android, the root component is an `Application`, which is defined by the `s:Application` element in Listing 6–19. Running this application on the desktop requires a different root element, as shown in Listing 6–22.

> **TIP:** MXML files include a lot of different namespaces in the root element. Think of these as Java import statements: they allow you to use components from different libraries, including your own.

Listing 6–22. *Main.mxml*

```
<?xml version="1.0" encoding="utf-8"?>
<s:WindowedApplication xmlns:fx="http://ns.adobe.com/mxml/2009"
                       xmlns:s="library://ns.adobe.com/flex/spark"
                       xmlns:ns="org.orb_quest.*"
                       width="400"
                       height="500">
```

```
        <ns:OrbQuest/>
</s:WindowedApplication>
```

Listing 6–22 shows the entry point for this application when it is run on the desktop. The only difference is that the root element is of type s:WindowedApplication. While it is not ideal that the root element is different for various platforms, it turns out to be a minor inconvenience, since both entry points have a single child element called ns:OrbQuest. The element ns:OrbQuest is a component defined by this project. In both the Android and desktop version it represents the layout of the application and the game logic. Listing 6–23 shows the portion of the OrbQuest.mxml file that defines the UI layout.

Listing 6–23. *OrbQuest.mxml (Layout)*

```
<s:Group xmlns:fx="http://ns.adobe.com/mxml/2009"
         xmlns:s="library://ns.adobe.com/flex/spark"
         xmlns:mx="library://ns.adobe.com/flex/mx"
         width="100%" height="100%"
         color="0xFFFFFF"
         creationComplete="init()"
         resize="layoutOrbs()"
         >
//ommited code and non-visual components

    <s:Rect width="100%" height="100%">
        <s:fill><s:SolidColor color="0x555555" /></s:fill>
    </s:Rect>

    <s:Group y="5" x="5">
        <s:layout>
            <s:TileLayout>
                <s:requestedColumnCount>2</s:requestedColumnCount>
            </s:TileLayout>
        </s:layout>
        <s:Label text="Score:"/>
        <s:Label id="scoreLabel" text="{score}"/>
        <s:Label text="High Score:"/>
        <s:Label id="highScoreLabel" text="{highScore}"/>
    </s:Group>

    <s:Group id="gameGroup" y="40" x="20" click="clicked(event)">
        <s:Rect width="100%" height="100%">
            <s:fill><s:SolidColor color="0x999999" /></s:fill>
        </s:Rect>
    </s:Group>
</s:Group>
```

In Listing 6–23 we see that the root element is of type Group. A Group is a basic container for other components. Each of the three top-level elements describes a component in the application. The first Rect simply defines a gray rectangle that fills the screen. The first Group element has a TileLayout and holds the text Labels used to display the score and high score. The last Group is where the application is going to dynamically add and animate the elements for the orbs.

This simple layout conveys some of the basic concepts of Flex. First, it is a bit like HTML in the way components are nested and described in XML. Second, it is a bit like

JavaScript as elements can be defined by setting the id attribute and events can be registered with event attributes, like the click attribute of the second `Group`. However, there are some important differences.

One thing that makes Flex different from HTML is that a much larger component set is available out of the box. While not immediately obvious from this example, a quick scan of the documentation shows many different types of layouts, something that is almost missing from HTML. But the real power of Flex is how the declarative XML is able to interact with the driving ActionScript code. Note the `Label`, with the id of `scoreLabel`, has its text attribute set to the value {score}. These curly brackets indicate that the text of this label should be whatever the value of the variable `score` is. We will look at how `score` is defined in a moment. In the meantime, know that it is of type int and that the application logic will be updating that variable as the games score increases. This is called "binding" in Flex terms. By binding the `text` attribute to the variable `score`, the developer no longer has to be concerned with updating the UI; the relationship between the UI and model (score) has been defined. However, binding should be used with care, since every time you use binding the ActionScript compiler inserts monitoring logic into your compiled code. This additional logic can become a performance issue if it is used frequently.

Writing ActionScript

We now have a basic UI laid out and we know that some of the components have a relationship with some code. For example, in Listing 6–21 we know that the `Label` `scoreLabel` is bound to the variable `score`, and the `Group` with id `gameGroup` should call the method `clicked` when it is clicked by a mouse or touched by a finger. The variable `score` and the method `clicked` obviously needs to be defined. One place where code can be defined is right in the MXML file. Flex allows ActionScript to be included in an MXML file inside of a CDATA block. Listing 6–24 shows the CDATA block from OrbQuest.mxml.

Listing 6–24. *OrbQuest.MXML (ActionScript, partial)*

```
<fx:Script>
            <![CDATA[
import flashx.textLayout.formats.Float;
import mx.collections.ArrayCollection;
import mx.core.IVisualElement;
import mx.events.EffectEvent;
import spark.effects.Animate;
import spark.effects.animation.Keyframe;
import spark.effects.animation.MotionPath;
import spark.primitives.BitmapImage;

[Embed(source="images/blue_orb.png")]
[Bindable]
public var blueOrbImage:Class;
[Embed(source="images/green_orb.png")]
[Bindable]
public var greenOrbImage:Class;
[Embed(source="images/red_orb.png")]
```

```
[Bindable]
public var redOrbImage:Class;
private var images:ArrayCollection = new ArrayCollection();
private var orbsAdded:Boolean = false;
private var numColsAndRows:int = 5;
private var imageWidth:int = 512;
[Bindable]
private var orbScale:Number = 0.1;
[Bindable]
private var firstOrb:Orb;
[Bindable]
private var secondOrb:Orb;
[Bindable]
private var score:int;
[Bindable]
private var highScore:int;

private var sharedObj:SharedObject;

public function init():void{
        sharedObj = SharedObject.getLocal("myTasks");
        if (sharedObj.size > 0) {
                highScore = sharedObj.data.highScore;
        }

        scaleDownAnimate.addEventListener(EffectEvent.EFFECT_END, scaleDownDone);
        swapAnimateSecond.addEventListener(EffectEvent.EFFECT_END, swapDone);
        scaleUpAnimateSecond.addEventListener(EffectEvent.EFFECT_END, scaleUpDone);

        images.addItem(blueOrbImage);
        images.addItem(greenOrbImage);
        images.addItem(redOrbImage);


        for (var i:int=0;i<numColsAndRows*numColsAndRows;i++){
                var image:BitmapImage = new BitmapImage();
                image.source = randomImage();
                var orb:Orb = new Orb(image);
                orb.scaleX = orbScale;
                orb.scaleY = orbScale;
                gameGroup.addElement(orb);
        }
        orbsAdded = true;
        layoutOrbs();
}
private function clicked(event:MouseEvent):void{
        if (!isAnimating()){

                trace("x: " + event.localX + " y: " + event.localY + " c: " +↵
 event.target.toString());

                var col:int = getColOrRowFromCoord(event.localX);
                var row:int = getColOrRowFromCoord(event.localY);

                var index:int = getIndexFromCoord(col, row);
                var orb:Orb = gameGroup.getElementAt(index) as Orb;
```

```
            if (firstOrb){
                if (firstOrb != orb){
                    secondOrb = orb;
                    scaleDownAnimate.target = orb;
                    scaleDownAnimate.play();
                }
            } else {
                firstOrb = orb;
                scaleDownAnimate.target = orb;
                scaleDownAnimate.play();
            }
        }
```

Listing 6–24 shows that the CDATA block must be declared in an `fx:Script` tag. Inside the CDATA block, we see some very ordinary looking code. We see import statements, variable declarations, and functions. In fact, this MXML file is not just defining a layout, it is defining a class called OrbQuest, which extends Group and has all of the fields and functions defined in the CDATA block. A quick scan of the code reveals the variable score; this is the variable that the Label scoreLabel is bound to. In Java terms, it is reasonable to think of Label being bound to this.score, where this is any instance of an OrbQuest class. Likewise, when a user clicks the Group gameGroup, the clicked method shown in Listing 6–24 is called on this OrbQuest object.

Some of the variables in Listing 6–24 have [bindable] above them; the square bracket annotation is similar to annotations in Java. The bindable annotation itself tells the compiler that this variable can be bound to. Variables by default are not eligible for binding unless they are declared to be. This is because there is some overhead when variables are bound. Under the covers, the logic must be inserted into the compiled code to update anything that is "listening" to the variable.

The other annotation used in Listing 6–24 is Embed. This annotation tells the compiler to generate code that loads the image file defines as the source. This is more than just a short hand for loading an image file; it is a way of telling the compiler that an external file is required. As an exercise, rename one of the image files and notice that the compiler complains that a resource is missing. This is a powerful tool, something I wish was in more languages, any time the compiler can tell me something is wrong, the better in my book.

The init function in Listing 6–24 does a lot of the same things as the JavaScript version. The highScore is read out of a SharedObject object. The SharedObject class is how Flex stores simple data from a user session. In a browser the SharedObject class is basically in interface to cookies. As an AIR application it is a convenient way to store user data, taking advantage of a shared API. There are a bunch of event listeners being register with Animate objects. Flex provides a powerful set of animation tools that we will explore shortly. By registering an event listener a particular function will be called every time these animations complete. The last section of the init method preloads a bunch of orbs and lays them out.

The clicked function in Listing 6–24 is purposefully similar to the user event handing found in the JavaScript version, as is much of the rest of the application. It is not worth going over all of the methods in detail, but it is worth taking a look at the `Animate` class. Note that toward the end of the `clicked` method, the `scaleDownAnimate` has a `target` set and then is told to play. Let's take a look at another declarative aspect of MXML in Listing 6–25.

Listing 6–25. *OrbQuest.mxml (Declarations)*

```
<fx:Declarations>
            <s:Animate id="scaleDownAnimate" >
                    <s:motionPaths>
                            <s:MotionPath property="scaleX">
                                    <s:keyframes>
                                            <s:Keyframe time="0"↵
 value="{orbScale}"/>
                                            <s:Keyframe time="500"↵
 value="{orbScale/4}"/>
                                    </s:keyframes>
                            </s:MotionPath>
                            <s:MotionPath id="scaleYPath" property="scaleY">
                                    <s:keyframes>
                                            <s:Keyframe time="0"↵
 value="{orbScale}"/>
                                            <s:Keyframe time="500"↵
 value="{orbScale/4}"/>
                                    </s:keyframes>
                            </s:MotionPath>
                    </s:motionPaths>
            </s:Animate>
```

In Listing 6–25 we see one of the `Animate` objects defined in the `Declarations` section of the MXML file. The `Declarations` section provides a space in an MXML file to define objects using the same technique as the visual components. The objects declared in the Declarations section are by nature not visual, but of course they may affect visual components. The `Animate` class is a good example: it defines an animation for visual components. Animations are described by stating which property of a component is going to be modified (`scaleX` in this case) and describing a collection of `KeyFrames`. Each `KeyFrame` states a time at which the given property will have a specific value. When the animation runs, the `KeyFrames` will determine the value of the property before and after the current time. This is much like the simple API in the JavaScript version, but much more complete. It might not be immediately clear why you would want to define an `Animate` with this XML syntax. It is definitely possible to create a similar `Animate` object by simply calling `new Animate` and filling out the correct properties. The advantage here is that it turns out to be a lot less typing to define this structure, and the structure is immediately obvious when the XML is well formatted. The other advantage is that we can use binding. Each `KeyFrame` has the `value` attribute bound to the variable `orbScale`. This is done because `orbScale` is recalculated every time the screen is resized. It ensures that these KeyFrames are always using the correct value.

In conclusion, the Flash, Flex, and AIR ecosystem is a powerful tool for developing applications for many platforms. If it is a technology you know, it is very easy to use with Android. In my experience so far, there does seem to be a performance decline when using AIR on Android, but if performance is not critical for your application this may not be an issue. There is also the problem of AIR availability. As mentioned, AIR is fully supported on Android 2.2 and later, but there are a lot of devices out there which do not run that version. At least in the United States, the cell phone carriers are packaging up their own version of Android and preventing users from updating their OSes. This sort of vendor lockout may be a stumbling block to using AIR as your deployment. Time will tell if this will be a growing issue or not.

Summary

The first half of this chapter was dedicated to using web-based tools like HTML and JavaScript to create an application that can easily be ported to another platform, or simply put on the web. We looked at some of the interoperability features Android provides for communicating with JavaScript. The second half of the chapter explored AIR, which is Adobe's deployment technology for Flash and Flex. We examined a simple Flex application and learned how MXML and ActionScript work together. Both technologies offer cross-platform advantages, but both technologies also have their own limitations.

One of the great things about writing applications for Android is that you can assume the device has a network connection most of the time. In the next chapter we will learn how to write an Android application that consumes a web service and explore how that expands what an Android application can do.

Chapter 7

Using REST with Facebook and Twitter

It has been said that every generation of software developers reinvents remote procedure calls (RPC). There are probably hundreds of technologies that have been created to get one computer to run a function for another. Representational State Transfer (REST) might seem like just another new type of RPC—this generation's version—especially considering how popular it is these days. But that's not the case; REST is really a collection of guidelines for using the existing HTTP 1.1 protocol to communicate information between a client and a server.

In this chapter we will explore how REST takes advantage of the HTTP methods (POST, GET, and so forth), as well as statelessness and caching, to suggest a simple, scalable architecture suitable for a large number of web services. The authors of REST would like you to consider the World Wide Web as the largest implementation of REST, taken as an entire application. Clearly, REST is scalable.

After an overview of REST, we will see how to consume a REST web service provided by Twitter. This will include creating a request, sending it to a server, and responding to the result. In this example we will also learn a little about JavaScript Object Notation (JSON), a popular data-interchange format.

Twitter exposes a lot of web services that don't require authentication, and a lot that do. It uses a protocol called Open Authentication (OAuth) for authentication, which is also used by Facebook and Google, among others. We will explore how to implement a simple authentication workflow in an Android application.

While composing a REST request and handling the details of OAuth is an interesting exercise, it can be a bit tedious. We will take a look at the Android APIs that Twitter and Facebook provide, which wrap a lot of the complexity around making REST calls. These APIs help developers interact with the many services exposed by Twitter and Facebook. After all, when working with Twitter, we want to *tweet*, not POST.

Understanding REST

REST is a strategy of using HTTP methods to create an API suitable for client-server communication. This is exactly how a web browser works: using a URL to make a request to a server, which returns an HTML file. Of course, browsers make requests for things besides HTML files; they also request CSS files, images, and a slew of other files types. It thus makes sense that this flexible protocol can also be used for communicating data that might not have a visual component. At the end of the day, the REST architecture simply takes advantage of the fact that HTTP is both pervasive and capable, making it an excellent candidate for a data transfer protocol.

Applications communicating over HTTP are nothing new. For example, the Simple Object Access Protocol (SOAP) uses HTTP to send and receive XML documents. While SOAP clearly uses HTTP, SOAP authors are encouraged to define XML documents for each type of action that can take place. For example, they will have one document type for adding users and another for listing movies. Both types of documents might be sent to the server using a POST method. When creating a set of REST services, authors are encouraged to use the various HTTP methods as the verbs that define the service. Listing movies, for example, would best be accomplished with a GET request, while adding a new user would use a POST request. Table 7–1 shows some example services and the HTTP methods used.

Table 7–1. *Example REST Service*

Service Name	Service URL	Method	Param
List Movies	http://example.com/movies	GET	
Get Single Movie	http://example.com/movies/[1]	GET	1) id of movie
Update Movie Info	http://example.com/movies/[1]	PUT	1) id of movie
Add Movie	http://example.com/movies	POST	
Clear All Movies	http://example.com/movies	DELETE	
Clear Single Movie	http://example.com/movies[1]	DELETE	1) id of movie

Table 7–1 shows six services. Each has a name for human reference, a URL where the resource is provided, the HTTP method used to perform the action, and a note about required parameters. This very simple example highlights how the HTTP methods can be used to describe a number of likely functions. By using four different methods and a single URL we have defined complete CRUD (Create Read Update Delete) services for a single data type. If we wanted a similar set of services for a different data type, we could simply define a new URL.

In some cases, REST is simply too poor syntactically for a given service. It would be unrealistic to suggest that all web services could or should be boiled down to just 4 verbs. Transactions, for example, are completely missing from the REST terminology.

You could argue that a transaction is just another object to be acted on by REST verbs, but the implementation would still be left to the developer. When we look at the examples for Twitter and Facebook, keep in mind the volume of data these companies process in a day. I suspect the simplicity of their services contributes, in part, to their success in processing the enormous number of requests they receive.

REST and JSON

So far we've described how REST defines services, but not what is actually sent and received when using these services. In fact there is no single answer to that question, since REST does not try to dictate how a client or server should accomplish a particular task. Of course, some services will return text and others will return binary data, like when a web browser asks for an image.

In practice, a lot of services return text when binary data is not required. This often takes the form of XML, JSON, RSS, or ATOM. All four of these formats are used to structure text data and have excellent support in all major languages. While many binary formats are more efficient in terms of size, the use of plain text is very common and very helpful when it comes to debugging. Let's take a closer look at JSON, since both Facebook and Twitter use it. Listing 7–1 shows some example JSON.

> **NOTE:** Twitter's web services actually allow you to specify which format you want your data returned in. Twitter may not have invented this idea, but it deserves praise for including this feature.

Listing 7–1. *A Simple JSON Example*

```
{
"height":128,
"name":"Fred"
}
```

This is a very simple JSON object with two key/value pairs. The first has a key of "height" and a number value of 128. The second has a key of "name" and a string value of "Fred". JSON objects are just collections of key/value pairs. Given JavaScript's dynamic nature this makes a lot of sense, as objects in JavaScript behave in exactly the same way. In fact, JSON is valid JavaScript and can be passed to the eval function to create a fully populated JavaScript object. For security reasons, though, this is not advised since third parties could put arbitrary code in the JSON string.

In our example, the values of the two keys are simple types, but this is not required. You can use another object for a value, or even an array. Listing 7–2 shows a more complete example.

Listing 7–2. *A More Complex JSON Example*

```
{
"firstName":"Lucas",
"lastName":"Jordan",
```

```
        "age":33,
        "favoriteColors":["Red, "Blue"],
        "address":{
                "street":"640 Nednil St."
                "city":"Rochester"
                        "state":"NY"
        },
        "phoneNumber":[
                {
                        "type":"mobile",
                        "number":"555 555-6666"
                }
                {
                        "type":"home",
                        "number":"555 555-7777"
                }
        ]
}
```

The JSON in Listing 7–2 describes a person object. We see the keys "firstName", "lastName", and "age", which have simple values. The value for the key "address" is another JSON object that contains its own key/value pairs. The key "favoriteColors" corresponds to an array of strings, while the key "phoneNumber" corresponds to an array of objects. See Figure 7–1 for a real example of JSON being used as the result of a web service.

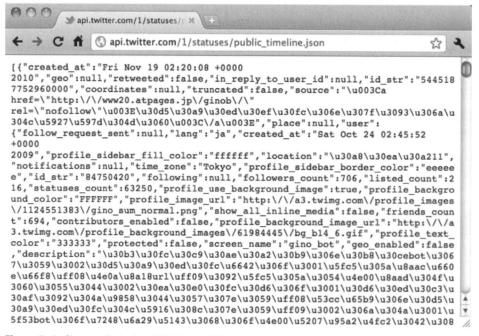

Figure 7–1. *Chrome displaying JSON from a GET request*

In Figure 7–1, we see a simple REST call made to Twitter using the browser. The URL shows that "json" was specified as the result type. The JSON displayed represents the

20 most recent tweets on Twitter. I am not sure who uses this service, but it is an interesting snapshot of a live web service.

REST from an Android Application

Now that we've seen how a REST service is defined and what type of data we can expect to get as a result, let's look at a sample Android application that performs a number of REST calls through a number of different APIs. Figure 7–2 shows the sample application running.

Figure 7–2. *The FaceTweet demo application*

The FaceTweet Android application displays the most recent tweet from the Twitter account "lucasljordan," as well as two buttons that let the user login to Facebook and Twitter. Below the authentication buttons are a pair of action buttons that become enabled after the user authenticates, to allow the user to interact with a Facebook or Twitter service. The tweet at the top of the screen is produced by the code in Listing 7–3.

Listing 7–3. *TweetFace.java (partial)*

```
private final static String URL_STATUSES_USER_TIMELINE = "http://api.twitter.com/1/↵
statuses/user_timeline.json";

private HttpClient client = new DefaultHttpClient();
//…
public JSONObject readStatus(String screenName)
            throws ClientProtocolException, IOException, JSONException {
    StringBuilder fullUrl = new StringBuilder(URL_STATUSES_USER_TIMELINE);
    fullUrl.append("?screen_name=");
    fullUrl.append(screenName);
```

```
            HttpGet get = new HttpGet(fullUrl.toString());
            HttpResponse response = client.execute(get);

            int statusCode = response.getStatusLine().getStatusCode();

            if (statusCode == 200) {
                    HttpEntity entity = response.getEntity();
                    String json = EntityUtils.toString(entity);
                    JSONArray bunchOfTweets = new JSONArray(json);
                    JSONObject mostRecentTweet = bunchOfTweets.getJSONObject(0);
                    return mostRecentTweet;
            } else {
                    String reason = response.getStatusLine().getReasonPhrase();
                    throw new RuntimeException("Trouble reading status(code="
                                    + statusCode + "):" + reason);
            }
    }
```

Listing 7–3 shows a method named readStatus that takes a string named screenName as an argument. The first thing we need to do is create a URL describing the resources we want to work with. This is done by creating a StringBuilder and concatenating the base URL defined in URL_STATUSES_USER_TIMELINE with the parameter screen_name set to the variable screenName. Once the URL is constructed, an HttpGet object is created with the URL. The HttpGet class is from the Apache commons code base, which is built into the Android Java environment. The get variable is passed to the execute method of the variable client, which is of type HttpClient, another class from the Apache networking libraries. The execute method is where the actual network call is made, and this method blocks until a result from the server is received.

Once the execute method returns, we check the status of the request. A statusCode of 200 means we have successfully received the requested information. If you take a closer look at the URL URL_STATUSES_USER_TIMELINE, you'll see that at the end of the String we specified a reply formatted in JSON. So when we use the toString method of EntityUtils to convert the response's HttpEntity into a string, we know we have a JSON string. This particular service is defined to return a JSONArray as a result, so we know to first create a JSONArray object, passing in the string json. Lastly, we pull out the first (index 0) JSONObject from the JSONArray and return it.

Both the JSONArray and the JSONObject are classes from the package org.json. These classes are built into the Android environment and don't require any external jars to use. JSONArray contains a list of valid JSON values, while JSONObject contains a mapping of keys to valid JSON values. Listing 7–4 shows the returned JSONObject in its raw form.

Listing 7–4. *A Tweet in JSON*

```
{
   "in_reply_to_user_id":null,
   "truncated":false,
   "in_reply_to_user_id_str":null,
   "id_str":"29482242963",
   "favorited":false,
   "geo":null,
   "created_at":"Tue Nov 02 15:52:36 +0000 2010",
   "contributors":null,
```

```
    "in_reply_to_screen_name":null,
    "source":"web",
    "coordinates":null,
    "retweet_count":null,
    "in_reply_to_status_id":null,
    "place":null,
    "user":{
      "description":null,
      "id_str":"211193291",
      "verified":false,
      "time_zone":null,
      "profile_text_color":"333333",
      "url":null,
      "follow_request_sent":null,
      "lang":"en",
      "created_at":"Tue Nov 02 15:50:19 +0000 2010",
      "profile_link_color":"0084B4",
      "location":null,
      "notifications":null,
      "profile_use_background_image":true,
      "profile_sidebar_fill_color":"DDEEF6",
      "listed_count":0,
      "following":null,
      "profile_background_image_url":"http:\/\/s.twimg.com\/a\
/1289502323\/images\/themes\/theme1\/bg.png",
      "favourites_count":0,
      "statuses_count":1,
      "profile_sidebar_border_color":"C0DEED",
      "followers_count":0,
      "protected":false,
      "profile_image_url":"http:\/\/s.twimg.com\/a\
/1289502323\/images\/default_profile_1_normal.png",
      "show_all_inline_media":false,
      "profile_background_tile":false,
      "friends_count":0,
      "name":"Lucas L Jordan",
      "contributors_enabled":false,
      "screen_name":"lucasljordan",
      "id":211193291,
      "geo_enabled":false,
      "utc_offset":null,
      "profile_background_color":"C0DEED"
    },
    "retweeted":false,
    "id":29482242963,
    "in_reply_to_status_id_str":null,
    "text":"Looks like REST on Android uses the apache libraries, that makes
 life easier!"
}
```

In Listing 7–4 we see the JSON representing a tweet. Note that there's a lot more information returned than just 140 characters. In addition to some extra information about the tweet, such as creation data and geo-location, there is also information about the user who authored the tweet. In our case, we are only interested in the very last key, "text".

Asynchronous Tasks

When creating an Android application, it's important not to have long-running tasks in the main thread of the application as this makes the application unresponsive. Making a network call should always be considered a long-running task, and making a REST call to Twitter is a network call, so we want to find a way to move this task to another thread. Android supplies a class called AsyncTask, which provides an easy way to move long-running tasks off of the main thread. In Listing 7–3 we saw the method readStatus, which does the work of calling Twitter. Listing 7–5 shows a subclass of AsyncTask that makes the call to readStatus.

Listing 7–5. *ReadTweet Extends AsyncTask*

```
private class ReadTweet extends AsyncTask<String, Integer, String> {
        @Override
        protected String doInBackground(String... screenNames) {
                try {
                        tweet = readStatus(screenNames[0]);
                        return tweet.getString("text");
                } catch (Exception e) {
                        Log.w("FaceTweet", e);
                        return "error reading tweet";
                }
        }

        protected void onPostExecute(final String result) {
                runOnUiThread(new Runnable() {
                        @Override
                        public void run() {
                                tweetView.setText(result);
                        }
                });
        }
}
```

Here we see that ReadTweet extends AsyncTask with three generics specified. The first generic, String, specifies the type passed into the method doInBackground. Note that more than one String can be passed in. The second generic type, Integer, is used for tracking progress, but we don't use it in this example. The last generic, String, is used to specify the return type of doInBackground and the type passed to onPostExecute as the result. Given these three points of customization, AsyncTask can be extended to accommodate a large number of use cases.

The doInBackground method is where we'll do the actual work—in this case, make a call to readStatus. As shown in Listing 7–3, readStatus returns a JSONObject containing the latest tweet. To get the actual content of the tweet out of the JSONObject, we call getString and pass in "text" as the key. Once we have the text of the tweet, we simply return it as the result of the method doInBackground. That result is passed to onPostExecute. In the method onPostExecute, we define a new Runnable that does the work of updating the UI. The Runnable is passed to the method runOnUiThread, which makes sure the Runnable gets executed on the UI thread so we don't have any multi-threading issues. Listing 7–6 shows the initialization code of this Android application and how the ReadTweet class is executed.

Listing 7-6. *onCreate*

```
@Override
public void onCreate(Bundle savedInstanceState) {
        super.onCreate(savedInstanceState);

        setContentView(R.layout.main);

        tweetView = (TextView) findViewById(R.id.tweetView);
        statusView = (TextView) findViewById(R.id.statusView);

        loginTwitterButton = (Button) findViewById(R.id.loginTwitterButton);
        loginFacebookButton = (Button) findViewById(R.id.loginFacebookButton);
        replyOnTwitterButton = (Button) findViewById(R.id.replyOnTwitterButton);
        facebookWallButton = (Button) findViewById(R.id.facebookWallButton);

        loginTwitterButton.setOnClickListener(this);
        loginFacebookButton.setOnClickListener(this);
        replyOnTwitterButton.setOnClickListener(this);
        facebookWallButton.setOnClickListener(this);

        new ReadTweet().execute("lucasljordan");
}
```

The onCreate method handles a number of initializing tasks. The first thing this method does is identify the UI components defined in the layout file for this Activity. The component we are most interested in right now is tweetView, which displays the current tweet on the screen. As you can see, tweetView's setText method is not called in the onCreate method. setText is called in the Runnable defined in the onPostExecute method of the class ReadTweet. At the bottom of the onCreate method, an instance of ReadTweet is created and the execute method is called. This causes the work defined in the ReadTweet object to be executed in the background and ultimately call the setText method on the tweetView object, displaying th latest tweet.

Twitter

We saw a simple example that used Twitter, but we haven't yet looked at authenticating an app with Twitter. Most Twitter services require that a client be authenticated before it can make a request. Twitter uses a technology called OAuth to authenticate a user. OAuth is an emerging standard for authenticating users so client applications can make request on their behalf. There is some specific terminology that must be covered to understand OAuth, but before we get to the technical information, let's consider Figure 7–3, which depicts the user experience when using OAuth with a web application.

Web Client Example

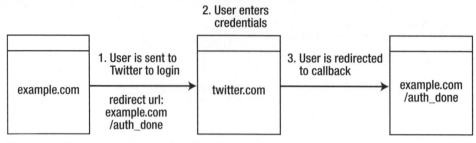

Figure 7-3. *The user experience when using OAuth with a web application*

> **TIP:** There's a lot more to learn about OAuth. Check out http://hueniverse.com/oauth/ to find out more about it.

The user starts out at a web page hosted at example.com. The web page at example.com asks the user to authenticate with Twitter so it can perform some action for that user. To facilitate this, the web application directs the user to a special web page at Twitter used for authenticating. When the web application directs the user to Twitter, it makes sure to include information about itself, including a callback URL. The callback URL is the URL that Twitter will send the user back to when the authentication is complete. This callback URL will also contain additional information the web application will use during future authenticated calls to Twitter services. However, we are not writing a web application; Figure 7–4 shows the equivalent in terms of Android.

Android Example

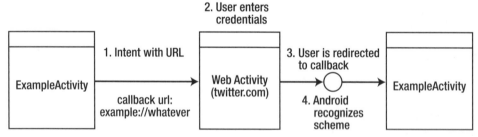

Figure 7-4. *OAuth user experience on Android*

With Android, a user starts out in some Activity that asks the user to authenticate with Twitter. This is done by creating an Intent with the URL of Twitter's authentication page. The callback URL is a URL where the scheme has been registered by the example Activity. The Intent causes the Android OS to switch the user to a Web Activity displaying the Twitter web page. Once the user has authenticated, the Web Activity redirects to the user to the callback URL. Since the callback URL has a scheme registered by the original example Activity, Android directs the user back the original Activity.

If you want to work with the example code, you must do a couple of things. First you must create a Twitter account, then you must create a Twitter application. Once you create an application you'll be given a *consumer key* and a *consumer secret*. These are values you'll need to paste into the class `FaceTweet` for the placeholder constants `CONSUMER_KEY` and `CONSUMER_SECRET`. Figure 7–5 shows the Twitter control panel for Twitter applications.

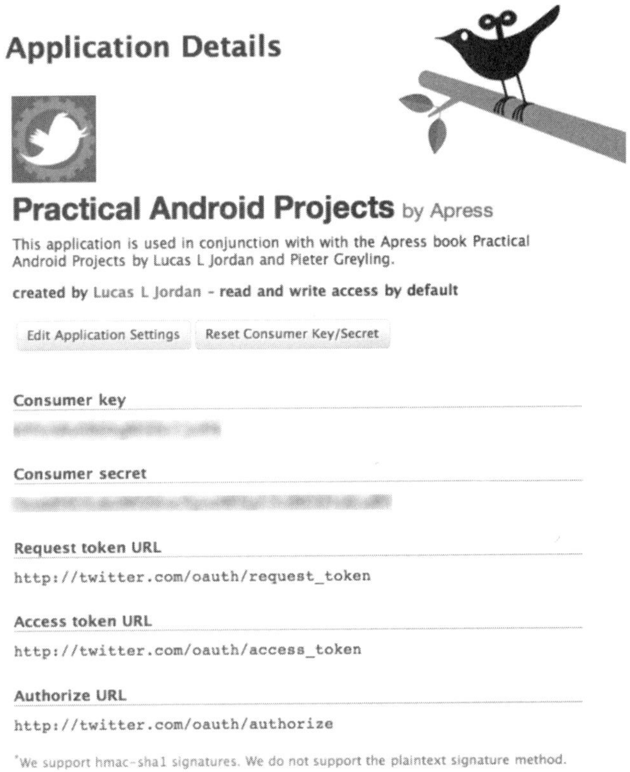

Figure 7–5. *Twitter application control panel*

Figure 7–5 shows the Twitter application created to accompany this example. You can see that the consumer key and consumer secret are blurred out. There's also a button for resetting these values in case I forget to delete them from the example code that accompanies this book. We shall see if I remember.

Examples in Code

In our sample application, the user can click on a button to authenticate with Twitter. Listing 7–7 shows the method this action calls.

Listing 7-7. *TweetFace.java (loginTwitter)*

```java
private final static String URL_OAUTH_REQUEST_TOKEN = "https://api.twitter.com/oauth/⤶
request_token";
private final static String URL_OAUTH_ACCESS_TOKEN = "http://twitter.com/oauth/⤶
access_token";
private final static String URL_OAUTH_AUTHORIZE = "http://twitter.com/oauth/authorize";

//Twitter provides these values.
private final static String CONSUMER_KEY = "XXXXXXXXXXXXXXXXXXXX";
private final static String CONSUMER_SECRET = "YYYYYYYYYYYYYYYYYYYY";

public final static String URL_CALLBACK = "tweetface://twitter";

//..
private OAuthProvider provider = new CommonsHttpOAuthProvider(
        URL_OAUTH_REQUEST_TOKEN, URL_OAUTH_ACCESS_TOKEN,
        URL_OAUTH_AUTHORIZE);
private CommonsHttpOAuthConsumer consumer = new CommonsHttpOAuthConsumer(
        CONSUMER_KEY, CONSUMER_SECRET);
//..
private void loginTwitter() {
    try {
        String authUrl = provider.retrieveRequestToken(consumer,
                URL_CALLBACK);
        startActivity(new Intent(Intent.ACTION_VIEW, Uri.parse(authUrl)));
    } catch (Exception e) {
        Log.e(APP, e.getMessage());
        throw new RuntimeException(e);
    }
}
```

As you can see, a number of URLs are stored as constants, as defined by the Twitter API. The consumer key and consumer secret are also provided with your Twitter application. And there are two variables named `provider` and `consumer` that are supplied by an open source project called Signpost (oauth-signpost). Signpost provides a simple API for working with OAuth. Using Signpost is not technically required, but OAuth requires that HTTP requests be constructed in a very particular way and cryptographically signed. Writing code to accomplish these tasks is educational, but not practical, when a library like Signpost exists to do it for you.

> **NOTE:** Signpost can be downloaded from `http://code.google.com/p/oauth-signpost/`

The method `loginTwitter` creates a URL using the `provider` variable. This URL is where the user will be directed to authenticate. The `provider` variable has properly encoded the URL with all of the information Twitter needs to trust who is sending the message and to redirect the user when the authentication is done. Figure 7-6 shows the web page where the user will authenticate with Twitter.

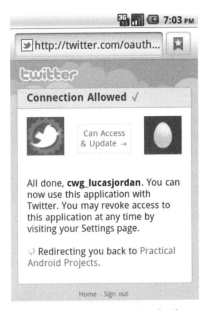

Figure 7-6. *The Twitter authentication page*

The Twitter authentication page shows where the user can enter her username and password to authenticate with Twitter. Once she hits the Allow button, Twitter sends her to the URL stored in the URL_CALLBACK constant. Note that the scheme for this URL is "tweetface," which is handled by the TweetFace Activity. Listing 7-8 shows how the TweetFace Activity in the AndroidManifest.xml file registers this protocol.

Listing 7-8. *AnrdoidManifest.xml*

```xml
<?xml version="1.0" encoding="utf-8"?>
<manifest xmlns:android="http://schemas.android.com/apk/res/android"
      package="org.ljordan.facetweet"
      android:versionCode="1"
      android:versionName="1.0">
    <application android:icon="@drawable/icon" android:label="@string/app_name" >
        <activity android:name=".FaceTweet"
                android:label="@string/app_name"
                android:launchMode="singleInstance">
            <intent-filter>
                <action android:name="android.intent.action.MAIN" />
                <category android:name="android.intent.category.LAUNCHER" />
            </intent-filter>

            <intent-filter>
                        <action android:name="android.intent.action.VIEW"/>
                            <category android:name="android.intent.category.DEFAULT"/>
                            <category android:name="android.intent.category.BROWSABLE"/>
                            <!-- URL_CALLBACK = "tweetface://twitter" -->
                            <data android:scheme="tweetface" android:host="twitter"/>
                </intent-filter>
```

```xml
    </activity>
</application>
    <uses-permission android:name="android.permission.INTERNET" />

</manifest>
```

The AndroidManifest.xml file has two intent-filter elements. The first is what you'd expect for most Android applications. The second is used to associate this Activity with the callback URL used in authentication. If you look at the data element, you can see that the scheme and host match our callback URL.

Normally, when an Activity passes control to another Activity, the original Activity may be shut down. To prevent state from being lost when our Activity passes control to the authentication web page, we set the `launchMode` to `singleInstance` on the activity element. This prevents Android from destroying the original TweetFace Activity and creating a new one when the callback URL is encountered.

When the TweetFace Activity is reactivated by the callback URL, the application must carry out a few last steps to complete the authentication process and be authorized to perform actions on the user's behalf. Listing 7–9 shows the onNewIntent method that's called when the intent is activated.

Listing 7–9. *TweetFace.java (onNewIntent)*

```java
@Override
protected void onNewIntent(Intent intent) {
        super.onNewIntent(intent);

        Uri uri = intent.getData();
        if (uri != null) {
                String uriString = uri.toString();
                if (uriString.startsWith(URL_CALLBACK)) {
                        try {
                                String verifier = uri
                                                .getQueryParameter(OAuth.OAUTH_VERIFIER);
                                provider.retrieveAccessToken(consumer, verifier);
                                statusView.setText("Authenticated with Twitter!");
                                replyOnTwitterButton.setEnabled(true);
                        } catch (Exception e) {
                                throw new RuntimeException(e);
                        }
                }
        } else {
                //probably the first time Activity is loaded.
        }
}
```

The onNewIntent method is called when the application is first loaded, as well as when it is loaded after the user authenticates. When the application first starts, the intent has no data and is simply ignored. When onNewIntent is called after user authentication, the intent contains the URL that Twitter constructed to make the callback. As you can see in Listing 7–10, there is some additional information.

Listing 7–10. *Callback From Twitter*

```
tweetface://twitter?oauth_token=kO1BQ...cWqI&oauth_verifier=kkOgu2Dxi5...3XRsKlZPM8
```

Besides the expected scheme and domain our application supplied, we can see some new information. The oauth_verifier parameter is used by the provider, from Listing 7–9, to retrieve an access token. This is the last step in authenticating. The TweetFace application is now able to perform operations on the user's behalf.

Tweeting on Behalf of the User

The authentication workflow required to post a tweet for a user is a bit complex, both from a developer's viewpoint and from a user experience perspective. However, once all the pieces are in place, interacting with the many web services that Twitter provides is very straightforward, as long as you use the Twitter4J library. Listing 7–11 shows how to update the status of a user with this library.

Listing 7–11. *TweetFace.java (updateStatus)*

```java
public void updateStatus() {
    try {
        Configuration conf = new ConfigurationBuilder()
                .setOAuthConsumerKey(consumer.getConsumerKey())
                .setOAuthConsumerSecret(consumer.getConsumerSecret())
                .build();

        AccessToken accessToken = new AccessToken(consumer.getToken(),
                consumer.getTokenSecret());
        Twitter twitter = new TwitterFactory(conf)
                .getOAuthAuthorizedInstance(accessToken);

        String tweetText = "@lucasljordan is trying to count up to: "
                + System.currentTimeMillis();

        // finally, we can update twitter.
        twitter.updateStatus(tweetText);
    } catch (Exception e) {
        throw new RuntimeException(e);
    }
}
```

In Listing 7–11, a Configuration object is created with the consumer key and consumer secret. An AccessToken is also created, containing the token and token secret. Both the AccessToken and Configuration classes are from the Twittter4J library and are used to initialize a Twitter object via a TwitterFactory. Once the Twitter object is created, it is ready to interact with the Twitter web services. By calling updateStatus on the Twitter object, a new tweet is created for the logged-in user. The tweet text in this example includes a timestamp to make sure the text is unique each time this code is run. Twitter does not post duplicate tweets, so when debugging a Twitter application, make sure you change the text each time to make sure your application is actually working.

Confirming the User Wants to Tweet

In this example application, we pop up a dialog asking the user if he wants to tweet. We do this because we are using a service on the user's behalf and don't want to perform any action he is not aware of. Of course, this isn't strictly necessary, but it brings up the topic of using dialogs in Android, which is worth understanding. Figure 7–7 shows the confirmation dialog.

Figure 7–7. *Confirmation dialog*

This is a simple dialog with a yes or no option. The dialog is modal, meaning it blocks all input to the background application. To indicate its modal nature, it darkens the background application, focusing the user on the dialog itself. Dialogs in Android are a bit different from those in other UI libraries. One thing that makes them different is that they are tightly bound to an Activity and are invoked by calling the special showDialog method. Listing 7–12 contains the code required to show a dialog.

Listing 7–12. *Showing A Dialog*

```
private final static int DIALOG_CONFIRM_TWEET = 10;
private final static int DIALOG_CONFIRM_WALL = 20;

//...
@Override
public void onClick(View v) {
        if (v == loginTwitterButton) {
                loginTwitter();
        } else if (v == loginFacebookButton) {
                facebook.authorize(this, new String[] { "publish_stream" },
                                authorizeListener);
        } else if (v == replyOnTwitterButton) {
                showDialog(DIALOG_CONFIRM_TWEET);
        } else if (v == facebookWallButton) {
```

```
                showDialog(DIALOG_CONFIRM_WALL);
        }
        //unknown button.
}

//...
@Override
protected Dialog onCreateDialog(int id) {
        if (id == DIALOG_CONFIRM_TWEET) {
                AlertDialog.Builder builder = new AlertDialog.Builder(this);
                builder.setMessage("Do you want to create a tweet?")
                        .setCancelable(false)
                        .setPositiveButton("Yes",
                                new DialogInterface.OnClickListener() {
                                        public void onClick(DialogInterface dialog, int id) {
                                                statusView.setText("Creating tweet...");
                                                new UpdateStatus().execute("Not Used");
                                        }
                                })
                        .setNegativeButton("No",
                                new DialogInterface.OnClickListener() {
                                        public void onClick(DialogInterface dialog, int id) {
                                                dialog.cancel();
                                        }
                                });
                return builder.create();
        } else if (id == DIALOG_CONFIRM_WALL) {
        //.. method continues
```

The code shows two methods. The first is `onClick`, which handles all of the button actions in the application. If the user clicks the `replyOnTwitterButton`, we make a call to `showDialog` and pass in the constant `DIALOG_CONFIRM_TWEET`. The `showDialog` method is defined by the class Activity and performs a number of operations to make sure the dialogs created in the method `onCreateDialog` are correctly associated with the Activity. In `onCreateDialog` we have to see which dialog is being asked for, which we do by checking the value of the argument id. In this application we create a confirmation dialog before interacting with Twitter or Facebook. The code in Listing 7–12 creates the dialog for Twitter. The dialog for the Facebook workflow looks almost exactly the same and is omitted for brevity.

Dialogs are created by creating a new instance of `AlertDialog.Builder` and passing in an Activity. Once the builder is instantiated, we can use it to create the `AlertDialog` and return it. The builder object is an object that implements the builder pattern. In the builder pattern, the set methods return the builder object. In this way, commands can be chained together. In the example in Listing 7–12, we see that `setCancelable` is called on the object returned from `setMessage`; this is because `setCancelable` is returning the builder object. In fact, the calls to `setMessage` and `setCancelable` could be reversed, so that `setMessage` is called on the result of `setCancelable`.

The method `setPositiveButton` accepts the text to be displayed and an instance of `DialogInterface.OnClickListener`. The listener is called when the positive button is clicked, in our case creating an `UpdateStatus` object and executing it. Since creating a tweet is a network call, we want to make sure we do it in a background thread. The class `UpdateStatus` is very much like the class `ReadTweet` from Listing 7–5, and simply calls `updateStatus` from Listing 7–11.

Once the builder is configured correctly, it is used to actually create a Dialog object and return it. Android handles the details of getting it on the screen and providing the nice fade effects.

In conclusion, Twitter on Android is very easy to use when you take advantage of the excellent third-party libraries available. The Signpost project makes using OAuth a lot easier and is real time-saver for developers. Twitter offers about 40-50 different web services; each is represented in the Twitter4J project and provides an elegant API.

Understanding the Facebook API

At one point, Facebook had the most confusing API I had ever seen, riddled with exceptions and secretly deprecated APIs. However, the company recently introduced the Social Graph API, which provides a comprehensive view into Facebook data with just a handful of services and data types. In addition to enhancing the API as a whole, Facebook now has a number of official libraries to help facilitate working with it on a number of platforms. Android is one of these supported platforms, and we would be foolish not to take advantage the official Android Facebook Library.

Under the hood the Facebook API is doing all the same things that are done in the Twitter example. It communicates with a web server by creating a GET or POST request, it parses a JSON response, and it handles authentication through OAuth. In this section we'll take a look at how Facebook improves the user's authentication experience. We will also explore the Social Graph API.

To work with the sample code for this project, download and install the Facebook Android SDK and make sure you include that project in your Eclipse workspace. This will enable the Facebook features to function properly.

> **NOTE:** You can download the Android Facebook API from https://github.com/facebook/facebook-android-sdk/.

Facebook and Authentication

The Android Facebook API authenticates users by bringing up a web page so they can log directly into Facebook, just like Twitter does. The Facebook API streamlines this process by bringing up a web view within a modal dialog. Figure 7–8 shows the Facebook authentication dialog.

Figure 7-8. *Facebook authentication screens*

The dialog on the left is for the sample application, with fields for entering your username and password. Facebook allows an application like ours to specify additional permissions when authenticating; in our case we want to be able to post to the user wall. Since we have requested this additional permission, users are shown the screen on the right, asking if they wish to allow this.

Once permissions are granted to an application, the user must explicitly revoke that permission through his Facebook privacy settings. Figure 7-9 shows the Facebook privacy settings for applications.

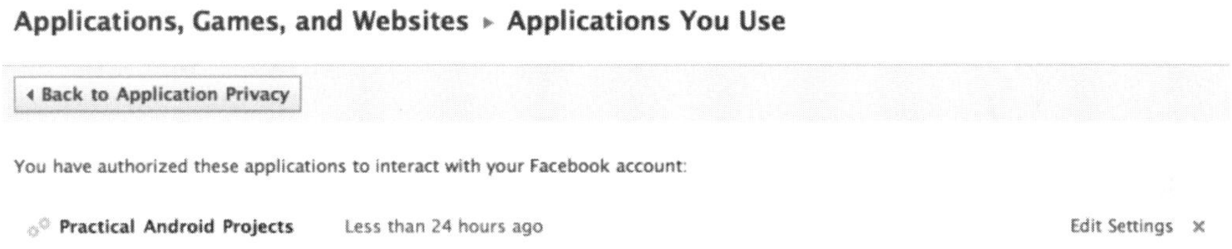

Figure 7-9. *Facebook application settings*

Finding the information shown in Figure 7-9 is pretty tricky. In the year I have worked with the Facebook API, the location of this page has changed a few times. Basically, start with the privacy settings in your Facebook account and look for a link directing you to application settings.

Since the granting of permissions from Facebook is effectively permanent, the user is prompted only once to grant permissions. In fact, authentication is effectively permanent as well. If you kill the application and restart it, you will notice that clicking the "Login to Facebook" button does not require you to log in again. Remember, to kill the FaceTweet application you have to kill it through the application manager or power cycle your device, since FaceTweet is a singleton application.

The rationale for making authentication permanent is questionable from a privacy standpoint, but very practical from a user experience perspective. Requiring users to authenticate only once means they will never be bothered to authenticate again, which removes an annoying step and increases participation. Listing 7–13 shows the code required to bring up the authentication dialog.

Listing 7–13. *Facebook Authentication Dialog*

```
public final static String FB_APPLICATION_ID = "158406107535204";
private Facebook facebook = new Facebook(FB_APPLICATION_ID);
private AuthorizeListener authorizeListener = new AuthorizeListener();
//...
facebook.authorize(this, new String[] { "publish_stream" }, authorizeListener);
```

As you can see, there's not much to authentication with Facebook. A Facebook object is created with an application id. The authorize method is called on the facebook object, passing on the Activity, a collection of permission strings, and an AuthorizeListener.

The array of strings in Listing 7–13 specifies which permissions we are requesting. Even though the granting of permissions is basically permanent, we want to pass this information in every time. The user experience does not change if the permissions are already granted and it is one less thing for our application to keep track of.

> **NOTE:** Facebook offers a lot of different extended permissions, a complete list can be found at http://developers.facebook.com/docs/authentication/permissions.

The AuthorizeListener class in Listing 7–13 is used for receiving callback calls from the Facebook authentication process. Listing 7–14 shows the implementation of this class.

Listing 7–14. *AuthorizeListener*

```
private class AuthorizeListener implements DialogListener {
        @Override
        public void onComplete(Bundle values) {
                statusView.setText("Authenticated with Facebook!");
                facebookWallButton.setEnabled(true);
        }
        @Override
        public void onFacebookError(FacebookError e) {
                Log.w("FaceTweet", e);
                statusView.setText("Trouble With FB, see logs");
        }
        @Override
        public void onError(DialogError e) {
                Log.w("FaceTweet", e);
                statusView.setText("Trouble With Dialog, see logs");
        }
        @Override
```

```
        public void onCancel() {
            statusView.setText("Did not authenticate.");
        }
}
```

This class has four methods, each of which is called depending on the user action or application error. The method onComplete is the happy path, where the user successfully authenticates and we update the UI appropriately. The method onCancel is called when the user cancels the authentication process. The other two methods are called when there is some sort of error. Our application basically ignores this case, but a more sophisticated application could do something smarter.

Just like in the Twitter example, you must create an application with Facebook in order to make API calls of any type. When an application is created, it is given an ID, which is the constant FB_APPLICATION_ID from Listing 7–13. The application's ID is public information, which is weird, since it means you can authenticate users for any Facebook application. Figure 7–10 shows the Facebook application page I used to develop this example.

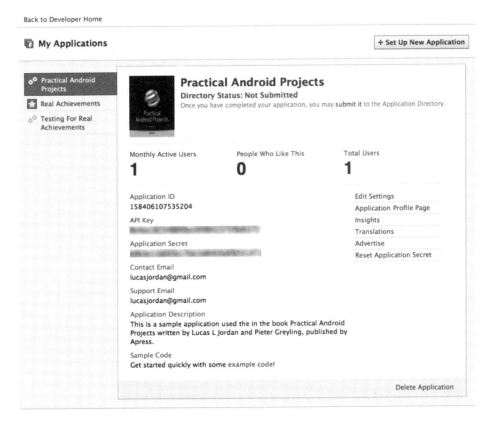

Figure 7–10. *Facebook application page*

This page shows an overview of the application as well as the application ID. There is a bunch of other information that goes along with a Facebook application, and this, as well as the picture, is used to identify the application to the user.

Facebook's Social Graph API

Once authenticated to Facebook, the application has access to the user's view of Facebook. This means, given the correct permissions, the application can perform any operation the user can perform, except changing privacy settings. In order to interact with the Facebook API, we must understand a little of how it is organized. Facebook obviously has users, but it also has pages, pictures, friend relationships, posts, and a lot more. Each of these entities has an ID and can be accessed through a REST service. To view a JSON presentation of a Facebook object, you use the URL `https://graph.facebook.com/ID`. Figure 7–11 is a screenshot showing the information for the application in Figure 7–10.

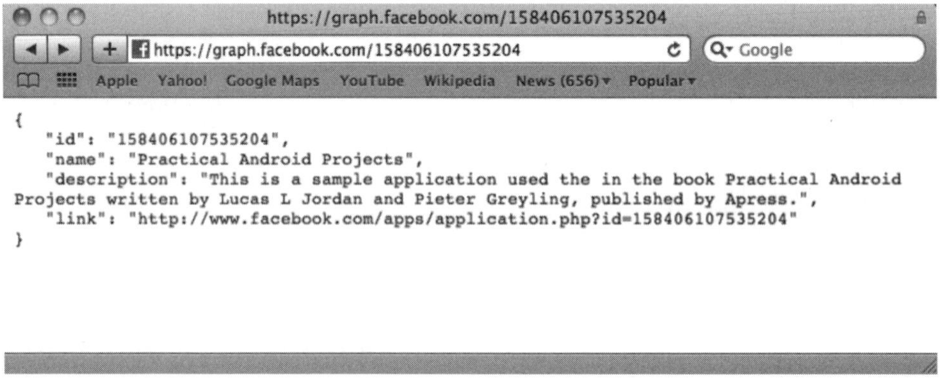
https://graph.facebook.com/158406107535204
https://graph.facebook.com/158406107535204
Google
Apple Yahoo! Google Maps YouTube Wikipedia News (656) Popular
{
"id": "158406107535204",
"name": "Practical Android Projects",
"description": "This is a sample application used the in the book Practical Android Projects written by Lucas L Jordan and Pieter Greyling, published by Apress.",
"link": "http://www.facebook.com/apps/application.php?id=158406107535204"
}

Figure 7–11. *Application details via Facebook Graph API*

Here we see that the URL specifies the ID of the application. In the window we see the JSON representation of the application. Try looking at the source of some different Facebook pages—you can usually pull out the ids of all kinds of things. Looking at the source for my Facebook home page, I learned my account has the id of 100001911096243. Just stick it at the end of the graph URL and there is a JSON representation of my account.

As a shortcut, you can replace the authenticated user's ID in the URL with the string 'me'. For example, `https://graph.facebook.com/me` will return the user's information. But to use the "me" shorthand, you must pass an access token in with the request.

Once you know the ID of something you can inspect that object further by appending a type to the end of the URL. Table 7–2 shows some examples.

Table 7-2. *Example Social Graph Calls*

Object Type Returned	URL
Friends	`https://graph.facebook.com/me/friends?access_token=…`
Home	`https://graph.facebook.com/me/home?access_token=…`
Likes	`https://graph.facebook.com/me/likes?access_token=`
Photo Tags	`https://graph.facebook.com/me/photos?access_token=`

This shows how simple this API is—we just add the type of thing we want to access to the URL and specify the access token.

In Facebook, when you create an item or update something, it is called publishing. To publish an object to Facebook, you simply POST your object to the same URL you'd expect to read it from. So, if you read a user's feeds from `https://graph.facebook.com/arjun/feed`, you would create a POST request and send it to the same URL. When you make the POST, you include the access token as well as the text of the feed item, in addition to any other values supported by the feed type.

> **NOTE:** To learn all about the different types of objects Facebook uses, go to `http://developers.facebook.com/docs/reference/api/`.

Though the Facebook Graph API is refreshingly simple to use, the Android Facebook API comes with a utility class for interacting with these services. In our sample application, we post to the user's wall. Listing 7-15 shows how this is done.

Listing 7-15. *postOnWall*

```
private void postOnWall() throws FileNotFoundException,
            MalformedURLException, IOException {
      Bundle bundle = new Bundle();
      bundle.putString("message",
                  "Working through the examples for the book Practical Android
 Projects.");
      bundle.putString("link",
                  "http://www.facebook.com/apps/application.php?id=
158406107535204");

      facebook.request("me/feed", bundle, "POST");
}
```

This code creates a `Bundle` object, which is a lot like a `JSONObject` in that is a utility for mapping keys to values. In this case, we are mapping the key "`message`" to the text we want displayed on the wall. We also want a link included, so we map the key "`link`" to the URL of the Facebook application page I created for this book. Lastly, we use the `facebook` object created in Listing 7-13 to send the request. Note that we use the POST method, since this is a write operation.

The Facebook Social Graph API is easy to use. The Android Facebook library makes it even easier. Facebook has a large investment in third-party application developers using its services. The simplicity of these services shows the fruits of this investment. Unfortunately, it does not take long working with the API to realize just how freewheeling the company is with user data.

Summary

In this chapter we reviewed the basic concepts of REST and how it uses HTTP methods as the "'verbs" in a web service. We looked at an example of constructing an HTTP request using the built-in Apache libraries to read a tweet. We explored using the Signpost library for managing the OAuth process, in addition to setting up our application for authenticating with OAuth. We used the Twitter4J library to make an authenticated web service call to Twitter. Lastly, we looked at Facebook, showing how the Android Facebook API improves the user login experience and how the Facebook Social Graph API works.

Chapter 8

Using the Google App Engine with Android

There are increasingly few applications written today that don't communicate with a web service of some type. Android applications are no exception: it is because an Android device is always connected to the Internet that it is such a compelling platform for application development. There are many options when it comes to developing the web services consumed by an Android device. From PHP to ASP, people have been creating web applications and services for many years. Java also offers a number of excellent web platforms, and if you find the use of Java attractive in Android, then you might find Java attractive for implementing your server-side logic. The traditional way of writing a web service in Java might include Java Enterprise Edition (J2EE) or Spring. These are powerful tools, but by definition they require a server or servers to run on, and servers require management.

Another consideration when creating a web service is scaling the application across a number of servers. This is a requirement for any application that becomes popular. I think it best to start planning for success from the beginning and choose a technology that is ready to scale. If you are going down the Spring or J2EE path, this means getting access to a number of servers, deploying your application, managing load balancing, and session handling. Not to mention setting up a database that can scale to hundreds of thousands of transactions a day – something that may require a commercial database, such as Oracle.

Although we have worked on many server-side projects and have spent time addressing the issues of scaling an application, we have grown a little tired of it all. In an ideal world, we would like to write our server-side logic and upload it to some service that simply handles the details of deployment, scaling, versioning, and high availability. The Google App Engine (GAE) is not perfect, but it is the closest thing we have found to an ideal server-side solution.

In this chapter we will cover GAE from a high level, exploring what it offers, how applications are developed to work with it, and some of its limitations. Following that, we will look at an example GAE project that serves a simple web service for tracking high scores. Lastly, we will see how to write an Android application to interact with this service, including displaying the location of users on a map.

Introducing Google App Engine

Google App Engine (GAE) is a service for running Internet-facing applications on Google hardware. This means you can write a web application using Java or Python, upload it to GAE, and have your application automatically scale up to meet user demand, in the same way Google's applications do. This is different from other hosting services, with which you are given a server or number of servers on which you can install and manage your application. Some people confuse GAE with services like Amazon's EC2, with which you can create and provision servers through a web service. Amazon's EC2 is an amazing service if your application requires access to the underlying OS – whether it is Windows, Linux, or something else. If your application fits nicely into the category of applications that don't require this level of access, GAE can save you the hassle of managing the hardware and OS your application is running on.

GAE supports two languages for handling the dynamic portion of your application: Java and Python. This chapter will focus on using Java and the Eclipse plugins that facilitate development and deployment. While GAE supports Java, it is not a full implementation of J2EE or any other web framework. GAE does support a subset of J2EE, allowing a lot of existing code and technologies to be used. For example, JSP is supported, along with most of the underlying technologies, like HttpServlets. If you are familiar with the basics of J2EE, you will be at home developing applications for GAE. As mentioned, GAE is a subset of J2EE, and a developer can get into trouble assuming a particular J2EE technology will work as expected or at all. After we discuss the basics of GAE, we will take a look at the portions of J2EE that are supported and to what extent.

GAE Java is also a subset of J2SE. Like Android, not all J2SE classes are present in the runtime. For example, AWT and Swing are missing. This makes sense because web applications do not use these libraries for rendering. However, AWT includes the Graphics2D classes, which are useful for image manipulation outside of a desktop environment. The absence of libraries like Graphics2D can be a bit of a shock when porting an existing an application. It is important to review the supported classes before committing to GAE.

> **NOTE:** The JRE classes supported by GAE are listed on the JRE Class White List, which can be found here: http://code.google.com/appengine/docs/java/jrewhitelist.html

Getting Started with GAE

You must sign up with Google to get access to GAE. Do so at http://code.google.com/appengine/. Once you are logged in to the GAE application, you will see a web page like the one shown in Figure 8-1.

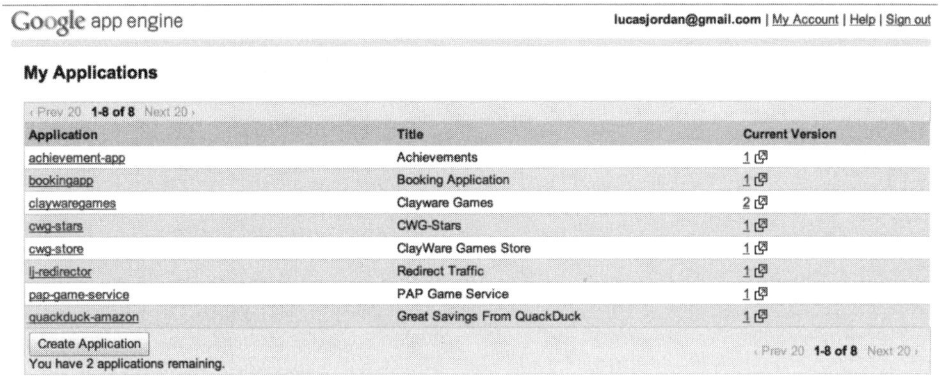

Figure 8–1. *List of applications*

Figure 8–1 lists a number of applications from my GAE account. When you first log in, no applications are listed, but the button at the bottom of the page allows you to create a new application. Figure 8–2 shows the page where a new application can be registered.

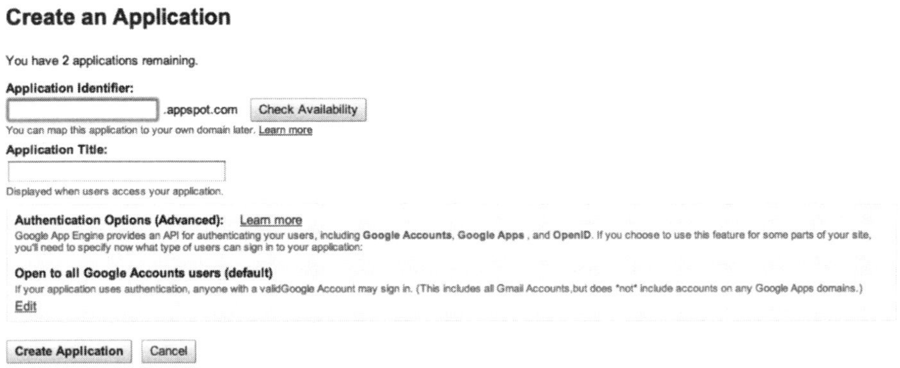

Figure 8–2. *Creating a new GAE application*

There is a place to enter a domain where your application will be available. By default, your application will be a sub-domain of the domain appspot.com. Your application will be available at this URL, but you can also set up your application to be any domain of your choosing. You are also prompted to enter an application title. This is just used to give your application a human readable name.

Once you create a new application, you will be brought to the dashboard view of the application. From this view, you can see statistics about your application as well as manage a number of settings. Figure 8–3 shows the dashboard for the GAE application we created to accompany this chapter.

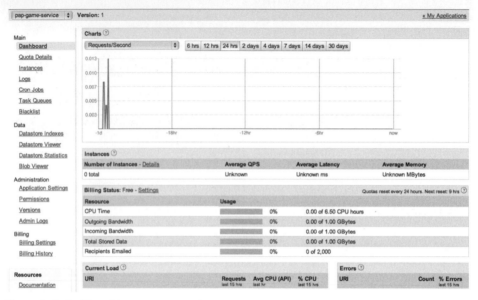

Figure 8–3. *Dashboard for pap-game-service*

The chart in Figure 8–3 shows the usage of the application in terms of request per second. As you can see, this application is not very active. As your usage increases, the data on this view becomes invaluable in understanding the usage of your application. On the left side of the page, you see a number of links that will display other details about your application.

Once you have an application set up with GAE, you will want to download and install the Eclipse plugin for GAE.

> **NOTE:** Install the Eclipse GAE plugin by following the directions found here:
> `http://code.google.com/appengine/docs/java/tools/eclipse.html`

Using Eclipse with GAE

Once Eclipse is configured with the GAE plugin, you can create a new GAE project by selecting Web Application Project from the New Projects menu. Figure 8–4 shows the dialog that is presented.

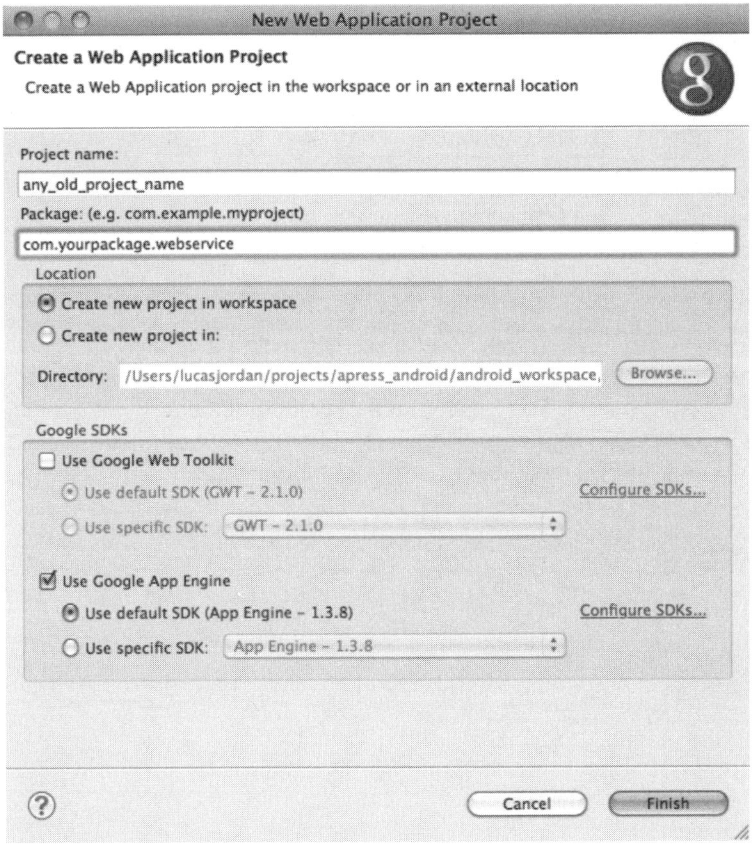

Figure 8–4. *Creating a web application project*

In this dialog, you must provide a project name and a package for the source code. The project name can be anything – it does not need to be the same as the application created with GAE. The package can also be anything you find useful. At the bottom of Figure 8–4, you have the option to use two possible Google SDKs. At minimum you must select Use Google App Engine in order for this project to work with GAE. The option Use Google Web Toolkit allows you to use GWT with your application. GWT or Google Web Toolkit is a framework for writing your client-side logic in Java. We won't be covering GWT, but the combination of GWT and GAE is a powerful one. We encourage any Java developer to check out GWT, as it makes your Java skills relevant in the domain of web-based, client-side application development.

Once your application is created, you run it locally by right-clicking on your project and selecting Run As and then Web Application, as shown in Figure 8–5.

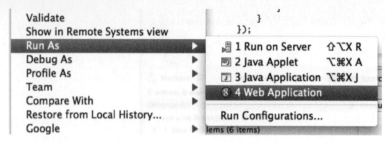

Figure 8–5. *Running GAE locally*

When you are developing your GAE application, you do so by running a version of it locally. Eclipse handles the details of this, but basically the GAE plug in launches a local web server and deploys your application. The local web server includes an implementation similar to the live GAE, and can reliably used to test your application. Once you run your application, it will be available at http://localhost:8888.

GAE Project Structure

Java-based GAE projects are organized like most typical Java web applications. Figure 8–6 shows how a project is organized in Eclipse.

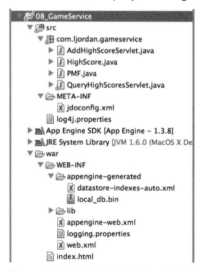

Figure 8–6. *GAE Project structure in Eclipse*

In Figure 8–6, you see the file called index.html under the 'war' directory. This file is the default web page served by this application. The war directory is used to store all static content for the web application; this includes html, css, image files, and JSP files. Also under the 'war' directory is a directory called WEB-INF. This contains a web.xml file, which is used to describe the dynamic resources for this application. There is nothing special about a web.xml file used by GAE versus a web.xml from other Java web applications. It contains the definition of servlets, their access points, and other information one would expect in a web.xml file. In addition to the web.xml file in the WEB-INF directory, there is a folder called appengine-genereated. This contains a number of configuration files that are automatically generated. In general, these files can be ignored.

The rest of the project includes the Java source code and a file called jdoconfig.xml, which is used to configure a technology called Java Data Objects (JDO). JDO is a relational object mapping technology like Hibernate or JPA. We will take a closer look at the persistence features of GAE later.

A new GAE project is uninteresting, but is ready to be deployed once it is configured to your GAE account. Figure 8–7 shows the panel used to configure your project for deployment.

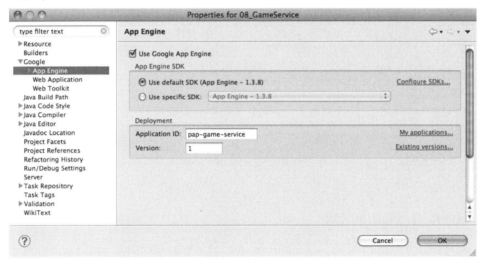

Figure 8–7. Configure GAE application for deployment

In Figure 8–7 the GAE-specific project settings are displayed. To prepare for deployment, you must fill out the Application ID field. The Application ID is the value you filled out when you created a new GAE application. It is the value you entered as the Application Identifier, as shown in Figure 8–7. The version should be the value 1. GAE has the ability to upload multiple versions of an application and then switch between them. This is a handy feature as an application grows in complexity, but we are going to work with a single version.

Once you have the GAE project settings filled out, the application can be deployed by right-clicking on your project and selecting Google, then Deploy to App Engine. Figure 8–8 shows the menu item.

CHAPTER 8: Using the Google App Engine with Android

Figure 8-8. *Deploy menu item*

After selecting the menu item as shown in Figure 8-8, the dialog shown in Figure 8-9 is displayed. In this dialog, you must enter the credentials you used to create you GAE account.

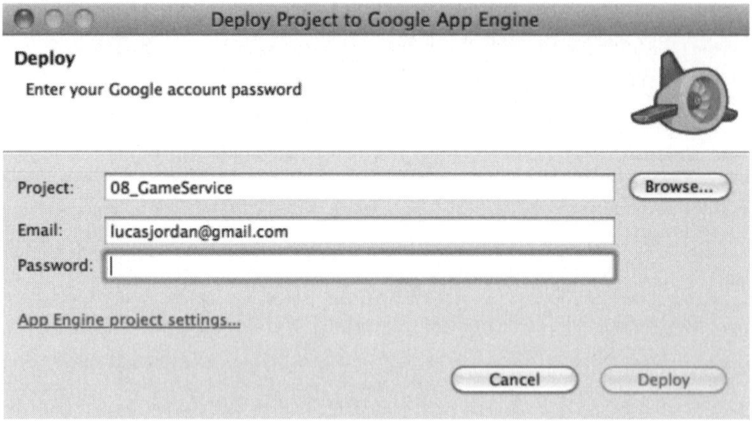

Figure 8-9. *Entering your Google credentials*

After hitting the Deploy button, the GAE plugin will perform a number of steps to prepare your application for deployment, and then deploy it. Figure 8-10 shows the type of output you should expect in the Eclipse Console.

```
*****************************************
Creating staging directory
Scanning for jsp files.
Scanning files on local disk.
Initiating update.
Cloning 1 static files.
Cloning 19 application files.
Uploading 2 files.
Uploaded 1 files.
Uploaded 2 files.
Initializing precompilation...
Deploying new version.
Will check again in 1 seconds.
Will check again in 2 seconds.
Will check again in 4 seconds.
```

Figure 8-10. *Output from a successful deployment*

Eclipse and the GAE plugin provide a simple way to get a web page deployed on GAE. However, the default application is little more then a stub of an application. It is worth exploring some of the details of GAE so it can be appropriately evaluated as a possible solution for implementing a web service consumed by an Android application.

Charges for the Google App Engine Service

GAE is free to set up and free to deploy your application on. Google does charge for this service, but not until your application has consumed more than its daily quota for a particular service. This is handy for start-ups, which only have to pay once their application becomes popular enough to exceed the quota. Hopefully, a web application that exceeds its quota is profitable enough to at least cover those addition charges. The current costs and quotas for the most important GAE resources are shown in Table 8–1. GAE does have a number of other quotas for less commonly used resources.

Table 8–1. *Google app engine quotas and costs for major resources*

Resource	Free Quota	Unit Cost
CPU Time	6.5 CPU hours	$0.10/CPU hour
Bandwidth Out	1.00 GBytes	$0.12/GByte
Bandwidth In	1.00 GBytes	$0.10/Gbyte
Stored Data	1.00 GBytes	$0.005/GByte-day
Recipients Emailed	2,000 Emails	0.0001/Email

GAE does not charge for overages; you just get a warning that you have exceeded your quota. But we are sure that you would be shut off at some point. In order to increase the amount of a particular resource available, you set a budget and select how you want that money spent. For example, you can choose to spend an additional $5.00 a day and select the Bandwidth Intensive budget preset. This option makes the most sense for a site one of us runs, because the Bandwidth Out resource was maxing out, while the CPU Time barely changed when the number of users increased. This was due to the large number of images and the limited amount of dynamic content. The Bandwidth Intensive budget distributes that $5.00 as shown in Table 8–2.

Table 8–2. *Bandwidth Intensive budget preset for $5.00*

Resource	Budget ($5.00)	Unit Cost	Paid Quota	Free Quota	Total Daily Quota
CPU Time	$0.50	$0.10	5.00	6.50	11.50 CPU hours
Bandwidth Out	$2.80	$0.12	23.33	1.0	24.33 GBytes
Bandwidth In	$0.70	$0.10	6.99	1.0	7.99 GBytes
Stored Data	$1.00	$0.005	200.00	1.0	201.00 GBytes
Recipients Emailed	$0.00	$0.0001	0	2000	2000 Emails

By setting a budget and increasing your daily quotas, Google will continue to server your application and only charge for the resources you consume over the free quotas. The budget presents are as follows:

- Standard (evenly distribute your budget over the available resources)
- CPU Intensive
- Bandwidth Intensive
- Storage Intensive
- Custom (select how your budget is applied to resources)

Google App Engine Services

Any web application of reasonable complexity will have to do more than just serve static content. In order to enable more complex applications, Google offers a number of services. Most of these are things you would expect from any application container, such as sending email. The GAE services use the normal Java classes to perform these functions where available. For example, to send email, your application would use the normal J2EE classes from the javax.mail package for most operations. But again, using the email example, there are some differences and limitations when running your code in GAE. These differences exist because any coding running on GAE must be scalable, so Google has removed the portions of each Java API that don't make sense in a massively distributed application. The biggest assumption GAE makes about your application is that it is stateless. Since your GAE application will be distributed among any number of servers and client requests will be disturbed evenly among these servers, your application must never assume that client request will be sent to the same server twice.

In some cases, Google's decisions make sense. In other cases, the limitations seem arbitrary or incomplete. The next section is an overview of each service, giving high-level detail and some notes on limitations.

App Engine Datastore

In a tiered web application, each server uses a database to store data. This database is queried to respond to users' requests and updated by their actions according to the application's business logic. When creating an application for GAE, Google provides access to a powerful, scalable data persistence service called the App Engine datastore. The App Engine datastore is a schema-less object datastore that supports custom queries and atomic transactions.

The App Engine datastore is what people are calling a No-SQL database, much like CouchDB or MongoDB. Basically each "row" in the App Engine datastore is a collection of key-value pairs. The key can be thought of as the column name, but this can lead to some confusion, because not all rows in a given table have to have the same keys. There are good reasons for this, and Google's track record for storing and serving data is proof that it knows what it's doing.

Not every developer is going to want to learn this new API for storing data, so GAE offers two wrappers around their App Engine datastore to make life easier for Java developers. The first wrapper is the Java Data Objects (JDO) API and the second is Java Persistence API (JPA). Neither of these two specifications is fully implemented by Google, and both offer only cursory functionality. Don't expect to be able to easily port an existing application that uses either of these technologies. However, if all you want to do is persist a handful of Plain Old Java Objects (POJOs), then Google's implementation of JDO and JPA will suffice.

Blobstore Java API

The Blobstore Java API is an API that allows GAE applications to store data that is too large for the App Engine datastore. In addition to storing larger chunks of data, the Blobstore API allows portions of a blob to be served without reading the entire blob into memory. This feature allows GAE applications to create scalable and efficient streaming applications, which might otherwise be impossible given GAE's stateless nature.

The Blobstore Java API does not have any particular limitations, since it is in effect a service to overcome the limitations of the App Engine datastore.

Channel API

The Channel API is used to create a persistent connection between your application and the client. This is done in many applications so messages or other data can be pushed from the server to the client. Historically, the client polling the server for messages has accomplished this, but in recent years, this has been accomplished by not closing a connection on the server side and sending new bytes to the client when available. With the advent of HTML5, this client-server behavior has been further refined and standardized. It makes sense that Google would want to support this type of messaging, given its support for HTML5 as a whole. It is interesting, though, that the HTML5 technology WebSockets is not used to implement this. We suspect that will change in the future, as HTML5 becomes more common.

Since GAE blocks access to a lot of the low level functions that would normally be used to accomplish this type of communication, they have provided a dedicated service to implement this. We don't consider this a limitation at all, since the API provided is the easiest we have ever used, when a comet-like service is required.

Images API

As mentioned, the AWT packages are absent from the Java implementation available on GAE. Since AWT contains a fully functionally image manipulation stack, this is a pretty big hole in the GAE runtime. Many simple web applications require some level of image manipulation, even if it is just to scale images before they are saved. To help plug this hole, GAE provides a number of canned functions for manipulating images. These include

- Resize
- Rotate
- Flip Horizontally
- Flip Vertically
- Crop
- I'm Feeling Lucky

The I'm Feeling Lucky function enhances dark and bright colors, which generally improves the visual quality of the image. The GAE supports the manipulation of images in the JPEG, PNG, GIF, BMP, TIFF, and ICO formats. If you application has no or limited image manipulation requirements, then GAE might still be valid option.

Mail API

The Mail API allows GAE applications to send and receive email. When it comes to sending email, a GAE application uses the standard javax.mail package. Your application can respond to any email address of the form [anyname]@appid.appspotmail.com. Emails sent to these types of addresses are treated as HTTP POST requests sent to the URL /_ah/mail/address.

The only limitation with the Mail API is that a quota governs the number of emails sent by your application, and incoming emails are counted toward your Bandwidth In quota. The limit on the number of emails that can be sent out makes sense, as this prevents the GAE from being a powerful tool to spammers.

Memcache

Web applications often make use of a shared, in-memory cache to improve performance when dealing with common data. GAE provides this functionality as the Memcache service. The GAE API for working with Memcache is identical to the JCache API specified by JSR 107. Memcache is important in GAE applications, not only through providing a caching API, but also through providing a way to store session data, since GAE is largely stateless. Calls to Memcache are governed by a Mamcache API Quota, which can be increased as needed.

Task Queues

The GAE JRE does not allow threads to be created or run. In order to create a background process, the Task Queues API must be used. The Task Queue API allows the developer to define a task by specifying an HTTP request be sent to given URL at a given time. In order to actually do the work of the task, the developer implements a Servlet that listens to the given URL. Since the Task API allows you to define repeating tasks, you can set up scheduled work, much like a CRON service.

Users and Authentication

At the time of this writing, GAE provides applications with the ability to authenticate users with OpenID and OAuth. This is a real value add, since you can have users simply use their existing Google (or other) account to log in to your application. Users can be marked as admins, allowing you some basic roll-based authentication.

XMPP

The XMPP service provides an API communicating with other XMPP services. XMPP services are things like Google Talk: you can send messages, receive messages, request invitations, and do other chat-related things. This is an interesting feature and a simple API to use; it is purely a value add for GAE application.

The Google App Engine is a unique development environment that offers a rich set of features and some inconvenient shortcomings. If your application fits with its limitations, it can be a powerful tool, freeing you from managing your own servers.

Examining a Sample GAE Application

In the accompanying source code to this chapter you will find an Eclipse project called 08_GameService. This project is a GAE application that provides a simple service for recording and querying high scores. These two services end points are defined by two Servlets. Let's take a look at the web.xml file for this project, shown in Listing 8-1.

Listing 8–1. *web.xml*

```xml
<?xml version="1.0" encoding="utf-8"?>
<web-app xmlns:xsi="http://www.w3.org/2001/XMLSchema-instance"
xmlns="http://java.sun.com/xml/ns/javaee"
xmlns:web="http://java.sun.com/xml/ns/javaee/web-app_2_5.xsd"
xsi:schemaLocation="http://java.sun.com/xml/ns/javaee
http://java.sun.com/xml/ns/javaee/web-app_2_5.xsd" version="2.5">

	<servlet>
		<servlet-name>AddHighScoreServlet</servlet-name>
		<servlet-class>com.ljordan.gameservice.AddHighScoreServlet</servlet-class>
	</servlet>

	<servlet>
		<servlet-name>QueryHighScoresServlet</servlet-name>
		<servlet-class>com.ljordan.gameservice.QueryHighScoresServlet</servlet-class>
	</servlet>

	<servlet-mapping>
		<servlet-name>AddHighScoreServlet</servlet-name>
		<url-pattern>/add_high_score</url-pattern>
	</servlet-mapping>

	<servlet-mapping>
		<servlet-name>QueryHighScoresServlet</servlet-name>
		<url-pattern>/query_high_scores</url-pattern>
	</servlet-mapping>

	<welcome-file-list>
		<welcome-file>index.html</welcome-file>
	</welcome-file-list>

</web-app>
```

As shown in Listing 9-1, there are two servlets defined, AddHighScoreServlet and QueryHighScoresServlet. These servlets respond to HTTP request at the URLs add_high_score and query_high_scores, respectively. In addition to the servlets, the web.xml file also indicates that the index.html file should be served when no page is specified. The index.html file contains a number of links that that can be used to interact with these services. Listing 8–2 shows a partial listing of the index.html file.

Listing 8–2. *Links from index.html*

```
//Add Highscore
<a href="
add_high_score?highscore=%7B%22username%22%3A%22ljordan%22%2C%22score%22%3A50%2C%22
longitude%22%3A-77.67%2C%22latitude%22%3A43.12%2C%22date%22%3A12345678%2C%22
gameName%22%3A%22orb+quest%22%7D
">Add Score: ljordan(50)</a>

//Query Highscores
<a href="query_high_scores">All</a>
<a href="query_high_scores?game_name=orb%20quest&username=ljordan">ljordan's orb quest
```

```
scores'</a>
a href="query_high_scores?game_name=orb%20quest&username=ljordan&gtr_score=↵
100">ljordan's orb quest scores' higher then 100</a>
```

In Listing 8–2, the first link will add a high score to the service. This is done by sending an HTTP GET to the URL add_high_score and specifying the parameter highscore. The value of highscore is a URL-encoded string, which in turn is a JSON representation of a HighScore object. To query for high scores, send an HTTP GET to the URL query_high_score and specify a number of parameters. The first query specifies no parameters and returns all high score values. The second query request high scores for the game "orb quest" that were earned by the user ljordan. The last query is similar to the previous, but restricts the high scores to those over the value 100. We will take a look at how these services are implemented, but first let's take a look at the Java representation of the HighScore class, as shown in Listing 8–3.

Listing 8–3. *HighScore.java*

```
@PersistenceCapable(identityType = IdentityType.APPLICATION)
public class HighScore {

        @PrimaryKey
        @Persistent(valueStrategy = IdGeneratorStrategy.IDENTITY)
        private Long key;
        @Persistent
        private String username;
        @Persistent
        private Long score;
        @Persistent
        private String gameName;
        @Persistent
        private Double longitude;
        @Persistent
        private Double latitude;
        @Persistent
        private Long date;

        public HighScore() {

        }

        public HighScore(JSONObject jsonObject) throws JSONException {
                if (jsonObject.has("key")) {
                        key = jsonObject.getLong("key");
                }
                if (jsonObject.has("username")) {
                        username = jsonObject.getString("username");
                }
                if (jsonObject.has("score")) {
                        score = jsonObject.getLong("score");
                }
                if (jsonObject.has("gameName")) {
                        gameName = jsonObject.getString("gameName");
                }
                if (jsonObject.has("longitude")) {
                        longitude = jsonObject.getDouble("longitude");
                }
```

```java
                if (jsonObject.has("latitude")) {
                        latitude = jsonObject.getDouble("latitude");
                }
                if (jsonObject.has("date")) {
                        date = jsonObject.getLong("date");
                }
        }

        public JSONObject toJSONObject() throws JSONException {
                JSONObject result = new JSONObject();
                result.put("key", key);
                result.put("username", username);
                result.put("score", score);
                result.put("gameName", gameName);
                result.put("longitude", longitude);
                result.put("latitude", latitude);
                result.put("date", date);

                return result;
        }
//get/set methods omitted
```

In Listing 8–3 we see the interesting parts of the HighScore class. The HighScore class is a simple POJO annotated with some JDO specific annotations. As mentioned, JDO is an object-relation mapping tool. What this means is that JDO provides a way for you to specify a class as persistable, and JDO handles the details of setting up a table in a database to store instances of this class. In general, this happens by creating a table with the same name as the class, and creating columns for each field. There is a lot more to how object relational mapping technologies work, but for now, you just have to know that JDO marks a class as persistable by annotating it with PersistenceCapable. Each persistable class also requires a field to be used as the primary key for the table backing the class. In this case, we use the field called key of type Long. Lastly, JDO requires you to specify exactly which fields should be included when an Object is persisted. This is done by adding the annotation Persistable to each field that should be included.

There is a special constructor that takes a JSON object. It is used to create a HighScore object from any JSON sent by the client. Conversely, the method toJSONObject is used to serialize a HighScore object so it can be sent back to the client in valid JSON.

Adding the HighScore Service

The first service we should look at is the one for adding high scores. The class AddHighScoreServlet implements this service. Let's take a look at the source code, shown in Listing 8–4.

Listing 8–4. *AddHighScoreServlet*

```java
@SuppressWarnings("serial")
public class AddHighScoreServlet extends HttpServlet {

        public final static String PARAM_HIGHSCORE = "highscore";
```

```
        public void doGet(HttpServletRequest req, HttpServletResponse resp)
                    throws IOException {
            String json = req.getParameter(PARAM_HIGHSCORE);

            resp.setContentType("application/json");
            Writer writer = resp.getWriter();

            PersistenceManager pm = PMF.get().getPersistenceManager();
            try {

                HighScore highScore = new HighScore(new JSONObject(json));

                pm.makePersistent(highScore);

                writer.write(highScore.toJSONObject().toString());
            } catch (Exception e) {
                throw new IOException(e);
            } finally {
                pm.close();
                writer.close();
            }

        }
}
```

The AddHighScoreServlet class in Listing 8–4 extends HttpServlet and responds to GET request in the method doGet. The method doGet looks for a JSON object as the value of the parameter highscore. The JSON text is parsed by creating a JSONObject, which is in turn used to create a new HighScore object. As the name of this class implies, its job is to write a HighScore object to the database. This is done by first getting an instance of PersistenceManager from the PFM factory class. The PersistenceManager, named pm, is used to write the object highScore to the database by calling makePersistent. Since adding the variable highScore to the database populates its key field, the object is written back to the client with the writer object.

Once JDO is set up, it is really easy to write objects to a database, or in this case, to the App Engine datastore. Getting JDO setup requires a little boilerplate. Let's start by taking a look at the PMF class, shown in Listing 8–5.

Listing 8–5. *PMF.java*

```
public final class PMF {
        private static final PersistenceManagerFactory pmfInstance = JDOHelper
                    .getPersistenceManagerFactory("transactions-optional");

        private PMF() {
        }

        public static PersistenceManagerFactory get() {
            return pmfInstance;
        }
}
```

In Listing 8–5 we see the class PMF, which is a simple class implementing a factory pattern. The whole point of the PMF class is to provide a convenient way to get at a PersistenceManagerFactory singleton from anyplace in your code. A

PersistenceManagerFactory is the main class for interacting with the underlying datastore. As such, it is important to only create one per datastore, since scanning the persistent classes and validating the datastore is a lot of work.

The example project 08_GameService was created with the GAE tool in Eclipse, and by default JDO is automatically configured to work with JDO. The configuration is found in the file jdoconfig.xml as shown in Listing 8–6.

Listing 8–6. *jdoconfig.xml*

```xml
<?xml version="1.0" encoding="utf-8"?>
<jdoconfig xmlns="http://java.sun.com/xml/ns/jdo/jdoconfig"
    xmlns:xsi="http://www.w3.org/2001/XMLSchema-instance"
    xsi:noNamespaceSchemaLocation="http://java.sun.com/xml/ns/jdo/jdoconfig">

    <persistence-manager-factory name="transactions-optional">
        <property name="javax.jdo.PersistenceManagerFactoryClass"
            value="org.datanucleus.store.appengine.jdo.↵
DatastoreJDOPersistenceManagerFactory"/>
        <property name="javax.jdo.option.ConnectionURL" value="appengine"/>
        <property name="javax.jdo.option.NontransactionalRead" value="true"/>
        <property name="javax.jdo.option.NontransactionalWrite" value="true"/>
        <property name="javax.jdo.option.RetainValues" value="true"/>
        <property name="datanucleus.appengine.autoCreateDatastoreTxns" value="true"/>
    </persistence-manager-factory>
</jdoconfig>
```

In Listing 8–6 we can see that some assumptions are made by GAE. The first is that non-transactional reads and writes are enabled. This is not a big deal in our simple application, but more complex, more data sensitive applications my find this setting problematic. As mentioned previously, there are some holes in Google's JDO implementation. If transactional reading and writing is required, be sure to read Google's documentation closely. They are adding features all the time. Another thing to notice is that the ConnectionURL is set to appengine. Figure 8–11 shows this URL for a local version of the app engine.

CHAPTER 8: Using the Google App Engine with Android

Figure 8–11. *Local datastore*

In Figure 8–11 we see the local datastore that is used while developing a GAE application. On the right, you can see instances of HighScore that have been persisted through the SaveHighScoreServlet. This view into persisted object is handy when debugging your application, as you can write little scripts that populate this datastore with sample data. On the left side of Figure 8–11 we can see that there are options for interacting with a local version of a Task Queue, XMPP, and Inbound Mail. These other tools allow you to simulate running your code on the live GAE.

Querying the HighScore Service

To query for high scores, an HTTP GET request is sent to the QueryHighScoresServlet. This servlet converts the HTTP GET request into a valid JDO query and returns the results. Listing 8–7 shows the doGet method of QueryHighScoresServlet.

Listing 8–7. *QueryHighScoresServlet.doGet()*

```
@SuppressWarnings("serial")
public class QueryHighScoresServlet extends HttpServlet {

    private static final String PARAM_COUNT = "count";
    private static final String PARAM_GTR_LAT = "gtr_lat";
    private static final String PARAM_LST_LAT = "lst_lat";
    private static final String PARAM_GTR_LON = "gtr_lon";
    private static final String PARAM_LST_LON = "lst_lon";
    private static final String PARAM_GTR_SCORE = "gtr_score";
    private static final String PARAM_USERNAME = "username";
    private static final String PARAM_LST_SCORE = "lst_score";
    private static final String PARAM_GAMENAME = "game_name";

    public void doGet(HttpServletRequest req, HttpServletResponse resp)
```

```
            throws IOException {
        String count = req.getParameter(PARAM_COUNT);
        String gtrLat = req.getParameter(PARAM_GTR_LAT);
        String lstLat = req.getParameter(PARAM_LST_LAT);
        String gtrLon = req.getParameter(PARAM_GTR_LON);
        String lstLon = req.getParameter(PARAM_LST_LON);
        String username = req.getParameter(PARAM_USERNAME);
        String gtrScore = req.getParameter(PARAM_GTR_SCORE);
        String lstScore = req.getParameter(PARAM_LST_SCORE);
        String gameName = req.getParameter(PARAM_GAMENAME);

        List<HighScore> highScores = queryHighScores(count, lstLat, gtrLat,
                    lstLon, gtrLon, username, lstScore, gtrScore, gameName);

        resp.setContentType("application/json");
        Writer writer = resp.getWriter();

        try {

            JSONArray result = new JSONArray();
            for (HighScore highscore : highScores) {
                    result.put(highscore.toJSONObject());
            }
            writer.write(result.toString());

        } catch (Exception e) {
            throw new IOException(e);
        } finally {
            writer.close();
        }
    }
```

In Listing 8–7, the doGet method finds all parameters passed in with the request. The values of these parameters are passed to the queryHighScores method. The result of the queryHighScores method is converted into JSONObjects, added to a JSONArray, and returned to the client. The heavy lifting of the doGet method is done in the queryHighScores method, shown in Listings 8–8 and 8–9.

Listing 8–8. *QueryHighScoresServlet.queryHighScores()*

```
        private List<HighScore> queryHighScores(String count, String lstLat,
                    String gtrLat, String lstLon, String gtrLon, String username,
                    String lstScore, String gtrScore, String gameName) {

            List<HighScore> results = new ArrayList<HighScore>();

            PersistenceManager pm = null;
            try {
                pm = PMF.get().getPersistenceManager();

                Map<String, String> paramNameToType = new HashMap<String, String>();

                Map<String, Object> paramNameToValue = new HashMap<String, Object>();

                List<String> filters = new ArrayList<String>();
```

```java
                        if (lstLat != null) {
                                filters.add("latitude < plstLat");
                                paramNameToType.put("plstLat", "Double");
                                paramNameToValue.put("plstLat",↵
Double.parseDouble(lstLat));
                        }
                        if (gtrLat != null) {
                                filters.add("latitude > pgtrLat");
                                paramNameToType.put("pgtrLat", "Double");
                                paramNameToValue.put("pgtrLat",↵
Double.parseDouble(gtrLat));
                        }
                        if (lstLon != null) {
                                filters.add("longitude < plstLon");
                                paramNameToType.put("plstLon", "Double");
                                paramNameToValue.put("plstLon",↵
Double.parseDouble(lstLon));
                        }
                        if (gtrLon != null) {
                                filters.add("longitude > pgtrLon");
                                paramNameToType.put("pgtrLon", "Double");
                                paramNameToValue.put("pgtrLon",↵
Double.parseDouble(gtrLon));
                        }
                        if (username != null) {
                                filters.add("username == pusername");
                                paramNameToType.put("pusername", "String");
                                paramNameToValue.put("pusername", username);
                        }
                        if (lstScore != null) {
                                filters.add("score < plstScore");
                                paramNameToType.put("plstScore", "Long");
                                paramNameToValue.put("plstScore",↵
Double.parseDouble(lstScore));
                        }
                        if (gtrScore != null) {
                                filters.add("score > pgtrScore");
                                paramNameToType.put("pgtrScore", "Long");
                                paramNameToValue.put("pgtrScore",↵
Long.parseLong(gtrScore));
                        }
                        if (gameName != null) {
                                filters.add("gameName == pgameName");
                                paramNameToType.put("pgameName", "String");
                                paramNameToValue.put("pgameName", gameName);
                        }

                        Query query = pm.newQuery(HighScore.class);

                        query.setOrdering("score desc");
                        if (count != null) {
                                query.setRange(0, Long.parseLong(count));
                        }
```

In Listing 8–8 we must figure out which parameters are passed from the client. If a parameter is null, the client has not included that it in their query string. If a parameter is not null, append the appropriate String to the variable filters and populate the maps paramNameToType and paramNameToValue. These maps will be used later to propertyl construct our JDO query, as shown in Listing 8–9.

Listing 8–9. *QueryHighScoresServlet.queryHighScores() (continued)*

```
                    if (filters.size() == 0) {
                        for (Object obj : (List) query.execute()) {
                            results.add((HighScore) obj);
                        }
                        return results;
                    } else {
                        StringBuffer filter = new StringBuffer();

                        ListIterator<String> li = filters.listIterator();
                        while (li.hasNext()) {
                            filter.append(li.next());
                            if (li.hasNext()) {
                                filter.append(" & ");
                            }
                        }

                        List values = new ArrayList();
                        StringBuffer parameters = new StringBuffer();
                        Iterator<Map.Entry<String, String>> i = paramNameToType
                                    .entrySet().iterator();

                        while (i.hasNext()) {
                            Map.Entry<String, String> param = i.next();
                            parameters.append(param.getValue());
                            parameters.append(' ');
                            parameters.append(param.getKey());
                            if (i.hasNext()) {
                                parameters.append(',');
                            }
                            values.add(paramNameToValue.get↵
(param.getKey())));
                        }
                        query.setFilter(filter.toString());
                        query.declareParameters(parameters.toString());

                        for (Object obj : (List) query.executeWithArray(values
                                    .toArray())) {
                            results.add((HighScore) obj);
                        }
                        return results;
                    }
            } finally {
                    pm.close();
            }
    }
```

Listing 8–9 uses the bookkeeping done by Listing 8–8 to construct a JDO query with the correct information. The filters are basically the 'where' clause from SQL. The map paramNameToType is used to tell JDO which strings in the filter are parameters and what their expected type is. Lastly, the map paramNameToValue is used to assign the parameters in the query their correct values. This is more complicated than simply constructing a big query string from the parameters because this technique prevents security threats similar to SQL injection. Once the query object is created with all the parts and pieces of the query, it is executed by calling executeWithArray. The method executeWithArray returns an untyped list containing the desired HighScore objects, which are returned to the client as JSON.

Creating a simple service to be run on GAE is not much different from creating a web application that lives in a servlet container like Tomcat, Glassfish, or the many other servlet containers. Taking advantage of the App Engine datastore is made easy by the preconfigured JDO setup. To help simulate other GAE services, the local version of the app engine provides a simple UI. We have several applications running on GAE, and every once in a while we are annoyed at GAEs' idiosyncrasies, but then we remember that it has never gone down in the three years we have used it.

Consuming GAE Services with Android

We have looked at the Google App Engine and a sample web service designed to run on it. We are now going to look at an Android application that uses this service. No, it is not a game – that's coming in another chapter. It is an application designed to give the user an overview of the high scores stored in the service. This sample Android project is called 09_GameManager. Figure 8–12 shows the first screen of the app.

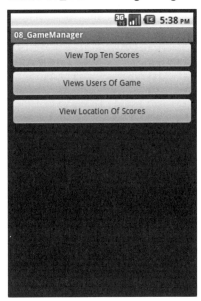

Figure 8–12. *09_GameManager*

In Figure 8–12 we see three buttons. The first allows the user to view the top ten highest scores. The second allows the user to view scores based on user name and the game played. The last button displays a map of the top 100 high scores. Let's start by looking at the layout for the starting activity that is defined in main.xml, as shown in Listing 8–10.

Listing 8–10. *main.xml*

```xml
<?xml version="1.0" encoding="utf-8"?>
<LinearLayout
        xmlns:android="http://schemas.android.com/apk/res/android"
    android:orientation="vertical"
    android:layout_width="fill_parent"
    android:layout_height="fill_parent"
    >
<Button
        android:id="@+id/viewTopTen"
    android:layout_width="fill_parent"
    android:layout_height="wrap_content"
    android:text="View Top Ten Scores"
/>
<Button
        android:id="@+id/usersOfGame"
    android:layout_width="fill_parent"
    android:layout_height="wrap_content"
    android:text="Views Users Of Game"
/>
<Button
        android:id="@+id/viewLocation"
    android:layout_width="fill_parent"
    android:layout_height="wrap_content"
    android:text="View Location Of Scores"
/>
</LinearLayout>
```

In Listing 8–10 we see a very simple layout, starting with a vertically oriented LinearLayout and then adding a button for each sub-activity. Listing 8–11 shows how these buttons are wired up to display different activities.

Listing 8–11. *GameManager.java*

```java
public class GameManager extends Activity implements View.OnClickListener {

    public final static String SERVICE_URL = "http://pap-game-service.appspot.com/";

    private Button topTenButton;
    private Button usersOfGameButton;
    private Button locationButton;

    /** Called when the activity is first created. */
    @Override
    public void onCreate(Bundle savedInstanceState) {
        super.onCreate(savedInstanceState);
        setContentView(R.layout.main);

        topTenButton = (Button) findViewById(R.id.viewTopTen);
        usersOfGameButton = (Button) findViewById(R.id.usersOfGame);
        locationButton = (Button) findViewById(R.id.viewLocation);

        topTenButton.setOnClickListener(this);
        usersOfGameButton.setOnClickListener(this);
```

```
                locationButton.setOnClickListener(this);
        }

        @Override
        public void onClick(View button) {
                if (button == topTenButton) {
                        Intent intent = new Intent(this, TopTenActivity.class);
                        startActivity(intent);
                } else if (button == usersOfGameButton) {
                        Intent intent = new Intent(this, UsersOfGameActivity.class);
                        startActivity(intent);
                } else if (button == locationButton) {
                        Intent intent = new Intent(this, UsersLocationActivity.class);
                        startActivity(intent);
                }
                //unknown button.
        }
}
```

In Listing 8–11 we see the content of main.xml is set as the content by calling setContentView. Once the content has been set, each of the three buttons is found by passing their IDs to the method findViewById. In order to respond to a user clicking a button, we register this instance of GameManager as the click listener for each button by calling setOnClickListener.

> **NOTE:** The sample project 08_GameManager is configured to use a live version of the 08_GameServices deployed at http://pap-game-service.appspot.com. You can change this to localhost:8888 and run game services locally if you wish.

When the user does click a button, the onClick method is called, where we test to see which button was pressed. Each button has a new activity associated with it and is started by first creating a new Intent and then calling startActivity. Each activity is declared in the AndroidManafest.xml file, as shown in Listing 8–12.

Listing 8–12. *AndroidManafest.xml*

```xml
<?xml version="1.0" encoding="utf-8"?>
<manifest xmlns:android="http://schemas.android.com/apk/res/android"
      package="org.ljordan.gamemanager"
      android:versionCode="1"
      android:versionName="1.0">
    <application android:icon="@drawable/icon" android:label="@string/app_name">
        <uses-library android:name="com.google.android.maps" />

        <activity android:name=".GameManager"
                    android:label="@string/app_name">
            <intent-filter>
                <action android:name="android.intent.action.MAIN" />
                <category android:name="android.intent.category.LAUNCHER" />
            </intent-filter>
        </activity>

            <activity android:name=".TopTenActivity"   android:label="Top Ten
Scores!" />
```

```
            <activity android:name=".UsersOfGameActivity"   android:label="Top Scores
For User of Game" />
            <activity android:name=".UsersLocationActivity"  android:label="Location
of Best Players" />

              UserAndGameActivity
  </application>

     <uses-permission android:name="android.permission.INTERNET" />

</manifest>
```

The three sub-activities are defined within the element application, under the main activity. Activities are defined in the AndroidManafiest.xml file are given a name and a label. The label is displayed at the top of the activity when it is active. Also in this AndroidManafest.xml file we see that we require the INTERNET permission, this is done because we want to make an external service call to retrieve the high score information. We also want to use a map. This permission allows us to download the map tiles displayed in the MapView component.

Exploring the Top Ten Activity

Lets take a look at each of the three sub activities in turn, starting with the top ten scores as shown in Figure 8–13.

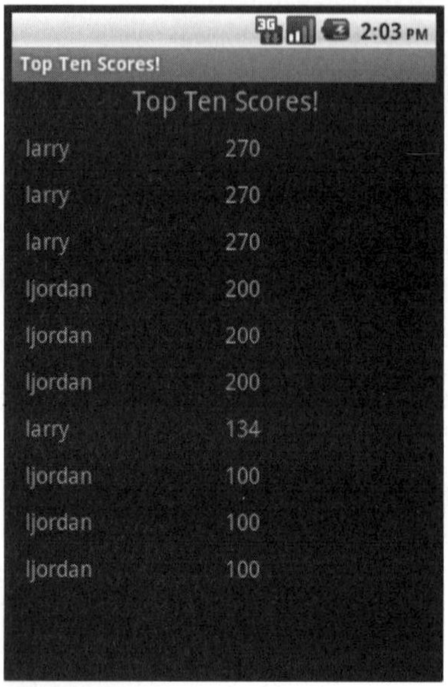

Figure 8–13. *Top ten activity*

In Figure 8–13 we see a simple list of scores. The highest at the top. This data was retrieved by the live GAE application described earlier in this chapter. Let's take a look at the source code for this activity and piece together how this information was retrieved and displayed. See Listing 8–13.

Listing 8-13. *TopTenActivity.java (Constructor)*

```java
public class TopTenActivity extends Activity {

        public HttpClient client = new DefaultHttpClient();

        private TableLayout tableLayout;

        /** Called when the activity is first created. */
        @Override
        public void onCreate(Bundle savedInstanceState) {
                super.onCreate(savedInstanceState);
                setContentView(R.layout.topten);

                tableLayout = (TableLayout) findViewById(R.id.tableLayout);

                new GetTopTen().execute(10);

        }
//class continues…
```

In Listing 8–13 we see that the class TopTenActivity extends Activity and its onCreate method is called when it is displayed. The layout for this class is very simple; it just contains a TableLayout that is found in the onCreate method and stored in the variable tableLayout. The last thing done in the onCreate method is to create a new GetTopTen and call execute on it. GetTopTen is an AsyncTask that is responsible for making the service call. GetTopTen is shown in Listing 8–14.

Listing 8-14. *TopTenActivity (GetTopTen class)*

```java
private class GetTopTen extends AsyncTask<Integer, Integer, JSONArray> {
        @Override
        protected JSONArray doInBackground(Integer... counts) {
                try {
                        StringBuilder fullUrl = new StringBuilder(
                                        GameManager.SERVICE_URL);

                        fullUrl.append("query_high_scores?count=");
                        fullUrl.append(counts[0]);

                        HttpGet get = new HttpGet(fullUrl.toString());
                        HttpResponse response = client.execute(get);

                        int statusCode = response.getStatusLine().getStatusCode();

                        if (statusCode == 200) {
                                HttpEntity entity = response.getEntity();
                                String json = EntityUtils.toString(entity);
                                return new JSONArray(json);
                        } else {
                                String reason =
response.getStatusLine().getReasonPhrase();
                                throw new RuntimeException("Trouble getting
scores(code="
                                                + statusCode + "):" + reason);
                        }
```

```
                } catch (Exception e) {
                        Log.w("TopTenActivity", e);
                        throw new RuntimeException(e);
                }
        }

        protected void onPostExecute(final JSONArray result) {
                runOnUiThread(new Runnable() {
                        @Override
                        public void run() {
                                try {
                                        displayResults(result);
                                } catch (JSONException e) {
                                        Log.w("TopTenActivity", e);
                                }
                        }
                });
        }
}
```

Listing 8–14 shows that TopTenActivity extends AsyncTask. The doInBackground is called in a separate thread from the UI, and is responsible for getting the top ten scores from the sample services. This is done by first creating an HttpGet object with the desired URL and then passing it into an HttpClient to execute. The URL is constructed concatenating the base URL defined as GameManager.SERVICE_URL with the service name query_high_scores. The number of results is specified by including the parameter count in the URL set to the first integer in the array counts.

An HttpResponse is the result of calling client.execute(). If this response has a successful return code (200), then we parse the result by constructing a new JSONArray and returning it.

The method onPostExecute is passed the JSONArray that was created at the end of doInBackground. This JSONArray then passed to the displayResults method by creating a new Runnable and passing it to the runOnUiThread. The method displayResults is shown in Listing 8–15.

Listing 8–15. *TopTenActivity.java (displayResults())*

```
protected void displayResults(JSONArray result) throws JSONException {
        tableLayout.removeAllViews();

        TableRow row = new TableRow(this);
        row.setLayoutParams(new LayoutParams(LayoutParams.FILL_PARENT,
                        LayoutParams.FILL_PARENT));

        TextView userTitleView = new TextView(this);
        userTitleView.setText("Username:");
        userTitleView.setTextSize(18);
        userTitleView.setPadding(10, 10, 100, 2);
        row.addView(userTitleView);

        TextView scoreTitleView = new TextView(this);
        scoreTitleView.setText("Score:");
        scoreTitleView.setTextSize(18);
        row.addView(scoreTitleView);
```

```java
        for (int i = 0; i < result.length(); i++) {
            HighScore highscore = new HighScore(result.getJSONObject(i));

            row = new TableRow(this);
            row.setLayoutParams(new LayoutParams(LayoutParams.FILL_PARENT,
                        LayoutParams.FILL_PARENT));

            TextView userView = new TextView(this);
            userView.setText(highscore.getUsername());
            userView.setTextSize(16);
            userView.setPadding(10, 10, 100, 2);
            row.addView(userView);

            TextView scoreView = new TextView(this);
            scoreView.setText("" + highscore.getScore());
            scoreView.setTextSize(16);
            row.addView(scoreView);
            tableLayout.addView(row, new TableLayout.LayoutParams(
                        LayoutParams.FILL_PARENT, LayoutParams.FILL_PARENT));
        }
    }
}
```

The displayResults method first creates a TableRow containing TextViews that will serve as headers for each column. Once the first row is created, a loop iterates over each entry in the JSONArray called result. Each entry in result is a JSONObject representing a single high score entry. This JSONObject is used to create HighScore object. The class HighScore is identical to the HighScore class used on the server, from Listing 8–3, except that all of the JDO related annotations are removed. Once we have a HighScore object, we simply create another TableRow and populate it with TextViews displaying the username and their score.

Viewing the Users of a Game

The second Activity available in this sample application allows the user to view the high scores for a particular user, for a particular game. Our purely utilitarian interface is displayed in Figure 8–14.

Figure 8-14. *Users of game activity*

In Figure 8-14 we see a place for the user to enter the their username and the name of a game. By clicking the button, the top ten scores for that user for that game are displayed. Much of the code for this Activity is identical, or only slightly different from the TopTenActivity. There are few differences worth pointing out, and these are found in the AsyncTask called GetUsersOfGame, which is analogous to the class GetTopTen from Listing 8-14. Listing 8-16 shows the AsyncTask GetUsersOfGame.

Listing 8-16. *UsersOfGameActivity.java (GetUsersOfGame class)*

```
private class GetUsersOfGame extends AsyncTask<Integer, Integer, JSONArray> {
        @Override
        protected JSONArray doInBackground(Integer... counts) {
                try {

                        String username = usernameEditText.getText().toString();
                        String gamename = gamenameEditText.getText().toString();

                        StringBuilder fullUrl = new StringBuilder(
                                        GameManager.SERVICE_URL);

                        fullUrl.append("query_high_scores?count=10");
                        fullUrl.append("&username=");
                        fullUrl.append(URLEncoder.encode(username, "UTF-8"));
                        fullUrl.append("&game_name=");
                        fullUrl.append(URLEncoder.encode(gamename, "UTF-8"));

                        HttpGet get = new HttpGet(fullUrl.toString());
                        HttpResponse response = client.execute(get);

                        int statusCode = response.getStatusLine().getStatusCode();

                        if (statusCode == 200) {
```

```
                                HttpEntity entity = response.getEntity();
                                String json = EntityUtils.toString(entity);
                                return new JSONArray(json);
                        } else {
                                String reason =
response.getStatusLine().getReasonPhrase();
                                throw new RuntimeException("Trouble getting
scores(code="
                                                                + statusCode + "):" + reason);
                        }

                } catch (Exception e) {
                        Log.w("TopTenActivity", e);
                        throw new RuntimeException(e);
                }
        }

        protected void onPostExecute(final JSONArray result) {
                runOnUiThread(new Runnable() {
                        @Override
                        public void run() {
                                try {
                                        displayResults(result);
                                } catch (JSONException e) {
                                        Log.w("TopTenActivity", e);
                                }
                        }
                });
        }
}
```

Listing 8–16 shows the class GetUsersOfGame that is responsible for making the network call to our GAE services. The interesting thing about this class is how it constructs the query. The variable fullUrl is a StringBuilder that is constructed by appending the service name the base URL found in the variable GameManager.SERVICE_URL. The values for the parameters username and game_name are pulled from the EditText variables usernameEditText and gamenameEditText. Once the query is constructed and executed, the UI is updated in exactly the same way as the TopTenActivity.

Viewing a User's Location (MapView)

The UsersLocationActivity allows the user to view the location in the world where the highest scores are achieved. This gives us a real-time look at which region of the world is currently getting the highest scores. Figure 8–15 shows this activity.

Figure 8–15. *User's location activity*

The map displayed in Figure 8–15 is from an optional Android package that provides a MapView component. On the map, you can see there is a circle over western New York. This is the location of the highest scored at the time of this writing. As people work through the example in this book, we should see the locations of other Android developers if they choose to submit scores to this service.

In order to enable an optional package, information must be entered into the AndroidManifest.xml file. Listing 8–12 shows the AndroidManifest.xml file for this project and the use-library element directs Android to include the map API.

In order to use a MapView, you must obtain a key from Google and include that key in your layout xml file. If you don't get a key, the example code for this project will not work correctly when you run it. The steps to generate a key for use with Google's Map API is different if you want to use the API on Android rather than a web page. In order obtain a key for use with Android, you first have to find the certificate fingerprint of the keystore you are using to sign your Android application. If you have not set up your own keystore, then chances are you are using the default one. Check in your home directory for a folder named ".android." This should contain a file named "debug.keystore" that is used to sign applications while you are debugging your application. Figure 8–16 shows a terminal on a development machine.

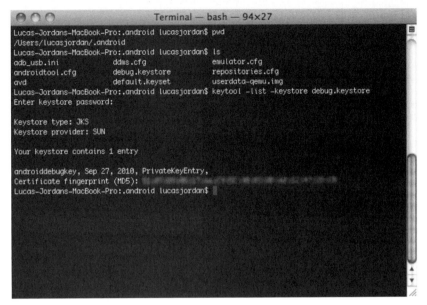

Figure 8–16. *Terminal showing content of debug.keystore*

In Figure 8–16, you can see the command keytool was used to inspect the debug keystore. The command keytool comes with your JDK and should be on your command path if java is. The fuzzy bit at the bottom is where the md5 certificate fingerprint is displayed. You use this fingerprint at http://code.google.com/android/maps-api-signup.html to generate your Android Maps API key. Once you have that key, you can set up a MapView to work properly. In this example, this was done in the layout xml file called user_location.xml as shown in Listing 8–17.

Listing 8–17. *user_location.xml*

```
<?xml version="1.0" encoding="utf-8"?>
<LinearLayout
    xmlns:android="http://schemas.android.com/apk/res/android"
    android:layout_width="wrap_content"
    android:layout_height="wrap_content">

    <com.google.android.maps.MapView
        android:id="@+id/mapview"
        android:layout_width="fill_parent"
        android:layout_height="fill_parent"
        android:clickable="true"
        android:apiKey="YOUR_MAP_API_KEY_GOES HERE"
    />

</LinearLayout>
```

In Listing 8–17 we see a single MapView element in a LinearLayout. The apiKey attribute of the MapView is where we want to stick our Android Map API key. If you run the application and no map tiles are displayed, there is a good chance something is wrong with your key.

The next thing to take a look at is the activity, and see how we add items to the map. Listing 8–18 shows this activity is setup in code.

Listing 8–18. *UsersLocationActivity.java (partial)*

```
public class UsersLocationActivity extends MapActivity {

        private MapView mapView;
        public HttpClient client = new DefaultHttpClient();

        /** Called when the activity is first created. */
        @Override
        public void onCreate(Bundle savedInstanceState) {
                super.onCreate(savedInstanceState);
                setContentView(R.layout.user_location);
                mapView = (MapView) findViewById(R.id.mapview);
                mapView.setBuiltInZoomControls(true);

                new GetTopTen().execute(100);
        }

        @Override
        protected boolean isRouteDisplayed() {
                // TODO Auto-generated method stub
                return false;
        }
}
```

In Listing 8–18 we see UsersLocationActivity extends MapActivity. MapActivity is a special subclass of Activity that must be used in order to display a MapView object. MapActivity is abstract and does not contain an implementation of the method isRouteDisplayed, so we must include an implementation in UsersLocationActivity. The isRouteDisplayed method simply returns false, since we don't want to display a route.

In the onCreate method of UsersLocationActivity the mapView variable is located in the layout in the usual way. Once the map view is found, we add the default controls by calling setBuiltInZoomControls to true. Lastly, we create a GetTopTen and execute it. GetTopTen is an AsyncTask and is shown in Listing 8–14. When GetTopTen is done running it passes the top 100 high scores to the method displayResults that adds the high scores to the map. Listing 8–19 shows this method.

Listing 8–19. *UsersLocationActivity (displayResults)*

```
protected void displayResults(JSONArray result) throws JSONException {
        Drawable drawable = this.getResources().getDrawable(
                        R.drawable.green_orb);

        HighscoreOverlay highscoreOverlay = new HighscoreOverlay(drawable);

        for (int i = 0; i < result.length(); i++) {
                HighScore highscore = new HighScore(result.getJSONObject(i));

                String username = highscore.getUsername();
                String score = "" + highscore.getScore();
                int latitude = (int) highscore.getLatitude().doubleValue() * 1000000;
                int longitude = (int) highscore.getLongitude().doubleValue() * 1000000;

                List<Overlay> mapOverlays = mapView.getOverlays();
```

```
            GeoPoint point = new GeoPoint(latitude, longitude);

            OverlayItem item = new OverlayItem(point, username, "Score: "
                        + score);

            highscoreOverlay.addOverlay(item);
            mapOverlays.add(highscoreOverlay);
        }
    }
```

In Listing 8–19, the displayResults method takes a JSONArray called result. The result variable contains a number of JSONObjects that are used to construct HighScore objects. For each HighScore object, an OverlayItem is created and added to an instance of HighScoreOverlay, which we will look at in a moment. Each OverlayItem is constructed with a GeoPoint, specifying the location of the OverlayItem, and the username and score. The HighScoreOverlay class is used to aggregate multiple OverlayItems that share an icon. The icon used to display each point on the map is defined by the Drawable that is passed to the constructor of HighScoreOverlay. HighScoreOverlay is shown in Listing 8–20.

Listing 8–20. *HighScoreOverlay Class*

```
public class HighscoreOverlay extends ItemizedOverlay<OverlayItem> {

        private ArrayList<OverlayItem> mOverlays = new ArrayList<OverlayItem>();

        public HighscoreOverlay(Drawable defaultMarker) {
                super(boundCenterBottom(defaultMarker));
        }

        public void addOverlay(OverlayItem overlay) {
                mOverlays.add(overlay);
                populate();
        }

        @Override
        protected OverlayItem createItem(int i) {
                return mOverlays.get(i);
        }

        @Override
        public int size() {
                return mOverlays.size();
        }

        @Override
        protected boolean onTap(int index) {
                OverlayItem item = mOverlays.get(index);
                AlertDialog.Builder dialog = new AlertDialog.Builder(
                                UsersLocationActivity.this);
                dialog.setTitle(item.getTitle());
                dialog.setMessage(item.getSnippet());
                dialog.show();
                return true;
        }
}
```

Listing 8–20 shows that HighScoreOverlay extends the class ItemizedOverlay. ItemizedOverlay is class provided by the Android Maps API and is used as a starting point for creating collections of MapOverlays. In the constructor of HighScoreOverlay, we see that a Drawable is passed in and is used as the icon drawn on the map. The method boundCenterBottom is used to indicate that the bottom center of the icon should be drawn at the actual point on the map described by the longitude and latitude of the OverlayItems. The onTap method brings up a small dialog, displaying the name of the user and the high score they achieved, as shown in Figure 8–17.

Figure 8–17. *Dialog for single map item*

Consuming a web service hosted by Google App Engine is no different than consuming a service hosted on any platform. The advantage to using GAE with android is the simplicity of deployment and using Google's Eclipse plugins. If you want a low-cost, high availability server backing your Android application, GAE is an excellent choice.

Summary

In this chapter we explored Google App Engine in some detail. We looked at how an application is set up to run on Google's hardware and what tools are available to create that application. We also looked at some of the limitations of the Google App Engine, and a number of the services Google offers to help offset these limitations. The sample Google App Engine application in this chapter implements a simple web service for recording high scores earned by users. This service utilizes JDO and the App Engine datastore in order to save and serve HighScore objects. In the last section, we looked at an Android application that queries this service and displays information about user's high scores in different ways, including displaying the high scores on map.

Chapter 9

Game Development: Graphics

Casual games were once the domain of Flash and the Web. Today, casual gaming is making big waves in the mobile space. While there have been mobile gaming devices for some time, the advent of smartphones that are capable of playing games has in effect put a gaming device in the pockets of millions of people who would never buy a dedicated gaming devices. By definition, this new group of game players is casual; they play games while waiting in line or on the bus. At least at first, these folks are not interested in big name titles with huge budgets; they want to check in on their virtual farms or solve a few puzzles. As a result, most casual games are 2D.

The first thing a game developer must do is select which technology they will use to implement their game. Basically, the developer has to choose between 2D and 3D. If 3D is required for the design of the game, they choose OpenGL ES because that library offers everything they will need to develop their game. If 2D is the choice, they can still use OpenGL ES, but the complexity of OpenGL ES might get in their way. The other choice for 2D is to use the graphics capabilities built into the Androids Java runtime.

In this chapter we will take a look at implementing a 2D game, this will serve the many developers looking to ride the wave of mobile casual game development. We will learn that there are really two ways of drawing things on the screen and will explore both. We will also take a look at some of the fundamentals of dealing with different size screens as well some other odds and ends that turn up while writing a game.

Figure 9-1 shows the starting screen of the game on the left and the game itself on the right. The starting screen allows players to start a new game, view their high scores or view the About screen. The user plays the game by trying to create vertical or horizontal lines of similar, orbs. They can rearrange orbs by selecting two to be swapped. When a matching line is created the orbs are animated off-screen and their score is incremented.

Figure 9-1. Orb Quest

Introducing the Android View Package

The most basic way to render a scene in Android is to use the component library provided with the Android software development kit (SDK). This SDK includes all the basic widgets one would expect in a modern user interface (UI) library, including dynamic layouts, buttons, sliders, and so on. The core class for getting content onto the screen is the View class, which is found on the android.view package. This package and its subpackages contain all classes required to draw whatever you want onto the screen. These packages also contain methods for layout, intercepting user actions, binding the UI to data, and applying style. The class itself is not particularly useful in and of itself, but it does provide a base functionality inherited by all its subclasses. These subclasses include both Views that the user interacts with, like a Button, and Views used for layout, like a LinearLayout. There are two basic methods for getting content onto the scene: the first is to use XML files to describe the layout of a View and the second is to describe the layout of a scene with code. Both techniques use the same application programming interface (API), but there are advantages and disadvantages to both techniques. Most applications will use a combination of these techniques. Let's start by looking at how layouts are described in XML.

Understanding XML Layout

Most developers are familiar with the concept of the Model View Controller (MVC) pattern. The idea with MVC is to separate the Model (the raw data) from the code that is responsible for controlling and validating the data. Further, the controller is separated from how the data is actually rendered to the screen. This separation of interests is helpful because it allows for code reuse and divides the responsibility of the application into common divisions of labor. Let's consider a hypothetical web page as an example of MVC.

Say you have a web page that displays a table containing all upcoming events for an office. The data for this page is probably a number of rows returned from a database. Each row contains the name and time for each event. This data is considered the Model; the people actually putting the web page together don't know exactly what the data will be on each given day, but they know there will be data and it will be of a particular type, so they can move forward with their work, even before the database is fully set up and populated.

The finished web page will be composed of HTML, CSS, and JavaScript. The CSS is solidly in the camp of the View because it describes the color of the page; nothing in the CSS should care about the data that is being returned or even that there is data. The HTML will provide the table itself, and the JavaScript will be responsible for populating the table with rows. This means that the HTML and the table it provides is part of the View while the JavaScript is the controller since it interprets the data in way that is meaningful to the table.

With Android, we have the ability to break up our application in a way similar to the web page we described. This is done in part by describing the layout of an application in a special XML file. The XML files that describe layout are generally stored in the layout directory under the res directory. An application can have any number of XML files describing layout, and each file contains an element describing a single root View (and possibly sub-Views). In general, each element in the XML file describes a View class that will be instantiated at runtime. Figure 9–2 shows a dialog from our example application that is defined by one of these XML files.

Figure 9–2. *The Score dialog is defined by XML*

Figure 9–2 shows a dialog with the title "High Score." This dialog is displayed to users after the end of the game; it gives them the option of entering a username and deciding whether they want their score sent to a web service. The XML used to describe the layout of the text and buttons is shown in Listing 9–1 (taken from the example code accompanying this chapter).

Listing 9–1. *score_dialog.xml*

```xml
<?xml version="1.0" encoding="utf-8"?>
<LinearLayout
  xmlns:android="http://schemas.android.com/apk/res/android"
  android:id="@+id/dialogRoot"
  android:layout_width="fill_parent"
  android:layout_height="fill_parent"
  android:orientation="vertical"
  android:gravity="center"
  android:padding="20px"
  android:background="#333333"
  >
        <TextView
                android:text="Share Your Score With The World?"
                android:textColor="#FBB040"
                android:textStyle="bold"
                android:textSize="24px"
                android:layout_width="wrap_content"
                android:layout_height="wrap_content"/>
        <LinearLayout
                android:layout_width="wrap_content"
                android:layout_height="wrap_content"
                android:orientation="horizontal"
                android:gravity="center">
                <TextView
                        android:text="Player Name: "
                        android:textColor="#FBB040"
                        android:textStyle="bold"
                        android:textSize="18px"
                        android:layout_width="wrap_content"
                        android:layout_height="wrap_content"/>
                <EditText
                        android:text="User Name"
                        android:id="@+id/playerNameEditText"
                        android:layout_width="wrap_content"
                        android:layout_height="wrap_content"/>
        </LinearLayout>
        <LinearLayout
                android:layout_width="wrap_content"
                android:layout_height="wrap_content"
                android:orientation="horizontal"
                android:gravity="center">
                <Button
                        android:id="@+id/noButton"
                        android:text="No"
                        android:textSize="24px"
                        android:textStyle="bold"
                        android:layout_width="fill_parent"
                        android:layout_height="wrap_content"
                />
```

```
            <Button
                    android:id="@+id/yesButton"
                    android:text="Yes"
                    android:textSize="24px"
                    android:textStyle="bold"
                    android:layout_width="fill_parent"
                    android:layout_height="wrap_content"
            />
    </LinearLayout>

</LinearLayout>
```

Listing 9–1 shows a root element called `LinearLayout`, which is an Android class that extends `GroupView`. `GroupView` extends `View` and is the root class for any `View` that contains children. So in the case of `LinearLayout`, we know that this class is intended to contain child `Views` and lay them out in a line. The attribute orientation (of namespace android) is set to `vertical`, which directs the `LinearLayout` to place each child `View` lower on the screen then its predecessor. The other possible value for the attribute orientation is `horizontal`, which would lay out the children from left to right.

The attributes `layout_width` and `layout_height` are required attributes and describe the size of this `View`. The size being set is not absolute and is either driven by the size of its parent or its children. This is done to allow the description of a layout independent of the size of the screen or region where this component is being drawn. The possible values for these attributes are the following:

- **fill_parent**: This directs the `View` to consume as much space as is available within the bounds of its parent `View`. If the `View` using this layout directive is the only child of its parent, it will be the same size as its parent, minus any padding.

- **wrap_content**: This directs the `View` to be the minimum size required to display its children `Views`. So if a `View` has two `Buttons` in it, it will take up just enough screen space to display those two children, plus any padding on the children.

- **match_parent**: This directs the `View` to use the same value for either `layout_width` or `layout_height` used by the parent.

The children of a `View` might not take up all the space a `View` takes up, especially if the parent `View` is using `fill_parent` for either `layout_width` or `layout_height`, so there needs to be a way of describing where the children should go. When this is the case, the gravity attribute can be used to indicate where in the parent `View` the children should be located. The root `LinearLayout` in Listing 9–1 has its gravity attribute set to `center`, which indicates that space taken up by all its children should be in the middle, both vertically and horizontally. The gravity attribute can also be set to lay out the children so they are aligned with the top, right, bottom, or left edge of the parent `View`, or just centered vertically or horizontally.

> **TIP:** Each View class has a number of attributes that can be set, these are all well documented on the Android website (http://developer.android.com/reference/packages.html), but remember, for quick reference, code completion works in Eclipse when editing layout XML files.

The LinearLayout root in Listing 9-1 also has its padding and background attributes set. The padding attribute indicates how much space should be left between itself and any containing View. The background attribute specifies how the background should be drawn; in this case, a solid gray color. The background can also be set to an image or any other Drawable class. More on the Drawable class later.

In Listing 9-1, the three children Views of the LinearLayout root contain the content of this View. The first View is a TextView, which displays text on the screen. In this case, the TextView is displaying a question to the user: "Share Your Score With The World?" The layout_width and layout_height are set to wrap_content, which indicate that the TextView should be the minimum size to display its text, given the length of the text and the attributes textSize and textStyle. The other two children Views of the root LinearLayout contain additional Views laid out horizontally. The first child LinearLayout contains another TextView and an EditText view. EditText is a View that allows the user to enter text; in this case, the name they wish to associate with their score. EditText, along with the two buttons in the second LinearLayout, have their id attributes set. The id attribute is a way of naming a View with the XML so it can be accessed programmatically. We will look at how View IDs are used in the following section, when we look at the Java side of things.

Beyond LinearLayout there are a host of other layouts available in Android, each providing the developer with unique layout options. The following is a selection of the most popular layouts with a brief description:

- **FrameLayout**: FrameLayout is the simplest layout; it just draws all its children at the upper-left corner (0,0). This layout is handy when you want to provide a container for a single View. For example, say you have a spot in your application where you display an image that needs to change. You can use a FrameLayout to mark the location where the image should be displayed; then remove the old image and add a new one when required.

- **LinearLayout**: As mentioned, LinearLayout is used to lay out Views either vertically or horizontally. This is a very common strategy for laying out Views.

- **TableLayout**: `TableLayout`, as the name suggests, is a `View` that is used to lay out `Views` in a table-like way. `TableLayout` is different from the other layout `Views` in that it expects its children to be of type `TableRow`. A `TableRow` can contain zero or more `Views`, where each `View` is a cell in that row. `TableLayout` is like an HTML table in that it is organized by rows (`<tr>` in HTML), but it is unlike the HTML table because cells cannot span more than one column.

- **RelativeLayout**: `RelativeLayout` provides a mechanism for laying out children relative to each other. This is a layout mechanism I have never run across on other platforms, but the idea is that you can say things like "place this button to the right of this text".

- **AbsoluteLayout**: If you want to specify the exact location of a child, you can use `AbsoluteLayout`. It should be noted that this class is deprecated because this layout can easily break when used on devices with different screen sizes.

The previous layouts may seem limiting compared with other UI libraries, but Android makes up for this by making the creation of custom layouts pretty simple. We will take a look at an example of a custom layout later in this chapter.

Layout in Code

Know we have our layout declared in XML we will want to display this content on the screen. Displaying content from an XML file is very similar to laying out a screen programmatically. Let's take a look at both these techniques and how they can be used. Listing 9–2 shows the constructor of `ScoreDialog`, which is the dialog displayed in Figure 9–2.

Listing 9–2. *ScoreDialog.java (constructor)*

```java
public class ScoreDialog extends Dialog implements
            android.view.View.OnClickListener {

    public final static String PREF_USER_NAME = "PREF_USER_NAME";

    public final static String SERVICE_URL = "http://pap-game-service↵
.appspot.com/add_high_score?highscore=";

    private EditText playerNameEditText;
    private Button yesButton;
    private Button noButton;

    private GameActivity activity;

    public ScoreDialog(GameActivity activity) {
        super(activity);
        this.activity = activity;

        setContentView(R.layout.score_dialog);
        setTitle("High Score");
```

```
            playerNameEditText = (EditText) findViewById(R.id.playerNameEditText);
            yesButton = (Button) findViewById(R.id.yesButton);
            noButton = (Button) findViewById(R.id.noButton);

            SharedPreferences settings = getContext().getSharedPreferences(
                        HighScoreView.PREFS_ORB_QUEST, 0);
            String unsername = settings.getString(PREF_USER_NAME, "User Name");
            playerNameEditText.setText(unsername);

            yesButton.setOnClickListener(this);
            noButton.setOnClickListener(this);

            LinearLayout rootLayout = (LinearLayout) findViewById(R.id.dialogRoot);

            BitmapDrawable bitmapDrawable = (BitmapDrawable) activity
                        .getResources().getDrawable(R.drawable.dialog_graphic);

            ImageView imageView = new ImageView(activity);
            imageView.setImageDrawable(bitmapDrawable);

            rootLayout.addView(imageView);

     }
```

In Listing 9–2 we see that the constructor requires a `GameActivity` object. A `GameActivity` is the class defined in our example project. At this point, the only thing we need to know about `GameActivity` is that it extends `Context` and is passed to the required superconstructor. The first thing the constructor does, as related to layout, is to call the `setContentView()` method and pass in the constant `R.layout.score_dialog`. `R` is a class that is automatically generated by the Android SDK and is used as a way to reference the artifacts declared in the `res` folder of an Android project. In Listing 9–1 we showed the content of the file `score_dialog.xml`. Because this file is located in the subfolder layout, the Android SDK creates a constant called `score_dialog` in the inner class layout. Listing 9–3 shows `R.java` and should help explain what is going on here.

Listing 9–3. *R.java*

```
/* AUTO-GENERATED FILE.   DO NOT MODIFY.
 *
 * This class was automatically generated by the
 * aapt tool from the resource data it found.  It
 * should not be modified by hand.
 */

package org.ljordan.orb_quest;

public final class R {
    public static final class anim {
        public static final int scale_down=0x7f040000;
    }
    public static final class attr {
    }
    public static final class drawable {
        public static final int background=0x7f020000;
        public static final int blue_orb=0x7f020001;
```

```
        public static final int dialog_graphic=0x7f020002;
        public static final int green_orb=0x7f020003;
        public static final int icon=0x7f020004;
        public static final int nine_patch=0x7f020005;
        public static final int red_orb=0x7f020006;
    }
    public static final class id {
        public static final int aboutButton=0x7f060006;
        public static final int dialogRoot=0x7f060007;
        public static final int gameView=0x7f060000;
        public static final int highScoreButton=0x7f060005;
        public static final int noButton=0x7f060009;
        public static final int playGameButton=0x7f060004;
        public static final int playerNameEditText=0x7f060008;
        public static final int root=0x7f060001;
        public static final int scoreTextView=0x7f060003;
        public static final int turnsTextView=0x7f060002;
        public static final int yesButton=0x7f06000a;
    }
    public static final class layout {
        public static final int about=0x7f030000;
        public static final int game=0x7f030001;
        public static final int high_score=0x7f030002;
        public static final int main=0x7f030003;
        public static final int score_dialog=0x7f030004;
    }
    public static final class string {
        public static final int about_text=0x7f050005;
        public static final int about_text_title=0x7f050006;
        public static final int app_name=0x7f050001;
        public static final int hello=0x7f050000;
        public static final int play_game=0x7f050002;
        public static final int view_about=0x7f050004;
        public static final int view_highscores=0x7f050003;
    }
}
```

In Listing 9–3, the R class has a number of inner classes defined. Each of these classes corresponds with a type of resource defined in the res folder of the project. Continuing our example, we see that the score_dialog constant is defined in the class layout. Further, the constant yesButton is defined in the class id. So if we want to refer to either of these components, we have a handy constant available to do so. In Listing 9–2, we sent the content of the dialog to the content of the score_dialog.xml file by referring to R.layout.score_dialog. In that file we define a pair of buttons; one of them is the yes button for the dialog. Since we need access to this view in order to register a listener, we can call findViewById and pass in the constant R.id.yesButton and get a pointer to it.

Normally referring to an external resource by an int constant would be a very fragile design pattern. Imagine if one developer changed the file score_dialog.xml so that the yes button was referred to as the confirm button and did not change R.java to reflect this change. Normally, you would have a runtime error, but since R.java is automatically generated you get a compile time error (since R.id.yesButton would no longer be a valid symbol). In this way we have a tightly coupled relationship between the XML and the Java code.

So we know that calling `setContentView` and passing in the right constant will populate the dialog with the `Views` described in `score_dialog.xml`. And we know that we can find those sub-`Views` by calling `findViewById`. But what if we want to add a new `View` to the scene? At the end of Listing 9-2, we do this by adding the image with the three orbs on it, as seen in Figure 9-2.

In Listing 9-2 we see that the root layout is also pulled out by calling `findViewById` and passing in `R.id.dialogRoot`. Once we have a reference to this object, we can add `Views` to it, but first we need to construct one. In this case, we want to add an image, and the easiest way to add an image to the scene is to put an image in the res directly and get a handle to it by calling `Context.getResources().getDrawable()` and passing in the correct id. The returned object is of type `BitmapDrawable`. The `Drawable` class is a generic class that provides an abstraction for things that are drawn. As can be guessed, `BitmapDrawable` is a subclass of `Drawable` and is used to draw bitmaps. There are other types of `Drawables`, and we will get to them, but for now we just want `BitmapDrawable`, so we can create an `ImageView`.

Once we have created an `ImageView` and passed `bitmapDrawable` to its `setImageDrawable()` method, we are ready to add the image to the scene. This is done by calling `addView` on `rootLayout` and passing the `ImageView`. Conceptually, this is identical to declaring an `ImageView` within `score_dialog.xml`.

It is up to each developer to decide whether they prefer to lay out their application in XML or in Java code. Personally, I think using XML makes more sense when working on a team, since it helps enforce the MVC pattern.

Custom Component

The Score dialog shows us how to use the existing components and layouts to create a UI. For any game, it is unlikely that the out-of-the-box widgets will be sufficient. By definition, games provide some unique form of interaction. However, we can take advantage of the existing `View` classes as a foundation for our game. For our game, we are going to create an `Activity` called `GameActivity` that will have its layout defined in XML, but one of the `Views` we add will be of type `GameView`, which is defined by us. Figure 9-3 shows the `GameActivity`. In Figure 9-3 we see a big square area with 25 orbs drawn on it. This region is defined by the `GameView` class. We also see four `TextViews` for displaying the number of remaining turns as well as the current score. The background is composed of the big orbs and the text "Orb Quest" and "The Quest for Orbs."

Figure 9–3. *The GameActivity of Orb Quest*

Let's start by looking Listing 9–4, which shows the content game.xml. We will look at the GameView class after that.

Listing 9–4. *game.xml*

```xml
<?xml version="1.0" encoding="utf-8"?>
<LinearLayout
  xmlns:android="http://schemas.android.com/apk/res/android"
  android:id="@+id/root"
  android:layout_width="fill_parent"
  android:layout_height="fill_parent"
  android:gravity="center"
  android:background="@drawable/background" android:orientation="vertical">


<LinearLayout
        android:orientation="horizontal"
        android:layout_width="wrap_content"
        android:layout_height="wrap_content"
        android:paddingBottom="2px"
        >
        <TextView
            android:layout_width="wrap_content"
            android:text="Turns: "
            android:layout_height="wrap_content"
            android:textSize="24px"
            android:textStyle="bold"
            android:paddingBottom="5px"
            android:textColor="#FFFFFF"
            android:shadowColor="#000000"
            android:shadowRadius="2.0"
            android:shadowDx="1.0"
```

```xml
        android:shadowDy="1.0"
        />
    <TextView android:id="@+id/turnsTextView"
        android:layout_width="wrap_content"
        android:text="10"
        android:layout_height="wrap_content"
        android:textSize="24px"
        android:textStyle="bold"
        android:textColor="#FFFFFF"
        android:shadowColor="#000000"
        android:shadowRadius="2.0"
        android:shadowDx="1.0"
        android:shadowDy="1.0"
        />
    <TextView
        android:layout_width="wrap_content"
        android:text="Score: "
        android:layout_height="wrap_content"
        android:textSize="24px"
        android:textStyle="bold"
        android:textColor="#FFFFFF"
        android:shadowColor="#000000"
        android:shadowRadius="2.0"
        android:shadowDx="1.0"
        android:shadowDy="1.0"
        />
    <TextView android:id="@+id/scoreTextView"
        android:layout_width="wrap_content"
        android:text="10"
        android:layout_height="wrap_content"
        android:textSize="24px"
        android:textStyle="bold"
        android:textColor="#FFFFFF"
        android:shadowColor="#000000"
        android:shadowRadius="2.0"
        android:shadowDx="1.0"
        android:shadowDy="1.0"
        />

</LinearLayout>
<view class="org.ljordan.orb_quest.GameView"
        android:id="@+id/gameView"
        android:layout_width="wrap_content"
        android:layout_height="wrap_content"
/>

</LinearLayout>
```

In Listing 9–4, we see that the root View is again a LinearLayout. There are four TextViews in a LinearLayout with a horizontal orientation. Two of these TextViews have IDs set (turnsTextView and scoreTextView) and will be updated dynamically in code. The last component is a GameView. To use Views of your own design in an XML layout file, you simply create a View element and specify the class attribute with the fully qualified name of your class. Listing 9–5 shows the GameActivity class.

Listing 9–5. *GameActivity.java*

```java
public class GameActivity extends Activity {

        private final static int DIALOG_CONFIRM_SHARE = 10;

        private TextView turnsTextView;
        private TextView scoreTextView;
        private GameView gameView;

        @Override
        public void onCreate(Bundle savedInstanceState) {
                super.onCreate(savedInstanceState);
                requestWindowFeature(Window.FEATURE_NO_TITLE);
                getWindow().setFlags(WindowManager.LayoutParams.FLAG_FULLSCREEN,
                            WindowManager.LayoutParams.FLAG_FULLSCREEN);
                setContentView(R.layout.game);

                turnsTextView = (TextView) findViewById(R.id.turnsTextView);
                scoreTextView = (TextView) findViewById(R.id.scoreTextView);

                gameView = (GameView) findViewById(R.id.gameView);

                gameView.reset(this);
        }

        public void updateValues(int score, int turns) {
                scoreTextView.setText("" + score);
                turnsTextView.setText("" + turns + "   ");
        }

        public Long getScore() {
                return Long.parseLong(scoreTextView.getText().toString());
        }

        public void endGame() {
                showDialog(DIALOG_CONFIRM_SHARE);
        }

        @Override
        protected Dialog onCreateDialog(int id) {
                if (id == DIALOG_CONFIRM_SHARE) {
                        return new ScoreDialog(this);
                } else {
                        return null;
                }
        }

        public void dialogClosed() {
                gameView.reset(this);
        }
}
```

In Listing 9–5 we see that the class GameActivity extends Activity. In the onCreate() method, we call requestWindowFeature and pass the constant Windw.FEATURE_NO_TITLE so we don't have a title. We also call setFlags on the object returned by getWindow and pass the flag FLAG_FULLSCREEN with the mask FLAG_FULLSCREEN. This removes the default

Android status bar at the top of the screen, which is the bar that usually indicates the time and battery levels.

Once we have claimed as much screen real estate as possible, we add content by calling setContentView and passing R.layout.game. Finally we pull out the Views we will need access to later by calling findViewById and passing in the constants as defined by the R class. Calling gameView.reset at the very end simply prepares the GameView for the first round.

In Listing 9–5, we see a couple of convenience methods such as updateValues, getScore(), endGame(), and dialogClosed(). These are called by GameView and ScoreDialog during the lifecycle of the application. There is not much to GameActivity; the meat of the application is in the class GameView, and the first chunk of that class is shown in Listing 9–6.

Listing 9–6. *GameView.java (partial)*

```java
public class GameView extends ViewGroup implements View.OnClickListener {

        private int orb_ids[] = new int[3];
        private Random random = new Random();

        private OrbView selectedOrbView = null;
        private boolean acceptInput = true;

        private int score = 0;
        private int turns = 10;

        private GameActivity gameActivity;

        public GameView(Context context, AttributeSet attrs) {
                super(context, attrs);
                init();
        }

        public GameView(Context context) {
                super(context);
                init();
        }

        private void init() {
                setBackgroundDrawable(new Background());

                orb_ids[0] = R.drawable.red_orb;
                orb_ids[1] = R.drawable.green_orb;
                orb_ids[2] = R.drawable.blue_orb;
        }

        public void reset(GameActivity gameActivity) {
                this.gameActivity = gameActivity;
                score = 0;
                turns = 10;
                acceptInput = true;

                removeAllViews();
```

```
                for (int c = 0; c < 5; c++) {
                    for (int r = 0; r < 5; r++) {
                        OrbView orbView = new OrbView(getContext(), c, r,
                                    random.nextInt(3));
                        addView(orbView);
                    }
                }
                gameActivity.updateValues(score, turns);
        }
```

In Listing 9–6, we see that `GameView` extends `ViewGroup` and implements `View.OnClickListener`. `GameView` has a number of private fields. The field `orb_ids` is an array that stores the IDs of the three different orb images; they are set in the `init()` method. The field random is of type `Random` from the core Java classes. The fields `selectedOrbView` and `acceptInput` are used to track game state. The `score` and `turns` fields track the current score and number of remaining turns. Finally, a reference to the containing `GameActivity` is held so we can update the `TextViews` it maintains reference to.

In Listing 9–6, you see that `GameView` has two constructors: the first takes a `Context` and an `AttributeSet`; the second takes only a `Context`. The constructor that takes two arguments is the constructor that is called when a `View` is instantiated from XML and is required if you intend to do so. The second constructor is actually never called in our application, but is included to illustrate that you would require such a constructor if you want to create an instance of `GameView` programmatically.

The method reset in Listing 9–6 is called whenever a new game should be started (including the first time) and is responsible for setting up the game state. Beyond resetting the score and the number of turns, 25 `OrbViews` are added as children to the `GameView`, one for each row and column. Before you look at how the orbs are laid out in the grid pattern, take a look at the class `OrbView` in Listing 9–7.

Listing 9–7. *OrbView.java*

```
protected class OrbView extends ImageView {
        private int orbType;
        private int col;
        private int row;

        protected OrbView(Context context, int col, int row, int orbType) {
                super(context);
                this.col = col;
                this.row = row;
                this.orbType = orbType;

                Drawable image = getResources().getDrawable(orb_ids[orbType]);
                setImageDrawable(image);
                setClickable(true);
                setOnClickListener(GameView.this);
        }

        public int getOrbType() {
                return orbType;
        }
```

```java
        public void setRandomType() {
                orbType = random.nextInt(3);
                Drawable image = getResources().getDrawable(orb_ids[orbType]);
                setImageDrawable(image);
        }

        public int getCol() {
                return col;
        }

        public int getRow() {
                return row;
        }

        public void setCol(int col) {
                this.col = col;
        }

        public void setRow(int row) {
                this.row = row;
        }
}
```

Listing 9–7 shows the `OrbView` class, which is used to represent a single orb on the screen. `OrbView` extends `ImageView`, and in its constructor you can see that one of the three IDs for the images is used as the `OrbView` image. The `GameView` is also registered to receive click events by passing it to the `setOnClickListener()` method.

To understand how the `OrbViews` are laid out in a grid, look at two more methods from the `GameView` class, as shown in Listing 9–8 and Listing 9–9.

Listing 9–8. *GameView.java (onMeasure)*

```java
@Override
protected void onMeasure(int widthMeasureSpec, int heightMeasureSpec) {
        int parentWidth = MeasureSpec.getSize(widthMeasureSpec);
        int parentHeight = MeasureSpec.getSize(heightMeasureSpec);
        int size = Math.min(parentHeight - 20, parentWidth - 20);
        this.setMeasuredDimension(size, size);
}
```

Listing 9–8 shows the `onMeasure()` method, which is defined in the `View` class. We are overriding it for two reasons. First, we want to give ourselves a 20-pixel border. Second, and more importantly, we want to make the `GameView` square. The `onMeasure()` method, if overridden, requires that the `setMeasuredDimension()`method be called. Failing to do so will cause a runtime exception. The ints passed in as arguments to the onMeasure method describe the parent `View` requirements for how the child (`GameView`) may specify its size. The possible values for the specs are the dimension of the parent masked with either UNSPECIFIED, EXACTLY, or AT_MOST as defined by the class `View.MeasuredSpec`. The meaning of these masks is as follows:

- **UNSPECIFIED**: The parent does not care what size the child wants to be; any value will be honored.

- **EXACTLY**: Regardless of size the child wants to be, it will be set to precisely one size.
- **AT_MOST**: The child may specify any size as long as it is smaller then some size, probably the size of the parent.

Given specs for the required size, we can get the actual parent size by calling `MeasureSpec.getSize` and passing in the `widthMeasureSpec` and the `heightMeasureSpec`. In our case, the spec being passed for both dimensions is AT_MOST, so we can't specify an actual size any larger. That's fine; we just take the smaller of the two values (minus 20) and pass that as both the width and height to `setMeasuredDevice`. This makes our `GameView` square and fit within our parent `View`. Subtracting 20 gives us a bit of padding purely for aesthetics.

`onMeasure()` is called just before our `GameView` is laid out. The `onLayout()`method is called during the `GameView` parent's layout and gives us a chance to specify the location of any children `Views`. Listing 9–9 shows the `onLayout()` method.

Listing 9–9. *GameView (onLayout)*

```
@Override
protected void onLayout(boolean changed, int l, int t, int r, int b) {
        int size = getWidth();
        int oneFifth = size / 5;

        int count = getChildCount();
        for (int i = 0; i < count; i++) {
                OrbView orbView = (OrbView) getChildAt(i);
                int left = oneFifth * orbView.getCol();
                int top = oneFifth * orbView.getRow();
                int right = oneFifth * orbView.getCol() + oneFifth;
                int bottom = oneFifth * orbView.getRow() + oneFifth;
                orbView.layout(left, top, right, bottom);
        }
}
```

By the time `onLayout()` (from Listing 9–10) is called, we know there are 25 `OrbViews` that are sub-`Views` of this `GameView`. Since we assigned each `OrbView` a column and row value, we can simply iterate through them and use those values to calculate the space each `OrbView` should occupy.

In order to calculate the location for each `OrbView`, we note in the variable size the current size of the game `View` by calling `getWidth` (`getHeight` will return an identical value). Since we have five columns and rows, we record what one-fifth of the total size is and store it in the variable `oneFifth`. To place each `OrbView`, we calculate the number of pixels from the left and top of the `GameView` by multiplying the `OrbView` col and row by `oneFifth`, respectively. The `OrbView.layout()` method is used to set the location of each `OrbView`. The `layout()` method is defined by the `View` class (a superclass of `OrbView`) and takes four `ints`. The first two are the left and top distances relative to the origin of the parent; the second two are right and bottom, also relative to the origin of the parent `View`. So, by adding one-fifth to the left and top values, we can calculate the right and bottom values.

I find the View.layout() method sort of weird. Why doesn't it specify the x,y width and height values, like so many other UI libraries? Further, by naming the second two arguments right and bottom, I was confused when I first used this method, since in HTML, for example, right and bottom specify the distance from the *right* and *bottom* of the parent container. In View.layout(), right and bottom specify the distance from the origin (top,left/0,0) of the parent container. I have never seen it done this way.

The GameView class gives us a custom layout specific to the requirements of the game Orb Quest. We did this by first extending ViewGroup and then overriding onMeasure() and onLayout(). The background grid is draw using a custom Drawable and will be explored in the next section.

Understanding the Drawable Class

Android uses the View class and its subclasses to describe the layout of the components on the screen. This is pretty normal for a UI library. Android extends this common pattern by introducing the Drawable class. A class that extends Drawable represents content that can be drawn. This is an anemic definition I know; let me explain. Drawables are different from Views in that they don't specify a size or a layout and don't respond to user interaction. They simply represent content that can be displayed at different sizes. The idea is that Drawable provides an important abstraction that can be exploited to facilitate the rendering of content, agnostic of the size of the host devices screen or any of its display limitations.

We used Drawables earlier in this chapter (in Listing 9–2 we created a BitmapDrawable that presented an image stored in the res directory). Let's take a closer look at the Drawable class and learn what else it can do.

Drawable Class

The Drawable class extends Object and is abstract. It provides a number of useful methods that are useful for all its subclasses. Listing 9–10 shows a number of method signatures defined by the Drawable class (this code was taken from the Android source code).

Listing 9–10. *Methods from Drawable.java*

```java
public abstract void draw(Canvas canvas);
public void setBounds(int left, int top, int right, int bottom);
public void setDither(boolean dither);
public void setFilterBitmap(boolean filter);
public abstract void setAlpha(int alpha);
public abstract void setColorFilter(ColorFilter cf);
public boolean setState(final int[] stateSet);
public final boolean setLevel(int level);
public int getIntrinsicWidth();
public int getIntrinsicHeight();
public int getMinimumWidth();
public int getMinimumHeight();
```

In Listing 9–10 we see the signature for a number of important methods defined by the Drawable class. The draw() method takes a Canvas object and is where the actual drawing code for a particular Drawable resides. The Canvas class is analogous to the Graphics2D class from Swing and provides a number of low-level drawing commands. Each subclass if Drawable will implement the draw() method differently.

Before a Drawable is drawn, it will have its bounds set by the setBounds() method. The View using Drawable will ultimately define the bounds being passed to this method. The bounds set by the View may or may not have a direct relation to the content being drawn. For example, if we create a BitmapDrawable from an image, the Drawable has an intrinsic size: the width and height of the image. However, the BitmapDrawable class must honor whatever bounds are passed to it. In practical terms, BitmapDrawable simply scales the image to fit within the bounds. For other Drawables, this behavior may be different.

As mentioned, some Drawables have an intrinsic size; the getIntrinsicHeight() and getIntrinsicWidth() methods are used to query a Drawable object for this information. We used the example of a BitmapDrawable as a Drawable with an intrinsic size, since these methods are defined on Drawable, all Drawables may specify these intrinsic size values. If the Drawable does not have an intrinsic size, it may return -1 for either of these two methods. An example of a Drawable that does not have any intrinsic size is ColorDrawable, which simply fills its bounds with a given color.

Similarly, a Drawable may specify a minimum size by returning a value in either the getMinimumWidth() or getMinimumHeight() methods. The minimum size of a Drawable is simply a suggestion, and there are no guarantees that Drawable will not be passed bounds that are smaller then the defined minimums. If a Drawable has no need to specify a minimum, it returns 0 for both of these methods.

In Listing 9–10, the Drawable class has a number of methods for adjusting how the content is drawn. These methods include setAlpha(), setDither(), setFilterBitmap(), and setColorFilter(). The setAlpha() method allows the caller to specify a transparency level for any Drawable. The setDither() method instructs the Drawable to dither its colors when it is being drawn on a device with fewer than 8-bits per color. setDither() has no effect otherwise.

The setFilterBitmap() method instructs Drawable to filter any bitmap that is being drawn by Drawable when scaled or rotated. This is a rendering hint that will improve the visual quality of any image being drawn at something besides its native scale. There may be a performance hit when setting setFilterBitmap to true. If Drawable does not use any bitmap data to draw, this method does nothing.

The setColorFilter() method is used to apply a ColorFilter to a Drawable. The ColorFilter class is a class that describes some color adjustment or enhancement that should be applied when Drawable is drawn. An example of a ColorFilter is the PorterDuffColorFilter class. PorterDuffColorFilter allows you to specify how the alpha channel in an image is applied to the final result. If you have ever used Adobe's Photoshop or the GIMP, you know that each layer in the image can be set to things like ADD or MULTIPLY. This is what PorterDuffColorFilter does.

The remaining methods in Listing 9–10 to be talked about are `setState()` and `setLevel()`. The `setState()` method is used on `Drawables` that have different states, think buttons. A button may have a pressed state, a highlighted state, or even more states. The states and visual representations of a `Drawable` are not defined; it is up the implementation of a specific `Drawable` to handle these values. It is also not necessary for a `Drawable` to have a state; in that case, calls to the `setState()` method are ignored. The `setLevel()` method is used with `Drawables` that have some visual indication of level. A progress bar, for example, has a level. The `setLevel()` method could there for be used with a `Drawable` that represents a progress bar to set how far along it should be drawn.

As can be seen by the description of some of the methods of `Drawable` methods, not all methods make sense with all types of `Drawables`. It is sort of a weird design pattern to stick these methods in an abstract superclass. I think this can cause confusion when working with specific subclasses of `Drawable`, since we don't immediately know whether a given method will have any effect. It requires us to go to the documentation and check each class. This confusion also exists when using a third-party library that offers implementations of `Drawable`.

Drawable Subclasses

We have taken a look at the `Drawable` class and explored some of its features. Now let's take a look at some of the subclasses of `Drawable` available in the Android SDK. There is a host of different types, and we are going to look at some of the most common used `Drawables` to illustrate how these classes can be used and combined to create a number of platform-independent visual effects.

- **BitmapDrawable:** `BitmapDrawable` is a `Drawable` that draws an image to the screen. While a common use for `BitmapDrawable` is to draw an image provided as a resource to an application, `BitmapDrawable` is really used to describe *how* an image should be drawn. For example, `BitmapDrawable` is used to specify whether the image should be drawn with dithering or with antialiasing, or even if the image should be tiled.

- **AnimationDrawable:** To create a simple static animation in an application, it is common practice to create a sequence of images, where each image is a single frame of the animation. By replacing each image with the next image in the sequence. a sense of animation can be created. The `AnimationDrawable` class provides an API to handle this common use case. To use this class simply create it with a number of images and then call run on it.

- **ColorDrawable:** `ColorDrawable` is a `Drawable` that simply fills its bounds with specific color. A common use for this class is to set the background on a `View` to a specific color. Of course, it can be used anywhere a rectangular region should have a specific color.

- **GradientDrawable:** Much like `ColorDrawable`, `GradientDrawable` is used to fill its bounds with a gradient. `GradientDrawable` allows a number of different gradients to specify by setting the colors, shape, and gradient style. The gradient style can be any of the usual suspects: `LINEAR_GRADIENT`, `RADIAL_GRADIENT`, or `SWEEP_GRADIENT`.

- **PaintDrawable:** Android obviously allows you to define the colors of things. Sometimes, however, it is desirable to describe how a color should be drawn, which is where the `Paint` class comes in. The `Paint` class provides a way of designating a color and some other values about how those colors should be applied. For example, when drawing a line, the `Paint` class is used to specify what type of end caps the line should have. For another example, when drawing text, the `Paint` class can be used to specify that a strikethrough line or an underline should be used. The `PaintDrawable` class fills a rectangular region with the specified `Paint`, optionally with rounded corners with a particular `Paint`.

- **ShapeDrawable:** `ShapeDrawable` draws a `Shape` with a particular `Paint`. The `Shape` is a superclass to various classes that present different types of shapes, including basic shapes such as `OvalShape` and `RoundedRectShape`, and also complex shapes that can be defined by the `PathShape` class. When drawing a shape the `Paint` object defines the thickness of the lines and other shape-related properties.

- **RotateDrawable and ScaleDrawable:** `RotateDrawable` and `ScaleDrawable` are wrapper `Drawables` that apply a transformation to another `Drawable`.

- **LayerDrawable:** A `LayerDrawable` draws an array of `Drawables` from back (index 0) to front. When used with `RotateDrawable`, `ScaleDrawable`, and other `LayerDrawables`, combining more content-oriented `Drawables` together can render complex scenes.

Let's take a look at an example from the game Orb Quest and see how some of these `Drawable` classes can be used in an application. Figure 9–4 shows the grid rendered behind the orbs.

CHAPTER 9: Game Development: Graphics

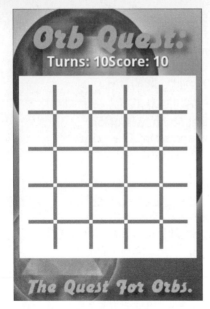

Figure 9–4. *Background grid*

Figure 9–4 shows a grid composed of eight lines, four running vertically and four running horizontally. This grid is defined in the Background class, as seen in Listing 9–11.

Listing 9–11. *Background.java*

```
public class Background extends LayerDrawable {

    public Background() {
        super(new Drawable[] { new ColorDrawable(Color.WHITE),
                    new GridDrawable() });
    }

    private static class GridDrawable extends ShapeDrawable {
        private GridDrawable() {
            super(createGridPath());
            getPaint().setColor(Color.GRAY);
            getPaint().setStrokeWidth(1.0f);
            getPaint().setStyle(Paint.Style.FILL);
        }
    }

    private static PathShape createGridPath() {
        float size = 1000;
        float colOrRowSize = size / 5.0f;
        float fivePercent = size * 0.05f;

        float onePercent = size * 0.01f;

        Path lines = new Path();
        for (int i = 0; i < 4; i++) {
            float x = i * colOrRowSize + colOrRowSize;
```

```
                lines.moveTo(x - onePercent, fivePercent);
                lines.lineTo(x + onePercent, fivePercent);
                lines.lineTo(x + onePercent, size - fivePercent);
                lines.lineTo(x - onePercent, size - fivePercent);
                lines.close();
            }
            for (int i = 0; i < 4; i++) {
                float y = i * colOrRowSize + colOrRowSize;

                lines.moveTo(fivePercent, y - onePercent);
                lines.lineTo(fivePercent, y + onePercent);
                lines.lineTo(size - fivePercent, y + onePercent);
                lines.lineTo(size - fivePercent, y - onePercent);
                lines.close();
            }

            return new PathShape(lines, size, size);
        }
    }
}
```

In Listing 9–11, the Background class extends LayerDrawable so we know that Background will be a composite of other Drawables. Looking at the constructor we see that we are creating an array of two Drawables. The first Drawable is the ColorDrawable type. Because this Drawable is the first in the array, it gives us a nice white background to draw our grid on. The second Drawable in the array is of type GridDrawable, an inner class of our own design. The GridDrawable class extends ShapeDrawable, and we are using the superclasses' constructor to pass in a PathShaped defined by the static createGridPath method. Before we look at the createGridPath() method, let's look at the rest of the GridDrawable constructor. Here we are modifying the ShapeDrawable Paint field by setting the color to gray, setting the stroke width to 1.0, and specifying that we want the shape filled.

The createGridPath() method creates a PathShaped used by GridDrawable. A PathShape object describes a shape in terms of paths. This is a pretty common abstraction in graphical libraries and similar to Java Swing class' GeneralPath. The first thing we do in this method is to define some values that we will use when describing the paths that make up the PathShape object. The first thing to note is that we declare the variable size as 1000. The value of size can be almost any value, since we want to describe this grid in a resolution-independent way. In fact, if you changed this value to 100, for example, you would not see any difference in the rendering. The other values colOrRowSize, fivePercent, and onePercent are derived from size.

To define the lines, we create a Path object in which we describe the paths that make up this shape. The paths are defined in two loops, one for the vertical lines and one for the horizontal line. In each loop, we describe the path a pen would take if it were outlining each line (describing a rectangle for each gray line). Once all these little rectangles are described in the object lines, we use it to create our result, the PathShape. Note that we also pass the size value to the constructor of the PathShape object, which tells the PathShape to draw the lines in terms of the size when PathShape is scaled.

So to create our background, we use the class `LayerDrawable` class to draw two other `Drawables`, one on top of the other. The first `Drawable` simply defines a colored region and provides our white background. The second `Drawable` extends `ShapeDrawable` and specifies a grid shape and how this grid should be drawn.

There are other `Drawables` available in Android; most are just extensions of the ideas presented previously. There is, however, a very useful type of `Drawable` called `NinePatchDrawable` that deserves special attention.

NinePatchDrawable

When creating buttons and other components for an application, it is common to include a decorative border and background to a component. It is often desirable for this decoration to be fairly elaborate, and the best way to create elaborate graphics is by creating a bitmap image. However, it can be time-consuming and difficult to create a background image for every component. For example, if an application has lots of buttons, each of a different size, you don't want to create a background image for each button. You want to be able to create a single image that somehow describes the border and background for all your buttons. This is where the `NinePatchDrawable` comes in. Figure 9–5 shows a close-up of three buttons using a `NinePatchDrawable` for their background.

Figure 9–5. *Buttons using a NinePatchDrawable*

Figure 9–5 shows the opening screen of the Orb Quest game. There are three buttons, each with a different size. They each share a common theme in terms of border and background. The image that describes the background of these three buttons is a special PNG image that describes how the image should be stretched and scaled in order to be visually consentient at different size. Android distinguishes images that should be used as a `NinePatchDrawable` from regular images by the extension of the file, which should be `.9.png`. The image used as the `NinePatchDrawable` is shown in Figure 9–6.

Figure 9–6. *The nine_patch.9.png file zoomed in*

Figure 9–6 shows the `nine_patch.9.png` file zoomed in; it looks like a square button from Figure 9–5. What makes this file different from other PNG files are the black bars along the sides of the image. These black bars are never drawn in the application; they simply describe how the image should be cut up so it can be displayed correctly as a border and background. Figure 9–7 shows a graphical depiction of how these black lines break the image up.

Figure 9–7. *Regions of a nine-patch PNG file*

Figure 9–7 shows the image from Figure 9–6 twice. On the left, we have extended four imaginary lines coming from the ends of the top and left black lines. These four lines break the image up into nine regions. These nine regions are then used to draw this image at different sizes. The four corner regions are used as is, to draw the corners of the buttons. The four edge areas are scaled to fill in any extra space along the sides of each button. Finally the center region is scaled to fill in the middle of the button.

On the right of Figure 9–7 is a rectangular region that is described drawing imaginary lines from the ends of the right and bottom black lines. This rectangular region describes the area where content (the text of the button) can be drawn without requiring the image to be scaled. In this particular case, the right and bottom lines allow text to get closer to the top of the image than to the sides. The right and bottom black lines are optional; if they are omitted, the region described by the top and left lines will describe the region where scaling is not required.

Specifying a `NinePatchDrawable` as the background of a `View` is easiest in XML, as Listing 9–12 shows.

Listing 9–12. *main.xml (partial)*

```
<Button
          android:id="@+id/playGameButton"
          android:layout_width="wrap_content"
          android:layout_height="wrap_content"
          android:text="@string/play_game"
          android:background="@drawable/nine_patch"
          android:textSize="24px"
          android:textStyle="bold"
/>
```

In Listing 9–12, the background of a button is being set to use out the `nine_patch.9.png` file by assigning the attribute background to "@drawable/nine_patch". Note that the extension of the filename is not used. This also assumes that the `nine_patch.9.png` file is stored in the `drawable` directory found in the `res` directory.

Direct Rendering

We have looked at two related techniques for using Android's built-in components for drawing content on the screen: `Views` and `Drawables`. Using these technologies can be a huge time-saver when creating an application since they offer a wide range of features, including layout and resolution-independent drawing. There are plenty of times, however, when greater control is required. In these cases, we want to use the `Canvas` class to get direct access to pixel-level rendering.

A `View` customizes how it is drawn by overriding the `onDraw()` method. The `onDraw()` method takes a `Canvas` object as its only parameter. The `Canvas` class is much like the Java Swing `Graphics2D` class in that it provides a number of low-level graphics functions for drawing line, shapes, text, and images. For demonstration purposes, the `HighScoreView` of the Orb Quest application was written to draw itself using a `Canvas` object. Figure 9–8 shows the `HighScoreView`.

Figure 9–8 shows the title "Your High Scores" drawn at the top of the screen. The title is drawn along a curved path and has a shadow. Just below the title is a horizontal bar that looks a little like an indent. Finally there are 10 scores, comprised of a username (Lucas) and a score value. Listing 9–13 shows the `HighScoreView` class and how we use the `onDraw()` method to achieve these visual effects.

Figure 9–8. *HighScoreView rendered within onDraw with Canvas*

Listing 9–13. *HighScoreView.java*

```java
public class HighScoreView extends View {

    public final static String PREFS_ORB_QUEST = "PREF_ORB_QUEST";
    public final static String PREF_HIGH_SCORE = "PREF_HIGH_SCORE";

    private List<HighScore> highscores;

    public HighScoreView(Context context, AttributeSet attrs) {
        super(context, attrs);
        init();
    }

    public HighScoreView(Context context) {
        super(context);
        init();
    }

    private void init() {
        SharedPreferences settings = getContext().getSharedPreferences(
                    PREFS_ORB_QUEST, 0);
        String json = settings.getString(PREF_HIGH_SCORE,
                    HighScore.createDefaultScores());
        try {
            JSONArray jsonArray = new JSONArray(json);

            highscores = HighScore.toList(jsonArray);
        } catch (JSONException e) {
            throw new RuntimeException(e);
        }
    }
```

```java
@Override
public void onDraw(Canvas canvas) {
        int width = getWidth();
        int height = getHeight();

        //Draw Background
        canvas.drawColor(Color.GRAY);

        Rect innerRect = new Rect(5, 5, width - 5, height - 5);
        Paint innerPaint = new Paint();
        LinearGradient linearGradient = new LinearGradient(0, 0, 0, height,
                        Color.LTGRAY, Color.DKGRAY, Shader.TileMode.MIRROR);
        innerPaint.setShader(linearGradient);

        canvas.drawRect(innerRect, innerPaint);

        //Draw Title
        Path titlePath = new Path();
        titlePath.moveTo(10, 70);
        titlePath.cubicTo(width / 3, 90, width / 3 * 2, 50, width - 10, 70);

        Paint titlePaint = new Paint(Paint.ANTI_ALIAS_FLAG);
        titlePaint.setColor(Color.RED);
        titlePaint.setTextSize(38);
        titlePaint.setShadowLayer(5, 0, 5, Color.BLACK);

        canvas.drawTextOnPath("Your High Scores", titlePath, 0, 0, titlePaint);

        //Draw Line
        Paint linePaint = new Paint();
        linePaint.setStrokeWidth(10);
        linePaint.setColor(Color.WHITE);
        linePaint.setStrokeCap(Cap.ROUND);

        float[] direction = new float[] { 0, -5, -5 };
        EmbossMaskFilter maskFilter = new EmbossMaskFilter(direction, .5f,
 8, 3);
        linePaint.setMaskFilter(maskFilter);

        canvas.drawLine(15, 100, width - 15, 100, linePaint);

        //Draw Scores
        Paint scorePaint = new Paint(Paint.ANTI_ALIAS_FLAG);
        scorePaint.setShadowLayer(5, 0, 5, Color.BLACK);
        scorePaint.setTextSize(20);

        RadialGradient radialGradient = new RadialGradient(width / 2,
                        height / 2, width, Color.WHITE, Color.GREEN,
 TileMode.MIRROR);
        scorePaint.setShader(radialGradient);

        int index = 0;
        for (HighScore score : highscores) {
                canvas.drawText(score.getUsername(), 40, 150 + index * 30,
                                scorePaint);
                canvas.drawText("" + score.getScore(), width - 115,
```

```
                          150 + index * 30, scorePaint);
                index++;
            }
        }
    }
}
```

Listing 9–13 shows the `HighScoreView` class that is responsible for reading the current high scores from the user preferences and then drawing them on the screen. The high scores are found in the `init()` method where a `SharedPreferences` object is retrieved from the context. The `SharedPreferences` object called `settings` is used to get a json-encoded string representation of a collection of `HighScore` objects. The `String` json is converted to a `List` containing `HighScore` objects by using the `HighScore.toList()` utility method.

Once we have our list of `HighScore` objects, we can focus on the actual drawing. The first thing done in the `onDraw()` method is to call `drawColor` and pass in the color gray. This fills the entire screen with a gray color; in our final rendered scene, it winds up just being a gray border around the rest of the content.

The next step in the `onDraw()` method is to draw the large rectangle with the gradient. Drawing a rectangle is pretty straightforward; we simply create a `Rect` object called `innerRect` and pass it to the `drawRect()` method of the `Canvas` object. The gradient effect is created by the second parameter passed to the `drawRect()` method: the `innerPaint` variable, which is a `Paint` object that has had its shader set to a `LinearGradient`. The first four parameters to the `LinearGradient` constructor tell `LinearGradient` that it should draw the gradient starting at the top left and complete at the bottom left. The constants `Color.LTGRAY` and `Color.DKGRAY` are the start and end colors, respectively. The last parameter indicates what the `LinearGradient` should do when drawing pixels outside of the region defined by the start and end points. In our case we don't really care because we have included the entire screen in the region specified by our points. The possible values are as follows:

- **CLAMP:** Pixels that are before the start of the gradient line should be the color of the first color. Conversely, pixels past the end of the gradient line should be the color of the last color in the gradient.

- **MIRROR:** Pixels beyond the range of the gradient line should be colored as if a mirror of the current gradient were applied. This creates a seamless gradation with no obvious indication of where the gradient starts and stops.

- **REPEAT:** This indicates that the pixels beyond the range of the gradient line should be colored as if an identical gradient existed just beyond the range of the line. This can create an abrupt edge in the gradation if the start and end colors are dissimilar.

The title text at the top of the screen is drawn along a curve, which is specified by creating a `Path` object and calling `moveTo`, followed by `cubicTo`. Figure 9–9 shows the drawn path.

Figure 9-9. *Line for the title text*

Figure 9-9 shows the black line that the text is drawn on using the `drawTextOnPath()` method of the `Canvas` class. The `Paint` object specified for this drawing operation is called `titlePaint` and is constructed with the rendering flag `ANTI_ALIAS_FLAG`. This flag is important as it greatly improves the visual quality of text. The `titlePaint` `Paint` object is set to be red and size 38. The last thing you need to do to modify the `titlePaint` object is to specify a shadow by calling `setShadowLayer`. The first parameter indicates the radius of the blurred shadow, the next parameters indicate the *x* and *y* offset for the shadow, and the last parameter sets the color to black.

In Figure 9-8 there is a horizontal line under the title text. This line has two distinct decorations applied to it. First is the fact that it looks like it is recessed into the background, which is accomplished by creating an `EmbossMaskFilter` and assigning it the `Paint` object named `linePaint`. Second, the ends of the line are rounded, which is accomplished by calling `setStrokeCap` in `linePaint` and passing in the constant `Cap.ROUND`.

Once the `linePaint` is set up the way we want, we simply call `drawLine` on `Canvas` and pass in coordinates for the line and the `linePaint` object.

The last thing we need to do to is to draw the scores. To do this, we create a new `Paint` object called `scorePaint`. We set a shadow on `scorePaint` by calling `setShadowLayer` in the same way we did the title. For `scorePaint`, we will apply a subtle radial gradient to help break up the visual impact of the text, creating a `RadialGradient` object. When creating a `RadialGradient` object, the first two parameters specify a center point, and the third parameter specifies a radius. The last parameter indicates how pixels should be drawn outside the defined circle. The same options apply here as they did the `LinearGradient`.

Once the `scorePaint` object is all set up, we simply iterate through each `HighScore` object and draw its username and its score by calling the `drawText()` method.

Summary

In this chapter, we used the example application Orb Quest to explore how `Views` can be laid out using subclasses of `ViewGroup` such as `LinearLayout`. You looked at how the objects that define a set of `Views` can be defined in XML or constructed in code. You looked at the `Drawable` class and its many subclasses to understand how to define resolution-independent graphical content. Finally, you looked at direct pixel-level rendering with the `Canvas` class.

Chapter 10

Game Development: Animation

There are really two types of animations in any application—one that can be described during the development of the application and another that is dynamically defined at runtime. Depending on the type of game you are creating, you may find that all of your animations can be defined beforehand, or you may realize that the location of each game element must be calculated frame by frame. There are no hard and fast rules that tell us which type of animations will be required for a given game. In fact, any game of any complexity will have both types.

In this chapter we are going to look at two strategies for creating animations in Android. The first will be to use the existing View framework to describe the location and animations of our game elements. The second strategy will show how to create an animation in which each frame is drawn by our code. The first offers simplicity while the second allows control.

Android Animations

In Chapter 9 we looked at the View class, which is the base class for all user interface elements. The Android SDK provides a number of classes for animating Views within their parent ViewGroup. The base class for animations is Animation, which can be found in the package android.view.animation.

The class Animation defines the duration, repeat count, start time offset, and a number of other related properties. Subclasses of Animation define the specific visual effect that will be applied to a View. These subclasses include:

- AlphaAnimation: This animation describes a change in the transparency of a view over time. You can use it to make a view fade out or in, or to create some other visual experience involving transparency.

- **RotateAnimation**: This animation describes the rotation of a view over time. The point about which the rotation happens can be described in terms of the View on which the rotation is happening, or its parent View. This flexibility makes the RotateAnimation class nice to use.

- **ScaleAnimation**: If you want your View to change size over time, ScaleAnimation will get the job done. Like RotateAnimation, ScaleAnimation allows you to define the point about which the scaling happens in terms of the current View or its parent.

- **TranslateAnimation**: Moving a View from one place to another is an extremely common use case, which TranslateAnimation lets you describe. A TranslateAnimation can be constructed to describe either the changes in the x and y position of the View or an animation over a fixed start and end point. The fixed point can be described in terms of the View's coordinate space or the parent View's coordinate space.

- **AnimationSet**: Use the class AnimationSet to combine animations. Any number of Animations can be added to an AnimationSet, including other AnimationSets. Since each Animation describes a period of time during which the Animation is applied, AnimationSet can be used to describe a sequence of animations by adjusting the starting offset for each Animation added. When adding Animations to an AnimationSet, keep mind that the order in which they are added describes the order in which they are *applied*, not the order in which they happen over time.

As mentioned, each Animation describes a period of time in which the animation affects the View. During this period, specifying an Interpolator can further refine the animation. For example, if we have a TranslateAnimation that describes a View moving from an x value of 0 to an x value of 100, we can specify an Interpolator to control whether the View simply moves at a constant speed or some other rate.

The interface Interpolator defines a single method, getInterpolation, that takes a value ranging from 0.0 to 1.0. It is up to implementing classes to define how this input value should be modified to control how the View moves. The following built-in classes allow a developer to easily pick from a number of prebuilt functions.

- **LinearInterpolator**: The default Interpolator for an Animation is the LinearInterpolator. In this class's implementation of the method getInterpolation, the input value is simply returned as the result. This causes the Animation to apply its effects evenly during the active period of its animation.

- **AccelerateDecelerateInterpolator**: In real life, when an object starts moving it must accelerate from its stopped state. Likewise, when an object stops moving it must decelerate to a stop. The AccelerateDecelerateInterpolator provides a short period of acceleration at the beginning of the animation and short period of deceleration at the end. Using this Interpolator instead of a LinearInterpolator can provide a subtle elegance to an animation. An

AccelerateInterpolator and a DecelerateInterpolator are also available if you only want this effect at just the start or end of an animation.

- AnticipateOvershootInterpolator: The AnticipateOvershootInterpolator starts by going backwards a little before going forward. Just before the end the animation this Interpolator goes past the maximum value before returning to the maximum. This Interpolator is a great way to make an Animation feel more energetic. Both an AnticipateInterpolator and an OvershootInterpolator are available if only the starting or ending behavior is desired.

- BounceInterpolator: The BounceInterpolator reaches its maximum value a little before the end of the animation period, at which point it reverses and then reversed again, finally ending at the maximum value. This gives the impression of a bounce for TranslateAnimations and RotateAnimations, but can be used with any Animation to create interesting visual results.

There are a number of other built-in interpolators, and implementing Interpolator can easily create more. Now that we've described the type of animations available in Android, let's continue looking at our sample game, Orb Quest, and see how these classes are used in code.

Creating Views and Animations

In Orb Quest, we have elected to use the View class to represent each orb in our game. In Chapter 9 we saw how to lay out these orbs in a 5×5 grid. Now let's look at the code that animates these orbs when the user clicks on them. Figure 10–1 shows an animation sequence in the game Orb Quest.

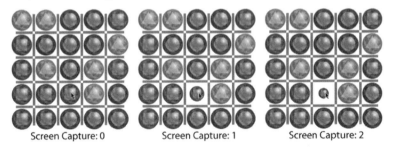

Figure 10–1. *Screen captures 0, 1, and 2—an orb shrinking*

As you can see, there are twenty five orbs laid out in a grid. The cursor is over the orb in the middle column, second-to-last row. The orb starts at its base size in Screen Capture 0. When the user clicks on the orb, it shrinks over half a second to the size shown in Screen Capture 2. Screen Capture 1 shows the animation about half way through. Recall from Listing 9-7 in Chapter 9 that each orb in Figure 10–1 is an OrbView object and that it uses the containing GameView as the click listener. Listing 10–1 shows the onClick method of GameView.

Listing 10–1. *GameView.java (onClick)*

```
@Override
public void onClick(View v) {
        if (acceptInput) {
                if (v instanceof OrbView) {
                        OrbView orbView = (OrbView) v;
                        if (selectedOrbView == null) {
                                selectedOrbView = orbView;
                                Animation scale = AnimationUtils.loadAnimation(
                                                getContext(), R.anim.scale_down);

                                orbView.startAnimation(scale);
                        } else {
                                if (orbView != selectedOrbView) {
                                        swapOrbs(selectedOrbView, orbView);
                                        selectedOrbView = null;
                                } else {
                                        Animation scale = AnimationUtils.loadAnimation(
                                                        getContext(), R.anim.scale_up);

                                        orbView.startAnimation(scale);
                                        selectedOrbView = null;
                                }
                        }
                }
        }
}
```

This is the method that is called when a user clicks (or touches) an orb. The first thing this method does is check if the variable `acceptInput` is true. This variable is set to false whenever there is an animation in progress, and set back to true when the animation is over, thus preventing user interaction during an animation. If we are accepting user input, we have to check whether this is the first or second of a pair of orbs selected. We know it's the first if the variable `selectedOrbView` is equal to null.

When the user clicks on the first of two orbs, we set the variable `selectedOrb` to be the `orbView` that was clicked. We then want to scale the orb down to indicate that it is selected. To do this, we want to use a `ScaleAnimation` that defines a starting scale and an ending scale. Animations can be created programmatically or defined in XML. In this case, we are using the class `AnimationUtils` to load an animation called `scale_down` from an XML file. The Animation called `scale` is applied to our `OrbView` by calling `startAnimation` and passing it the `Animation`. Like all resources in an Android project, these are defined in the `res` directory of a project. Listing 10–2 shows the `scale_down.xml` file from the anim directory, found in the `rest` directory.

Listing 10–2. *scale_down.xml*

```
<?xml version="1.0" encoding="utf-8"?>
<scale xmlns:android="http://schemas.android.com/apk/res/android"
    android:fromXScale="1.0"
    android:toXScale="0.5"
    android:fromYScale="1.0"
    android:toYScale="0.5"
    android:pivotX="50%"
```

```
        android:pivotY="50%"
        android:duration="500"
        android:fillAfter="true"
        android:interpolator="@android:anim/anticipate_overshoot_interpolator"
/>
```

The root element in Listing 10–2 is a `scale` element. By setting attributes on this element, we can define a `ScaleAnimation` object. We are setting both `fromXScale` and `fromYScale` to 1.0. This indicates we want the animation to start with `scale` at its native value. The attributes `toXScale` and `toYScale` are set to 0.5, which indicates the `scale` the `View` should be at when the `Animation` is done. The attributes `pivotX` and `pivotY` specify a percentage that means the actual point is in the `View`'s coordinate space. The value of 50 percent for both `pivotX` and `pivotY` is, of course, the center of the `View`.

The attribute duration is the number of milliseconds the animation should take to complete. The attribute `interpolate` indicates we want to use an instance of `AnticipateOvershootInterpolator`. The effect of this interpolator is not visible in Figure 10–1, but if you run the code, you'll notice that the orb grows a little before it shrinks and shrinks past its final size briefly at the end of the animation.

The attribute `fillAfter` in Listing 10–2 tells the animation to apply itself to the transformation of the animated `View` when the animation is done. This means that when the animation is over, the orb will stay scaled down. If `fillAfter` is not set or is set to false, the orb would snap back to full size when the animation was over.

In Listing 10–1, if the variable `selectedOrbView` is not null, we want to check to see if the orb reporting the click event is the same orb as the `selectedOrbView`. If the user has selected the same orb twice, we want to scale the orb back up and set `selectedOrbView` to null. This basically allows users to change their minds about which orb they want to swap. If the user clicked on a different orb, we want to create an animation that swaps these orbs. Figure 10–2 shows a sequence of screen shots where two orbs are changing places.

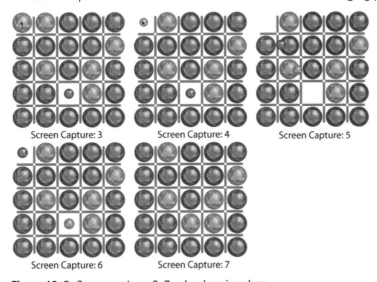

Figure 10–2. *Screen captures 3–7, orbs changing place*

In Figure 10–2, five screen shots depict the animation that occurs when two orbs trade place. Screen Capture 3 shows the user clicking on the top left orb, which will shrink down to the same size as the previously selected orb, as shown in Screen Capture 4. Screen Capture 5 shows the two orbs a little over half way through trading places. In Screen Capture 6, we see each node in its final destination, where it grows back to full size, as Screen Capture 7 shows. This animation consists of a series of individual animations; Listing 10–3 shows the code that creates this effect.

Listing 10–3. *GameView.java (swapOrbs)*

```
protected void swapOrbs(OrbView orb1, OrbView orb2) {
        turns--;

        acceptInput = false;
        //swap locations
        int col1 = orb1.getCol();
        int row1 = orb1.getRow();
        int col2 = orb2.getCol();
        int row2 = orb2.getRow();

        orb1.setCol(col2);
        orb1.setRow(row2);
        orb2.setCol(col1);
        orb2.setRow(row1);

        //Animate Orb1
        TranslateAnimation trans1 = new TranslateAnimation(0, orb2.getLeft()
                    - orb1.getLeft(), 0, orb2.getTop() - orb1.getTop());
        trans1.setDuration(500);
        trans1.setStartOffset(500);

        ScaleAnimation scaleUp1 = new ScaleAnimation(0.5f, 1.0f, 0.5f, 1.0f,
                    Animation.RELATIVE_TO_SELF, .5f, Animation.RELATIVE_TO_SELF,
                    .5f);
        scaleUp1.setDuration(500);
        scaleUp1.setStartOffset(1000);

        AnimationSet set1 = new AnimationSet(false);
        set1.addAnimation(scaleUp1);
        set1.addAnimation(trans1);

        orb1.startAnimation(set1);

        //Animate Orb2
        ScaleAnimation scaleDown2 = new ScaleAnimation(1.0f, 0.5f, 1.0f, 0.5f,
                    Animation.RELATIVE_TO_SELF, .5f, Animation.RELATIVE_TO_SELF,
                    .5f);
        scaleDown2.setDuration(500);
        scaleDown2.setInterpolator(new AnticipateOvershootInterpolator());

        TranslateAnimation trans2 = new TranslateAnimation(0, orb1.getLeft()
                    - orb2.getLeft(), 0, orb1.getTop() - orb2.getTop());
        trans2.setDuration(500);
        trans2.setStartOffset(500);

        ScaleAnimation scaleUp2 = new ScaleAnimation(1.0f, 2.0f, 1.0f, 2.0f,
```

```
                        Animation.RELATIVE_TO_SELF, .5f, Animation.RELATIVE_TO_SELF,
                        .5f);
        scaleUp2.setDuration(500);
        scaleUp2.setStartOffset(1000);

        AnimationSet set2 = new AnimationSet(false);
        set2.addAnimation(scaleDown2);
        set2.addAnimation(scaleUp2);
        set2.addAnimation(trans2);

        set2.setAnimationListener(new RunAfter() {
                @Override
                public void run() {
                        requestLayout();
                        checkMatches();
                }
        });
        orb2.startAnimation(set2);
}
```

The first thing we do here is take care of a little bookkeeping. We decrement the number of available turns, set acceptInput to false, and swap the row and column values for the two orbs. The method swapOrbs continues with an AnimationSet for each orb.

The first AnimationSet is called set1 and consists of a TranslateAnimation called trans1 and a ScaleAnimation called scaleUp1. The variable trans1 is constructed with a constructor that uses the starting and ending deltas for the x and y values. Since we want the animation to start at the current location of the orb, we pass 0s for the starting X and Y deltas. The ending deltas are calculated by subtracting the second orb's coordinate from the coordinate of the first for both X and Y. The duration and starting offset are set to 500. Setting the duration to 500 indicates that the translation from the starting location to the destination location should take half a second. Setting the starting offset to 500 causes this animation to wait half a second before starting, which gives the second orb time to shrink.

The second animation added to set1 in Listing 10-3 is a ScaleAnimation called scaleUp1. The constructor used to instantiate scaleUp1 contains the same sort of information used in the XML definition of a ScaleAnimation from Listing 10-2. We specify a starting scale of .5 for both the scale X and scale Y values. The end scale is set to 1.0 for both scale X and scale Y. We also use the constant RELATIVE_TO_SELF to indicate that the last two 0.5fs should indicate a point at 50 percent of the width and height of the orb. The duration for scaleUp1 is also set to half a second. The starting offset is set to 1000 milliseconds or a full second. We get the value of 1000 because trans1 will take 500 milliseconds and start after 500 milliseconds (500+500=1000).

Once both trans1 and scaleUp1 are defined, we add them to set1 by calling addAnimation. Note that we add scaleUp1 before we add trans1. We do this because the order in which Animations are added to addAnimations indicates the order in which underlying transformation matrixes are composed. If we swapped the order these two Animations were added, they would still affect the orb the same temporally, but the resulting location and scale would be messed up. Once set1 is fully configured, we call startAnimation on orb1 to kick off the animation we defined.

In Listing 10–3, we create a second `AnimationSet` called `set2` to describe the animation of the second orb. The second orb, `orb2`, is full size when this method is called, so we have to include an addition `ScaleAnimation` called `scaleDown2` to scale the orb down before it starts to move. The `ScaleAnimation scaleDown2` is constructed to animate the scale from 1.0 to .5 for both x and y, and the scale should use a point in the middle of the orb. The duration for `scaleDown2` is set to 500 milliseconds and the interpolator is set to a new `AntisipateOvershootInterpolator`. Though we used code to create `scaleDown2`, its functionality happens to be identical to the interpolator defined in XML in Listing 10–2.

To complete our setup of the `AnimationSet set2`, we construct a `TranslationAnimation` called `trans2` and a `ScaleAnimation` called `scaleUp2`. The animation `trans2` is slightly different from `trans1`; `trans2`'s ending deltas for x and y have signs opposite `trans1`'s. The `ScaleAnimation scaleUp2` is also different from `scaleUp1`— the scale range goes from 1.0 to 2.0. The reason for the difference is that `scaleUp2` must compensate for the fact that `scaleDown2` is added to `set2`. Remember that even after a given Animation's duration has passed, its ending value will still be applied. Figure 10–3 shows a time line for how these three Animations interact.

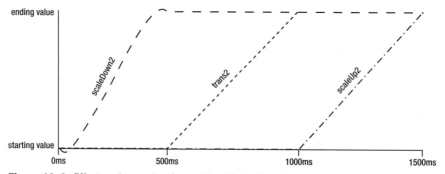

Figure 10–3. *Effect on three animations of the full duration of `set2`*

We see on the left that from time 0 to 500, the Animation `scaleDown2` is interpolating. The line is curved due to the use of the `AnticipateOvershootInterpolator`. During this first period of time, the resulting animation is the combination of the interpolated value for `scaleDown2`, the starting value for `scaleUp2`, and the starting value for `trans2`. From time 500 to 1000, the Animation `trans2` is interpolating and the resulting transformation is defined by the ending value of `scaleDown2`, the starting value of `scaleUp2`, and the interpolating value of `trans2`. During the last period of time, from 1000ms to 1500ms, the resulting transformation is defined by the end value of `scaleDown2`, the interpolating value of `scaleUp2`, and the end value of `trans2`.

The last thing to do in the `swapOrbs` method is to register a listener with `set2` so we know when the animation is done, at which point we will call `requestLayout` and `checkMatches`. The method `requestLayout` is defined by the class `View` and tells the system to call the method `onLayout` (see Listing 9-9). The method `checkMatches` will inspect the orbs and see if any columns or rows contain orbs of the same types. But let's look first at the class `RunAfter`, which we're using with the method `setAnimationListener`, as shown in Listing 10–4.

Listing 10-4. *GameView.java (RunAfter)*

```java
private abstract class RunAfter implements Animation.AnimationListener,
            Runnable {

    @Override
    public void onAnimationEnd(Animation animation) {
        run();
    }

    @Override
    public void onAnimationRepeat(Animation animation) {
    }

    @Override
    public void onAnimationStart(Animation animation) {
    }

}
```

Here we see an inner class named `RunAfter`, a utility class we're using to call methods after an animation is complete. As you can see, `RunAfter` implements the interfaces `Animation.AnimationListener` and `Runnable`. Thus, looking back to Listing 10-3, you can see we are creating a concrete instance of `RunAfter` and defining the method `run`, which is called from `onAnimationEnd`.

In Listing 10-3, we make sure `onLayout` gets called by calling `requestLayout` when the animation `set2` is complete. We have to do this because `Animations` are a little strange in Android. While it is true that they move where a `View` is drawn, they do not, for some reason, change where the `View` receives events. If we did not call `requestLayout` at the end of the animation, the orbs would appear in their new location, but clicking one of them would result in an event being generated for the other orb.

The other thing we do when the animation `set2`, from Listing 10-3, is complete is call `checkMatches`, as shown in Listing 10-5.

Listing 10-5. *GameView.java (checkMatches)*

```java
protected void checkMatches() {
    Set<OrbView> matchingRows = new HashSet<OrbView>();
    Set<OrbView> matchingCols = new HashSet<OrbView>();

    for (int r = 0; r < 5; r++) {
        Set<OrbView> oneSet = new HashSet<OrbView>();

        OrbView zero = findOrbView(0, r);
        boolean allSame = true;
        for (int c = 0; c < 5; c++) {
            OrbView orbView = findOrbView(c, r);
            if (orbView.getOrbType() != zero.getOrbType()) {
                allSame = false;
                break;
            }
            oneSet.add(orbView);
        }

        if (allSame) {
```

```java
                    matchingRows.addAll(oneSet);
            }
    }

    for (int c = 0; c < 5; c++) {
            Set<OrbView> oneSet = new HashSet<OrbView>();

            OrbView zero = findOrbView(c, 0);
            boolean allSame = true;
            for (int r = 0; r < 5; r++) {
                    OrbView orbView = findOrbView(c, r);
                    if (orbView.getOrbType() != zero.getOrbType()) {
                            allSame = false;
                            break;
                    }
                    oneSet.add(orbView);
            }

            if (allSame) {
                    for (OrbView orb : oneSet) {
                            if (!matchingRows.contains(orb)) {
                                    matchingCols.add(orb);
                            }
                    }
            }
    }

    if (matchingRows.size() == 0 && matchingCols.size() == 0) {
            doneAnimating();
            return;
    }

    int size = getWidth();
    boolean runAfterSet = false;

    final Set<OrbView> allOrbs = new HashSet<GameView.OrbView>(matchingCols);
    allOrbs.addAll(matchingRows);

    if (matchingRows.size() != 0) {
            for (OrbView orbView : matchingRows) {

                    ScaleAnimation scaleDown = new ScaleAnimation(1.0f, 0.5f, 1.0f,
                                    0.5f, Animation.RELATIVE_TO_SELF, 0.5f,
                                    Animation.RELATIVE_TO_SELF, 0.5f);
                    scaleDown.setDuration(500);
                    scaleDown.setFillAfter(true);

                    TranslateAnimation trans = new TranslateAnimation(0, size, 0, 0);
                    trans.setDuration(500);
                    trans.setStartOffset(500);
                    trans.setFillAfter(true);

                    AnimationSet set = new AnimationSet(false);
                    set.addAnimation(scaleDown);
                    set.addAnimation(trans);
```

```
                if (!runAfterSet) {
                        runAfterSet = true;
                        set.setAnimationListener(new RunAfter() {
                                @Override
                                public void run() {
                                        updateRemovedOrbs(allOrbs);
                                }
                        });
                }

                orbView.startAnimation(set);
            }
        }

        if (matchingCols.size() != 0) {
            for (OrbView orbView : matchingCols) {
                ScaleAnimation scaleDown = new ScaleAnimation(1.0f, 0.5f, 1.0f,
                        0.5f, Animation.RELATIVE_TO_SELF, 0.5f,
                        Animation.RELATIVE_TO_SELF, 0.5f);
                scaleDown.setDuration(500);
                scaleDown.setFillAfter(true);

                TranslateAnimation trans = new TranslateAnimation(0, 0, 0,
 size);
                trans.setDuration(500);
                trans.setStartOffset(500);
                trans.setFillAfter(true);

                AnimationSet set = new AnimationSet(false);
                set.addAnimation(scaleDown);
                set.addAnimation(trans);

                if (!runAfterSet) {
                        runAfterSet = true;
                        set.setAnimationListener(new RunAfter() {
                                @Override
                                public void run() {
                                        updateRemovedOrbs(allOrbs);
                                }
                        });
                }

                orbView.startAnimation(set);
            }
        }
    }
}
```

In Listing 10–5, we create two `HashSet`s where we record all `OrbView`s that are in matching rows or columns. By iterating over each row and testing if all of the orbs are of the same type, we can find the matching rows, and we repeat the process for each column as well. Once all of the rows and columns are inspected, we check to see if any columns or rows were found. If not, we call `doneAnimating` and return. If we do find matching rows and columns, we create an animation sequence for each `OrbView` to produce the sequence shown in Figure 10–4.

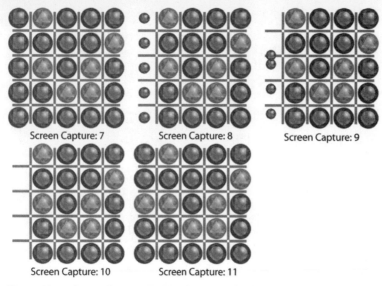

Figure 10-4. *Screen Captures 7–11, column match animation*

In Screen Capture 7, the left column contains all the same type. This triggers the animation starting in Screen Capture 8, where each orb shrinks. When the orbs have shrunk, they begin moving to a point off the bottom of the screen, as shown in Screen Capture 9. Screen Capture 10 shows that all of the matching orbs are gone, and Screen Capture 11 shows five fresh orbs filling the empty space. At this point, it is possible that the new orbs create new matches, in which case the animation would be repeated for the newly matching sets.

As Listing 10–5 shows, we create an animation for each OrbView in a match. The animation called set is an AnimationSet and is composed of a ScaleAnimation and a TranslateAnimation. These Animations are almost identical to the Animations we looked at in Listing 10–3. ScaleAnimation scales the orb from 1.0 to 0.5 over 500 milliseconds and TranslateAnimation moves the orb either off the right or the bottom of the screen.

We do have to do a little bookkeeping as we create these animations, since we only registered one RunAfter with one animation. To keep track of this, we use the variable runAfterSet to make sure we register only the one RunAfter. RunAfter is configured to call updateRemovedOrbs when the animations are complete (all of the animations complete at the same time). Listing 10–6 shows the method updateRemovedOrbs.

Listing 10–6. *GameView.java (updateRemovedOrbs)*

```
private void updateRemovedOrbs(Set<OrbView> allOrbs) {
        score += allOrbs.size() * 5;
        for (OrbView orbView : allOrbs) {
                orbView.setRandomType();
        }
        requestLayout();
        checkMatches();
}
```

The method `updateRemovedOrbs` is called when the animation that removes the nodes is complete. A `Set` called `allOrbs` is passed to `updateRemovedOrbs` and contains all orbs that were part of a matching column or row. The size of `allOrbs` is used to update the current score, then each `OrbView` in `allOrbs` is assigned a new random type. Lastly we call `requestLayout` to reset the location of the `OrbView`, and call `checkMatches` to see if any of the new orbs create matches. If no new matches are found, we call `doneAnimating` from `checkMatches`. The method `doneAnimating` is shown in Listing 10–7.

Listing 10–7. *GameView.java (doneAnimating)*

```
protected void doneAnimating() {
        requestLayout();
        acceptInput = true;
        gameActivity.updateValues(score, turns);
        if (turns <= 0) {
                gameActivity.endGame();
        }
}
```

The method `doneAnimating` is responsible for doing some clean-up. The call to `requestLayout` makes sure the correct orb responds to a touch event. We start accepting user input again by setting `acceptInput` to true. The method `updateValues` is called on `gameActivity` to update `TextViews` to show the score and remaining turns. Lastly, we check if any turns remain. If not, we call `endGame` to bring up the dialog described at the beginning of Chapter 9.

In conclusion, using `Views` and the related classes to implement a game can save a lot of time because you're using the same API for the game as for the rest of the application. The `Animation` classes are a little tricky at first, especially when creating sequences of animations. Perhaps the best part about using `Views` is that registering event listeners is taken care of for you. Nowhere in our code did we have to try to figure out what the user was interacting with; we simply listened for `onClick` events.

Overall, this strategy seems appropriate for games where a specific animation is generated for a specific user interaction. Basically, the state of the game oscillates between waiting for user interaction and running an animation. I would recommend this pattern for puzzle games, but probably not for games where there is continuous action driven by game logic.

Frame By Frame Animations

In Chapter 9 we explored how to override the `onDraw` method so we could do pixel-level rendering with an instance of the `Canvas` class. In this section we are going to extend this concept to create an animation where each frame of an animation is drawn using a `Canvas` object. Since we will want to redraw the scene many times a second, we have to do a little more work than simply overriding the `onDraw` method. We have to set up a rendering thread that correctly synchronizes with the underlying graphics system to create a smooth, performant animation. Figure 10–5 shows the animations will be implementing.

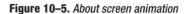

Figure 10–5. *About screen animation*

These are screen captures from Orb Quest's About screen. There are three orbs, each moving in a straight line. When an orb reaches the end of the screen, it bounces off the edge of the screen and changes direction. Behind the three balls is some text describing the game. Listing 10–8 shows the first part of the class `AboutView`.

Listing 10–8. *AboutView.java (partial)*

```java
public class AboutView extends SurfaceView implements SurfaceHolder.Callback {

        public static Random random = new Random();

        private boolean animating = true;
        private AnimationThread thread;

        private List<Sprite> sprites = new ArrayList<Sprite>();

        public AboutView(Context context, AttributeSet attrs) {
                super(context, attrs);

                SurfaceHolder surfaceHolder = getHolder();
                surfaceHolder.addCallback(this);
                thread = new AnimationThread(surfaceHolder);
        }

        @Override
        public void surfaceChanged(SurfaceHolder holder, int format, int width,
                        int height) {
                //called when the size of the surface changes, we are not handling⏎
 this case.
        }

        @Override
        public void surfaceCreated(SurfaceHolder holder) {
                animating = true;
                thread.start();
```

```
        }

        @Override
        public void surfaceDestroyed(SurfaceHolder holder) {
                boolean retry = true;
                animating = false;
                while (retry) {
                        try {
                                thread.join();
                                retry = false;
                        } catch (InterruptedException e) {
                        }
                }
        }
}
```

As you can see, AboutView extends SurfaceView and implements SurfaceHolder.Callback. The class SurfaceView is a special type of View that provides access to a Surface object, which is a handle to the raw bytes used by the underlying compositor. Basically, the Surface class gives us low-level access for rendering. The interface SurfaceHolder.Callback is used by any object interested in any changes in status of an underlying Surface object.

In the constructor, we see that we get access to a SurfaceHolder by calling getHolder. Once we have the holder we register this instance of AboutView as a callback to the SurfaceHolder. This causes the methods surfaceCreated, surfaceChanged, and surfaceDestroyed to be called when the Surface we are rendering is created, changes size, or is destroyed. The last thing done in the constructor is to create an instance of AnimationThread and pass in the surface holder. AnimationThread is a class of our own design and handles the rendering logic. Note that the thread is started in the surfaceCreated method; this prevents the thread from trying to draw to a Surface that does not yet exist. When the surface is destroyed, we stop the AnimationThread by setting animation to false, then we call join on it. The method join causes the calling thread to block until the AnimationThread stops execution. This is done to make sure AnimationThread is completely finished before exiting the surfaceDestroyed method, preventing an application crash.

As mentioned, the actual animation happens in the AnimationThread class, which is shown in Listing 10–9.

Listing 10–9. *AboutView.java (AnimationThread)*

```
private class AnimationThread extends Thread {
        private SurfaceHolder surfaceHolder;

        AnimationThread(SurfaceHolder surfaceHolder) {
                this.surfaceHolder = surfaceHolder;
        }

        @Override
        public void run() {
                while (animating) {
                        Canvas c = null;
                        try {
                                c = surfaceHolder.lockCanvas(null);
```

```
                    synchronized (surfaceHolder) {
                            doDraw(c);
                    }
            } finally {
                    if (c != null) {
                            surfaceHolder.unlockCanvasAndPost(c);
                    }
            }
        }
    }
}
```

Here we see that the constructor for the AnimationThread class simply keeps a reference to the SurfaceHolder passed in. As with most Thread classes, the interesting stuff is in the run methods, so let's take a look at that.

In the run method we create a while loop that will run as long as the variable animating is true. To get a reference to a Canvas object, we call lockCanvas on surfaceHolder. This method not only gives us access to a Canvas object, it also prevents SurfaceView from creating, modifying, or destroying the Canvas until unlockCanvasAndPost is called. This happens when we are done drawing and want the changed pixels to be displayed on the screen. Before we do any actual drawing in the doDraw method, we synchronize on surfaceHolder to prevent another instance of AnimationThread from drawing to the same canvas. This synchronization is a defensive measure, since our application never intentionally creates two instances of AnimationThread. To do the drawing, let's look at the method doDraw shown in Listing 10–10.

Listing 10–10. *AboutView.java (doDraw and addSprites)*

```java
public void doDraw(Canvas canvas) {
        addSprites();

        canvas.drawColor(Color.WHITE);

        for (Sprite sprite : sprites) {
                sprite.update(getWidth(), getHeight());
                sprite.draw(canvas);
        }

}

private void addSprites() {
        if (sprites.size() == 0) {
                Drawable rOrb = getResources().getDrawable(R.drawable.red_orb);
                Drawable gOrb = getResources()
                                .getDrawable(R.drawable.green_orb);
                Drawable bOrb = getResources().getDrawable(R.drawable.blue_orb);

                int width = getWidth();
                int height = getHeight();

                sprites.add(new Sprite(rOrb, width, height));
                sprites.add(new Sprite(gOrb, width, height));
                sprites.add(new Sprite(bOrb, width, height));
        }
}
```

Listing 10–10 shows two methods, doDraw and addSprites. The method addSprites is the first thing called in doDraw and it adds the three orbs the first time it is called. The orbs are instances of a class called Sprite that we define; each Sprite is constructed with a Drawable and the size of the region in which it is being drawn. The Sprite class encapsulates the visual component of the orb (the Drawable), where the Sprite should be drawn, and how the Sprite should move for each frame of the animation.

In the doDraw method, we clear the canvas by calling drawColor; then, for each Sprite, we update its location and then call draw in the Sprite. In this way, each time the while loop from Listing 10–9 iterates, doDraw clears the screen, updates the location of the orbs, and draws them in a new location. Listing 10–11 shows the Sprite class.

Listing 10–11. *Sprite.java*

```java
public class Sprite extends Drawable {
        public static Random random = new Random();

        //current location
        private float x;
        private float y;
        private float radius;

        //used for updates
        private float deltaX;
        private float deltaY;
        private float deltaRadius;

        //what the Sprite looks like
        private Drawable drawable;

        public Sprite(Drawable drawable, float width, float height) {
                this.drawable = drawable;

                //Randomize radius
                radius = 10 + random.nextFloat() * 30;

                //Randomize Location
                x = radius + random.nextFloat() * (width - radius);
                y = radius + random.nextFloat() * (height - radius);

                //Randomize Direction
                double direction = random.nextDouble() * Math.PI * 2;
                float speed = random.nextFloat() * .3f + .7f;

                deltaX = (float) Math.cos(direction) * speed;
                deltaY = (float) Math.sin(direction) * speed;

                //Randomize
                if (random.nextBoolean()) {
                        deltaRadius = random.nextFloat() * .2f + .1f;
                } else {
                        deltaRadius = random.nextFloat() * -.2f - .1f;
                }

        }
```

```java
        public void update(int width, int height) {
            if (radius > 40 || radius < 15) {
                deltaRadius *= -1;
            }
            radius += deltaRadius;

            if (x + radius > width) {
                deltaX *= -1;
                x = width - radius;
            } else if (x - radius < 0) {
                deltaX *= -1;
                x = radius;
            }

            if (y + radius > height) {
                deltaY *= -1;
                y = height - radius;
            } else if (y - radius < 0) {
                deltaY *= -1;
                y = radius;
            }
            x += deltaX;
            y += deltaY;

    }

    @Override
    public void draw(Canvas canvas) {

            Rect bounds = new Rect(Math.round(x - radius), Math.round(y - radius),
                            Math.round(x + radius), Math.round(y + radius));
            drawable.setBounds(bounds);

            drawable.draw(canvas);
    }

    @Override
    public int getOpacity() {
            return drawable.getOpacity();
    }

    @Override
    public void setAlpha(int alpha) {
            drawable.setAlpha(alpha);
    }

    @Override
    public void setColorFilter(ColorFilter cf) {
            drawable.setColorFilter(cf);
    }
```

The Sprite class has a number of fields. The x and y fields represent where the center of the Sprite should be drawn. The radius field describes how big it should be. The three fields starting with the word *delta* describe how the sprite should change for every frame of animation. The fields deltaX and deltaY indicate how much the x and y values should change and the field deltaRadius specifies how much the radius should change per call to update. The last field in Sprite is drawable, which is used to actually draw the Sprite. Even though our simple example only uses bitmaps for Drawables, this Sprite class could use any kind of Drawable.

The constructor for the Sprite class uses the static variable random to randomize the location, direction, speed, and how much the Sprite shrinks or grows. Once the sprite is constructed, future calls to update will cause it to change location based on the rules of our application. In the method update, we see that radius will fluctuate in value between 15 and 40. For the x and y, we simply add the deltaX and deltaY values to them. To implement the bouncing, we change the sign of the deltaX or deltaY values whenever the sprite reaches the sides of the screen.

The draw method in Listing 10–11 uses the x and y locations of the sprite, along with the radius, to define a Rect named bounds. This Rect is used to set the bounds of the drawable, so that the subsequent call to draw causes the drawable to draw in the correct location, at the correct size.

Mixing Views and SurfaceViews

The About view, shown in Figure10–5, displays text as well as orbs. The text is not being drawn by the rendering logic. The text is, in fact, just a normal TextView. Listing 10–12 shows the about.xml file that defines this layout.

Listing 10–12. *about.xml*

```
<?xml version="1.0" encoding="utf-8"?>
<FrameLayout
  xmlns:android="http://schemas.android.com/apk/res/android"
  android:layout_width="fill_parent"
  android:layout_height="fill_parent"
  android:background="#00000000"
  >
        <view class="org.ljordan.orb_quest.AboutView"
                android:id="@+id/gameView"
                android:layout_width="fill_parent"
                android:layout_height="fill_parent"
        />

        <LinearLayout
                android:layout_width="fill_parent"
                android:layout_height="fill_parent"
                android:gravity="center"
                android:orientation="vertical"
                >
                <TextView
                        android:layout_width="wrap_content"
                        android:layout_height="wrap_content"
                        android:textSize="24px"
                        android:text="@string/about_text_title"
                        android:textColor="#000000"
                />
                <TextView
                        android:layout_width="wrap_content"
                        android:layout_height="wrap_content"
```

```
                    android:text="@string/about_text"
                    android:textColor="#000000"
                    android:padding="30px"
            />
        </LinearLayout>
</FrameLayout>
```

Here we see that the root element is a `FrameLayout`. The class `FrameLayout` simply draws its children on top of each other. This is perfect for our About page, so we create a `view` element that will be an instance of our AboutView class. AboutView has its `layout_width` and `layout_height` attributes set to `fill_parent`, so it will take up the entire screen. The second child of the root `FrameLayout` is a `LinearLayout` that also fills the entire screen, but has its gravity set to `center`. This causes the two `TextViews` to be centered on the screen.

Mixing components in this way is very handy and speaks to the power of the Android compositing logic. However, I have noticed a significant performance hit when doing this. As an experiment, delete the `LinearView` (and its children) from `about.xml` and rerun the application. I think you'll find that it runs faster and smoother.

In conclusion, rendering a scene frame by frame provides the most control over an animation. Android makes it pretty painless to set up a rendering loop, giving you direct access to the screen. You will have to create your layout classes, like our `Sprite` class, but there are lots of Java libraries out there to help with this.

Summary

In this chapter, we explored creating animations using the `View` and `Animation` classes. We learned how to chain animations together and to create callback code to be run when the animations are complete. We also saw how to get a handle to the screen so we could create our own rendering thread. In this rendering thread we looked at a simple example of managing our own scene graph and how to draw the frames of our animation.

Chapter 11

App Inventor

There have been many attempts over the years to simplify the development process and allow more people to develop apps. Google's App Inventor is another tool that can bring software development to the masses, rather than being in the hands of a small number of professionals. The value of App Inventor can seem dubious to a professional developer with years of Java experience. Why use App Inventor at all? The answer to that lies in understanding that more and more non-technical people will discover App Inventor, and it behooves the professional developer to understand the tools these people will use. It gives us the ability to understand the challenges they face, and gives us a context for helping would-be software developers move to the next step. If you are working professionally with Java or Android, it is just a matter of time before you will be approached with demo or prototype developed with App Inventor.

App Inventor is a tool that allows people to drag and drop components together to create a fully functional Android app without writing a single line of code. Like most Google applications, App Inventor is a web page, though it does require the user to install a package on their local machine. On this web page, the user sees a mockup of an Android phone, along with a number of tools for creating applications.

This chapter will cover the basics of getting App Inventor up and running. We will explore the features of App Inventor so we can understand what it can do. We will finish by reviewing the current limitations of App Inventor and where it might go in the future.

Setting Up App Inventor

App Inventor is really a number of applications working together to provide the full set of functionality. There is a web page where you manage your applications and do the layout, and there is special version of the Android SDK called App Inventor Setup that must be installed. The App Inventor Setup provides the connectivity between a connected device or emulator. Lastly, there is Java application called App Inventor for Android Blocks Editor, which we will simply call the Blocks Editor. The Blocks Editor is where you "write" the code for your application. We put write in quotes because you don't write traditional code, you assemble graphical items (called blocks) that describes the behavior of your app.

Setting up App Inventor is pretty simple: just go to http://appinventor.googlelabs
.com/ and follow the directions for your platform. You will install App Inventor Setup,
which will be a native installer for Windows, Linux (Debian package), or OS X. This
installs a special version of the Android SDK. Figure 11–1 shows the installer running on
an OS X machine.

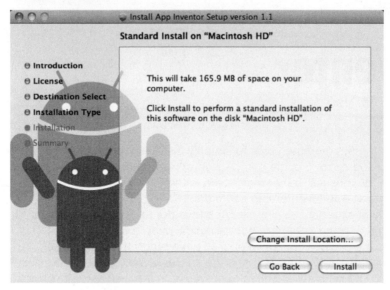

Figure 11–1. *Files installed on an OS X machine*

In Figure 11–2 we see a typical installation screen. When this installer runs, it will create
a number of files on your machine. Figure 11–2 shows the file structure installed on an
OS X machine.

- commands-for-Appinventor
  - adb
  - adbdevices
  - adbrestart
  - emulator
  - getversion
  - kill-emulator
  - mksdcard
  - run-emulator
  - unlock-emulator-keyboard
- extras
  - Appinventor-emulator-data
- from-Android-SDK
  - platforms

Figure 11–2. *App Inventor setup files*

In Figure 11–2 we see files that look familiar to a standard Android SDK installation. The App Inventor Setup is a subset of a full install, but it does come with an emulator preconfigured to be used during development. Once the installer is finished, it is time to log in to App Inventor and start creating your first application.

To log in to the App Inventor web page, go to the main App Inventor page and click My Projects. If you are not signed in with a Google account you will be prompted to do so. Once you log in, you will see a screen something like Figure 11–3.

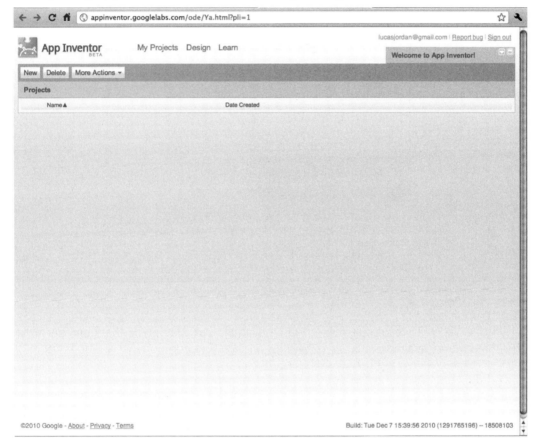

Figure 11–3. *Just logged in*

In Figure 11–3 we see an almost empty web page. There are a number of buttons at the top for managing your projects. You can either create a new project or, in the More Actions drop-down menu, you will find an option for uploading a project. The accompanying source code for this book contains the project used in this chapter. You can upload that project if want; it is a file called Sample_01.zip. Once you are actually working with a project, you will see something like Figure 11–4.

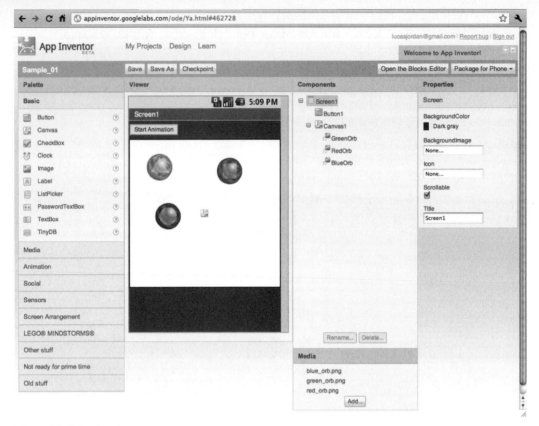

Figure 11-4. *Design view*

Figure 11–4 shows our sample project. On the left we see the palette that contains all of the components available in an App Inventor project. The components are both visual and non-visual elements of an application. As can be seen under Basic, there are things like buttons and also a TinyDB component. To add components to your application, simply drag it onto the View. When a visual component is added, it will be placed in the Viewer according the layout rules of the containing component. Non-visual components are listed below the screen area. All added components are also accessible from the Components section of the screen, which shows the hierarchy of the visual components in a tree. Selecting a component on either the Viewer or the Components section will display those components properties under the Properties section.

Up to this point, App Inventor is very much like any other visual design tool. It is perhaps lacking in the number of available components, but we should remember it is a work in progress.

For our sample application we added a Button, a Canvas, and three ImageSprites found under the Animation section. A button is pretty self-explanatory: it works just like any other button. The Canvas is special type of visual component that allows drawing commands to be defined and provides a container for ImageSprites. An ImageSprite is a component with a number of built-in animation behaviors. To specify an image for an ImageSprite, you must first upload your image under the Media section. Once uploaded, you can select the desired image from the ImageSprite's properties panel.

In our case we uploaded the now familiar orb images. This sample application is going to mimic the animation behavior found in Chapter 10 for the About View. Each orb will animate around the screen and bounce of the edges of the screen.

In order to make these ImageSprites animate the way we want, we have to set the property Interval to 33 for each orb. The Interval value is the number of milliseconds between each step in the animation. Setting it to 33 will cause the orb to animate at about 30 frames per second.

When we added the Canvas, we noticed that the layout rules didn't seem to be working as advertised. We had to specify a fixed size for this component. It's not a critical bug, but there are lots of little annoying quirks like this.

Now that the components are laid out, we are ready to specify some behaviors for our application.

Working with Blocks

App Inventor defines behavior using a visual programming application called App Inventor for Android Blocks Editor. The idea with visual programming is that you connect graphical components – called blocks – together to create your application. This is intended to make programming more accessible, because you can only connect the right types of components together. In this section we take a look at the Blocks Editor and work through a couple of examples of using blocks.

You launch this Blocks Editor application by clicking the Open the Blocks Editor button shown in Figure 11–4. Launching the Blocks Editor can be a little strange, since the button actually causes the browser to download a JNLP file. A JNLP file is a file used by Java's WebStart technology to install and run a Java application. Depending on your platform, your experience will be different. On OS X, each time you want to start the Blocks Editor you wind up downloading another copy of the JNLP file. Double-clicking on any of the downloaded files launched the application. No big deal, but if you have never worked with a WebStart application, it can be a little confusing.

Once the Blocks Editor has launched, you will be prompted by a dialog asking if you want to use a connected device, an emulator, or proceed without a device. Figure 11–5 shows this dialog.

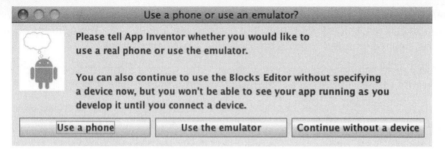

Figure 11-5. *Select your device*

Once you have made your device selection, the Blocks Editor will try and establish a connection with either your real device or a running emulator. If you selected emulator and no emulator is running, one will be started. You don't have to wait for the emulator to start before you can start exploring the Blocks Editor, as shown in Figure 11–6.

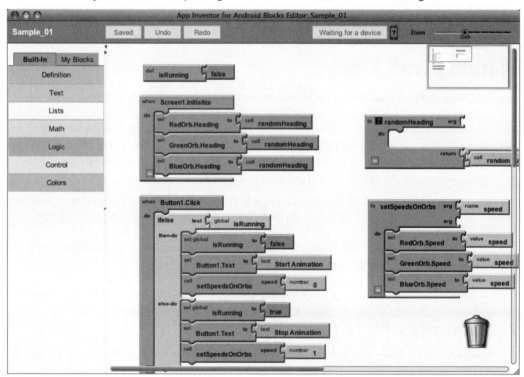

Figure 11-6. *Blocks editor*

The Blocks Editor has three parts. At the top are a number of buttons for managing your project and device. On the left is a tabbed panel containing all of the built-in blocks, as well as blocks we will define. If you started a fresh project, the area in the middle will be blank; if you uploaded the sample project, it will be populated with the blocks shown in Figure 11–6.

Before we take a look at the blocks defined in the sample project, we should take a closer look at some the built-in blocks so we know what we are working with.

Understanding the Types of Blocks

The fundamentals of an App Inventor application's behavior are defined by a relatively small set of built-in blocks. Blocks are grouped together by function, like Text and Logic as shown on the left side of Figure 11–6. Let's take a look these groups and a sample of blocks from each one.

Definition Blocks

The Definition group contains blocks that are used to define variables and procedures. These are the general organizational blocks used in any app. The Definition blocks are shown in Figure 11–7.

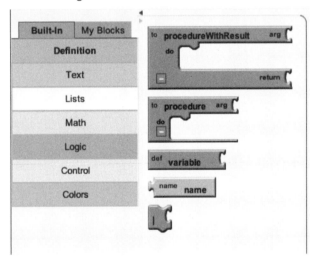

Figure 11–7. *Definition blocks*

Procedures: A procedure is a collection of procedure calls – think Java method. Like a Java method, a procedure can be defined to have a return type or not. A procedure can also take a number of arguments. When defining a procedure, you can draw other blocks into it to describe the program logic. If the procedure has a return type it must be specified in the result connector.

Variable: A variable is a block that defines a global variable. You create a variable by dragging it out into the center of the application and specifying a name. The value of the variable block is set by attaching a block to the right side of the variable block. Once a variable is created, it is used by dragging the value or setter block from the My Definitions group found under My Blocks. There does not seem to be any way to create variables that exist within the scope of a procedure.

Cap: Among the definition blocks is a block used to ignore the result of a procedure. Graphically it is depicted with a "|" char. This is a purely utility block and is used when you have defined a procedure with a return type, but you are using that procedure in a place that does not take a value.

Text Blocks

Text blocks are used to manipulate string values. There are a good number of them, and we suspect new ones are added regularly. Figure 11–8 shows most of the available text blocks.

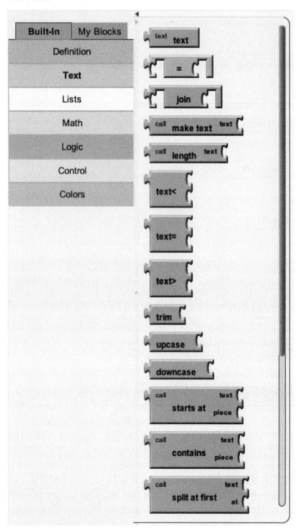

Figure 11-8. *Text blocks*

- **Text:** Text is the most basic text block; it is used to define a string value.
- **Make Text:** The Make Text block is used to concatenate two or more strings into a single string.
- **Length:** The Length block takes a string and returns the number of characters in the string.
- **Greater Than, Equal To, and Less Than:** The Equal To block takes two strings and evaluates their equality. The Greater Than and Less Than blocks will return true or false if the string arguments are in alphabetical order. These block returns a Boolean value that can be used with control blocks.
- **Upcase and Downcase:** These blocks are used to force a string to be either all uppercase or all lowercase, respectively.
- **Starts At:** The Starts At block is used to find the first index of a substring. If the substring is not present, a 0 is returned. Note that this is different from Java; with App Inventor the first letter in a string has an index of 1. In Java the index of the first letter would be 0.
- **Split:** The Split block is used to find all of the pieces of a string separated by a specified delimiter. The return type of this block is a list.

List Blocks

The group called Lists contains blocks for creating and querying lists. You will find blocks for determining the size as well as blocks for list manipulation. Figure 11-9 shows a selection of lists blocks.

- **Make a List:** Lists are created using the make a list block. Zero or more starting items can be added to a new list. In Figure 11-9, the Make a List block is shown with a single empty slot labeled item. When a value is placed in the spot, a new empty item slot is created, allowing you at add additional items.
- **Select List Item:** The Select List Item block is used to pull out a single item from a list by specifying the index of the desired item. Like strings, lists are not zero-based. The first item in a list has an index of 1.

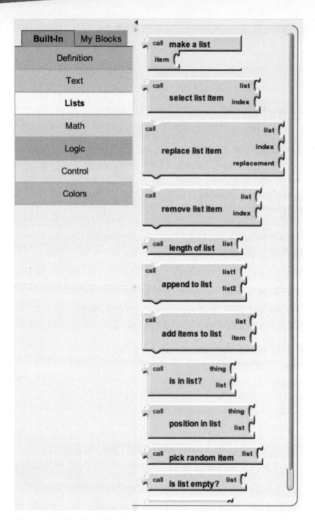

Figure 11-9. *Lists block*

- **Replace List Item:** The Replace List Item block is used to replace an item in the list. This block requires you to specify the list being modified, the index of the item to be replaced, and the replacement value.

- **Remove List Item:** The Remove List Item block removes an item from the list. Keep in mind that the first item has an index of 1.

- **Length of List:** The Length of List block reports the number of items in a list.

- **Append to List:** The Append to List block adds the contents of the second list to the first. The second list is unmodified by this operation.

- **Add Items to List:** The Add Items to List block allows any number of values to be added to a list. Like the Make a List block, the block will update after dragging a value into the item slot to make room for additional items.

- **Is in List:** The Is in List block tests to see if the given item is a member of the provided list.

- **Position in List:** The Position in List block will return the index of the given thing in the given list. A value of 0 is returned if the thing is not in the list.

- **Pick Random Item:** The Pick Random Item block returns one of the values from a provided list. This block could be reproduced blocks from the Math and List groups, but is provided for convenience.

- **Is List Empty:** The Is List Empty block returns true if the provided list has no items in it. This block prevents us from having to get the size of a list and see if it is 0 or not.

- **Is a List:** The Is a List block tests to see if the given value is a list at all. This is handy, because the type system in this graphical language is not very strict.

Math Blocks

The blocks in the Math group define a number of common mathematical functions. This includes blocks for testing equality and inequality, and blocks for creating new values through addition, subtraction, and the like. There are also blocks for all of the functions you would find in the Java class Math, in addition to blocks for creating random values. Figure 11–10 shows a number of blocks from the Math group.

- **123:** The block labeled 123 is used to create a new numeric value. After adding this block to the center are of the application, you can double-click on the value 123 and change it to any valid numeric value.

- **Equality and Inequality:** The block with the label = is used for testing if numbers are the same. There are four more blocks for testing inequality: greater than, greater than or equals, less than, and less than or equals, designated by the characters >, >=, <, and <=, respectively.

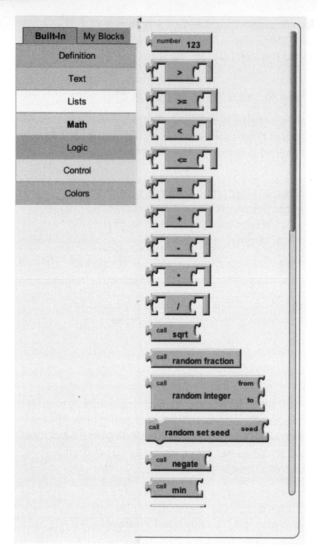

Figure 11-10. *Math blocks*

- **Addition, Subtraction, Multiplication, and Division:** For each basic numeric operation there is a corresponding block. When two number values are added to these blocks, they return a new value according to the function of the block. For example, to add to two numbers, create a block with the + symbol, and then drag a number value into each of the two open spots. The result is the sum.

- **Random Fraction:** The Random Fraction block returns a random value between 0.0 and 1.0. There is no indication in the documentation if this value is single or double precision.

- **Random Integer:** The Random Integer block takes two values and returns an integer value between the two provided values, inclusively.

- **Random Set Seed:** The Random Set Seed is used set the seed for the underlying random number generator.

- **Other Functions:** For each function found in the Java class Math, there is a corresponding block that performs the same functions. These include, sqrt, negate, min, max, quotient, remainder, modulo, abs, round, floor, ceiling, expt, exp, log, sin, cos, tan, asin, acos, atan, and atan2.

- **Is a Number:** The Is a Number block is used to test if a given value is a number. We don't see any way of testing if a value is an integer or floating point value.

Logic Blocks

The blocks found in the Logic group are used to test and manipulate Boolean values. Figure 11–11 shows the six Logic blocks.

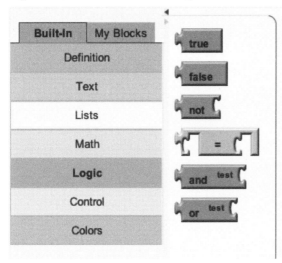

Figure 11–11. *Logic blocks*

- **True and False:** The True and False blocks are used to create a value of either true or false. Once you create a True or False block, you can change it by using a little pull-down menu to set the value. This is handy, because you don't have to drag out a new block just to swap values.

- **Not:** The Not block takes a Boolean value and inverts its value.

- **Equals:** The Logic group contains a block for testing equality. This seems to be the same as the one from the Math group; we suspect it is included in both groups so it is easy to find.

- **And and OR:** The And block and the OR block are used to apply the and or or function to two or more Boolean values. In Figure 11–11, they are shown with only a single connector for values. When a value is added, a new open connector appears for you to add additional values.

Control Blocks

Control blocks provide a way to control the flow of a program. This includes if-else statements as well as loops. There are also a few blocks used to interact with the environment your application is running in. Figure 11–12 shows the Control blocks.

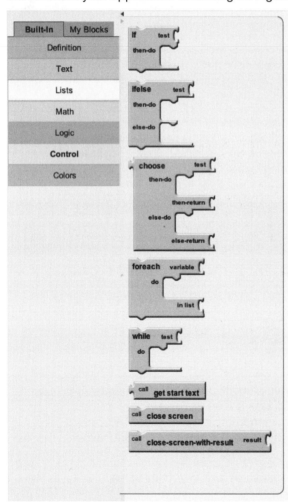

Figure 11–12. *Control blocks*

- **If:** The If block takes a test value and a number of command blocks to be executed of the test value is true.

- **Ifelse:** The Ifelse block is just like the if block, except it has an additional spot for adding blocks the test value is false.

- **Choose:** The Choose block is similar to the Ifelse block, except it is used to set a value. The Choose block is much like the ternary statement in Java.

- **Foreach:** The Foreach block is used to iterate over the contents of a list. The blocks in the do section are run for each item in a list.

- **While:** The While block executes the blocks in the do section until the value test is false. If the value test starts out as false, the do block is not executed.

- **Get Start Text:** The Get Start Text block is used to get any arguments passed to this application. This does not return a value during the normal App Inventor workflow.

- **Close Screen:** The Close Screen block is used to exit the application.

- **Close Screen with Result:** The Close Screen with Result block is used to exit the application with a particular value. This block is not used during the normal App Inventor workflow.

Color Blocks

App Inventor has a special set of blocks for presenting the available colors available to the application. Listing 11–13 shows the Color blocks.

In Figure 11–13 we see 14 color blocks – one for each color available to the application, including the color None. Each block is the color indicated by the text, e.g., the block Pink is displayed in a pink color. Note that there is no way to specify a custom color through RGB values or any other way. While images used in an App Inventor application seem to support a full range of colors, the components in the application can only use one of these colors. This seems like an odd limitation to us; hopefully it will be addressed in future version of App Inventor.

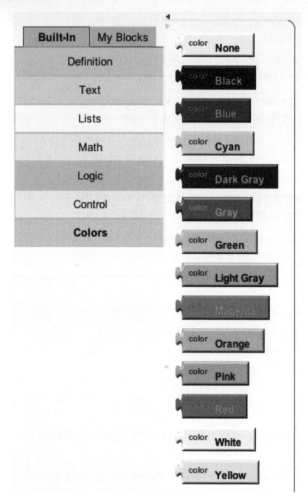

Figure 11-13. *Color blocks*

Creating Application Logic with the Block Editor

The example application that comes with this chapter includes some logic defined with the Block Editor application. The logic enables the button in the application to start and stop an animation. For every component you add to your application, a corresponding item is added the My Blocks tab in Block Editor. Figure 11-14 shows the My Blocks items.

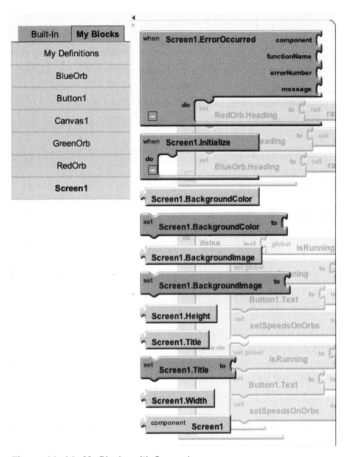

Figure 11-14. *My Blocks with Screen1 open*

On the left of Figure 11-14 we see an item for each component in our application, as well as an item called My Definitions. Clicking any of these items will open a panel containing the associated blocks for each item. In Figure 11-14 we see the contents of the Screen1 item. The first two blocks labeled Screen1.ErrorOccured and Screen1.Initialize are Event blocks, and will be executed when any error occurs in the application and when the application first launches. Figure 11-15 shows the Screen1.Initialize block used in our application.

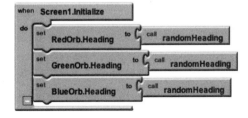

Figure 11-15. *Screen1.Initialize block*

By dragging the Screen1.Initialize block from Figure 11–14 out into the center of the Block Editor application, we can populate it so it looks like Figure 11–15. In the Initialize block we want to set the Heading property of each orb to a random value. So for the red orb, we open the block panel for the component RedOrb and drag out the block used for setting the Heading property and drop it into the do section of the Screen1.Initialize block. Any value can be dragged into the right side of the Heading block to set the value. In our case, we want to use a procedure of our own design called randomHeading, shown in Figure 11–16.

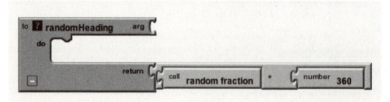

Figure 11–16. *randomHeading*

In Figure 11–16 we see the procedure randomHeading that we defined in our application. This is a very simple procedure and does not actually call any other blocks in the do section. It does however create a random value by adding three blocks to the return connector. The first of the three blocks is a Multiplier block that contains the other two blocks, a random value and the value 360. Once the randomHeading block is added to the application it becomes available under the My Definitions blocks found under the My Blocks tab, as shown in Figure 11–17.

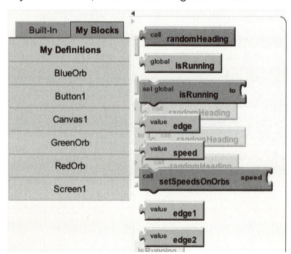

Figure 11–17. *My Definitions*

In Figure 11–17 we see all of the definitions in our application. At the top is the block randomHeading. This block is dragged out from here and added to the right side of the Heading blocks found as shown in Figure 11–15. When the application first launches, the Screen1.Initialize procedure is called, but there is no animation running yet, as shown in Figure 11–18.

Figure 11-18. *Running application in emulator*

Once the application launches, as shown in Figure 11–18, the application displays the three orbs and a button. When the user clicks the button, the text on the button will change and the orbs will start animating. In order to define the logic that is executed when the user clicks the button, we have to find the Click procedure for Button1, as shown in Figure 11–19.

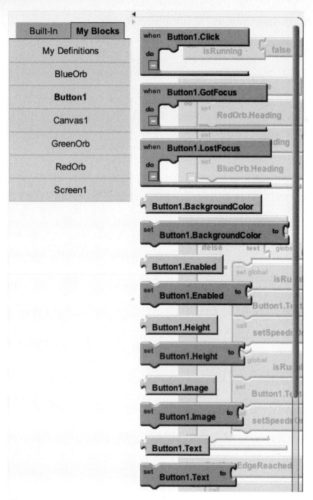

Figure 11-19. *Blocks for Button1*

In Figure 11-19 we see the blocks available for the component Button1. We can see that there are three blocks that correspond to an event: Click, GotFocus, and LostFocus. Under the Event blocks are a number of blocks for reading and setting the different properties for Button1. The bottom most block in Figure 11-19 is the block we are going to use to set the text of the button. Figure 11-20 shows our definition of the Button1.Click procedure.

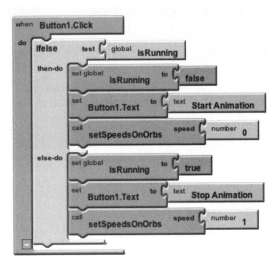

Figure 11-20. *Button1.Click procedure*

In Figure 11-20 we see our implementation of the Button1.Click procedure. There is a single block directly connected to the Button1.Click block that is an ifelse block. The ifelse block uses the value stored in the global variable isRunning. If isRunning is true we set isRunning to false, set the text of the button to say "Start Animation," and call the procedure setSpeedsOnOrbs and pass the value 0. If isRunning is false we do the opposite: we set isRunning to true, update the button text to say "Stop Animation," and use the setSpeedsOnOrbs procedure to set the orb's speed to 1. There are two blocks used in Figure 11-20 that are defined elsewhere by our application: the block isRunning and setSpeedsOnOrbs. These are shown in Figure 11-21.

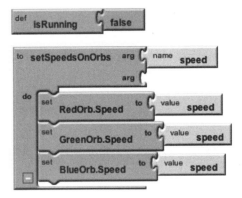

Figure 11-21. *The isRunning block and setSpeedsOnOrbs block*

In Figure 11-21 there are two blocks defined. The first is a global variable called isRunning and has an initial value of false. The second clock is a procedure called setSpeedsOnOrbs and takes a single argument called speed. The block speed is used to set the speed property of each of the three orbs. To use these blocks in other parts of the application, you drag them out of the panel shown in Figure 11–17.

When the speed of the orbs is set to 1, as is the case in Figure 11–20, the orbs will start moving according to the their heading and speed value. When the orbs reach the edge of the Canvas they are on, they bounce off the edge and continue animating. Each orb is a component of the type ImageSprite. The type ImageSprite has a number blocks associated with it. Figure 11–22 shows some of these blocks.

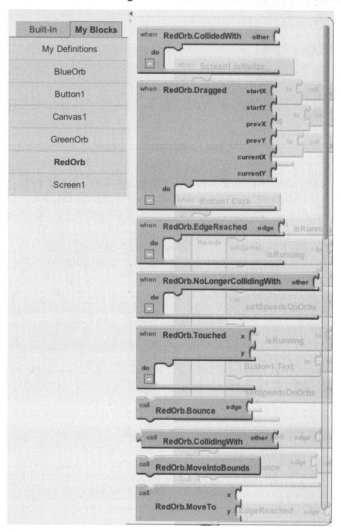

Figure 11–22. *Blocks for ImageSprites*

Figure 11–22 shows a number of blocks that are associated with the component RedOrb. RedOrb is an ImageSprite so a lot of its blocks deal with common uses of sprites. To implement our bouncing effect, we are interested in the blocks EdgeReached and Bounce for all three of our orbs. Figure 11–23 shows our use of the blocks EdgeReached and Bounces.

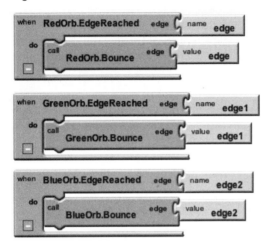

Figure 11–23. *EdgeReached and Bounce blocks*

In Figure 11–23 we see that we have define behavior for each of the three orbs. When they reach the edge of a Canvas, the corresponding procedure is executed calling Bounces on that orb. Make note that each of these three procedures has an argument defined. For the RedOrb.EdgeEached procedure the argument is called edge, while the version for the GreenOrb is called edge1 and the BlueOrb version is called edge2. If we were defining three Java methods we would be free to name the arguments the same thing. It might even be considered bad form to name them differently. In the Block Editor we must name all of the arguments differently. This is done, we think, so that there is a unique block created within the My Definitions panel, allowing the user to select the right block for the right procedure.

We have discussed all of the blocks required to get our application running the way we want. It is time to consider some of the limitations we have encountered along the way.

Limitations of App Inventor

App Inventor and the corresponding application Block Editor go a long way to simplify app development. But as can be clearly seen in this chapter, only a specific set functionality is exposed by the App Inventor components. There are also limitations brought about by the visual programming language, as well as generally bugginess of the current release. Let's explore each of these facets to understand the limitations of App Inventor.

Limited Set of Components

App Inventor provides the "developer" with a fixed set of components and each component brings a fixed set of functionality. If functionality outside of the provided components is required, the developer is out of luck: there is simply no way to extend the library of components in App Inventor. Figure 11–24 shows four sets of components out of the total of ten groups.

Figure 11–24. *Four out of ten component groups*

In Figure 11–24 we see four groups of components. The Basic group contains the fundamental widget components used to create an application. However, there are some big omissions. For example, there is no table component or a web view component. There is a check box, but no radio button. The Social group contains a number of interesting items. Providing access to the host device's contacts, email, and phone dialer definitely increases the scope of usefulness. The inclusion of the Twitter button is nice, but without the ability to create a component to work with other social media web sites, we are very limited.

The Media group provides controls for capturing and playing media. These are required components, and we are happy to see them included. Even when using the normal Android SDK, widgets for playing media are fully built components with little space for modification. The Sensor group extends the reach of the application into the domain of phone specific development that we consider the most interesting. Having access to the unique sensors available on phones is the one thing that really separates mobile development from desktop development.

All in all we look forward to seeing more components available in App Inventor, but more important, we want to see the ability to add new components.

Limitations in Block Editor

The Block Editor application provides a unique way of expressing programming logic. It is certainly a different way to program. The Block Editor is really bringing two things to the table. The first is the graphical nature of the tool, which allows users to click and drag blocks together. The second is the underlying language that Block Editor is writing.

The graphical nature of the Block Editor application is a little buggy, but when things are working as expected it can be pleasure to use. For example, the editor simply prevents you from making mistakes common to new developers. For example, you can't forget a semicolon because there are no semicolons. Basically your application is always in a compilable state, if not necessarily in a correct state.

The language being used by the Block Editor seems to be something called YAIL (Yet Another Intermediate Language) in combination with some custom XML. At least we think that is what it is using – the documentation from Google on the topic is very limited. If you unzip the project code that comes with this chapter, you will find a number of different files that describe the project. One of the files is a YAIL file and a couple of other oddball files types.

We don't mean to be critical of YAIL; frankly we know almost nothing about it. What concerns us is there is no Java code being produced at all. This is problematic because it reduces the value of App Inventor as a learning tool. A new developer using App Inventor is learning to put a program together with tools that are used by no one else. There is no path for them to extend their knowledge and move beyond App Inventor; they simply have to start over with Java.

Another concern we have with the language used by Block Editor is that there is no way to call a procedure on a component in a dynamic way. When we first put this application together, we tried to put all three orbs into a list. We were going to write the procedure that iterated over the orbs and set each orbs speed. We couldn't do this because the items returned by the foreach block are type-less values. There is no concept of variable for any type more complex than numbers, strings, and Booleans.

At the time of this writing, we would not recommend App Inventor for any real work. It is definitely worth keeping an eye on, and perhaps Google will open up its development process to third parties. This would allow the community to add new component types, which could catapult this experimental product into something really useful.

Summary

In this chapter we looked at the steps required to get App Inventor set up. We explored the web-based tool used for laying out the application, and how it connects with the Block Editor application. Using the Block Editor we took a detailed look at the types of functions – or blocks – that are available in that tool. We used those blocks to create a very simple animation. Lastly, we discussed the limitations of App Inventor and some hopes for the future.

Index

■Special Characters and Numbers

~/.android/avd/ directory, 52
123 math block, 371

■A

aapt utility, 25
About CocoaDroid menu item, 125
About menu item, 151
AboutView class, 354, 360
about.xml file, 359–360
AbsoluteLayout, 317
Abstract Window Toolkit (AWT), 106
AccelerateDecelerateInterpolator, 342
acceptInput field, 325
acceptInput variable, 344, 347, 353
AccessToken class, 265
ActionScript, for Flash applications, 246
.actionScriptProperties file, 241
Activity class, 11, 65, 76, 79, 95, 244
Activity class source files, 126–128
Activity Java source files, 79–81
activity tag, 75
ADB (Android Debug Bridge) shell, 95
adb help command, 50
adb install command, 25
adb install sl4a_r3.apk command, 197
adb logcat command, 84
adb tool, 242
Add (a New Software Site) button, Eclipse, 29
Add Items to List block, 371
Add menu item, 202
Add Movie service, 252
addAnimation, 347
AddHighScoreServlet class, 288, 290–291
Addition math block, 372

addJavascriptInterface method, 225
addSprites method, 357
addView( ) method, 88–89, 91
ADK (Android Development Kit), 1, 50–53
Adobe AIR, web applications with, 238–250
    ActionScript for, 246
    building and deploying, 240–244
    Flex UI for, 244–246
    overview, 239–240
Adobe Flash. *See* Flash, web applications with
ADT (Android Development Tools)
    Eclipse IDE, 29
    Google Eclipse official update site, 29
    migrating applications to, 97–104
        creating new projects from copies of projects, 97–98
        creating signed APKs of applications, 101
        deploying to devices, 99–101
        Eclipse with ADT plugin, 97
        making copies of projects, 97
    tools plugin for, 28
Advanced tab, System Properties dialog box, 5
alert dialogs, 90
AlertDialog class, 267
AlertDialog.Builder class, 90, 267
AlphaAnimation, 341
And logic block, 374
android-9 Android platform API Level, 120
Android APIs, 210
Android AsyncTask class, 176–177
android command, 53
android create avd command, 52
android create avd -n android23api9_hvga_32mb-t android-9 -c 32M command, 121
android create project command, 53, 59–60, 75
Android Debug Bridge (ADB), 17–18, 95

387

android delete avd -n android23api9_hvga_32mb command, 121
android delete command, 52
Android Development Kit (ADK), 1, 50, 52–53
Android Development Tools. See ADT
Android Device Chooser dialog box, 100
Android Devices node, NetBeans, 37
.android directory, 52, 306
Android emulator, 13
Android Facebook Library, 268, 274
Android GUI Manipulation Methods in KahluaDroid.java (partial), 180
android list avd command, 121
Android Manifest tab, 101
Android-Mode utility, 54
Android node, Eclipse, 31
Android Platform directory, 46
Android Preferences editor, Eclipse, 31
Android Project option, 31
Android SDK and AVD Manager tool, 14, 53
Android Toast, 212
android variable, 225, 231
Android Virtual Devices. See AVDs
android.bat command, 53
androidinterpreter, 162
AndroidMain-app.xml file, 240–241
AndroidMain.mxml file, 244
AndroidManifest.xml file, 12, 224–225, 241–242, 263–264, 299–300, 306
android_version function, 171
anim directory, 344
Animate class, 249–250
Animation class. See also frame by frame animations
  implementing, 343–353
  overview, 341–342
animation, in JavaScript, 231–235
Animation scaleDown2, 348
Animation section, App Inventor project, 364
Animation trans2, 348
Animation.AnimationListener interface, 349
AnimationDrawable, 330
AnimationSet, 342, 347–348, 352
AnimationThread class, 355–356
AnimationUtils class, 344
ANR Dialog box, 109
ANR state, 109
Ant Build Debug command, 60
Ant Build Debug tool, 53

Ant Build Install tool, 53
Ant Build Uninstall tool, 53
ant build.xml file, 53
ant clean command, 53
Ant Clean tool, 53
ant compile command, 53, 60
Ant Compile tool, 53
ant debug command, 53, 60
ant install command, 53
ant install process, 17
ant install step, 17, 25
ant uninstall command, 53
ant.bat clean command, 53
ant.bat compile command, 53
ant.bat debug command, 53
ant.bat install command, 53
ant.bat uninstall command, 53
ANTI_ALIAS_FLAG flag, 340
AnticipateOvershootInterpolator, 343, 345, 348
Apache Ant tool, 9
Apache Harmony JVM and DVM, 26–27
API (application programming interface), 5, 49, 312
apiKey attribute, 307
.apk application package, path to, 25–26
apk-debug utility, 241
apkbuilder utility, 25
APKs (application packages)
  creating signed, 101
  and SL4A
    downloading, 197
    installing, 197
    installing interpreters with archives, 208–209
App Engine datastore, GAE service, 285
App Inventor Setup, 361–363
App Inventor tool, 361–386
  Block Editor application in, 365–383
    Color blocks, 375
    Control blocks, 374–375
    creating logic, 376–383
    Definition blocks, 367–368
    List blocks, 369–371
    Logic blocks, 373–374
    Math blocks, 371–373
    Text blocks, 368–369
  limitations of, 383–386
    in Block Editor, 385–386
    components, 384–385
  setting up, 361–365

App Inventor web page, 363
Append to List block, 370
Application Framework, 22
Application Launcher icon, 64
application methods
    calling as Lua functions, KahluaDroid snippets file, 183–185
    exposing to KahluaDroid project, 180–183
        implementing small Lua callable runtime methods, 182–183
        sharing data between Java and Lua, 180–181
Application Not Responding state, 109
application packages. *See* APKs
application programming interface (API), 5, 49, 312
applications
    core files, 74–81
        default String table files, 78–79
        GUIs, 76
        layout file for example code, 76–77
        main Activity Java source file, 79–81
        main layout files, 75
        Manifest files, 74–75
        and View class, 76
    creating signed APKs, 101
    design, 112–113, 121–122
    example project, 58–59
    exiting activities, 86–87
    extending
        by embedding interpreters, 107–108
        interpreters by embedding, 108–109
    generating foundation projects, 59–61
    GUI initialization code, 85–86
    layer, 22–23
    loading asset resources, 144–145
    migrating to Eclipse/ADT, 97–104
        creating new projects from copies of projects, 97–98
        creating signed APKs of applications, 101
        deploying to devices, 99–101
        Eclipse with ADT plugin, 97
        making copies of projects, 97
    preparing to run, 61–66
        creating log filter in DDMS application, 64–66
        replacing default generated code, 63–64
        starting debugging session, 61–63
    private files for, 92–95
        browsing with ADB shell, 95
        browsing with DDMS File Explorer, 93–94
    running, 66–81, 122–153
        Activity class source file, 126–128
        application asset resources, 144–145
        BASIC code, 133–136, 151–153
        CocoaDroid, 123–125, 143–151
        core files, 74–81
        custom ArrayAdapter class, 128–129
        demo, 67–74
        desktop, 114–118
        Hello Android BASIC! script, 131–133
        main XML layout resource file, 125–126
        MenuInflater object, 131
        saving sessions in scratch files, 136–139
        viewing files in DDMS File Explorer, 142
        Work Files, 139–142
        XML menu layout resources, 130–131
        XML strings table, 129–130
    runtime, 22
architecture, 20–27
    components, 23
    platform stack, 21–23
        Application Framework, 22
        C/C++ runtime libraries, 22
        HALs, 21
    runtime platform, DVM, 23–27
ArrayAdapter class, implementing custom, 128–129
asset resources, loading, 144–145
assets directory, 144
assets folder, 183
Asynchronous Threading Implementation in KahluaDroid.java (partial), 177
AsyncTask class
    executing background code with, 177–178
    extending, 258–259
    running BASIC code asynchronously using, 133–136
atest2.bas file, 115
AT_MOST masks, 327
AttributeSet constructor, 325
authenticating users
    for GAE services, 287

with REST
   for Facebook, 268–272
   for Twitter, 261–265
AuthorizeListener class, 270
Automatic setting, Run Configuration, 100
Available Plugins tab, NetBeans, 36
Available Software dialog box, Eclipse, 30
AVDs (Android Virtual Devices)
   image locations, 52
   preparing, 51–52
AWT (Abstract Window Toolkit), 106

B

background attribute, 316
Background class, 332–333
background code, multi-threading for, 110
BaseLib runtime support library, 167
BASIC (Beginner's All-purpose Symbolic Instruction Code), 111
BASIC class, 113
Basic group, App Inventor, 384
BASIC language
   asynchronously running using AsyncTask class, 133–136
   CocoaDroid samples, 142–143
   programming with, 110–112
      background, 111
      Cocoa-BASIC interpreter for Java, 111–112
   running CocoaDroid
      sample programs, 149–151
      sample scripts, 145–148
BASIC.java file, 118
Beginner's All-purpose Symbolic Instruction Code (BASIC), 111
BitmapDrawable class, 320, 329–330
BitmapDrawable object, 320
Blobstore Java API, GAE (Google App Engine) service, 285
Block Editor application, 365–383
   Color blocks, 375
   Control blocks, 374–375
   creating logic, 376–383
   Definition blocks, 367–368
   limitations in, 385–386
   List blocks, 369–371
   Logic blocks, 373–374
   Math blocks, 371–373
   Text blocks, 368–369
block randomHeading, 378

Blocks Editor, 361, 366
Bluefish utility, 55
body element, 229
Bounce block, 383
BounceInterpolator, 343
boundCenterBottom method, 310
Build Commands, 56
Build tab, Project Properties dialog box, 56–57
Building utilities task, 195
build.xml file, 53
Button class, 87
Button Maker Button button, 68, 70
Button1. Click procedure, 380
Button1 component, 380
Button1.Click block, 381
Button1.Click procedure, 52, 381
buttons, disabling and enabling, 87–88

C

C/C++ runtime libraries, 22
C main function, 212
C Main Module for Accessing SL4A (ndk-to-sl4a.c) \b, 212
C Support Functions for Accessing SL4A (ndk-to-sl4a.c) \b, 213
Canvas class, direct rendering with, 336–340
canvas element, 228, 230, 233–236, 238
Canvas object, 336
canvas tag, 232
canvasClick function, 235
canvas.getContext("2d"), 232
Cap block, 368
Cap.ROUND constant, 340
cat command, 4
Categories list, NetBeans, 40
cert.p12 file, 241
Channel API, GAE (Google App Engine) service, 285–286
charges, for GAE (Google App Engine), 283–284
checkForGroups function, 236–237
checkForMatches function, 237
checkMatches method, 348–349, 353
Choose control block, 375
CLAMP value, 339
classes.dex file, 11, 25
Clear All Movies service, 252
Clear button, 124, 138

Clear Button (button_clear) control, 169
Clear Single Movie service, 252
clicked method, 246, 248–249
client variable, 256
client.execute( ) method, 302
cloning SL4A source code, Mercurial
        program, 216–218
Close Screen control block, 375
Close Screen with Result control block, 375
Cocoa-BASIC AWT project, 112–120
    application design, 112–113
    running desktop application, 114–118
    source code for, 118–120
cocoa-basic-awt.jar file, 114–115
Cocoa-BASIC interpreter for Java
        programming language, 111–112
CocoaDroid, 120–153
    application design, 121–122
    BASIC samples
        overview, 142–143
        programs, 149–151
        scripts, 145–148
    checklist, 120–121
    main Activity screen, 123–125
    running applications, 122–153
        Activity class source file, 126–128
        BASIC code asynchronously using
            Android AsyncTask class, 133–136
        custom ArrayAdapter class, 128–129
        Hello Android BASIC! script, 131–133
        loading application asset resources,
            144–145
        main XML layout resource file,
            125–126
        MenuInflater object, 131
        saving sessions in scratch files,
            136–139
        viewing files in DDMS File Explorer,
            142
        Work Files, 139–142
        XML menu layout resources,
            130–131
        XML strings table, 129–130
CocoaDroidActivity class, 122, 131
CocoaDroidActivity.java file, 132
CocoaDroidCommandInterpreter class, 122,
        124, 135
cocoadroid_main_menu.xml file, 131
code editors, 53–58
    configuring, 56–58
    selecting, 53–55

    editor alternatives, 54–55
    Geany code editor, 55
Code Input Text Field (edittext_input)
        control, 169
code repositories, SL4A, 195–196
coding techniques, 81–96
    centralizing application GUI initialization
        code, 85–86
    creating controls dynamically at runtime,
        88–89
    disabling buttons, 87–88
    enabling buttons, 87–88
    exiting application activities, 86–87
    Log API, 81–84
        methods, 81–82
        SDK log viewers, 83–84
        styles, 81–82
    making menus, 95–96
    making toasts, 90
    private application files, 92–95
        browsing with ADB shell, 95
        browsing with DDMS File Explorer,
            93–94
    showing alert dialogs, 90
    system notifications, 91
Color blocks, in Block Editor application,
        375
Color.DKGRAY constants, 339
ColorDrawable type, 330, 333
Color.LTGRAY constants, 339
colOrRowSize value, 333
com.example.myandroid.MyAndroidSdkApp
        Activity2 class, 75
command line, and AVDs, 51–52
CommandInterpreter class, 113, 119, 122
CommonAndroidCodeLibrary class, 122,
        145
Configuration class, 265
ConsoleWindow class, 113, 119
consumer varaible, 262
CONSUMER_KEY constant, 261
CONSUMER_SECRET constant, 261
Context constructor, 318, 325
Context.getResources( ) method, 320
contrib folder, 162
Control blocks, in Block Editor application,
        374–375
controls, creating dynamically at runtime in
        code, 88–89
Copy operation, 146
CoroutineLib runtime support library, 167

Create AVD button, 14
Create new Android Virtual Device form, 13
Create project from existing sample option, 32
Create project from existing source radio button, 32, 97
Create project from scratch option, IntelliJ IDEA, 44
Create Read Update Delete (CRUD), 252
createGridPath( ) method, 333
CRUD (Create Read Update Delete), 252
ctx variable, 235
currentTick variable, 232

D

Dalvik Debug Monitor Server. *See* DDMS
Dalvik Debug Monitor tool, 53
Dalvik Virtual Machine. *See* DVM
/data/data/ directory, 142
DataInputStream class, 113
ddms command, 53
DDMS (Dalvik Debug Monitor Server)
   application, creating log filter in, 64–66
   File Explorer
      accessing startup scripts from, 190
      browsing device file systems with, 93–94
      viewing files in, 142
ddms.bat command, 53
Debug logging level, 82
debugging starting session, 61–63
debug.keystore file, .android directory, 306
Definition blocks, in Block Editor application, 367–368
DELETE method, 252
deltaRadius field, 358
deltaX field, 358
deltaX value, 359
deltaY field, 358
deltaY value, 359
Deploy button, 282
development environment
   running SL4A in emulator, 196
   for using Kahlua2 in Java, 158
development tools, 49–104
   ADK, 52–53
   and code editors, 53–58
      configuring, 56–58
      selecting, 53–55
   coding techniques, 81–96

      centralizing application GUI initialization code, 85–86
      creating controls dynamically at runtime in code, 88–89
      disabling buttons, 87–88
      enabling buttons, 87–88
      exiting application activities, 86–87
      Log API, 81–84
      making menus, 95–96
      making toasts, 90
      private application files, 92–95
      showing alert dialogs, 90
   coding with SDK, 50
   environment dependencies, 50–52
      ensuring development kit locations are on path, 50
      preparing AVDs, 51–52
   example application project, 58–59
   generating foundation projects, 59–61
   migrating applications to Eclipse/ADT, 97–104
      creating new projects from copies of projects, 97–98
      creating signed APKs of applications, 101
      deploying to devices, 99–101
      making copies of projects, 97
      opening Eclipse with ADT plugin installed, 97
   preparing to run applications, 61–66
      creating log filter in DDMS application, 64–66
      replacing default generated code, 63–64
      starting debugging session, 61–63
   running applications, 66–81
      core files, 74–81
      demo, 67–74
.dex file, path to, 25–26
dialogClosed( ) method, 324
DIALOG_CONFIRM_TWEET constant, 267
DialogInterface.OnClickListener class, 268
direct rendering, with Canvas class, 336–340
directory structure, 60–61
displayResults method, 302–303, 308
Division math block, 372
doDraw method, 356–357
doGet method, 291, 293–294
doInBackground method, 134, 258, 302–303
domain specific languages (DSLs), 105

doneAnimating, 351, 353
Downcase block, 369
draw method, 359
Drawable class, game development with, 328–336
    methods for, 328–330
    and NinePatchDrawable class, 334–336
    subclasses of, 330–334
drawable directory, 336
drawRect( ) method, 339
drawText( ) method, 340
drawTextOnPath( ) method, 340
DSLs (domain specific languages), 105
DVM (Dalvik Virtual Machine), 23–27
    and Apache Harmony JVM, 26–27
    JVM performance, 27
    path to .apk application package, 25–26
    path to .dex file, 25–26
dx program, 24–25

E

easeboth function, 233
Eclim utility, 54
Eclipse
    download area, 28
    with GAE, 278–280
    home page, 28
Eclipse ADT (Android Development Tools)
    Eclipse IDE, 29
    Google ADT Eclipse official update site, 29
    plugin setup, 29–32
        creating projects, 31–32
        installing, 29–31
    tools plugin for, 28
Eclipse IDE (Integrated Development Environment), 28–32
    development with
        with ADT, 29
        Eclipse download area, 28
        Eclipse home page, 28
        Google ADT Eclipse update site, 29
        tools plugin for Eclipse ADT, 28
    migrating applications to, 97–104
        creating new projects from copies of projects, 97–98
        creating signed APKs of applications, 101
        deploying to devices, 99–101
        making copies of projects, 97

        opening with ADT plugin installed, 97
Eclipse IDE plugin, 216
Eclipse Mercurial plugin, 217
Eclipse plugin, using Mercurial program with, 217
EdgeReached block, 383
Edit button, 5
EditText field, 87
EditText view, 316
EditText View class, 124
Emacs utility, 54
embedding Kahlua2, 165–168
EmbossMaskFilter, 340
emulator, running SL4A in, 196–209
    development environment configuration, 196
    downloading APKs, 197
    installing APKs, 197
    installing interpreters, 202–209
endCheck function, 237–238
endGame( ) method, 324
environment dependencies, preparing AVDs
    deleting from command line, 51–52
    image locations, 52
Environment Variables button, System Properties dialog box, 5
Environment Variables window, 5
Equal To block, 369
Equality and Inequality math block, 371
Equals logic block, 374
Error logging level, 82
eval method, 135, 253
evalCodeString method, 134–135, 153
EvalCodeStringAsyncTask class, 133
evalCodeStringSync method, 151–153
EXACTLY masks, 327
exampleFunction function, 240
execute method, 134, 256, 259
executeSync method, 189
executeWithArray method, 297
exposeGlobalFunctions, 168, 180
extending AsyncTask class, 258–259
Extensible Markup Language. *See* XML

F

Facebook authentication dialog box, 268
Facebook Social Graph API, 274
Facebook, with REST
    authenticating user, 268–272
    overview, 268

Social Graph API for, 272
FaceTweet application, 270
FaceTweet class, 261
FB_APPLICATION_ID constant, 271
File Explorer menu item, DDMS application, 93
File Explorer tool, 142
file systems
    browsing with ADB shell, 95
    browsing with DDMS, 93–94
fillAfter attribute, 345
fill_parent attribute, 315
fillRect method, 234
Filter Name field, 64
findOrbForXY function, 236
findViewById method, 77, 299, 319–320, 324
fivePercent value, 333
FLAG_FULLSCREEN, 323
Flash Builder plug-in, Eclipse, 222
Flash, web applications with, 238–250
    ActionScript for, 246
    building and deploying, 240–244
    Flex UI for, 244–246
    overview, 239–240
Flex. *See* Flash, web applications with
Flex UI, for Flash applications, 244–246
.flexProperties file, 241
Foreach control block, 375
frame by frame animations, 353–360
FrameLayout class, 316, 360
FrameLayout root, 360
function keyword, 240
fx:Script tag, 248

G

GAE (Google App Engine), 275–310
    charges for, 283–284
    creating application in, 276–278
    Eclipse with, 278–280
    example using, 287–297
        accessing services with Android, 297–300
        adding HighScore service, 290–293
        querying HighScore service, 293–297
        querying top ten scores, 300–303
        querying top ten scores for user, 303–305
        viewing user location on map, 305–310
    project structure for, 280–283
    services of, 284–287
        App Engine datastore, 285
        authenticating users for, 287
        Blobstore Java API, 285
        Channel API, 285–286
        Images API, 286
        Mail API, 286
        Memcache, 287
        Task Queues API, 287
        XMPP, 287
    signing up, 276–278
game development, 311–360
    Animation class, 341–353
    direct rendering with Canvas class, 336–340
    with Drawable class, 328–336
        methods for, 328–330
        and NinePatchDrawable class, 334–336
        subclasses of, 330–334
    frame by frame animations for, 353–360
    with View class, 312–328
        custom classes, 320–328
        displaying layout in code, 317–320
        XML layout for, 312–317
GameActivity class, 318, 320, 322–323, 325
GameManager.SERVICE_URL variable, 305
game_name parameter, 305
gamenameEditText variable, 305
GameView class, 320–322, 324–328
GameView square, 326
gameView.reset, 324
game.xml file, 321
Geany code editor, 55
Geany utility, 53
GET method, 252
Get Single Movie service, 252
Get Start Text control block, 376
get variable, 256
getDrawable( ) method, 320
getHighScore function, 231
getInterpolation method, 342
getIntrinsicHeight( ) method, 329
getIntrinsicWidth( ) method, 329
getMinimumHeight( ) method, 329
getMinimumWidth( ) method, 329
getScore( ) method, 324
getScreenHeight method, 230–231
getScreenWidth method, 230–231
getString( ) method, 78, 129, 258

getTag( ) method, 89
GetTopTen class, 301, 304, 308
GetUsersOfGame class, 304
getView method, 129
getWidth, 327
getWindow, 323
Google ADT (Android Development Tools) Eclipse official update site, 29
Google Android Platform, 38
Google App Engine. *See* GAE
GradientDrawable, 331
graphical user interfaces (GUIs), 15, 49, 76, 176
Graphics2D class, 336
gravity attribute, 315
Greater Than block, 369
GridDrawable class, 333
GridDrawable constructor, 333
Group element, 245–246, 248
GroupView, 315
GUI threads, running Lua code on, 176–179
  executing background code with AsyncTask class, 177–178
  executing UI code on main thread, 178–179
GUIs (graphical user interfaces), 15, 49, 76, 176

H

HALs (hardware abstraction layers), 21
Heading blocks, 378
Heading property, 378
heightMeasureSpec, 327
Hello Android BASIC! script, 131–133
Hello World examples, with SL4A (Scripting Layer for Android), 219–220
HelloAndroidSdk directory, 9
Hg executable file, 216–217
hg -v command, 216
High Score dialog, 314
HighScore class, 289–290, 303
highscore element, 230
HighScore objects, 339–340
highscore parameter, 291
HighScore service, GAE example
  adding, 290–293
  querying, 293–297
highScore variable, 291
HighScoreOverlay class, 309–310
HighScore.toList( ) utility method, 339

HighScoreView class, 336, 339
History List, 124
HtmlOnAndroid class, 223
HtmlOnAndroid.java file, 225
HttpClient class, 256
HttpGet class, 256
HttpServlet class, 291

I

id attributes, 316
id class, 319
IDEs (Integrated Development Environments), 27, 49
If control block, 375
Ifelse control block, 375
I'm Feeling Lucky function, 286
image variable, 240
ImageButton View class, 124
Images API, GAE (Google App Engine) service, 286
ImageSprite type, 382
ImageSprites, App Inventor project, 364
ImageSprites properties panel, App Inventor project, 365
ImageView, 320, 326
index.html file, 227–229, 232, 280, 288
Information logging level, 82
init( ) method, 248, 325, 339
initialize( ) method, 85, 87, 128
innerPaint variable, 339
innerRect Rect object, 339
Input field, 124
Install button, NetBeans, 36
Install Selected button, 8
Installed tab, NetBeans, 36
installing, 2–9
  Eclipse ADT plugin setup, 29–31
  JDK, 3
  SDK, 3–9
    Apache Ant tool, 9
    API levels, 5
    platform setup, 6–9
install.sh script, 241
int constant, 319
int type, 246
Integrated Development Environment, Eclipse. *See* Eclipse IDE
IntelliJ IDEA
  Community Edition
    code repository, 43

home page, 42
project repository, 43
download areas, 42
Early Access Program, 42
IDE, development with, 42
official sites, 43
plugin, using Mercurial program with, 218
interface controls, user, 169–170
INTERNET permission, 225–226, 300
interpolate attribute, 345
interpreter project, 162–168
building
from console, 163
from IDEs, 163–164
embedding Kahlua2, 165–168
running, 164–165
setting up, 162–163
interpreters
extending applications by embedding, 107–108
extending by embedding applications, 108–109
for SL4A, installing, 202–209
Interpreters entry, 199
Interpreters screen, 202
Is a List block, 371
Is a Number math block, 373
Is in List block, 371
Is List Empty block, 371
isRouteDisplayed method, 308
isRunning block, 381
isRunning variable, 381
ItemizedOverlay class, 310

J

J2EE (Java Enterprise Edition), 275
J2SEPlatform constructor, 166
J2SEPlatform newEnvironment method, 166
J2SEPlatform newTable method, 168
J2SEPlatform.java class, 167
J2SEPlatform.java (partial) method, 166
Java
sharing data between Lua and, 180–181
using Kahlua2 in, 157–158
Java class math, 371
Java Data Objects (JDO), 281, 285
Java Development Kit (JDK), 3
Java Enterprise Edition (J2EE), 275
Java Native Interface (JNI), 23

Java Persistence API (JPA), 285
Java programming language, Cocoa-BASIC interpreter for, 111–112
Java SE (JSE), 23
Java Virtual Machine (JVM), 22, 27
javac utility, 25
JavaScript Object Notation. *See* JSON
JavaScript, web applications with, 222–238
animation in, 231–235
application files, 226–231
calling Android methods from, 225–226
overview, 238
project for, 223–225
user interaction in, 235–238
JavaScriptInterface class, 225–226, 231
javax.mail package, 284
JDK (Java Development Kit), 3
JDO (Java Data Objects), 281, 285
jdoconfig.xml file, 292
jEdit utility, 54
JetBrains IntelliJ IDEA IDE Community Edition, 42–47
JNI (Java Native Interface), 23
JNLP file, 365
JPA (Java Persistence API), 285
JRE Class White List, 276
JSE (Java SE), 23
JSON (JavaScript Object Notation), 209–210, 251, 253–255
json string, 256
json_array, 212
JSONArray class, 256
JSONObject class, 256, 258
JVM (Java Virtual Machine), 22, 27

K

Kahlua2
interpreter project, 162–168
building, 163–164
embedding, 165–168
running, 164–165
setting up, 162–163
Lua embedding with, 156–157
projects, 158–162
building, 160–161
runtime files, 159
runtime libraries, 161–162
using in Java, 157–158
kahlua2interpreter project root directory, 163
Kahlua2Interpreter.java, 162, 165

KahluaAsyncTask class, 177
KahluaConverterManager, 167
KahluaDroid executeAsync method, 177
KahluaDroid Load Snippets Menu, 183
KahluaDroid loaded snippets, 184
KahluaDroid Lua Code Snippets Asset
    File-lua_snippets.lua, 184
KahluaDroid Main Layout Resource
    main.xml, 170
KahluaDroid Main Menu Resource-
    kahluadroid_main_menu.xml menu
    latout resource file, 172
KahluaDroid Main String Table Resource-
    strings.xml, 174
KahluaDroid project, 168–192
    calling application methods as Lua
        functions, 183–185
    exposing application methods to,
    180–183
        implementing small Lua callable
            runtime, 182–183
        sharing data between Java and Lua,
            180–181
    implementing application startup scripts,
        185–192
            accessing from DDMS File Explorer,
            190
            removing broken, 191–192
            running applications with, 187–189
            saving Lua code as, 185–186
            using Lua comment blocks in,
            189–190
    running application, 169–176
        initialization code, 174–176
        menu, 172–173
        running Lua code, 170–172
        strings table, 174
        user interface controls, 169–170
    running Lua code on main GUI thread,
        176–179
            executing background code with
                AsyncTask class, 177–178
            executing UI code on main thread,
            178–179
    snippets file, 183–185
KahluaInterpreter.java, 162
KahluaThread instance, 168
KeyboardBuffer class, 113
keystore Alias, 102
Keystore selection dialog box, 102
Kurtz, 111

L

LAUNCHER category, 75
LayerDrawable class, 331, 334
Layout class, 76
layout files, 75–77
layout, for View class
    displaying in code, 317–320
    in XML, 312–317
layout( ) method, 327
layout_height attribute, 315–316
LayoutParams class, 89
layout_width attribute, 315–316
Length block, 369
Length of List block, 370
Less Than block, 369
libs subdirectory, 162
linear function, 233
LinearGradient constructor, 339
LinearInterpolator, 342
LinearLayout, 312, 315–316, 322
LinearView, 360
linePaint object, 340
List blocks, in Block Editor application,
    369–371
list command, 116
LIST command, 150
List Movies service, 252
LIST statement, 151
Load button, 124, 139
Load Samples menu item, 125, 143
Load Snippets, 183
Load Snippets (menu_itm_snippets_load)
    menu item, 172
Load Startup Script
    (menu_itm_startup_script_load)
    menu item, 172
Load Work menu item, 125, 139
loadUrl method, 224
localStorage varible, 231
Log API, 81–84
    methods, 81–82
    SDK log viewers, 83–84
    styles, 81–82
Log class, 65, 81
log filters, creating in DDMS (Dalvik Debug
    Monitor) application, 64–66
Log tab, DDMS application, 62
Log Tag, 64–65, 82
Log.d(String tag, String msg) method, 82
Log.d(String tag, String msg, Throwable tr)
    method, 82

Log.e(String tag, String msg) method, 82
Log.e(String tag, String msg, Throwable tr) method, 82
Logic blocks, in Block Editor application, 373–374
logic, creating with Block Editor application, 376–383
Login to Facebook button, 270
loginTwitter method, 262
Log.i(String tag, String msg) method, 82
Log.i(String tag, String msg, Throwable tr) method, 82
Log.v(String tag, String msg) method, 82
Log.v(String tag, String msg, Throwable tr) method, 82
Log.w(String tag, String msg) method, 83
Log.w(String tag, String msg, Throwable tr) method, 82
Lua
    calling application methods as functions, 183–185
    embedding of, 155–192
        with Kahlua2, 156–157
        Kahlua2 interpreter project, 162–168
        Kahlua2 project, 158–162
        KahluaDroid project, 168–192
        using Kahlua2 in Java, 157–158
    entering code, 170–172
    implementing small callable runtime methods, 182–183
    running code, 170–179
    sharing data between Java and, 180–181
    and startup scripts
        saving code as, 185–186
        using comment blocks in, 189–190
Lua Callable Android Runtime Methods in KahluaDroid.java (partial), 182
Lua Environment Variable Manipulation Methods in KahluaDroid.java (partial), 180
LuaCompiler runtime support library, 167
LuaJavaClassExposer class, 168, 180

M

Mail API, GAE (Google App Engine) service, 286
MAIN action, 75
Main-app.xml file, src directory, 240
Main Menu, 124
main method, 113
main thread, executing UI code on, 178–179
main.xml file, 298–299
Make a List block, 369
Make Text block, 369
make utility, 9
makePersistent method, 291
Maker button, 68
makeWideButton( ) method, 88–89
Manage apps menu item, 191
Manifest files, 74–75
manifest tag, 75
maps, viewing user location on, 305–310
mapView variable, 308
match_parent attribute, 315
Math blocks, in Block Editor application, 371–373
MathLib runtime support library, 167
McManis, Chuck, 111
MeasureSpec.getSize, 327
Media group, App Inventor, 384
Media section, App Inventor project, 365
Memcache, GAE (Google App Engine) service, 287
Menu Implementation Methods in KahluaDroid.java (partial), 173
MenuInflater object, 131
menus
    for KahluaDroid application, 172–173
    making, 95–96
Mercurial program
    installing, 216
    using Hg executable file, 216–217
    using with Eclipse plugin, 217
    using with IntelliJ IDEA, 218
Mercurial repository, 217
methods
    calling from JavaScript, 225–226
    for Drawable class, 328–330
MIRROR value, 339
modal dialogs, Twitter with REST example, 266–268
Model View Controller (MVC), 312–313
multi-threading, for background code, 110
Multiplication math block, 372
Multiplier block, 378
MVC (Model View Controller), 312–313
My Blocks tab, 376, 378
My Definitions blocks, 378
My Definitions panel, Block Editor, 383
MyAndroidSdkApp-debug.apk file, 11
MyAndroidSdkApp2-debug.apk package, 63

MyAndroidSdkAppActivity application, 19
MyAndroidSdkAppActivity2 log filter tab, DDMS application, 66
MyAndroidSdkAppActivity2.java file, 77, 79, 89
MyAndroidSdkAppActivity.java file, 11
/MyAndroidSdkAppProject/bin directory, 11
MyAndroidSdkAppProject folder, 16
MyAndroidSdkAppProject project, 59
MyAndroidSdkAppProject2 directory, 60, 63, 97
MyAndroidSdkAppProject2 project, 59
/MyAndroidSdkAppProject2_Eclipse directory, 97, 224
MyAndroidSdkAppProject2_Eclipse project, 97
MyButtonTagData class, 89

N

NBAndroid (NetBeans Android)
    creating projects, 40–41
    official update site, 34
    plugin, 33–34, 41
NetBeans
    download area, 33
    home page, 33
    with NBAndroid plugin, 33
    official update site, 34
NetBeans Android. *See* NBAndroid
NetBeans IDE, 33–41
    development with
        download area, 33
        home page, 33
        with NBAndroid plugin, 33
        official update site, 34
    NBAndroid plugin, 34–41
New Android Application screen, NetBeans, 41
New Project wizard, IntelliJ IDEA, 43–46
New Projects menu, GAE plugin, 278
newOrbAt function, 237
nine_patch.9.png file, 335–336
NinePatchDrawable class, 334–336
Not logic block, 373
Notification class, 91
NotificationManager class, 91
notifications, system, showing, 91
ns:OrbQuest element, 245

O

OAuth (Open Authentication), 251
oauth_verifier parameter, 265
onAnimationEnd, 349
onCancel method, 271
onClick events, 353
onClick method, 132, 267
OnClickListener class, 132
onComplete method, 271
onCreate( ) method, 85, 223, 231, 259, 301, 308, 323
onCreateDialog method, 267
onCreateOptionsMenu( ) method, 95
onDraw( ) method, 336, 339, 353
oneFifth variable, 327
onePercent value, 333
onLayout( ) method, 327–328
onLoad function, 229–230
onMeasure( ) method, 326–328
onNewIntent method, 264
onOptionsItemSelected( ) method, 95–96
onPostExecute method, 134–135, 258–259, 302
onProgressUpdate method, 134
onTap method, 310
Open Authentication (OAuth), 251
OR logic block, 374
Orb class, 240
Orb.as file, 239
orb_ids array, 325
OrbQuest class, 248
orb_quest.js file, 228–229
OrbQuest.mxml file, 245–246
orbScale variable, 249
OrbView class, 326, 351–352
OrbView image, 326
OrbView.layout( ) method, 327
OrbViews, 325–327
org.json package, 256
OsLib runtime support library, 167
Other Functions math block, 374
Output field, 124
OutputStringArrayAdapter class, 128
OvalShape, 331

P

p switch, 52
package tag, 75
package.sh script, 241

padding attribute, 316
Paint class, 331, 340
PaintDrawable, 331
Paste operation, 147
PATH entry, 197
Path object, 333, 339
PATH variable, 4–5, 216
PathShape class, 331, 333
Perl APK file, 208
Perl scripting interpreter, 208
PersistenceManager class, 291
PFM factory class, 291
Pick Random Item block, 371
Plain Old Java Objects (POJOs), 285
platform setup, 6–9
platform stack, 21–23
    Application Framework, 22
    applications
        layer, 22–23
        runtime, 22
    C/C++ runtime libraries, 22
    HALs, 21
platform.newEnvironment platform instance, 166
Please enter a message and save it field, 68
plugins
    JetBrains IntelliJ IDEA IDE Community Edition, 43–47
    NBAndroid, 33
    opening Eclipse with ADT, 97
    tools for Eclipse ADT, 28
PMF class, 291
POJOs (Plain Old Java Objects), 285
PorterDuffColorFilter class, 329
Position in List block, 371
POST method, 252, 273
PrintStream class, 113, 168
private application files, 92–95
    browsing with ADB shell, 95
    browsing with DDMS File Explorer, 93–94
Procedures calls, 367
Program class, 113, 122
PROGRAMS area, 142
program_templates directory, 144
program_templates/lua_snippets.lua code file, 183
Project Checks dialog box, 101
Project Properties dialog box, Geany utility, 56–57
project structure, for GAE (Google App Engine), 280–283
Properties section, App Inventor project, 364
provider variable, 262, 265
proxy implementations, using SL4A (Scripting Layer for Android), 211–215
PUT method, 252
Python interpreter files, 205
Python Module for Accessing the AndroidProxy, 211
Python script language, 206

Q

queryHighScores method, 294
QueryHighScoresServlet class, 288, 293

R

R class, 318–319, 324
RAD programming task, 194
RadialGradient object, 340
Random Fraction math block, 372
Random Integer math block, 373
Random Set Seed math block, 374
randomHeading block, 378
readStatus method, 258
ReadTweet class, 258–259, 268
RedOrb component, 378, 382
RedOrb.EdgeEached procedure, 383
RelativeLayout, 317
RELATIVE_TO_SELF constant, 347
remote procedure calls (RPC), 210, 251
Remove List Item block, 370
renderScene method, 232–234
REPEAT value, 339
Replace List Item block, 370
Representational State Transfer. *See* REST
requestLayout, 348–349, 353
res folder, 319
resource-constrained systems, designing for, 109–110
rest directory, 344
REST (Representational State Transfer), 251–274
    extending AsyncTask class, 258–259
    with Facebook, 268–274
        authenticating user, 268–272

Social Graph API for, 272
and JSON, 253–255
overview, 252–259
with Twitter, 259–268
    authenticating user, 261–265
    modal dialog to confirm user request, 266–268
    tweeting, 265
using in Android application, 255–257
restore method, 235
result variable, 309
Results Output Field (textview_output) control, 169
R.id.dialogRoot, 320
R.id.yesButton constant, 319
R.java file, 77–78, 318–319
R.layout.game, 324
R.layout.score_dialog, 318–319
root LinearLayout, 315
root View, 313
rootLayout, 320
RotateAnimation class, 342
RotateDrawable and ScaleDrawable, 331
RPC (remote procedure calls), 210, 251
RPC server, 210
Run button, 124, 131–132
Run Code Asynchronously Button (button_run_async) control, 169
Run Code Synchronously (on GUI Thread) Button (button_run_sync) control, 169
run command, 117
RUN command, 150
Run Configuration, 100
run configurations
    creating new, 98–99
    deploying to devices, 99–101
    testing, 98–99
Run logcat menu item, DDMS application, 83
run method, 356
Run on GUI Thread, 176
RunAfter class, 348–349, 352
Runnable interface, 349
running applications, role of View class, 76
runOnUiThread method, 244–245, 258
runtime methods, implementing small Lua callable, 182–183
runtime platform, DVM (Dalvik Virtual Machine), 23–27
    and Apache Harmony JVM, 26–27

JVM performance, 27
path to .apk application package, 25–26
path to .dex file (and APK), 25–26

■S

Sample_01.zip file, 363
Save button, 68, 124, 137
Save Message button, 67, 69
Save Startup Script menu item, 172, 185
Save Work menu item, 125
SaveHighScoreServlet class, 293
ScaleAnimation, 342, 345, 347–348
scaleDownAnimate method, 249
scale_down.xml file, 344
score element, 230
score variable, 237, 246, 248
ScoreDialog, 317, 324
score_dialog constant, 318–319
score_dialog.xml file, 318–320
scorePaint object, 340
scoreTextView, 322
scratch files, saving sessions in, 136–139
Screen1.ErrorOccured block, 377
Screen1.Initialize block, 377–378
Screen1.Initialize procedure, 379
screen_name parameter, 256
screenName string, 256
screenName variable, 256
scripting environment, 105–153
    BASIC language, 110–112
        background, 111
        Cocoa-BASIC interpreter for Java, 111–112
    Cocoa-BASIC AWT project, 112–120
        application design, 112–113
        reviewing source code, 118–120
        running desktop application, 114–118
    CocoaDroid project, 120–153
        application design, 121–122
        checklist, 120–121
        running application, 122–153
    code projects, 112
    designing, 106–110
        component roles in scripting systems, 107–109
        components of scripting systems, 106–107
        multi-threading for background code, 110

for resource-constrained systems, 109–110
Scripting Layer for Android. *See* SL4A
SCRIPTS area, 142
SDK Manager.exe utility, 8
SDK (software development kit), 3–9
    Apache Ant tool, 9
    API levels, 5
    platform setup, 6–9
    and programmer editors, coding with, 50
<sdk>/tools/ directory, 4
se.krka.kahlua.android, 163
Select List Item block, 369
Select Path dialog box, IntelliJ IDEA, 45
selectedOrb variable, 236, 344
selectedOrbView field, 325
selectedOrbView variable, 344–345
Sensor group, App Inventor, 384
services, of GAE, 284–287
    App Engine datastore, 285
    authenticating users for, 287
    Blobstore Java API, 285
    Channel API, 285–286
    Images API, 286
    Mail API, 286
    Memcache, 287
    Task Queues API, 287
    XMPP, 287
Services tab, NetBeans, 37
Set Build Commands menu item, Geany utility, 56
setAlpha( ) method, 329
setAnimationListener method, 348
setBounds( )method, 329
setBuiltInZoomControls method, 308
setButtonsEnabled( ) method, 87–88
setCancelable method, 267
setColorFilter( ) method, 329
setContentView( ) method, 244, 299, 318, 320, 324
setDither( ) method, 329
setEnabled( ) method, 87
setFilterBitmap( ) method, 329
setFlags, 323
setHighScore function, 231, 238
setImageDrawable( ) method, 320
setInterval("renderScene( )", 1000/30), 232
setLevel( ) method, 330
setMeasuredDevice, 327
setMeasuredDimension( )method, 326
setMessage method, 267

setOnClickListener( ) method, 299, 326
setPositiveButton method, 268
setScrollBarStyle method, 224
setShadowLayer, 340
setSpeedsOnOrbs procedure, 381
setState( ) method, 330
setTag( ) method, 89
setText method, 259
Settings main menu, 191
Settings tab, NetBeans, 34–35
SharedObject class, 248
SharedPreferences object, 339
Shell interpreter, 199–201
Show Details option, 36
show( ) method, 90
showDialog method, 266–267
showOkAlertDialog method, 137
signing up, for GAE (Google App Engine), 276–278
Signpost project, 262
Silly Exit Button button, 67, 86
Simple Object Access Protocol (SOAP), 252
SL4A APK file, 197
SL4A application Activity screen, 198
SL4A Application Launcher icon, 198
SL4A (Scripting Layer for Android), 193–220
    architecture, 210–211
    code repository, 195–196
    communicating using JSON data format, 209–210
    getting source code, 215–218
    Hello World examples, 219–220
    license for, 194
    local proxy implementations, 211–215
    overview, 194
    resources, 195
    running in emulator, 196–209
        development environment configuration, 196
        downloading APKs, 197
        installing APKs, 197
        installing interpreters, 202–209
    using, 194–195
SL4A toolbox, 202
sl4a_rpc function, 212
SOAP (Simple Object Access Protocol), 252
Social Graph API, for Facebook with REST, 272
Social group, App Inventor, 384
software development kit. *See* SDK
source code, reviewing, 118–120

Split block, 369
Sprite class, 357–360
Sprite variable, 232–235, 238
src folder, 162, 240
Start button, 15
startAnimation, 347
Starts At block, 369
Startup Script Implementation-KahluaDroid.java (partial), 187
startup scripts, implementing, 185–192
    accessing from DDMS File Explorer, 190
    removing broken, 191–192
    running applications with, 187–189
    saving Lua code as, 185–186
    using Lua comment blocks in, 189–190
String tables, default files, 78–79
stringFromAssetFile method, 144
stringFromInputStream method, 135, 145
stringFromPrivateApplicationFile method, 137
StringLib runtime support library, 167
strings table, for KahluaDroid application, 174
strings.xml file, 79, 129, 144
style.css file, 228
sub-Views, 327
subclasses, of Drawable class, 330–334
Subtraction math block, 372
surfaceCreated method, 355
SurfaceHolder.Callback interface, 355
SurfaceView class, mixing with View class, 359–360
swapOrbs method, 347–348
Synchronous Threading Implementation Methods in KahluaDroid.java (partial), 179
system notifications, 91
System Properties dialog box, Windows, 5

T

TableLayout, 317
TableLib runtime support library, 167
TableRow type, 317
target command, apk-debug utility, 241
Target tab, Run Configuration, 100
Task Queues API, GAE (Google App Engine) service, 287
text attribute, 246
Text blocks, in Block Editor application, 368–369

TextMate utility, 54
textSize, 316
textStyle, 316
TextViews, 316, 320, 322, 325, 359–360
Thread classes, 356
titlePaint Paint object, 340
Toast class, 90
toasts, 90
top command, 200
TopTenActivity class, 301–302
toString method, 256
toXScale attribute, 345
toYScale attribute, 345
<tr> rows, 317
Transformation function, 232–234, 236–237
TranslateAnimation, 342, 347, 352
True and False logic block, 373
turnsTextView, 322
TweetFace application, 265
Twitter, with REST, 259–268
    authenticating user, 261–265
    modal dialog to confirm user request, 266–268
    tweeting, 265
Twitter4J library, 265
Twitter4J project, 268

U

UI (User Interface) code, executing on main thread, 178–179
Uninstall button, 205
UNIX top command, 200
unlockCanvasAndPost, 356
UNSPECIFIED masks, 326
Upcase block, 369
Update Center Customizer, NetBeans, 34
Update Movie Info service, 252
updateRemovedOrbs method, 352–353
UpdateStatus class, 268
updateStatus method, 265, 268
updateValues method, 324, 353
URL_CALLBACK constant, 263
USB Debugging setting, 99
Use Google App Engine option, 279
Use the Export Wizard link, 101
user interaction, in JavaScript, 235–238
User Interface (UI) code, executing on main thread, 178–179
UserdataArray runtime support library, 167
user_location.xml file, 307

username parameter, 305
usernameEditText variable, 305
UsersLocationActivity class, 305, 308

V

value attribute, 249
value field, 233
var keyword, 240
Variable block, 368
Verbose logging level, 82
View class
    and Android GUIs, 76
    game development with, 312–328
        custom classes, 320–328
        displaying layout in code, 317–320
        XML layout for, 312–317
    mixing with SurfaceView class, for frame by frame animations, 359–360
View element, 322
View menu item, 199
ViewGroup class, 76, 325
ViewIDs, 316
View.layout( ) method, 328
View.MeasuredSpec class, 326
View.OnClickListener. GameView, 325
Views, 316
Vim utility, 54
Virtual Devices list, 15
virtual machines
    Apache Harmony JVM, 26–27
    DVM, 23–27
        and Apache Harmony JVM, 26–27
        JVM performance, 27
        path to .dex file (and APK), 25–26
    JVM performance, 27

W

war directory, 280
Warning logging level, 82
Web Application Project menu item, GAE plugin, 278
web applications, 221–250
    with Flash and AIR, 238–250
        ActionScript for, 246
        building and deploying, 240–244
        Flex UI for, 244–246
        overview, 239–240
    with JavaScript, 222–238
        animation in, 231–235
        application files, 226–231
        calling Android methods from, 225–226
        overview, 238
        project for, 223–225
        user interaction in, 235–238
WEB-INF directory, 280–281
WebStart application, 365
webView.getSettings( ).setJavaScriptEnabled(true) method, 224
web.xml file, 280–281, 287–288
whenDone function, 234
While control block, 375
while loop, 356–357
widthMeasureSpec, 327
Windows USB Driver package, 7, 99
windupovershoot function, 233
Windw.FEATURE_NO_TITLE constant, 323
Work Files, 139–142
wrap_content attribute, 315–316
write method, 168
Writing test scripts task, 194

X

XML (Extensible Markup Language)
    menu layout resources, 130–131
    strings table, 129–130
XML layout, for View class, 312–317
XML layout resource files, 125–126
XMPP, GAE (Google App Engine) service, 287

Y, Z

YAIL (Yet Another Intermediate Language), 385
yesButton constant, 319
    Yet Another Intermediate Language (YAIL), 385

You Need the Companion eBook

Your purchase of this book entitles you to buy the companion PDF-version eBook for only $10. Take the weightless companion with you anywhere.

We believe this Apress title will prove so indispensable that you'll want to carry it with you everywhere, which is why we are offering the companion eBook (in PDF format) for $10 to customers who purchase this book now. Convenient and fully searchable, the PDF version of any content-rich, page-heavy Apress book makes a valuable addition to your programming library. You can easily find and copy code—or perform examples by quickly toggling between instructions and the application. Even simultaneously tackling a donut, diet soda, and complex code becomes simplified with hands-free eBooks!

Once you purchase your book, getting the $10 companion eBook is simple:

❶ Visit **www.apress.com/promo/tendollars/**.

❷ Complete a basic registration form to receive a randomly generated question about this title.

❸ Answer the question correctly in 60 seconds, and you will receive a promotional code to redeem for the $10.00 eBook.

233 Spring Street, New York, NY 10013

All Apress eBooks subject to copyright protection. No part may be reproduced or transmitted in any form or by any means, electronic or mechanical, including photocopying, recording, or by any information storage or retrieval system, without the prior written permission of the copyright owner and the publisher. The purchaser may print the work in full or in part for their own noncommercial use. The purchaser may place the eBook title on any of their personal computers for their own personal reading and reference.

Offer valid through 8/11.